{ THE GREAT MOVIES }

OTHER BOOKS BY ROGER EBERT

An Illini Century

A Kiss Is Still a Kiss

Roger Ebert's Movie Home Companion (1986–1993)

A Perfect London Walk *(with Daniel Curley)*

Two Weeks in the Midday Sun: A Cannes Notebook

Behind the Phantom's Mask: A Serial

Roger Ebert's Video Companion (1994–1998)

Ebert's Little Movie Glossary

Roger Ebert's Book of Film: A Norton Anthology

Questions for the Movie Answer Man

Roger Ebert's Movie Yearbook (1999–)

Ebert's Bigger Little Movie Glossary

I Hated, Hated, Hated This Movie

DVD COMMENTARY TRACKS

Dark City

Citizen Kane

THE

{ GREAT MOVIES }

ROGER EBERT

Photo Stills Selected by Mary Corliss,
Assistant Film Curator, Museum of Modern Art

Broadway Books

New York

BROADWAY

Film stills appear courtesy of The Museum of Modern Art, New York/ Film Stills Archive.

Excerpt from "Cautious Man" by Bruce Springsteen, Copyright © 1987 by Bruce Springsteen (ASCAP). Reprinted by permission.

Broadway Books titles may be purchased for business or promotional use or for special sales. For information, please write to: Special Markets Department, Random House, Inc., 1540 Broadway, New York, NY 10036.

PRINTED IN THE UNITED STATES OF AMERICA

BROADWAY BOOKS and its logo, a letter B bisected on the diagonal, are trademarks of Broadway Books, a division of Random House, Inc.

Visit our website at www.broadwaybooks.com
Visit Roger Ebert's website at www.suntimes.com/ebert

Previous versions of these essays have appeared in the *Chicago Sun-Times*, 1996–2001.

Library of Congress Cataloging-in-Publication Data
Ebert, Roger.
    The great movies / by Roger Ebert.—1st ed.
        p.   cm.
    1. Motion pictures.   I. Title.
PN1994.E23 2002
791.43'75—dc21   2001043806

FIRST EDITION

Book design by Maria Carella

ISBN 0-7679-1032-X

10 9 8 7 6 5 4 3 2 1

This book is dedicated to

Daniel Curley
Manny Farber
Pauline Kael
Stanley Kauffmann
Arthur Knight
Dwight Macdonald
Donald Richie
Andrew Sarris

Teachers

CONTENTS

CONTENTS

CONTENTS

INTRODUCTION

We live in a box of space and time. Movies are windows in its walls. They allow us to enter other minds—not simply in the sense of identifying with the characters, although that is an important part of it, but by seeing the world as another person sees it. François Truffaut said that for a director it was an inspiring sight to walk to the front of a movie theater, turn around, and look back at the faces of the audience, turned up to the light from the screen. If the film is any good, those faces reflect an out-of-the-body experience: The audience for a brief time is somewhere else, sometime else, concerned with lives that are not its own. Of all the arts, movies are the most powerful aid to empathy, and good ones make us into better people.

Not many of them are very good, however. Yes, there are the passable Friday night specials, measured by critics including myself in terms of their value in entertaining us for two hours. We buy our tickets and hope for diversion, and usually we get it, but we so rarely get anything more. Especially in these latter days of the marketing-driven Hollywood, and a world cinema dominated by the Hollywood machine, films aim coarsely at low tastes. "If you put three thoughts into a movie you've broken the law and no one will come," Sean Penn told an audience at the Edinburgh Festival in 2001. The movies in this book have three thoughts, or more. They are not "the" 100 greatest films of all time, because all lists of great movies are a foolish attempt to codify works which must stand alone. But it's fair to say:

If you want to make a tour of the landmarks of the first century of cinema, start here.

I began writing these essays at a time when new Hollywood product seemed at a low ebb (it has ebbed lower) and many younger filmgoers seemed to have little sense of the cinema's past. Every spring since 1968 I have attended the Conference on World Affairs at the University of Colorado in Boulder, and conducted a week-long exploration of one film. We sit in the dark and use stop-action to creep through a film, sometimes at a shot-by-shot pace. At first we used 16mm; then laserdiscs and DVD made it easier. Everybody engages in the discussion. It is democracy in the dark, with an image frozen on the screen. In earlier years I did mostly classics (*Citizen Kane, The Third Man, La Dolce Vita, The General, Notorious, Persona, Ikiru, Taxi Driver*). In recent years, reflecting the death of film societies and the rise of home video, the students were less interested in the past. One year I suggested *Vertigo* and they begged me to do *Fight Club*.

We did both. *Fight Club* was not a film I approved of, although I recognized its skill and knew from countless e-mails how strong an impression it made on its admirers. Seeing it over the course of a week, I admired its skill even more, and its thought even less. It lacks an intelligent drawing-together of its themes, but that is not held against it in a time when audiences are assaulted with sound and motion, when shots get shorter and movies get louder, when special effects replace or upstage theme and performance. The ability of an audience to enter into the narrative arc of a movie is being lost; do today's audiences have the patience to wait for Harry Lime in *The Third Man*?

At Boulder and on other campuses, talking with the students, I found that certain names were no longer recognized. Even students majoring in film had never seen one by Buñuel, Bresson, or Ozu. They'd seen one or two titles by Ford and Wilder, knew a half-dozen Hitchcock classics, genuflected at *Citizen Kane*, knew the *Star Wars* pictures by heart, and sometimes uttered those words which marked them as irredeemably philistine: "I don't like black and white." Sixty of these films are in black and white, and three use b&w and color; you cannot know the history of the movies, or love them, unless you understand why b&w can give more, not less, than color.

I came to believe that the classics of earlier years were an unexplored country for many filmgoers, even the best ones. As a film critic for a daily newspaper, I didn't want to spend my life locked in the present. In 1997 I went to Nigel Wade, then the editor of the *Chicago Sun-Times*, and proposed a biweekly series of longer articles revisiting the great movies of the past. He gave his blessing. Not many editors would have; the emphasis in American film journalism is on "celebrity news," box office results, and other forms of bottom-feeding. Every other week since then, I have revisited a great movie, and the response has been encouraging. I received letters and e-mails from movie lovers; got into debates with other critics; heard from a university trustee and a teenager in Madison who both vowed to watch every movie on the list. The Library Media Project made discounted DVDs of the movies available to public libraries.

The relative invisibility of classic movies is directly related to the death of film societies. Until the rise of home video, every campus and many public libraries and community centers had film societies which held cheap and well-programmed 16mm screenings. My early film initiation took place at two such clubs at the University of Illinois, which also inspired me to see first-run films I might otherwise have avoided. I saw *Ikiru*, *The 400 Blows*, *The Maltese Falcon*, and *Swing Time* for the first time in those campus rooms—knowing little or nothing about them except that they cost only twenty-five cents, and that afterward people got together in the student union and drank coffee and talked about them.

In theory home video should be a godsend for lovers of great films, and indeed most of these titles are available on video in one form or another, and that is how most people will have to see them. But when you enter the neighborhood video chain store, display boxes near the door push the latest "new on video" Hollywood blockbusters, and you have to prowl in the shadows to find "foreign films" and "classics"—often a pitiful selection. Independent local video stores and Web-based operations like netflix.com and facets.org give access to a much larger range of films, but does the average moviegoer ever find them? In the 1960s Stanley Kauffmann coined the term "the film generation" to describe the phenomenon of younger filmgoers who were film-obsessed. I was a member of that generation, and can personally testify that I waited in line at ordinary theaters to get into sold-out performances of Resnais's *Last Year at Marienbad* and Godard's *Weekend*. Today even the most popular subtitled films are ignored by the national distribution oligarchy, mainstream movies are pitched at the teenage male demographic group, and the lines outside theaters are for Hollywood's new specialty, B movies with A budgets.

I've seen some of the movies in this book dozens of times, and have been through forty-seven of them a shot at a time. But I made a fresh viewing before writing each essay; that was the whole idea. I was reminded of a similar selection by the British critic Derek Malcolm, who said his list simply reflected films he could not bear the thought of never seeing again. I have revised and lengthened these pieces for book publication, and made adjustments where necessary—for example, discussing the new longer version of *Apocalypse Now*. The 100 titles were selected from about 150 I had written up to publication date, and the biweekly series continues.

Revising the essays, I realized what a wonderful task I'd set myself, because I remembered the circumstances under which I'd seen the films. There was a cold London night in January when I took the tube to Hampstead and saw *Written on the Wind* at the Everyman. I joined Donald Richie, the great expert on Japanese film, as we went through Ozu's *Floating Weeds* a shot at a time at the Hawaii Film Festival. At the Virginia Festival of American Film, I did *Raging Bull* with its editor, Thelma Schoonmaker (nobody knows a film quite as well as its editor). The cinematographer Haskell Wexler joined me for *Casablanca* on the Floating Film Festival. Peter Bogdanovich and I went through *Citizen Kane* together on the Telluride Film Festival's anniversary cruise on the *QE2*. I was at the world premiere of *2001: A Space Odyssey*, and saw it again in 70mm on a giant screen at my own Overlooked Film Festival at the University of Illinois. *Apocalypse Now Redux* was screened at Cannes 2001, in the best movie theater in the world. *Battleship Potemkin* I saw projected on a screen on the outside wall of the Vickers Theater in Three Oaks, Michigan, while the audience sat on folding chairs and Concrete, a group from Benton Harbor, played a score it had composed. At the Overlooked again, I saw *Nosferatu* with music by the Alloy Orchestra of Cambridge, Mass. I remembered seeing the original version of *The Big Sleep* on 16mm in the Los Angeles living room of the late David Bradley, a curmudgeonly and beloved film collector. The best time I saw *City Lights* was outdoors in Piazza San Marco in Venice, and after it was over Chaplin came out on a balcony and waved. The first time I saw *Gates of Heaven*, Milos Stehlik of Facets Multimedia in Chicago called me up and said he had a film I had to see and he would not tell me what it was about. That mysterious masterpiece has suffered all its life because people *think* they don't want to see a documentary about a pet cemetery.

What happens when you see a lot of good movies is that directorial voices and styles begin to emerge. You see that some movies are made by individuals, and others by committees. Some movies are simply about the personalities they capture (the Marx Brothers and Astaire and Rogers). Others are about the mastery of genre, from *Star Wars*, which attempts to transcend swashbuckling, to *Detour*, which attempts to hide in the shadows of noir. Most good movies are about the style, tone, and vision of their makers. A director will strike a chord in your imagination, and you will be compelled to seek out the other works. Directors become like friends. Buñuel is delighted by the shamelessness of human nature. Scorsese is charged by the lurid possibilities of Catholic guilt. Kurosawa celebrates individuals in a country that suspects them. Wilder is astonished by the things some people will do to be happy. Keaton is about the struggle of man's spirit against the physical facts of the world. Hitchcock creates images that have the quality of guilty dreams. Sooner or later every lover of the film arrives at Ozu, and understands that the movies are not about moving, but about whether to move.

ROGER EBERT

STILL AND MOVING

I live in the past.

My job, as assistant curator in the Department of Film and Media at the Museum of Modern Art in New York, is to operate the Film Stills Archive, one of the largest collections of film stills in the world. Scholars and journalists request photographs from important movies, or of notable film personalities; and, as I have for the past thirty-four years, I open those venerable filing cabinets in the archive and find a century's worth of art and folly, commerce and kitsch, invaluable documentation and, most of all, indelible memories.

Researching these stills for Roger Ebert's *The Great Movies* has given me a refreshed look at movie history—a century of cinematic miracles in a hundred photographs. Similarly, when I rummage through bulging "personality files" of movie-star stills, I can see a compressed life story: the freshness and gawky promise of a young actor; the radiant maturity as the star's appeal is complemented by the filmmakers' artistry; then, as age writes its cruel lines on a face, the poignant battle against decay, waged with heavy makeup and lighting that is ever more carefully soft-focus. Any of these personality files is a flip-book that grants me a God's-eye view into both the intoxicating nature of human beauty and the inevitability of mortality. In a film still, though, an actor can remain forever at the apogee of his appeal.

Such is the archival and emotional power of film stills, a relic of nineteenth-century technology that holds priceless treasures for the twenty-first. Like the images in a movie theater—which run through a projector and escape to lodge in the viewer's mind, sometimes forever—film stills document the cinematic event. They are the images of record, representing the movie when they are published in newspapers, books, and magazines. This is how generations of audiences—the readers of all that prose, the gazers at all those photos—were taught to remember movies. Film stills return movies to their basics: a succession of images. They are the equivalent of photos in an old family album, a face or a caress petrified in time. These are the pictures a moviegoer is likely to retain, in the portable museum of his or her own imagination.

As you look through this book, your eye will occasionally be seduced away from Roger's peerless prose to focus on the image accompanying each essay. Whether or not you are familiar with the films under discussion, you will find that the stills evoke the films' visual and emotional content. From *Casablanca*: Humphrey Bogart and Ingrid Bergman discussing times gone by. From *City Lights*: the sightless Virginia Cherrill offering a flower to the tramp Charles Chaplin, who would in turn offer his undying love to her. From *Psycho*: Anthony Perkins, as the cinema's most dutiful son, with his hand clasped onto his mouth in horror at the crime his mother has just committed. From *The Seventh Seal:* the Knight (Max von Sydow) in a confessional, whispering his most intimate fears to white-faced Death (Bengt Ekerot). From *Raging Bull:* Robert De Niro standing over a defeated foe, the men's bodies a Picasso assemblage of welts and bruises.

François Truffaut acknowledged the potency of the still image when he ended his first feature, *The 400 Blows*, with a freeze frame of his young hero. It captured Antoine Doinel (Jean-Pierre Léaud) in a moment in time, his future uncertain, his face seemingly asking "Now what?" at the end of the first turbulent chapter of his experiences. That's what film stills do. They freeze the emotion and excitement of an actor, a scene, a film, an era; they are the pin through the movie butterfly that somehow gives this lovely, ephemeral creature lasting life. Stills distill; stills preserve. Most of the stills in this book are not, exactly, from the films they accompany. That is to say, they are not frame enlargements—blowups of single 35mm frames.

They are usually the work of "unit photographers," men and women hired by the production company to take pictures on the set while the scenes are being shot. They are designed to sell the product: to whet the prospective ticket buyer's appetite with publicity photos of the stars and alluring scenes from the film.

But like much commercial art, film stills have their glories, both sentimental and aesthetic. A glance at a still from an old Hollywood film conjures up an era in an instant. The photo suggests the film's directorial style; it recalls the lavish, precise design of sets and costumes; it anatomizes the look and attitude of the stars and forgotten players of an age gone by.

The still photograph's density, its search for the perfect single image, lends it a unique grip on our memories. In the 1930s, plenty of newsreel footage was expended on the Depression's poor, but the most telling portraits were those taken by photographer Dorothea Lange for the Farm Security Administration. The artful rawness of these pictures—the panhandlers and dirt farmers, the families ravaged by poverty and staring into a bleak future—lodges in the mind like a doctor's sad diagnosis to an anxious patient. Here is the poetry of deprivation and despair.

Hollywood movies were after a different kind of poetry: inspiring, reassuring. They told fairy tales about gorgeous people chasing their dreams. And they did this by taking pictures of ordinary actors and turning them into icons. The movie still refined this process even further: it isolated the light fantastic. Its mission was to encapsulate, in a single frame, the enthrallment of movies—all the glamour, and much of the art. At its best, the film still captured the heart of a movie, and the essence of star quality.

Not all stars were suited to the still photograph. The more bustling type of performer—James Cagney, Gene Kelly, Jerry Lewis—might be only a blur in the shutter. But the still camera was ideal for celestial bodies like Greta Garbo and Marlene Dietrich, whose screen personalities suggested goddesses in watchful repose, aloof and attentive as they waited for their men to make a false move. These actresses had an allure that was literally statuesque; and for this stillness, the still camera was the ideal machine to record it and improve on it. The best actresses recognized this symbiosis and had some of their most productive professional relationships with stills photographers: Garbo with

Ruth Harriet Louise and Clarence Sinclair Bull, Dietrich with Eugene Robert Richee and William Walling, Jr. In his book *The Art of the Great Hollywood Portrait Photographers*, John Kobal says Dietrich believed "that her studio photographs were of greater importance to her than her films."

The basis for the Museum of Modern Art's Film Stills Archive is the collection of one million photographs from *Photoplay* magazine, which documents movies from the earliest experiments in cinema in the 1890s to 1948, near the end of Hollywood's Golden Age. The MoMA Archive now comprises some four million stills representing every major country, director, performer, film—and decade. Indeed, because of the care with which they were taken and the sturdy fiber paper stock on which they were printed, photos from the 1920s, '30s, and '40s remain in pristine condition. As long as there still are films, there will be film stills.

Sometimes, the stills outlive the films. Many works, especially from the silent years, are missing and presumed lost. For example, only one tantalizing reel exists of Victor Seastrom's *The Divine Woman*, starring Greta Garbo. The melancholy fact is that the nitrate stock on which pre-1948 films were released often deteriorates disastrously, whereas the paper on which photographs are printed may last for centuries. Thus, the only visual evidence for many movies is the collection of film stills made to publicize them. A 1968 MoMA exhibition, "Stills from Lost Films," organized by Gary Carey, devoted an entire gallery to mounted stills enlargements from the most famous lost films.

Fortunately, the studios that produced these films often instructed their unit photographers to document them fully—scene by scene, sometimes shot by shot—with several hundred stills for even "minor" films of the 1920s and '30s. The existence of this material has allowed scholars to "re-create" lost films. Historian Philip K. Riley published a book that reconstructed Lon Chaney's *London After Midnight*. Herman G. Weinberg did a similar book on Erich von Stroheim's 1928 *The Wedding March*. In 1999, for the TNT channel, Rick Schmidlin devised a four-hour film version of Stroheim's legendary *Greed* by interlacing the surviving footage with hundreds of film stills. These efforts attest to the importance of film stills in piecing together the precious artifacts of an endangered medium.

This book should prove the truths I recognize each working day in the Film Stills Archive. Film stills preserve more than a dusty historical record. They evoke, with precision and purity, the cinema's glorious past. They testify to the persistence of the filmmakers' vision, to the enticement of movie glamour. They validate the movie lover's fondest memories. The legacy of still photos shows just how moving moving pictures can be.

MARY CORLISS

{ THE GREAT MOVIES }

2001:
A SPACE ODYSSEY

The genius is not in how much Stanley Kubrick does in *2001: A Space Odyssey,* but in how little. This is the work of an artist so sublimely confident that he doesn't include a single shot simply to keep our attention. He reduces each scene to its essence and leaves it on-screen long enough for us to contemplate it, to inhabit it in our imaginations. Rare among science fiction movies, *2001* is not concerned with thrilling us, but with inspiring our awe.

No little part of his effect comes from the music. Although Kubrick commissioned an original score from Alex North, he used classical recordings as a temporary track while editing the film, and they worked so well that he kept them. This was a crucial decision. North's score, which is available on a recording, is a good job of film composition but would have been wrong for *2001* because, like all scores, it attempts to underline the action—to give us emotional cues. The classical music chosen by Kubrick exists *outside* the action; it uplifts, it wants to be sublime, it brings a seriousness and transcendence to the visuals.

Consider two examples. The Johann Strauss waltz "Blue Danube," which accompanies the docking of the space shuttle and the space station, is deliberately slow, and so is the action. Obviously such a docking process would have to take place with extreme caution (as we now know from experience), but other directors might have found the space ballet too slow, and punched it up with thrilling music, which would have been wrong. We are asked in the scene to contemplate the process, to stand in space and watch. We know the music. It proceeds as it must. And so, through a peculiar logic, the space hardware moves slowly because it's keeping the tempo of the waltz. At the same time, there is an exaltation in the music that helps us feel the majesty of the process.

Now consider Kubrick's famous use of Richard Strauss's *Thus Spake Zarathustra*. Inspired by the words of Nietzsche, its bold opening notes embody the ascension of man into spheres reserved for the gods. It is cold, frightening, magnificent. It is associated in the film with the first entry of man's consciousness into the universe—and with the eventual passage of that consciousness onto a new level, symbolized by the Star Child at the end of the film. When classical music is associated with popular entertainment, the result is usually to trivialize the music (who can listen to the *William Tell* Overture without thinking of the Lone Ranger?). Kubrick's film is almost unique in *enhancing* the music by its association with his images.

I was present at the Los Angeles premiere of the film, in 1968, at the Pantages Theater. It is impossible to adequately describe the anticipation in the audience. Kubrick had been working on the film in secrecy for some years, in collaboration, the audience knew, with the author Arthur C. Clarke, the special effects expert Douglas Trumbull, and consultants who advised him on the specific details of his imaginary future—everything from space station design to corporate logos. Fearing to fly and facing a deadline, Kubrick had sailed from England on the *Queen Elizabeth,* using an editing room on board, and had continued to edit the film during a cross-country train journey. Now it was finally ready to be seen.

To describe that first screening as a disaster would be wrong, for many of those who remained until the end knew they had seen one of the greatest films ever made. But not everyone remained. Rock Hudson stalked down the aisle, audibly complaining, "Will someone tell me what the hell this is about?" There were many other walkouts, and some restlessness at the film's slow pace (Kubrick immediately cut about seventeen minutes, including a pod sequence that essentially repeated another one). The film did not provide the clear narrative and easy entertainment cues the audience expected. The closing sequences, with the astronaut inexpli-

cably finding himself in a bedroom somewhere beyond Jupiter, were baffling. The overnight Hollywood judgment was that Kubrick had become derailed, that in his obsession with effects and set pieces, he had failed to make a movie.

What he had actually done was make a philosophical statement about man's place in the universe, using images as those before him had used words, music, or prayer. And he had made it in a way that invited us to contemplate it—not to experience it vicariously as entertainment, as we might in a good conventional science fiction film, but to stand outside it as a philosopher might, and think about it.

The film falls into several movements. In the first, prehistoric apes, confronted by a mysterious black monolith, teach themselves that bones can be used as weapons, and thus discover their first tools. I have always felt that the smooth artificial surfaces and right angles of the monolith, which was obviously *made* by intelligent beings, triggered the realization in an ape brain that intelligence could be used to shape the objects of the world.

The bone is thrown into the air and dissolves into another weapon, an orbiting bomb platform (this has been called the longest flash-forward in the history of the cinema). We meet Dr. Heywood Floyd (William Sylvester), en route to a space station and the moon. This section is willfully antinarrative; there are no breathless dialogue passages to tell us of his mission, and instead Kubrick shows us the minutiae of the flight: the design of the cabin, the details of in-flight service, the effects of zero gravity.

Then comes the docking sequence, with its waltz, and for a time even the restless in the audience are silenced, I imagine, by the sheer wonder of the visuals. On board, we see familiar brand names, we participate in an enigmatic conference among the scientists of several nations, we see such gimmicks as a videophone and a zero-gravity toilet.

The sequence on the moon (which looks as real as the actual video of the moon landing a year later) is a variation on the film's opening sequence. Man is confronted with a monolith, just as the apes were, and is drawn to a similar conclusion: *This must have been made.* And as the first monolith led to the discovery of tools, so the second leads to the employment of man's most elaborate tool: the space ship *Discovery,* employed by man in partnership with the artificial intelligence of the onboard computer, named HAL 9000.

Life on board the *Discovery* is presented as a long, eventless routine of exercise, maintenance checks, and chess games with HAL. Only when the astronauts fear that HAL's programming has failed does a level of suspense emerge; their challenge is to somehow get around HAL, which has been programmed to believe "This mission is too important for me to allow you to jeopardize it." Their efforts lead to one of the great shots in the cinema, as the men attempt to have a private conversation in a space pod, and HAL reads their lips. The way Kubrick edits this scene so that we can discover what HAL is doing is masterful in its restraint: He makes it clear but doesn't insist on it. He trusts our intelligence.

Later comes the famous "star gate" sequence, a sound and light journey in which the astronaut Dave Bowman (Keir Dullea) travels through what we might now call a wormhole, into another place, or dimension, that is unexplained. At journey's end is the comfortable bedroom suite in which he grows old, eating his meals quietly, napping, living the life (I imagine) of a zoo animal who has been placed in a familiar environment. And then the Star Child.

There is never an explanation of the other race that presumably left the monoliths and provided the star gate and the bedroom. *2001* lore suggests Kubrick and Clarke tried and failed to create plausible aliens. It is just as well. The alien race exists more effectively in negative space: We react to its invisible presence more strongly than we possibly could to any actual representation.

2001: A Space Odyssey is in many respects a silent film. There are few conversations that could not be handled with title cards. Much of the dialogue exists only to *show* people talking to one another, without much regard to content (this is true of the conference on the space station). Ironically the dialogue containing the most feeling comes from HAL, as it pleads for its "life" and sings "Daisy."

The film creates its effects essentially out of visuals and music. It is meditative. It does not cater to us, but wants to inspire us, enlarge us. More than thirty years after it was made, it has not dated in any important detail, and although special effects have become more versatile in the computer age, Trumbull's work remains completely convincing—more convincing, perhaps, than more sophisticated effects in later films, because it looks more plausible, more like documentary footage than like elements in a story.

Only a few films are transcendent and work upon our minds and imaginations like music or prayer or a vast belittling landscape. Most movies are about characters with a goal in mind, who obtain it after difficulties either comic or dramatic. *2001: A Space Odyssey* is not about a goal, but about a quest, a need. It does not hook its effects on specific plot points, nor does it ask us to identify with Dave Bowman or any other character. It says to us: We became men when we learned to think. Our minds have given us the tools to understand where we live and who we are. Now it is time to move on to the next step, to know that we live not on a planet, but among the stars, and that we are not flesh, but intelligence.

{ THE 400 BLOWS }

I demand that a film express either the joy of making
cinema or the agony of making cinema. I am not at all interested
in anything in between.
TRUFFAUT

François Truffaut's *The 400 Blows* (1959) is one of the most intensely touching stories ever made about a young adolescent. Inspired by Truffaut's own early life, it shows a young, resourceful boy growing up in Paris and apparently dashing headlong into a life of crime. Adults see him as a troublemaker. We are allowed to share some of his private moments, as when he lights a candle before a little shrine to Balzac in his bedroom. The film's famous final shot, a zoom in to a freeze-frame, shows him looking directly into the camera. He has just run away from a house of detention and is on the beach, caught between land and water, between past and future. It is the first time he has seen the sea.

Antoine Doinel was played by Jean-Pierre Léaud, who has a kind of solemn detachment, as if his heart had suffered obscure wounds long before the film began. This was the first in a long collaboration between actor and director; they returned to the character in the short film *Antoine and Collette* (1962) and three more features: *Stolen Kisses* (1968), *Bed and Board* (1970), and *Love on the Run* (1979).

The later films have their own merits, and *Stolen Kisses* is one of Truffaut's best, but *The 400 Blows,* with all its simplicity and feeling, is in a class by itself. It was Truffaut's first feature, and one of the founding films of the French New Wave. We sense that it was drawn directly out of Truffaut's heart. It is dedicated to André Bazin, the influential French film critic who took the fatherless Truffaut under his arm at a time when the young man seemed to stand between life as a filmmaker and life in trouble.

Little is done in the film for pure effect. Everything adds to the impact of the final shot. We meet Antoine when he is in his early teens, living with his mother and stepfather in a crowded walk-up where they always seem to be squeezing out of each other's way. The mother (Claire Maurier) is a blonde who likes tight sweaters and is distracted by poverty, by her bothersome son, and by an affair with a man from work. The stepfather (Albert Rémy) is a nice enough sort, easygoing, and treats the boy in a friendly fashion although he is not deeply attached to him. Both parents are away from home a lot, and neither has the patience to play close attention to the boy: They judge him by appearances and by the reports of others who misunderstand him.

At school, Antoine has been typecast by his teacher (Guy Decomble) as a troublemaker. His luck is not good. When a pinup calendar is being passed from hand to hand, his is the hand the teacher finds it in. Sent to stand in the corner, he makes faces for his classmates and writes a lament on the wall. The teacher orders him to diagram his offending sentence, as punishment. His homework is interrupted. Rather than return to school without it, he skips. His excuse is that he was sick. After his next absence, he says his mother has died. When she turns up at his school, alive and furious, he is marked as a liar.

And yet we see him in the alcove that serves as his bedroom, deeply wrapped in the work of Balzac, whose chronicles of daily life helped to create France's idea of itself. He loves Balzac. He loves him so well, indeed, that when he's assigned to write an essay on an important event in his life, he describes "the death of my grandfather" in a close paraphrase of Balzac, whose words have lodged in his memory. This is seen not as homage, but as plagiarism, and leads to more trouble and eventually to a downward spiral: He

and a friend steal a typewriter; he gets caught trying to return it and is sent to the juvenile detention home.

The film's most poignant moments show him set adrift by his parents and left to the mercy of social services. His parents discuss him sadly with authorities as a lost cause ("If he came home, he would only run away again"). And so he is booked in a police station, placed in a holding cell, and put in a police wagon with prostitutes and thieves, to be driven through the dark streets of Paris, his face peering out through the bars like a young Dickensian hero. He has a similar expression at other times in the film, which is shot in black and white in Paris in a chill season; Antoine always has the collar of his jacket turned up against the wind.

Truffaut's film is not a dirge or entirely a tragedy. There are moments of fun and joy (the title is an idiom meaning "raising hell"). One priceless sequence, shot looking down from above the street, shows a physical education teacher leading the boys on a jog through Paris; two by two they peel off, until the teacher is at the head of a line of only two or three boys. (This is homage to Jean Vigo's *Zero for Conduct* [1933].) The happiest moment in the film comes after one of Antoine's foolish mistakes. He lights a candle to Balzac, which sets the little cardboard shrine on fire. His parents put out the flames, but then for once their exasperation turns to forgiveness, and the whole family goes to the movies and laughs on the way home.

There is a lot of moviegoing in *The 400 Blows,* with Antoine's solemn face turned up to the screen. We know that young Truffaut himself escaped to the movies whenever he could, and there is a shot here that he quotes later in his career. As Antoine and a friend emerge from a cinema, Antoine steals one of the lobby photos of a star. In *Day for Night* (1973), which stars Truffaut himself as a film director, there is a flashback memory to the character, as a boy, stealing down a dark street to snatch a still of *Citizen Kane* from the front of a theater.

The cinema saved François Truffaut's life, he said again and again. It took a delinquent student and gave him something to love, and with the encouragement of Bazin he became a critic and then made this film by his twenty-seventh birthday. If the New Wave marks the dividing point between classic and modern cinema (and many think it does), then Truffaut is likely the most beloved of modern directors—the one whose films resonated with the deepest, richest love of moviemaking. He liked to resurrect old effects (the iris shots in *The Wild Child* [1969], narration in many of his films) and pay tribute; *The Bride Wore Black* (1967) and *Mississippi Mermaid* (1969) owe much to his hero, Alfred Hitchcock.

Truffaut (1932–84) died too young, of a brain tumor, at fifty-two, but he left behind twenty-one films, not counting shorts and screenplays. His *Small Change* (1976) returns to the sharply remembered world of the classroom, to students younger than Doinel, and recalls the almost unbearable tension as the clock on the wall creeps toward the final bell. Even while directing a film a year, he found time to write about other films and directors and did a classic book-length, film-by-film interview with Hitchcock.

One of his most curious, haunting films is *The Green Room* (1978), based on the Henry James story "The Altar of the Dead," about a man and a woman who share a passion for remembering their dead loved ones. Jonathan Rosenbaum, who thinks *The Green Room* may be Truffaut's best film, told me he thinks of it as the director's homage to the auteur theory. That theory, created by Bazin and his disciples (Truffaut, Godard, Resnais, Chabrol, Rohmer, Malle), declared that the director was the true author of a film—not the studio, the screenwriter, the star, the genre. If the figures in the green room stand for the great directors of the past, perhaps there is a shrine there now to Truffaut. One likes to think of Antoine Doinel lighting a candle before it.

{ 8 ½ }

The conventional wisdom is that Federico Fellini went wrong when he abandoned realism for personal fantasy—that, starting with *La Dolce Vita* (1960), his work ran wild through jungles of Freudian, Christian, sexual, and autobiographical excess. The precise observation in *La Strada* (1954) was the high point of his career, according to this view, and then he abandoned his neorealist roots. *La Dolce Vita* was bad enough, *8 ½* (1963) was worse, and by the time he made *Juliet of the Spirits* (1965), he was completely off the rails. Then all is downhill, in a career that lasted until 1987, except for *Amarcord* (1974), with its memories of Fellini's childhood; that one is so charming that you have to cave in and enjoy it, regardless of theory.

This conventional view is completely wrong. What we think of as Felliniesque comes to full flower in *La Dolce Vita* and *8 ½*. His later films, except for *Amarcord*, are not as good, and some are positively bad, but they are stamped with an unmistakable maker's mark. The earlier films, wonderful as they often are, have their Felliniesque charm weighted down by leftover obligations to neorealism.

The critic Alan Stone, writing in the *Boston Review*, deplores Fellini's "stylistic tendency to emphasize images over ideas." I celebrate it. A filmmaker who prefers ideas to images will never advance above the second rank, because he is fighting the nature of his art. The printed word is ideal

for ideas; film is made for images, and images are best when they are free to evoke many associations and are not linked to narrowly defined purposes. Here is Stone on the complexity of *8 ½*: "Almost no one knew for sure what they had seen after one viewing." True enough. But true of all great films, whereas you know for sure what you've seen after one viewing of a shallow one. ("The thing that depresses me the most," Robert Altman told me, "is that people say they've seen one of my films when what they mean is, they've seen it once.")

8 ½ is the best film ever made about filmmaking. It is told from the director's point of view, and its hero, Guido (Marcello Mastroianni), is clearly intended to represent Fellini. It begins with a nightmare of asphyxiation and a memorable image in which Guido floats off into the sky, only to be yanked back to earth by a rope pulled by his associates, who are hectoring him to organize his plans for his next movie. Much of the film takes place at a spa near Rome and at the enormous set Guido has constructed nearby for his next film, a science fiction epic he has lost all interest in.

The film weaves in and out of reality and fantasy. Some critics complained that it was impossible to tell what was real and what was taking place only in Guido's head, but I have never had the slightest difficulty, and there is usually a clear turning point when Guido escapes from the uncomfortable present into the accommodating world of his dreams.

Sometimes the alternate worlds are pure invention, as in the harem scene where Guido rules a house occupied by all of the women in his life— his wife, his mistresses, and even those he has only wanted to sleep with. In other cases, we see real memories that are skewed by imagination. When little Guido joins his schoolmates at the beach to ogle the prostitute Saraghina, for example, she is seen as the towering, overpowering, carnal figure a young adolescent would remember. When he is punished by the priests of his Catholic school, one entire wall is occupied by a giant portrait of Dominic Savio, a popular symbol of purity in that time and place; the portrait, too large to be real, reflects Guido's guilt that he lacks the young saint's resolve.

All of the images (real, remembered, invented) come together into one of the most tightly structured films Fellini ever made. The screenplay is meticulous in its construction—and yet, because the story is about a confused director who has no idea what he wants to do next, *8 ½* itself is often described as the flailings of a filmmaker without a plan. "What happens," asks a web-based critic, "when one of the world's most respected directors runs out of ideas, and not just in a run-of-the-mill kind of way, but whole hog, so far that he actually makes a film about himself not being able to make a film?" But *8 ½* is not a film *by* a director out of ideas—it is a film filled to bursting with inspiration. Guido is unable to make a film, but Fellini manifestly is capable of making a film about him.

Mastroianni plays Guido as a man exhausted by his evasions, lies, and sensual appetites. He has a wife (Anouk Aimée), chic and intellectual, whom he loves but cannot communicate with, and a mistress (Sandra Milo), cheap and tawdry, who offends his taste but inflames his libido. He manages his affairs so badly that both women are in the spa town at the same time, along with his impatient producer, his critical writer, and uneasy actors who hope or believe they will be in the film. He finds not a moment's peace. "Happiness," Guido muses late in the film, "consists of being able to tell the truth without hurting anyone." That gift has not been mastered by Guido's writer, who tells the director his film is "a series of completely senseless episodes" and "doesn't have the advantage of the avant garde films, although it has all of the drawbacks."

Guido seeks advice. Aged clerics shake their heads sadly and inspire flashbacks to childhood guilt. The writer, a Marxist, is openly contemptuous of his work. Doctors advise him to drink mineral water and get rest, a lot of rest. The producer begs for quick rewrites; having paid for the enormous set, he insists that it be used. And from time to time Guido visualizes his ideal woman, who is embodied by Claudia Cardinale: cool, comforting, beautiful, serene, uncritical, with all the answers and no questions. This vision, when she appears, turns out to be a disappointment (she is as hopeless as all of the other actors), but in his mind he transforms her into a Muse and takes solace in her imaginary support.

Fellini's camera is endlessly delighting. His actors often seem to be dancing rather than simply walking. I visited the set of his *Satyricon* (1969) and was interested to see that he played music during every scene (like most Italian directors of his generation, he didn't record sound on the set but post-synced the dialogue). The music brought a lift and subtle rhythm to their movements. Of course many scenes have music built into them. In *8 ½*, orchestras, dance bands, and strolling musicians are seen, and the actors move in a subtly choreographed way, as if they're synchronized. Fellini's scores, by Nino Rota, combine snatches of pop tunes with dance music, propelling the action.

Few directors make better use of space. One of his favorite techniques is to focus on a moving group in the background and track with them past foreground faces that slide in and out of frame. He also likes to establish a scene with a master shot, which then becomes a close-up when a character stands up into frame to greet us. Another of his favorite techniques is to follow his characters as they walk, photographing them in three-quarter profile as they turn back toward the camera. And he likes to begin dance sequences with one partner smiling invitingly toward the camera before the other partner joins in the dance.

All of these moves are brought together in his characteristic parades. Inspired by a childhood love of the circus, Fellini used parades in all his films—not structured parades, but informal ones, people moving together toward a common goal or to the same music, some in the foreground, some farther away. *8 ½* ends with a scene that has deliberate circus overtones, a parade of musicians, major characters, and the grotesques, eccentrics, and "types" that Fellini loved to cast in his films.

I have seen *8 ½* over and over again, and my appreciation only deepens. It does what is almost impossible: Fellini is a magician who discusses, reveals, explains, and deconstructs his tricks, while still fooling us with them. He claims he doesn't know what he wants or how to achieve it, and the film proves he knows exactly, and rejoices in his knowledge.

{ AGUIRRE, THE WRATH OF GOD }

On this river God never finished his creation.

The captured Indian speaks solemnly to the last remnants of a Spanish expedition seeking the fabled El Dorado, the city of gold. A padre hands him a Bible, "the word of God." He holds it to his ear but can hear nothing. Around his neck hangs a golden bauble. The Spanish rip it from him and hold it before their eyes, mesmerized by the hope that now, finally, at last, El Dorado must be at hand. "Where is the city?" they cry at the Indian, using their slave as an interpreter. He waves his hand vaguely at the river. It is farther. Always farther.

Werner Herzog's *Aguirre, the Wrath of God* (1973) is one of the great haunting visions of the cinema. It tells the story of the doomed expedition of the conquistador Gonzalo Pizarro, who led a body of men into the Peruvian rain forest, lured by stories of the lost city. The opening shot is a striking image: A long line of men snakes its way down a steep path to a valley far below, while clouds of mist obscure the peaks. These men wear steel helmets and breastplates and carry their women in enclosed sedan chairs. They are dressed for a court pageant, not for the jungle.

The music sets the tone. It is haunting, ecclesiastical, human and yet something else. It is by Florian Fricke, whose band Popol Vuh (named for the Mayan creation myth) has contributed the sound tracks to many

Herzog films. For this opening sequence, Herzog told me, "we used a strange instrument which we called a choir-organ. It has inside it three dozen different tapes running parallel to each other in loops . . . All these tapes are running at the same time, and there is a keyboard on which you can play them like an organ so that [it will] sound just like a human choir but yet, at the same time, very artificial and really quite eerie."

I emphasize the music because the sound of a Herzog film is organically part of its effect. His stories begin in a straightforward manner, but their result is incalculable, and there is no telling where they may lead: They conclude not in an "ending" but in the creation of a mood within us—a spiritual or visionary feeling. I believe he wants his audiences to feel like detached observers, standing outside time, saddened by the immensity of the universe as it bears down on the dreams and delusions of humankind.

If the music is crucial to *Aguirre, the Wrath of God,* so is the face of Klaus Kinski. He has haunted blue eyes and wide, thick lips that would look sensual if they were not pulled back in the rictus of madness. Here he plays the strongest-willed of the conquistadors. Herzog told me that he was a youth in Germany when he saw Kinski for the first time: "At that moment I knew it was my destiny to make films, and his to act in them."

When Pizarro fears that his expedition is a folly, he selects a small party to spend a week exploring farther upriver. If they find nothing, he says, the attempt will be abandoned. This smaller party is led by the aristocrat Don Pedro de Ursua, with Aguirre (Kinski) as his second-in-command. Also in the party, along with soldiers and slaves, are a priest, Gaspar de Carvajal; the fatuous nobleman Fernando de Guzman; Ursua's wife, Flores; Aguirre's daughter, Inez; and Baltasar, an Indian slave, who sadly tells one of the women, "I was born a prince, and men were forbidden to look on me. Now I am in chains."

Herzog does not hurry their journey or fill it with artificial episodes of suspense and action. What we feel above all is the immensity of the river and the surrounding forest; there is no shore to stand on because the waters have risen and flooded it. Consider how Herzog handles an early crisis, when one of the rafts is caught in a whirlpool. The slaves row furiously, but the raft cannot move. Herzog's camera stays across the river from the endangered rafters; their distress seems distant and insoluble. Aguirre con-

temptuously dismisses any attempt to rescue them, but a party is sent out to try to reach them from the other side. In the morning, the raft still floats in place; everyone on it is dead.

How did they die? I have an idea, but so do you. The point is that death is the destiny of this expedition. Ursua, the leader, is put under arrest. Aguirre arranges the selection of Guzman as their new leader. Soon both are dead. Guzman's last meal is fish and fruit, which as acting "emperor" he eats greedily while his men count out a few kernels of corn apiece. A horse goes mad, he orders it thrown overboard, and men mutter darkly that it would have supplied meat for a week. Guzman's dead body is found soon after.

Aguirre rules with a reign of terror. He stalks about the raft with a curious lopsided gait, as if one of his knees will not bend. There is madness in his eyes. When he overhears one of the men whispering of plans to escape, he cuts off his head so swiftly that the dead head finishes the sentence it was speaking. Death occurs mostly offscreen, or swiftly and silently, as arrows fly softly out of the jungle and into the necks and backs of the men. The film's final images, among the most memorable I have ever seen, are of Aguirre alone on his raft, surrounded by corpses and by hundreds of chattering little monkeys, still planning his new empire.

The filming of *Aguirre* is a legend in film circles. Herzog, a German director who speaks of the "voodoo of location," took his actors and crew into a remote jungle district where fever was frequent and starvation seemed like a possibility. It is said Herzog held a gun on Kinski to force him to continue acting, although Kinski, in his autobiography, denies this, adding darkly that he had the only gun. The actors, crew members, and cameras were all actually on rafts like those we see, and often, Herzog told me, "I did not know the dialogue ten minutes before we shot a scene."

The film is not driven by dialogue anyway, or even by the characters, except for Aguirre, whose personality is created as much by Kinski's face and body as by words. What Herzog sees in the story, I think, is what he finds in many of his films: men haunted by a vision of great achievement who commit the sin of pride by daring to reach for it and are crushed by an implacable universe. One thinks of his documentary about the ski jumper Steiner, who wanted to fly forever and became so good that he was in danger of overshooting the landing area and crushing himself against stones and trees.

Of modern filmmakers, Werner Herzog is the most visionary and the most obsessed with great themes. Little wonder that he has directed many operas. He does not want to tell a plotted story or record amusing dialogue; he wants to lift us up into realms of wonder. Only a handful of modern films share the audacity of his vision; I think of *2001* and *Apocalypse Now*. Among active directors, the one who seems as messianic is Oliver Stone. There is a kind of saintly madness in the way they talk about their work; they cannot be bothered with conventional success, because they reach for transcendence.

The companion film to *Aguirre* is Herzog's *Fitzcarraldo* (1982), also starring Kinski, also shot in the rain forest, also about an impossible task: a man who wants to physically move a steamship from one river system to another by dragging it across land. Of course Herzog literally dragged a real ship across land to make the film, despite urgent warnings by engineers that the cables would snap and slice everyone in half. A documentary about the shooting of that film, *Burden of Dreams* (1982), by Les Blank, is as harrowing as the film itself.

ALI: FEAR
EATS THE SOUL

The first shots set up the theme: them against us. An older woman, dumpy and plain, walks into an unfamiliar bar and takes a seat at the table inside the door. The barmaid, an insolent blonde in a low-cut dress, strolls over. The woman says she will have a Coke. At the bar, a group of customers turns to stare at her, and the camera exaggerates the distance between them. Back at the bar, the blonde tauntingly dares one of her customers to ask the woman to dance. He does. And now the camera groups the man and woman together on the dingy dance floor, while the others stare.

Ali: Fear Eats the Soul (1974) tells the story of these two people. Emmi Kurowski (Brigitte Mira) is about sixty, a widow who works two shifts as a building cleaner, and whose children avoid her. Ali (El Hedi ben Salem) is about forty, a garage mechanic from Morocco, who lives in a room with five other Arabs and describes his life simply: "Always work, always drunk." Ali is not even his real name; it's a generic name for dark-skinned foreign workers in Germany.

Rainer Werner Fassbinder told their story in a brief film that he dashed off in fifteen days in 1974, between the big-budget productions *Martha* and *Effi Briest*. He shot it on a shoestring. Mira was a little-known supporting player, and Salem, then Fassbinder's lover, had played only bit parts. The story was inspired by *All That Heaven Allows*, the 1955 Douglas Sirk film starring Jane Wyman as an older woman who falls in love with her

young gardener (Rock Hudson). Fassbinder said he made the film just to fill the time between bigger pictures, yet *Ali* may be the best of his forty or so films; it certainly belongs on the short list with *The Marriage of Maria Braun* (1979) and *Merchant of the Four Seasons* (1972).

The film is powerful but very simple. It is based on a melodrama, but Fassbinder leaves out all of the highs and lows and keeps only the quiet desperation in the middle. The two characters are separated by race and age, but they have one valuable thing in common: They like one another, and care for one another, in a world that otherwise seems coldly indifferent to both of them. When Emmi shyly confesses she is a building cleaner, she says many people look down on her for that. Ali, whose German is limited, expresses his position more directly: "German master, Arab dog."

Fassbinder often made films about characters cynically exploiting one another through sexuality. In *Ali,* there is a startling tenderness. The tall, bearded Moroccan offers to walk the cleaning woman home. It is raining, so she invites him in for coffee. He has a long tram journey to the district where he lives. She asks him to spend the night. He cannot sleep and wants to talk. She tells him to sit on her bed. As often as I've seen the film, I've never quite noticed the precise moment when he takes her hand and begins to caress her arm.

Of course she studies herself in the mirror the next morning. She knows she is old and lined. We see something of the world she lives in, and hear the casual racist conversations of her fellow cleaners, who talk about how filthy the foreign workers are. Emmi's defense is indirect: "But they work! That's what they're here for." True. Germans don't like their foreign workers but don't want to collect their own garbage or dig their own ditches. This fastidiousness is not limited to Germany.

Emmi and Ali, simply by being together, offend everyone who sees them. Fassbinder provides scenes in which Emmi's neighbors gossip spitefully; the grocer across the street is deliberately rude to Ali; a waiter is aloof in a restaurant ("Hitler's favorite restaurant!" Emmi tells Ali); and guests in a café mock them. The most unforgettable scene comes when Emmi informs her children that she has gotten married. Using a zoom lens to flatten the shot, as if its subjects are sandwiched between microscope slides, Fassbinder pans across the faces of her two sons, her daughter, and her son-in-law (played by himself). Then her son Bruno whirls around in his chair, stands up, and kicks in the screen of her TV set.

The movie's best scenes are the more subtle ones that follow. Ali and Emmi are contented when they're alone with each other, but they live in a toxic society. Soon Emmi is ganging up with her fellow workers to exclude the new cleaner, a woman from Yugoslavia. Soon her disapproving neighbors are happy to have Emmi's strong new husband help them shift furniture. Soon the coworkers are admiring Ali, and Emmi is letting them feel his muscles. Soon Ali is back in the bar with his "Arab mates" and upstairs with the buxom blonde—and not for sex. Posed in the doorway like the model for a Mickey Spillane paperback, she asks what he wants, and he replies, "Couscous."

Fassbinder was himself an outsider. His father died when he was young, his mother used the movie theater as a baby-sitter, he was gay when that was not acceptable, he was short and unattractive. It is not much of a stretch to see *Ali: Fear Eats the Soul* as the story of his own love affair with the tall, handsome El Hedi ben Salem. And not difficult to see self-criticism in the way he has Emmi unthinkingly reflect her society's prejudices against foreigners.

But the movie cuts its politics with irony. Emmi Kurowski's first husband was a Polish worker in Germany; when they see her with a Moroccan, the neighbors sniff, "She's not a real German with that name." The grocer and his daughter snub Ali, but soon realize they need the business, and flatter Emmi to get her back in the store. Bruno, the son, sends a check for the smashed TV set and turns up to ask his mother to baby-sit every afternoon. And Ali's infidelity with the barmaid is more sad than passionate: When they go to bed together, he lies unmoving, exhausted, and she simply comforts him.

The phrase "fear eats the soul" is one that Arabs often use, Ali tells Emmi. Certainly it is eating his soul. The film's ending, as sudden and melodramatic as life can be, is a reflection of the unendurable tension Ali experiences as a stranger in a hostile land. But Emmi is able to suggest a solution: "When we're together, we must be nice to one another."

There are times when Fassbinder uses deliberately mannered visuals to make a point. He often separates Emmi and Ali from the rest of society with alternating long shots: First they are distant, then those who watch them are distant. He crowds them into close two-shots in claustrophobic little rooms. He makes use of the Moroccan's natural stiffness before the camera. When Emmi comes into the bar toward the end and requests "that gypsy song" she and Ali first danced to, the song acts as Ali's cue, and he stands, walks toward her, and asks her to dance as if he were a robot triggered by the song. Would it be better if he were more natural? No, because Fassbinder's style throughout the movie is one in which movements and decisions are dictated to his characters by the world they live in.

At the very end of the film, there's dialogue about the condition of foreign workers in Germany: not a "message," but a reflection of reality. A few months after Fassbinder died (in 1982, at thirty-seven, of drugs and alcohol), I was on the Montreal Film Festival jury with Daniel Schmid, a Swiss-German director who knew Fassbinder very well. He told me the rest of the story of El Hedi ben Salem, who came to Germany from the mountains of North Africa and drifted into Fassbinder's orbit. "Germany was a strange world to him," Schmid told me. "He started drinking, the tension built up, and one day he went to a place in Berlin and stabbed three people. Then he came back to Rainer and said, 'Now you don't have to be afraid anymore.' He hanged himself in jail."

Ali: Fear Eats the Soul might sound like improbable, contrived soap opera. It doesn't play that way. The reason it gathers so much power, I think, is that Fassbinder knew exactly what was meant by the title and made the film so quickly he only had time to tell the truth.

{ ALL ABOUT EVE }

Growing older was a smart career move for Bette Davis, whose personality was adult, hard-edged, and knowing. Never entirely comfortable as an ingenue, she was glorious as a professional woman, a survivor, or a bitchy predator. Her veteran actress Margo Channing in *All About Eve* (1950) was her greatest role; it seems to show her defeated by the wiles of a younger actress, but in fact marks a victory, the triumph of personality and will over the superficial power of beauty. She never played a more autobiographical role.

Davis's performance as a star growing older is always paired with another famous 1950 performance—Gloria Swanson's aging silent star in *Sunset Boulevard*. Both were nominated for best actress, but neither won; the Oscar went to Judy Holliday for *Born Yesterday*, although Davis's fans claimed she would have won if her vote hadn't been split, ironically, by Anne Baxter, who plays her rival in the film and was also nominated for best actress. When you compare the performances by Davis and Swanson, you see different approaches to similar material. Both play great stars, now inexorably aging. Davis plays Margo Channing realistically, while Swanson plays Norma Desmond as a gothic waxwork. *Sunset Boulevard* seems like the better film today, maybe because it fits our age of irony, maybe because Billy Wilder was a better director than Joseph Mankiewicz. But Davis's performance is stronger than Swanson's, because less mad and more touching.

Davis *was* a character, an icon with a grand style, so even her excesses are realistic.

The movie, written by Mankiewicz, begins like *Sunset Boulevard* with a narration by a writer—the theater critic Addison DeWitt (George Sanders), bemused, cynical, manipulative. He surveys the room at a theatrical awards dinner, notes the trophy reserved for Eve Harrington (Baxter), and describes the survivors of Eve's savage climb to the top: her director, Bill Simpson (Gary Merrill); her writer, Lloyd Richards (Hugh Marlowe); and Lloyd's wife, Karen (Celeste Holm), who was her greatest supporter. And the idol she cannibalized, Margo. As the fatuous old emcee praises Eve's greatness, the faces of these people reflect a different story.

The movie creates Margo Channing as a particular person and Eve Harrington as a type. Eve is a breathless fan, eyes brimming with phony sincerity. She worms her way into Margo's inner circle, becoming her secretary, then her understudy, then her rival. Faking humility and pathos is her greatest role, and at first only one person sees through it: crusty old Birdie (Thelma Ritter), Margo's wardrobe woman. "What a story!" she snaps. "Everything but the bloodhounds snappin' at her rear end."

Margo believes Eve's story of hard luck and adoration; no actor has much trouble believing others would want to devote their lives to them. Good, sweet Karen also sympathizes with the girl and arranges to strand Margo in the country one weekend so that Eve can go on as her understudy. Karen is repaid when Eve tries to steal her playwright husband, after an earlier, unsuccessful attempt to steal Margo's fiancé, Bill (played by Davis's real-life husband), who turns her away with a merciless put-down. "What I go after, I want to go after. I don't want it to come after me."

Eve Harrington is a universal type. Margo Channing plays at having an ego but is in love with her work—a professional, not an exhibitionist. She's the real thing. But the sardonic tone of the film is set by George Sanders, as the critic Addison DeWitt. He's the principal narrator, and with his cigarette holder, his slicked-down hair, and his flawless evening dress, he sees everything with deep cynicism. He has his own agenda: While Eve naively tries to steal the men who belong to the women who helped her, Addison calmly schemes to keep Eve as his own possession. Sanders, who won the Oscar for best supporting actor, lashes out at her in one of the

movie's most savage speeches: "Is it possible, even conceivable, that you've confused me with that gang of backward children you play tricks on? That you have the same contempt for me as you have for them?" And: "I am no-body's fool. Least of all, yours."

Glittering in the center of *All About Eve* is a brief supporting appearance by Marilyn Monroe. This film, and John Huston's *The Asphalt Jungle* earlier the same year, put her on the map; she was already "Marilyn Monroe" in every detail. She appears at Margo's party as DeWitt's date, and he steers her toward the ugly but powerful producer Max Fabian (Gregory Ratoff), advising her, "Now go and do yourself some good." Monroe sighs, "Why do they always look like unhappy rabbits?"

It has been observed that no matter how a scene was lighted, Monroe had the quality of drawing all the light to herself. In her brief scenes here, surrounded by actors much more experienced, she is all we can look at. Do we see her through the prism of her legend? Perhaps not; those who saw the movie in 1950, when she was unknown, also singled her out. Mankiewicz helped create her screen persona when he wrote this exchange after the Monroe character sees Margo's fur coat:

"Now there's something a girl could make sacrifices for," Monroe says.

"And probably has," says the director.

"Sable," Monroe explains.

"Sable?" asks the producer. "Did she say sable or Gable?"

Monroe: "Either one."

If Monroe steals her own scenes, the party sequence contains Davis's best work in the movie, beginning with her famous line, "Fasten your seat belts. It's going to be a bumpy night." Drinking too much, disillusioned by Eve's betrayal, depressed by her fortieth birthday, she says that admitting her age makes her "feel as if I've taken all my clothes off." She looks at Bill, her fiancé, and bitterly tells Lloyd, "Bill's thirty-two. He looks thirty-two. He looked it five years ago. He'll look it twenty years from now. I hate men."

It was believed at the time that Davis's performance as Margo was inspired by Tallulah Bankhead. "Tallulah, understandably enough, did little to dispel the assumption," Mankiewicz tells Gary Carey in the book *More*

About All About Eve. "On the contrary, she exploited it to the hilt with great skill and gusto." Press agents manufactured a feud between Davis and Bankhead, but Mankiewicz says neither he nor Davis was thinking of Bankhead when the movie was made. Davis could have found all the necessary inspiration from her own life.

Davis smokes all through the movie. In an age when stars used cigarettes as props, she doesn't smoke as behavior, or to express her moods, but because she wants to. She inhales needfully. The smoking is invaluable in setting her apart from others, making her separate from their support and demands; she is often seen within a cloud of smoke, which seems like her charisma made visible.

The movie's strength and weakness is Anne Baxter, whose Eve lacks the presence to be a plausible rival to Margo Channing, but is convincing as the scheming fan. When Eve understudies for Margo and gets great reviews, Mankiewicz wisely never shows us her performance; better to imagine it, and focus on the girl whose look is a little too intense, whose eyes are a little too focused, whose modesty is somehow suspect.

Mankiewicz (1909–93) came from a family of writers; his brother, Herman, wrote *Citizen Kane.* He won back-to-back twin Oscars for writing and directing *A Letter to Three Wives* in 1949 and *All About Eve* in 1950, and is also remembered for *The Ghost and Mrs. Muir* (1947), *The Barefoot Contessa* (1954), and *Guys and Dolls* (1955). He remained sharp-tongued all of his days. When *All About Eve* was recycled into the Broadway musical *Applause,* Mankiewicz observed that the studio had received "infinitely more" in royalties than it paid him for writing and directing the film. He said he had no complaints. The reason they have the "no refunds" sign in the theater ticket window, he said, is to keep the rubes from calling the cops.

{ THE APARTMENT }

There is a melancholy divide over the holidays between those who have someplace to go and those who do not. *The Apartment* is so affecting partly because of that buried reason: It takes place on the shortest days of the year, when dusk falls swiftly and the streets are cold, when after the office party some people go home to their families and others go home to apartments where they haven't even bothered to put up a tree. On Christmas Eve, more than any other night of the year, the lonely person feels robbed of something that was there in childhood and isn't there anymore.

Jack Lemmon plays C. C. Baxter, a definitive lonely guy, in *The Apartment*, with the ironic twist that he is not even free to go home alone, because his apartment is usually loaned out to one of the executives at his company. He has become the landlord for a series of their illicit affairs; they string him along with hints about raises and promotions. His neighbor Dr. Dreyfuss (Jack Kruschen) hears the nightly sounds of passion through the wall and thinks Baxter is a tireless lover, when in fact Baxter is pacing the sidewalk out in front, looking up resentfully at his own lighted window. Baxter has no girlfriend and, apparently, no family. Patted on the back and called "buddy boy" by the executives who use him, he dreams of a better job and an office of his own. One day he even gets up his nerve and asks out one of the elevator girls, Miss Kubelik (Shirley MacLaine), but she stands him up at the last moment because of a crisis in her relationship with the

big boss, Mr. Sheldrake (Fred MacMurray). She thought her affair with Sheldrake was over, but now apparently it's on again; he keeps talking about divorcing his wife but never does.

When Billy Wilder made *The Apartment* in 1960, the "organization man" was still a current term. One of the opening shots in the movie shows Baxter as one of a vast horde of wage slaves, working in a room where the desks line up in parallel rows almost to the vanishing point. This shot is quoted from King Vidor's silent film *The Crowd* (1928), which is also about a faceless employee in a heartless corporation. Cubicles would have come as revolutionary progress in this world. The screenplay, executed as a precise balance between farce and sadness, has been constructed by Wilder and I. A. L. Diamond to demonstrate that while Baxter and Miss Kubelik may indeed like one another—may feel genuine feelings of the sort that lead to true love—they are both slaves to the company's value system. He wants to be the boss's assistant, she wants to be the boss's wife, and both of them are so blinded by the concept of "boss" that they can't see Mr. Sheldrake for an untrustworthy rat.

The movie has been photographed in wide-screen black and white. The b&w dampens down any jollity that might sweep in with the decorations at the Christmas parties, bars, and restaurants where the holidays are in full swing. And the wide screen emphasizes space that separates the characters or surrounds them with emptiness. The design of Baxter's apartment makes his bedroom door, in the background just to the left of center, a focal point; in there reside the secrets of his masters, the reasons for his resentments, the arena for his own lonely slumber, and eventually the stage on which Miss Kubelik will play out the crucial transition in her life. Other shots track down Manhattan streets and peer in through club windows, and isolate Miss Kubelik and the phony-sincere Mr. Sheldrake in their booth at the Chinese restaurant, where he makes earnest protestations of his good intentions and glances uneasily at his watch.

By the time he made *The Apartment*, Wilder had become a master at a kind of sardonic, satiric comedy that had sadness at its center. *Double Indemnity* (1944) was about a man (MacMurray again) who trusted that one simple crime would solve his romantic and financial troubles. *Sunset Boulevard* (1950) has William Holden as a paramour to a grotesque aging movie queen (Gloria Swanson), but there was pathos in the way her former husband (Erich von Stroheim) still worshiped at the shrine of her faded greatness. Wilder was fresh off the enormous hit *Some Like It Hot* (1959), his first collaboration with Lemmon, and Lemmon was headed toward *Days of Wine and Roses* (1962), which along with *The Apartment* showed that he could move from light comedian to tragic everyman. This movie was the summation of what Wilder had done to date and the key transition in Lemmon's career.

It was also a key film for Shirley MacLaine, who had been around for five years in light comedies and had interesting scenes in *Some Came Running* (1958) but here emerged as a capable actress who would flower in the 1960s. What is particularly good about her Miss Kubelik is the way she doesn't make her a ditzy dame who falls for a smooth talker, but suggests a young woman who has been lied to before, who has a good heart but finite patience, who is prepared to make the necessary compromises to be the next Mrs. Sheldrake. The underlying seriousness of MacLaine's performance helps anchor the picture; it raises the stakes and steers it away from any tendency to become musical beds.

What's particularly perceptive is the way, after her suicide attempt, she hauls herself together and actually gives Sheldrake another chance. Like Baxter, she has not been forced into job prostitution, but has chosen it. One of the ways this is an adult picture and not a sitcom is the way it takes Baxter and Miss Kubelik so long to make the romantic leap; they aren't deluded fools, but jaded realists who have given up on love and are more motivated by paychecks. There is a wonderful, wicked delicacy in the way Wilder handles the final scene and finds the right tender-tough note in the last lines of the screenplay. ("Shut up and deal" would become almost as famous as "Nobody's perfect," the immortal closing line of *Some Like It Hot*.)

As it happened, I watched *The Apartment* not long after Jack Lemmon's death in June 2001 and looked at Blake Edwards's *Days of Wine and Roses* and James Foley's *Glengarry Glen Ross* (1992) at the same time. The side-by-side viewings were an insight into Lemmon's acting and into changing styles in movies. *Days of Wine and Roses* has dated; the greenhouse scene looks more like overacting than alcoholism. Wilder's *The Lost Weekend* (1945) was made seventeen years earlier but feels more contemporary in his treatment of the disease. *Glengarry Glen Ross* contains probably Lemmon's best performance. His aging, desperate real estate salesman is deserving of comparison with anyone's performance of Willy Loman in *Death of a Salesman,* and it is interesting how Lemmon, who famously began with directors asking him to dial down and give "a little less," was able here to hit the precise tones needed for the David Mamet dialogue, which is realism cloaked in mannerism.

In observing that *The Lost Weekend* hasn't dated, I could be making a comment about Wilder's work in general. Even a lightweight romantic comedy like *Sabrina* (1954) holds up better than its 1990s remake, and the great Wilder pictures don't play as period pieces, but look us straight in the eye. *Some Like It Hot* is still funny, *Sunset Boulevard* is still a masterful noir character comedy, and *The Apartment* is still tougher and more poignant than the material might have indicated. The valuable element in Wilder is his adult sensibility; his characters can't take flight with formula plots, because they are weighted down with the trials and responsibilities of working for a living. In many movies, the characters hardly even seem to have jobs, but in *The Apartment,* they have to be reminded that they have anything else.

{ APOCALYPSE NOW }

Francis Ford Coppola's *Apocalypse Now* was inspired by *Heart of Darkness*, a novel by Joseph Conrad about a European named Kurtz who penetrated to the farthest reaches of the Congo and established himself like a god. A boat sets out to find him, and on the journey the narrator gradually loses confidence in orderly civilization; he is oppressed by the great weight of the jungle all around him, a pitiless Darwinian testing ground in which each living thing tries every day not to be eaten.

What is found at the end of the journey is not Kurtz so much as what Kurtz found: that all of our days and ways are a fragile structure perched uneasily atop the hungry jaws of nature which will thoughtlessly devour us. A happy life is a daily reprieve from this knowledge. A week before seeing the film, I had been in Calcutta, where I saw mile upon square mile of squatter camps in which hundreds of thousands live generation after generation in leaky huts of plastic, cardboard, and scrap metal, in poverty so absolute it is impossible to see any hope of escape. I do not mean to equate the misery of those hopeless people with a movie; that would be indecent. But I was deeply shaken by what I saw, and realized how precious and precarious is a happy life. And in such a mood I watched *Apocalypse Now* and came to the scene where Colonel Kurtz (Marlon Brando) tells Captain Willard (Martin Sheen) about "the horror."

Kurtz is a decorated hero who has created a jungle sanctuary upriver inside enemy territory and rules Montagnard tribesmen as his private army. He tells Willard about a day when his Special Forces men inoculated the children of a village against polio: "This old man came running after us and he was crying, he couldn't see. We went back there, and they had come and hacked off every inoculated arm. There they were in a pile, a pile of little arms."

What Kurtz learned is that the Viet Cong was willing to go to greater lengths to win: "Then I realized they were stronger than we. They have the strength, the strength to do that. If I had ten divisions of those men, then our troubles here would be over very quickly. You have to have men who are moral and at the same time who are able to utilize their primordial instincts to kill without feeling, without passion, without judgment." This is "the horror" that Kurtz has found, and it threatens to envelop Willard too. The whole movie is a journey toward Willard's understanding of how Kurtz, one of the Army's best soldiers, penetrated the reality of war to such a depth that he could not look any longer without madness and despair.

The film has one of the most haunting endings in cinema, a poetic evocation of what Kurtz has discovered, and what we hope not to discover for ourselves. The river journey creates enormous anticipation about Kurtz, and Brando fulfills it. When the film was released in 1979, his casting was criticized and his then-enormous paycheck of $1 million was much discussed, but it's clear he was the correct choice, not only because of his stature as an icon but because of his voice, which enters the film from darkness or half-light, repeating the words of T. S. Eliot's despairing "The Hollow Men." That voice sets the final tone of the film.

Another crucial element in the ending is the photojournalist (Dennis Hopper) who has somehow found Kurtz's camp and stayed there, stoned, as a witness. He blathers to Willard that Kurtz is "a poet-warrior in the classic sense" and "we're all his children." In the photographer's spaced-out ravings, we hear mangled snatches of the poetry he must have heard Kurtz reciting: "I should have been a pair of ragged claws scuttling across floors of silent seas." The photographer is the guide, the clown, the fool, providing the balance between Willard and Kurtz.

Why has *Apocalypse Now* been so long bedeviled by rumors that

Coppola was not happy with this ending? At the film's premiere at Cannes, I saw how the confusion began. Coppola originally intended to show the movie as a 70mm road show with no credits (they would be printed in a booklet). But the 35mm release would need end titles. After he was finished filming on the huge set of the Kurtz compound, Coppola was required by the Philippines government to destroy it, and he photographed it being blown up. He decided to use this footage over his closing 35mm credits, even though (this is crucial) he did not intend the destruction of the compound as an alternative "ending" to the film. Alas, confusion about the endings spread from Cannes into movie folklore, and most people thought that by "ending" he meant all of the material involving Kurtz.

In any event, seen again at a distance of twenty years, *Apocalypse Now* is more clearly than ever one of the key films of the century. Most films are lucky to contain a single great sequence. *Apocalypse Now* strings together one after another, with the river journey as the connecting link. The best is the helicopter attack on a Vietnam village, led by Lieutenant Colonel Kilgore (Robert Duvall), whose choppers use loudspeakers at top volume to play Wagner's "Ride of the Valkyries" as they swoop down on a yard full of schoolchildren. Duvall won an Oscar nomination for his performance and its unforgettable line, "I love the smell of napalm in the morning." His emptiness is frightening: A surfing fanatic, he agrees to the attack only to liberate a beach said to offer great waves ("Charlie don't surf").

There is also the sequence where the patrol boat stops a small fishing boat with a family on board. A little girl makes a sudden dash, and the jumpy machine gunner (a young Laurence Fishburne) opens fire, wiping out the entire family. It turns out the girl was running for her puppy. The mother is not quite dead. The boat chief (Albert Hall) wants to take her for medical treatment. Willard puts a bullet into her; nothing can delay his mission. He and "Chief" are the only two seasoned military men on the boat, trying to do things by the book. Later, in a scene with peculiar power, the chief is astonished to be killed by a spear.

For me, the most remarkable visuals in the film occur when Chef (Frederic Forrest), one of Willard's crew members, insists on venturing into the forest in search of mangoes. Willard can't stop him, so joins him. The great cinematographer Vittorio Storaro shows them as little human specks at the foot of towering trees, and this is a Joseph Conrad moment, showing how nature dwarfs us.

The rock and roll sound track opens and closes with "The End" by the Doors and includes disc jockeys on transistor radios ("Good morning, Vietnam!"). The music underlines surrealistic moments, as when Lance (Sam Bottoms), one of Willard's crew, water-skis behind the boat. It also shows how the soldiers try to use the music of home, and booze and drugs, to ease their loneliness and apprehension.

Other important films like *Platoon, The Deer Hunter, Full Metal Jacket,* and *Casualties of War* take their own approaches to Vietnam. Once at the Hawaii Film Festival, I saw five North Vietnamese films about the war. (They never mentioned "America," only "the enemy," and one director told me, "It is all the same—we have been invaded by China, France, the U.S. . . .") But *Apocalypse Now* is the best Vietnam film, one of the greatest of all films, because it pushes beyond the others, into the dark places of the soul. It is not about war so much as about how war reveals truths we would be happy never to discover. In a way I cannot quite explain, my thoughts since Calcutta prepared me to understand the horror that Kurtz found. If we are lucky, we spend our lives in a fool's paradise, never knowing how close we skirt the abyss. What drives Kurtz mad is his discovery of this.

TWO NOTES

1. In my review of his *The 400 Blows,* I quoted the French director François Truffaut: "I demand that a film express either the joy of making cinema or the agony of making cinema. I am not at all interested in anything in between." Coppola's joy and agony are revealed in *Hearts of Darkness,* a 1991 documentary by Fax Bahr and George Hickenlooper about the making of *Apocalypse Now,* with personal footage and journal entries by Coppola's wife, Eleanor Coppola, who made secret recordings of Coppola expressing his doubts and discouragement as the project threatened to swamp him.

2. *Apocalypse Now Redux,* shown at Cannes in May 2001 and released the next month, adds forty-nine minutes of footage, including a long sequence at a French plantation, additional footage on the river journey, another meeting with the Playboy Playmates, and more dialogue by Brando and Hopper. I was happy to see the additional footage, and indeed had seen it before, in outtake form. But did the movie require it?

Some of the footage enters seamlessly into the work and disappears, enriching it. That would include the river footage and some moments with the photographer. The new Brando footage, including more savagely pointed analysis of the war, is a valuable addition. The Playmate footage simply doesn't work; it was left out of the original, Coppola explains, because a typhoon prevented him from completing its filming, but his editor, Walter Murch, "found a way to get in and out of the sequence." Perhaps, but no reason to be there.

It is the French plantation sequence that gives me the most pause. It is long enough, I think, to distract from the overall arc of the movie. The river journey sets the rhythm, and too much time on the banks interrupts it. Yet the sequence is effective and provoking (despite the inappropriate music during the love scene). It helps me to understand it when Coppola explains that he sees the French like ghosts; I questioned how they had survived in their little enclave, and accept his feeling that their spirits survive as a cautionary specter for the Americans. Longer or shorter, redux or not, *Apocalypse Now* is one of the central events of my life as a filmgoer.

THE APU TRILOGY

The great, sad, gentle sweep of the Apu Trilogy remains in the mind of the moviegoer as a promise of what film can be. Standing above fashion, it creates a world so convincing that it becomes, for a time, another life we might have lived. The three films, which were made in India by Satyajit Ray between 1950 and 1959, swept the top prizes at Cannes, Venice, and London and created a new cinema for India, whose prolific film industry had traditionally stayed within the narrow confines of swashbuckling musical romances. Never before had one man had such a decisive impact on the films of his culture.

Ray (1921–92) was a commercial artist in Calcutta with little money and no connections when he determined to adapt a famous serial novel about the birth and young manhood of Apu—born in a rural village, formed in the holy city of Benares, educated in Calcutta, then a wanderer. The legend of the first film is inspiring: how on the first day Ray had never directed a scene, his cameraman had never photographed one, his child actors had not even been tested for their roles—and how that early footage was so impressive it won the meager financing for the rest of the film. Even the music was by a novice, Ravi Shankar, later to be famous.

The trilogy begins with *Pather Panchali*, filmed between 1950 and 1954. Here begins the story of Apu when he is a young boy, living with his parents, older sister, and ancient aunt in the ancestral village to which his father, a priest, has returned despite the misgivings of the practical mother. The second film, *Aparajito* (1956), follows the family to Benares, where the father makes a living from pilgrims who have come to bathe in the holy Ganges. The third film, *The World of Apu* (1959), finds Apu and his mother living with an uncle in the country; the boy does so well in school he wins a scholarship to Calcutta. He is married under extraordinary circumstances, is happy with his young bride, then crushed by the deaths of his mother and his wife. After a period of bitter drifting, he returns at last to take up the responsibility of his son.

This summary scarcely reflects the beauty and mystery of the films, which do not follow the punched-up methods of conventional biography, but are told in the spirit of the English title of the first film, *The Song of the Road*. The actors who play Apu at various ages from about six to twenty-nine have in common a moody, dreamy quality; Apu is not sharp, hard, or cynical, but a sincere, naive idealist, motivated more by vague yearnings than concrete plans. He reflects a society that does not place ambition above all, but is philosophical, accepting, optimistic. He is his father's child, and in the first two films we see how his father is eternally hopeful that something will turn up—that new plans and ideas will bear fruit. It is the mother who frets about money owed the relatives, about food for the children, about the future. In her eyes, throughout all three films, we see realism and loneliness, as her husband and then her son cheerfully go away to the big city and leave her waiting and wondering.

The most extraordinary passage in the three films comes in the third when Apu, now a college student, goes with his best friend, Pulu, to attend the wedding of Pulu's cousin. The day has been picked because it is astrologically perfect—but the groom, when he arrives, turns out to be stark mad. The bride's mother sends him away, but then there is an emergency because Aparna, the bride, will be forever cursed if she does not marry on this day, and so Pulu, in desperation, turns to Apu—and Apu, having left Calcutta to attend a marriage, returns to the city as the husband of the bride.

Sharmila Tagore, who plays Aparna, was only fourteen when she made the film. She projects exquisite shyness and tenderness, and we consider how odd it is to be suddenly married to a stranger. "Can you accept a

life of poverty?" asks Apu, who lives in a single room and augments his scholarship with a few rupees earned in a printshop. "Yes," she says simply, not meeting his gaze. She cries when she first arrives in Calcutta, but soon sweetness and love shine out through her eyes. Soumitra Chatterjee, who plays Apu, shares her innocent delight, and when she dies in childbirth, it is the end of his innocence and, for a long time, of his hope.

The three films were photographed by Subrata Mitra, a still photographer whom Ray was convinced could do the job. Starting from scratch, at first with a borrowed 16mm camera, Mitra achieves effects of extraordinary beauty: forest paths, river vistas, the gathering clouds of the monsoon, water bugs skimming lightly over the surface of a pond. There is a fearsome scene as the mother watches over her feverish daughter while the rain and winds buffet the house, and we feel her fear and urgency as the camera dollies again and again across the small, threatened space. And a moment after a death, when the film cuts shockingly to the sudden flight of birds.

I heard a distant echo of the earliest days of the filming, perhaps, when Subrata Mitra was honored at the Hawaii Film Festival in the early 1990s, and in accepting a career award he thanked not Satyajit Ray, but his camera and his film. On those first days of shooting, it must have been just that simple, the hope of these beginners that their work would bear fruit.

What we sense all through the Apu Trilogy is a different kind of life than we are used to. The film is set in Bengal in the 1920s, when in the rural areas life was traditional and hard. Relationships were formed with those who lived close by; there is much drama over the theft of some apples from an orchard. The sight of a train, roaring at the far end of a field, represents the promise of the city and the future, and trains connect or separate the characters throughout the film, even offering at one low point a means of possible suicide.

The actors in the films have all been cast from life, to type; Italian neorealism was in vogue in the early 1950s, and Ray would have heard and agreed with the theory that everyone can play one role: himself. The most extraordinary performer in the films is Chunibala Devi, who plays the old aunt, stooped double, deeply wrinkled. She was eighty when shooting began; she had been an actress decades before, but when Ray sought her out, she was living in a brothel and thought he had come looking for a girl.

When Apu's mother becomes angry with her and tells her to leave, notice the way she appears at the door of another relative, asking, "Can I stay?" She has no home, no possessions except for her clothes and a bowl, but she never seems desperate because she embodies complete acceptance.

The relationship between Apu and his mother observes truths that must exist in all cultures: how the parent makes sacrifices for years, only to see the child turn aside and move thoughtlessly away into adulthood. The mother has gone to live with a relative, as little better than a servant ("they like my cooking"), and when Apu comes to visit during a school vacation, he sleeps or loses himself in his books, answering her with monosyllables. He seems in a hurry to leave, but has second thoughts at the train station and returns for one more day. The way the film records his stay, his departure, and his return says whatever can be said about lonely parents and heedless children.

I watched the Apu Trilogy recently over a period of three nights and found my thoughts returning to it during the days. It is about a time, place, and culture far removed from our own, and yet it connects directly and deeply with our human feelings. It is like a prayer, affirming that this is what the cinema can be, no matter how far in our cynicism we may stray.

{ BATTLESHIP POTEMKIN }

Eisenstein's *Battleship Potemkin* (1925) has been so famous for so long that it is almost impossible to come to it with a fresh eye. It is one of the fundamental landmarks of cinema. Its famous massacre on the Odessa Steps has been quoted so many times in other films (notably in *The Untouchables*) that it's likely many viewers will have seen the parody before they see the original. The film once had such power that governments actually believed it could incite audiences to action. If today it seems more like a technically brilliant but simplistic "cartoon" (Pauline Kael's word in a favorable review), that may be because it has worn out its element of surprise—that, like the Twenty-third Psalm or Beethoven's Fifth, it has become so familiar we cannot perceive it for what it is.

Having said that, let me say that *Potemkin*, which I have seen many times and taught with the shot-by-shot approach, did come alive for me one June night in 1998 in an unexpected way. The movie was projected on a big screen hanging from the outside wall of the Vickers Theater in Three Oaks, Michigan, and some three hundred citizens settled into their folding chairs in the parking lot to have a look at it. The simultaneous musical accompaniment was by Concrete, a southwestern Michigan band. Under the stars on a balmy summer night, far from film festivals and cinematheques, Eisenstein's 1925 revolutionary call generated some of its legendary rabble-rousing power. It's not that anybody stood up and sang the "Internationale."

The folding chairs for this classic exercise in Soviet propaganda were on loan from the local Catholic church. Some audience members no doubt drove over to Oink's in New Buffalo afterward for ice cream cones. But the film did have headlong momentum, thrilling juxtapositions, and genuine power to move—most especially during the Odessa Steps sequence, which had some viewers gasping out loud.

The movie was ordered up by the Russian revolutionary leadership for the twentieth anniversary of the *Potemkin* uprising, which Lenin had hailed as the first proof that troops could be counted on to join the proletariat in overthrowing the old order. As sketched by Eisenstein's film, the crew members of the battleship, cruising the Black Sea after returning from the war with Japan, are mutinous because of poor rations. There is a famous close-up of their breakfast meat, crawling with maggots. After officers throw a tarpaulin over the rebellious ones and order them to be shot, a firebrand named Vakulinchuk cries out, "Brothers! Who are you shooting at?" The firing squad lowers its guns, and when an officer unwisely tries to enforce his command, full-blown mutiny takes over the ship. Onshore, news of the uprising reaches citizens who have long suffered under czarist repression. They send food and water out to the battleship in a flotilla of skiffs. Then, in one of the most famous sequences ever put on film, czarist troops march down a long flight of steps, firing on the citizens, who flee before them in a terrified tide. Countless innocents are killed, and the massacre is summed up in the image of a woman shot dead trying to protect her baby in a carriage—which then bounces down the steps, out of control.

That there was, in fact, no czarist massacre on the Odessa Steps scarcely diminishes the power of the scene. The czar's troops did shoot innocent civilians elsewhere in Odessa, and Eisenstein, in concentrating those killings and finding the perfect cinematic setting for them, was doing his job as a director. It is ironic that he did it so well that today the bloodshed on the Odessa Steps is often referred to as if it really happened.

News of the uprising reaches the Russian fleet, which speeds toward Odessa to put it down. The *Potemkin* and a destroyer, also commanded by revolutionaries, steam out to meet them. Eisenstein creates tension by cutting between the approach fleet, the brave *Potemkin*, and details of the onboard preparation. At the last moment, the men of the *Potemkin* signal their comrades on the fleet to join them—and the ship steams through the fleet without a shot being fired at it.

Battleship Potemkin is conceived as class-conscious revolutionary propaganda, and Sergei Eisenstein deliberately avoids creating any three-dimensional individuals (even Vakulinchuk is seen largely as a symbol). Instead, masses of men move in unison, as in the many shots looking down at the *Potemkin*'s foredeck. The people of Odessa, too, are seen as a mass made up of many briefly glimpsed but starkly seen faces. The dialogue (in title cards) is limited mostly to outrage and exhortation. There is no personal drama to counterbalance the larger political drama.

Eisenstein (1898–1948) was one of the creators of Soviet theories of film montage, which argued that film has its greatest impact not by the smooth unrolling of images, but by their juxtaposition. Sometimes the cutting is dialectical: point, counterpoint, fusion. Cutting between the fearful faces of the unarmed citizens and the faceless troops in uniform, he created an argument for the people against the czarist state. Many other cuts are as abrupt: After *Potemkin*'s captain threatens to hang mutineers from the yardarm, we see ghostly figures hanging there. As the people call out, "Down with the tyrants!" we see clenched fists. To emphasize that the shooting victims were powerless to flee, we see one revolutionary citizen without legs. As the troops march ahead, a military boot crushes a child's hand. In a famous set of shots, a citizen is seen with eyeglasses; when we cut back, one of the lenses has been pierced by a bullet.

Eisenstein felt that montage should proceed from rhythm, not story. Shots should be cut to lead up to a point and should not linger because of personal interest in individual characters. Most of the sound tracks I've heard with *Potemkin* do not follow this theory, and instead score the movie as a more conventional silent drama. Concrete, the Michigan band (Boyd Nutting, Jon Yazell, Andrew Lersten), underlined and reinforced Eisenstein's approach with an insistent, rhythmic, repetitive score, using keyboards, half-heard snatches of speech, cries, and choral passages, percussion, martial airs, and found sounds. It was an aggressive, insistent approach, played loud, by musicians who saw themselves as Eisenstein's collaborators, not his meek accompanists.

It was the music, I think, along with the unusual setting, that was able to break through my long familiarity with *Battleship Potemkin* and make me understand, better than ever before, why this movie was long considered dangerous. (It was banned in various American states and in France, and for a longer time than any other film in British history; even Stalin banned it, at a time when mutiny was against the party line.)

The fact is, *Potemkin* doesn't really stand alone, but depends for its power upon the social situation in which it is shown. In prosperous peacetime, it is a curiosity. If it had been shown in China at the time of Tiananmen Square, I imagine it would have been inflammatory. It was voted the greatest film of all time at the Brussels World's Fair in 1958 (ironically the very year *Citizen Kane* had its great rerelease and quickly took possession of the crown). The cold war was at its height in 1958, and many European leftists still subscribed to the Marxist prescription for society; *Potemkin* for them had a power too.

But it suffers when it is seen apart from its context (just as *The Graduate,* by striking the perfect note for 1967, strikes a dated note now). It needs the right audience. In a sense, the band Concrete supplied a virtual audience; the loud, passionate, ominous music by the three young musicians worked as an impassioned audience response does, to carry and hurry the other watchers along. *Battleship Potemkin* is no longer considered the greatest film ever made, but it is obligatory for anyone interested in film history, and that night in the small-town parking lot I got a sense, a stirring, of the buried power it still contains, awaiting a call.

BEAUTY
AND THE BEAST

Before Disney's 1991 film and long before the Beast started signing autographs in Orlando, Jean Cocteau filmed *Beauty and the Beast* in 1946, in France. It is one of the most magical of all films. Before the days of computer effects and modern creature makeup, here is a fantasy alive with trick shots and astonishing effects, giving us a Beast who is lonely like a man and misunderstood like an animal. Cocteau, a poet and surrealist, was not making a "children's film," but was adapting a classic French tale that he felt had a special message after the suffering of World War II: Anyone who has an unhappy childhood may grow up to be a Beast.

Those familiar with the 1991 cartoon will recognize some of the elements of the story, but certainly not the tone. Cocteau uses haunting images and bold Freudian symbols to suggest emotions at a boil in the subconscious of his characters. Consider the extraordinary shot where Belle waits at the dining table in the castle for the Beast's first entrance. He appears behind her and approaches silently. She senses his presence and begins to react in a way that some viewers have described as fright, although it is clearly orgasmic. Before she has even seen him, she is aroused to her very depths, and a few seconds later, as she tells him she cannot marry—a Beast!—she toys with a knife that is more than a knife.

The Beast's dwelling is one of the strangest ever put on film— Xanadu crossed with Dalí. Its entrance hall is lined with candelabra held by living human arms that extend from the walls. The statues are alive, and their eyes follow the progress of the characters (are they captives of the Beast, imprisoned by spells?). The gates and doors open themselves. As Belle first enters the Beast's domain, she seems to run dreamily a few feet above the floor. Later, her feet do not move at all, but she glides, as if drawn by a magnetic force (this effect has been borrowed by Spike Lee). She is disturbed to see smoke rising from the Beast's fingertips—a sign that he has killed. When he carries her into her bed chamber, she has common clothes on one side of the door and a queen's costume on the other.

Belle has come to the castle as a hostage. She lives at home with her father, two unkind sisters, and a silly brother, whose handsome friend wants to marry her. But she cannot marry, for she must care for Papa. His business is threatened, and he learns on a trip to a seaport that he has lost everything. On his way home, through a forest on a stormy night, he happens upon the Beast's castle and is taken prisoner and told he must die. The Beast offers a deal: He can go home if he will return in three days, or he can send one of his daughters. The other sisters, of course, sniff and make excuses, and their father says he is old and nearly dead and will return himself. But Belle slips out and rides the Beast's white horse, which knows the way to the castle. And the Beast's first words are "You are in no danger."

Indeed she is not. The Beast has perhaps intuited that a daughter who would take her father's place has a good heart. He tells her that every night at seven he will ask her the same question: "Will you be my wife?" She shudders and says she will never marry him, but eventually her heart softens, and she pities him and sees that he is good. He gives her a magical glove that allows her to travel instantly between the castle and her home (emerging whole from the wall), and there is intrigue involving the key to the garden where his fortune is held. The sisters plot and scheme, but Belle, of course, prevails. Her father rises up from his deathbed, the Beast sinks into a final illness instead, and when she begs him to rally, his dying words are pathetic: "If I were a man, perhaps I could. But the poor beasts who want to prove their love can only grovel on the ground, and die."

Then there is another death, of the faithless family friend who wanted to marry her, and as his body turns into that of the Beast, the Beast comes back to life and turns into a prince who looks uncannily like the dead

friend. And no wonder, because all three—friend, Beast, and prince—are played by Jean Marais. Odd, how appealing Marais is as the Beast, and how shallow and superficial he seems as the pompadoured prince. Even Belle doesn't leap cheerfully into his arms, but looks quizzically at her new catch and confesses she misses the Beast. So did Marlene Dietrich, who held Cocteau's hand during the suspenseful first screening of the film at a Paris studio. As the prince shimmered into sight and smilingly presented himself as Belle's new lover, she called to the screen, "Where is my beautiful Beast?"

Although he made many films, Cocteau (1889–1963) did not consider himself primarily a filmmaker, but a poet who also painted, sculpted, wrote novels and plays, and stirred the currents of the Paris art scene. His first film, the surrealistic *Blood of a Poet*, was made in 1930, the same year as Salvador Dalí and Luis Buñuel's notorious *L'Age d'Or*. Both films were produced by the Viscount de Noailles, who delayed the release of Cocteau's after the other film inspired riots. Cocteau's film included images that became famous, as when a mirror turns into a pool of water and when a mouth wiped off a painting affixes itself to his hand.

Blood of a Poet was an art film made by a poet. *Beauty and the Beast* was a poetic film made by an artist. He made it at the urging of Marais, his lover of many years, who was tall and imposing, with an extraordinary profile and matinee-idol looks—a contrast to the skinny, chain-smoking Cocteau, whose months of shooting the film were made a misery because of a painful skin disease that required penicillin every three hours.

Because Cocteau was not sure he had the technical mastery for such an ambitious production, he recruited the director René Clément *(Purple Noon, Diabolique)* as his technical adviser, the gifted cameraman Henri Alekan to handle the tricky changes between outdoor realism and indoor fantasy, and the theatrical designer Christian Bérard to design the makeup, sets, and costumes (his ideas were based on the illustrations of Gustave Doré). The costumes were so elaborate they were said to be "as much as the actors could stand up in." All of Cocteau's thoughts on this process are preserved in his journal, *Beauty and the Beast: Diary of a Film*, which shows him persevering despite his health. His entry for October 18, 1945: "Woke up with unbearable pain. As I can neither sleep nor walk up and down, I calm myself by picking up this notebook and trying to shout my pain to the unknown friends who will read these lines."

We exist. His film has made us the friends. Watching it again tonight, I felt an unusual excitement. Its devices penetrate the usual conventions of narrative and appeal at a deeper psychic level. Cocteau wanted to make a poem, wanted to appeal through images rather than words, and although the story takes the form of the familiar fable, its surface seems to be masking deeper and more disturbing currents. It is not a "children's film." Is it even suitable for children? Some will be put off by the black-and-white photography and the subtitles (brief, however, and easy to read). Those who get beyond those hurdles will find a film that may involve them much more deeply than the Disney cartoon, because it is not just a jolly comic musical but deals, as all fairy tales do, with what we dread and desire. Brighter and more curious children will be able to enjoy it very much, I suspect, although if they return as adults, they may be amazed by how much more is there.

{ BELLE DE JOUR }

In the days after I first saw Stanley Kubrick's *Eyes Wide Shut* (1999), another film entered my mind again and again. It was Luis Buñuel's *Belle de Jour* (1967), the story of a respectable young wife who secretly works in a brothel one or two afternoons a week. Actors sometimes create "back stories" for their characters—things they know about them that we don't. I became convinced that if Nicole Kidman's character in the Kubrick film had a favorite film of her own, it was *Belle de Jour*.

It is probably the best-known erotic film of modern times, possibly the best. That's because it understands eroticism from the inside out—understands how it exists not in sweat and skin, but in the imagination. *Belle de Jour* is seen entirely through the eyes of Séverine, the proper twenty-three-year-old surgeon's wife played by Catherine Deneuve. Buñuel, who was sixty-seven when the film was released, had spent a lifetime making sly films about the secret terrain of human nature, and he knew one thing most directors never discover: For a woman like Séverine, walking into a room to have sex, the erotic charge comes not from who is waiting in the room, but from the fact that she is walking into it. Sex is about herself. Love, of course, is another matter.

The subject of Séverine's passion is always Séverine. She has an uneventful marriage to a conventionally handsome young surgeon named Pierre (Jean Sorel), who admires her virtue. She is hit upon by an older family friend, the saturnine Henri (Michel Piccoli, who was born looking insinuating). He's

also turned on by her virtue—by her blond perfection, her careful grooming, her reserve, her icy disdain for him. "Keep your compliments to yourself," she says when she and Pierre have lunch with him at a resort.

Her secret is that she has a wild fantasy life, and Buñuel cuts between her enigmatic smile and what she is thinking. Buñuel celebrated his own fetishes, always reserving a leading role in his films for feet and shoes, and he understood that fetishes have no meaning *except* that they are fetishes. Séverine is a masochist who likes to be handled roughly, but she also has various little turn-ons that the movie wisely never explains, because they are hers alone. The mewling of cats, for example, and the sound of a certain kind of carriage bell. These sounds accompany the film's fantasy scenes, including the opening in which she rides with Pierre out to the country, where he orders two carriage drivers to assault her. In another scene, she is tied helplessly, dressed in an immaculate white gown, as men throw mud at her.

The turning point in Séverine's sexual life comes when she learns of exclusive Paris brothels where housewives sometimes work in the afternoons, making extra money while their husbands are at the office. Henri, who has her number, gives her the address of one. A few days later, dressed all in black as if going to her own funeral, she knocks at the door and is admitted to the domain of Madame Anaïs (Geneviève Page), an experienced businesswoman who is happy to offer her a job. Séverine runs away but returns, intrigued. At first she wants to pick and choose her clients, but Anaïs gives her a push, and when she answers, "Yes, madame," the older woman smiles to herself and says, "I see you need a firm hand." She understands Séverine's need and is pleased that it will bring her business.

There is no explicit sex in the movie. The most famous single scene—those who have seen it describe it again and again—involves something we do not see and do not even understand. A client has a small lacquered box. He opens it and shows its contents to one of the other girls and then to Séverine. We never learn what is in the box. A soft buzzing noise comes from it. The first girl refuses to do whatever the client has in mind. So does Séverine, but the movie cuts in an enigmatic way, and a later scene leaves the possibility that something happened. What's in the box? The literal truth doesn't matter. The symbolic truth, which is all Buñuel cares about, is that it contains something of great erotic importance to the client.

Into Madame Anaïs's come two gangsters. One of them, young and swaggering, with a sword-stick, a black leather cape, and a mouthful of hideous steel teeth, is Marcel (Pierre Clémenti). "For you there is no charge," Séverine says quickly. She is turned on by his insults, his manner, and no doubt by the notion of her cool perfection being defiled by his crude street manners. They have an affair, which leads up to the deep irony of the final melodramatic scenes—but what Marcel never understands is that while Séverine is addicted to what he represents, she hardly cares about him at all. He is a prop for her fantasy life, the best one she has ever found.

Buñuel (1900–83), one of the greatest of all directors, was almost contemptuous of stylistic polish. A surrealist as a young man, a collaborator with Salvador Dalí on the famous *Un Chien Andalou* (1928), he was deeply cynical about human nature, but with amusement, not scorn. He was fascinated by the way in which deep emotional programming may be more important than free will in leading us to our decisions. Many of his films involve situations in which the characters seem free to act, but are not. He believed that many people are hardwired at an early age into lifelong sexual patterns. Séverine is such a person. "I can't help myself," she says at one point. "I am lost." She has a kind of resignation late in the film. She knows she has betrayed Pierre. For that matter, she knows she has used Marcel shamefully, even though that's what he thought he was doing to her. In the words of Woody Allen, which contain as much despair as defiance, "the heart wants what the heart wants."

The film is elegantly mounted—costumes, settings, decor, hair, clothes—and languorous in its pacing. Séverine's fate seems predestined. So does that of her husband, who as a weak man is swept away by the implacable strength of his wife's desire. The best stylistic touches are the little ones, which someone unfamiliar with Buñuel might miss (although they work even if you don't notice them). The subtle use of meows on the sound track—what do they represent? Only Séverine knows. The weary wisdom about human nature: After Séverine refuses an early client, Anaïs sends in another girl, then takes Séverine into the next room to watch through a peephole and learn. "That is disgusting," Séverine says, turning away. Then she turns back and looks through the peephole again.

Belle de Jour and *Eyes Wide Shut* are both about similar characters—

about staid middle-class professionals whose marriages do not satisfy the fantasy needs of the wives. The long story about the naval officer that Nicole Kidman's character tells her husband is closely related to the scenarios that play out in Séverine's imagination. Both husbands remain clueless because what their wives desire is not about them, but about needs and compulsions so deeply engraved they function at the instinctive level. Like a cat's meow.

{THE BICYCLE THIEF}

The Bicycle Thief is so well entrenched as an official masterpiece that it is startling to visit it again after many years and realize that it is still alive and has strength and freshness. Given an honorary Oscar for 1949, routinely voted one of the greatest films of all time, revered as one of the foundation stones of Italian neorealism, it is a simple, powerful film about a man who needs a job.

The film was directed by Vittorio De Sica, who believed that everyone could play one role perfectly: himself. It was written by Cesare Zavattini, the writer associated with many of the great European directors of the 1940s through the 1970s. In his journals, Zavattini writes about how he and De Sica visited a brothel to do research for the film—and later the rooms of the Wise Woman, a psychic, who inspired one of the film's characters. What we gather from these entries is that De Sica and his writer were finding inspiration close to the ground in those days right after the war, when Italy was paralyzed by poverty.

The story of The Bicycle Thief is easily told. It stars Lamberto Maggiorani, not a professional actor, as Ricci, a man who joins a hopeless queue every morning looking for work. One day there is a job—for a man with a bicycle. "I have a bicycle!" Ricci cries out, but he does not, for it has been pawned. His wife, Maria (Lianella Carell), strips the sheets from their bed, and he is able to pawn them to redeem his bicycle; as he glances through a window at the pawnshop, we see a man take the bundle of linen and climb up a ladder to a towering wall of shelves stuffed with other people's sheets.

The bicycle allows Ricci to go to work as a poster-hanger, slapping paste on walls to stick up cinema advertisements (a large portrait of Rita Hayworth provides an ironic contrast between the world of Hollywood and the everyday lives of neorealism). Maria, meanwhile, goes to thank the Wise Woman, who predicted that Ricci would get a job. Ricci, waiting for her impatiently, finally leaves his bicycle at the door while he climbs upstairs to see what's keeping her; De Sica is teasing us, since we expect the bike to be gone when Ricci returns, but it is still there.

Then, of course, it is stolen, no doubt by another man who needs a job. Ricci and his small, plucky son, Bruno (Enzo Staiola), search for the bicycle, but that's an impossible task in the wilderness of Rome, and the police are no help. Finally Ricci gives up: "You live and suffer," he tells Bruno. "To hell with it! You want a pizza?" In a scene of great cheer, they eat in a restaurant, Bruno even allowed to drink a little wine; the boy looks wistfully at a family eating platters of pasta and is told by his father, "To eat like that, you need a million lire a month at least." A little later, to his astonishment, Ricci spots the bicycle thief and pursues him into a brothel. An ugly crowd gathers. A cop arrives but can do nothing, because there is no evidence and only Ricci as witness. And then, in the closing sequence of the movie, Ricci is tempted to steal a bicycle himself, continuing the cycle of theft and poverty.

This story is so direct it plays more like a parable than a drama. At the time it was released, it was seen as a Marxist fable (Zavattini was a member of the Italian Communist Party). Later, the leftist writer Joel Kanoff criticized the ending as "sublimely Chaplinesque but insufficiently socially critical." David Thomson found the story too contrived, and wrote, "The more one sees *Bicycle Thief,* the duller the man becomes and the more poetic and accomplished De Sica's urban photography seems."

True, Ricci is a character entirely driven by class and economic need. There isn't a lot else to him, although he comes alive in the pizzeria scene. True, the movie doesn't make a point of contrasting his poverty with high-living millionaires (wealth is illustrated as the ability to buy a plate of spaghetti). But if the film is allowed to wait long enough—until the film-

makers are dead, until neorealism is less an inspiration than a memory—*The Bicycle Thief* escapes from its critics and becomes, once again, a story. It is happiest that way.

And its influence isn't entirely in the past. One of the 1999 Oscar nominees for best foreign film was *Children of Heaven,* from Iran, about a boy who loses his sister's shoes. In it there is a lovely passage where the father lifts his boy onto the crossbar of his bicycle and pedals to a rich neighborhood, looking for work. The sequence resonates for anyone who has seen *The Bicycle Thief.* Such films stand outside time. A man loves his family and wants to protect and support it. Society makes it difficult. Who cannot identify with that?

Vittorio De Sica (1901–74) was a handsome man, much in demand as an actor, whose first films as a director were light comedies like the ones he often worked in. Perhaps the harsh reality of World War II jarred the optimism necessary to make such stories, and in 1942 he made *The Children Are Watching Us,* a film that came soon after Visconti's *Ossessione.* The Visconti film, based on James M. Cain's hard-boiled novel *The Postman Always Rings Twice,* is often named as the first of the neorealist films, although even in silent days there were films that boldly looked at everyday life in an unvarnished way.

De Sica and others often used real people instead of actors, and the effect, after decades of Hollywood gloss, was startling to audiences. Pauline Kael remembers going to see De Sica's first great film, *Shoeshine,* in 1947, just after a lovers' quarrel that had left her in a state of despair:

> I came out of the theater, tears streaming, and overheard the petulant voice of a college girl complaining to her boyfriend, "Well, I don't see what was so special about that movie." I walked up the street, crying blindly, no longer certain whether my tears were for the tragedy on the screen, the hopelessness I felt for myself, or the alienation I felt from those who could not experience the radiance of *Shoeshine.* For if people cannot feel *Shoeshine,* what *can* they feel?

Neorealism, as a term, means many things, but it often refers to films of working-class life, set in the culture of poverty, and with the im-

plicit message that in a better society wealth would be more evenly distrib-
uted. *Shoeshine* told the story of two shoeshine boys sent to reform school
for black-marketing; Kael's description of it could function as a definition
of the hope behind neorealism: "It is one of those rare works of art which
seem to emerge from the welter of human experience without smoothing
away the raw edges, or losing what most movies lose—the sense of confusion and accident in human affairs."

The Bicycle Thief, De Sica's next film, was in the same tradition, and
after the lighthearted *Miracle in Milan* in 1951, he and Zavattini returned
to the earlier style with *Umberto D*, in 1952, about an old man and his dog,
forced out onto the streets. Then, in the view of most critics, De Sica put
his special gift as a director on hold for many years, turning out more light
comedies (*Marriage, Italian Style* [1964]; *Yesterday, Today and Tomorrow*
[1963]). The two important exceptions are *Two Women* (1961), which won
Sophia Loren an Oscar for her portrait of a homeless woman during the
war, and *The Garden of the Finzi-Continis* (1971), about an Italian Jewish
family that tries to ignore the gathering clouds of doom. Both screenplays
were by Zavattini.

The Bicycle Thief had such an impact on its first release that when
the British film magazine *Sight & Sound* held its first international poll of
filmmakers and critics in 1952, it was voted the greatest film of all time. The
poll is held every ten years; by 1962, it was down to a tie for sixth, and then
it dropped off the list. The 1999 release of a restored print allowed a new
generation to see how simple, direct, and true it is—"what was so special
about it."

{ THE BIG SLEEP }

Two of the names mentioned most often in Howard Hawks's *The Big Sleep* (1946) are Owen Taylor and Sean Regan. One is the chauffeur for the wealthy Sternwood family. The other is an Irishman hired by old General Sternwood "to do his drinking for him." Neither is ever seen alive; Regan has disappeared mysteriously before the movie begins, and Taylor's body is hauled from the Pacific after his Packard runs off a pier. Were they murdered? And does it even matter, since there are five other murders in the film?

One of the best known of all Hollywood anecdotes involves the movie's confusing plot, based on the equally confusing novel by Raymond Chandler. Lauren Bacall recalls in her autobiography, "One day Bogie came on the set and said to Howard, 'Who pushed Taylor off the pier?' Everything stopped." As A. M. Sperber and Eric Lax write in *Bogart*, "Hawks sent Chandler a telegram asking whether the Sternwood's chauffeur, Owen Taylor, was murdered or a suicide. 'Dammit I didn't know either,' Chandler recalled. And Chandler later wrote to his publisher, 'The girl who played the nymphy sister [Martha Vickers] was so good she shattered Miss Bacall completely. So they cut the picture in such a way that all her best scenes were left out except one. The result made nonsense and Howard Hawks threatened to sue . . . After long argument, as I hear it, he went back and did a lot of re-shooting.' "

It is typical of this most puzzling of films that no one agrees even on why it is so puzzling. Yet that has never affected *The Big Sleep*'s enduring popularity, because the movie is about the process of a criminal investigation, not its results. The process follows private eye Philip Marlowe (Humphrey Bogart) as he finds his way through the jungle of gamblers, pornographers, killers, and blackmailers who have attached themselves to the rich old general (Charles Waldron) and his two randy daughters (Bacall and Vickers). Some bad guys get killed and others get arrested, and we don't much care—because the *real* result is that Bogart and Bacall end up in each other's arms. *The Big Sleep* is a lust story with a plot about a lot of other things.

That can be seen more clearly now that an earlier version of the film has surfaced. *The Big Sleep* was finished by Warner Bros. in 1945, but held out of release while the studio rushed to play off its backlog of World War II movies. The 1945 print has a complicated history. It was sent out by the USO to be shown to troops in the Pacific, and I was shown a copy of that version one Sunday afternoon in 1980 by the legendary film archivist David Bradley, whose house in the Hollywood Hills had a concrete-block bunker behind it, jammed with film prints. Bradley said it was rare for a film to be supplied to troops while withheld from theaters, and wondered if the studio immediately started thinking about beefing up the Bacall role.

At any rate, ongoing events greatly affected its future. Hawks's *To Have and Have Not* (1944), Bacall's screen debut, was an enormous hit, and the on-screen chemistry between her and Bogart was sizzling ("You know how to whistle, don't you, Steve? You just put your lips together and blow"). Bacall then starred opposite Charles Boyer in *Confidential Agent* (1945) and got withering reviews. And she and Bogart were married (she was twenty, he was forty-four).

Bacall's powerful agent, Charles Feldman, who disliked the original version of *The Big Sleep*, wrote studio head Jack Warner in desperation, asking that scenes be eliminated, added, and reshot. Otherwise, he warned, Bacall was likely to get more bad reviews, damaging the career of a promising star who was married to the studio's biggest moneymaker. Warner agreed, and Hawks returned to the soundstages with his actors for reshoots. Bacall's book minimizes this process: "Howard . . . did need one more scene between Bogie and me." Actually he needed a lot more than that; the 1945 release, restored by archivists at UCLA and available on video, is accompanied by a detailed documentary showing what was left out and what was brand-new when the movie was finally released in 1946.

What Feldman missed, he said in his letter to Warner, was the "insolence" that Bacall showed in *To Have and Have Not*. In the original version of *The Big Sleep*, the relationship between Bogart and Bacall is problematical: Marlowe isn't sure whether he trusts this cool, elegant charmer. The 1946 version commits to their romance, and adds among other scenes one of the most daring examples of double entendre in any movie up until that time. The new scene puts Bacall and Bogart in a nightclub, where they are only ostensibly talking about horse racing:

> *Bacall:* . . . speaking of horses, I like to play them myself. But I like to see them work out a little first. See if they're front-runners or come from behind . . . I'd say you don't like to be rated. You like to get out in front, open up a lead, take a little breather in the back stretch, and then come home free . . .
>
> *Bogart:* You've got a touch of class, but I don't know how far you can go.
>
> *Bacall:* A lot depends on who's in the saddle.

What you sense here is the enjoyable sight of two people who are in love and like toying with one another. The new scenes add a charge to the film that was missing in the 1945 version; this is a case where "studio interference" was exactly the right thing. The only reason to see the earlier version is to go behind the scenes, to learn how the tone and impact of a movie can be altered with just a few scenes. (The accompanying documentary even shows how dialogue was redubbed to get a slightly different spin.)

As for the 1946 version that we have been watching all of these years, it is one of the great film noirs, a black and white symphony that exactly reproduces Chandler's ability, on the page, to find a tone of voice that keeps its distance, and yet is wry and humorous, and cares. Working from Chandler's original words and adding spins of their own, the writers

(William Faulkner, Jules Furthman, and Leigh Brackett) wrote one of the most quotable of screenplays: It's unusual to find yourself laughing in a movie not because something is funny, but because it's so wickedly clever. (Marlowe on the "nymphy" kid sister: "She tried to sit in my lap while I was standing up.") Unlike modern crime movies which are loaded with action, *The Big Sleep* is heavy with dialogue. The characters talk and talk, just like in the Chandler novels; it's as if there's a competition to see who has the most verbal style.

Martha Vickers was indeed electric as the kid sister, and Dorothy Malone all but steals her scene as a book clerk who finds Marlowe intriguing. But the 1945 version makes it clear Bacall was by no means as bad as Feldman feared she was—she is adequate in most scenes and splendid in others—but the scenes themselves didn't give her the opportunities that the reshoot did. In scenes like the "racing" conversation, she has the dry reserve, the private amusement, the way of sizing up a man and enjoying the competition, that became her trademark. It's astonishing to realize she was twenty, untrained as an actor, and by her own report scared to death.

Bogart himself made personal style into an art form. What else did he have to work with? He wasn't particularly handsome, he wore a rug, he wasn't tall ("I try to be," he tells Vickers), and he always seemed to act within a certain range. Yet no other movie actor is more likely to be remembered a century from now. And the fascinating subtext in *The Big Sleep* is that in Bacall he found his match.

You can see it in his eyes. Sure, he's in love, but there's something else too. He was going through a messy breakup with his wife, Mayo, when they shot the picture. He was drinking so heavily he didn't turn up some days, and Hawks had to shoot around him. He saw this coltish twenty-year-old not only as his love but perhaps as his salvation. That's the undercurrent. It may not have been fun to live through, but it creates a kind of joyous, desperate tension on the screen. And since the whole idea of film noir was to live through unspeakable experiences and keep your cool, this was the right screenplay for this time in his life.

Howard Hawks (1896–1977) is one of the great American directors of pure movies (*His Girl Friday* [1940], *Bringing Up Baby* [1938], *Red River*

[1948], *Rio Bravo* [1959]) and a hero of auteur critics because he found his own laconic values in many different kinds of genre material. He once defined a good movie as "three great scenes and no bad scenes." Comparing the two versions of *The Big Sleep* reveals that the reshoots inserted one of the great scenes and removed some of the bad ones, proving his point.

{ BLOWUP }

Michelangelo Antonioni's *Blowup* opened in America two months before I became a film critic, and colored my first years on the job with its lingering influence. It was a wake-up call for what Stanley Kauffmann named "the film generation," which quickly lined up outside *Bonnie and Clyde, Weekend, Battle of Algiers, Easy Rider,* and *Five Easy Pieces.* It was the highest-grossing art film to date, was picked as the best film of 1966 by the National Society of Film Critics, and got Oscar nominations for screenplay and direction. Today you rarely hear it mentioned.

Young audiences aren't interested anymore in a movie about a "trendy" London photographer who may or may not have witnessed a murder, who lives a life of cynicism and ennui, and who ends up in a park at dawn, watching college kids play tennis with an imaginary ball. The children of the audiences that bought tickets for *Blowup* prefer ironic, self-referential slasher movies. Americans flew to "swinging London" in the 1960s; today's Londoners pile onto charter jets to Orlando.

Over three days at the University of Virginia, I revisited *Blowup* in a shot-by-shot analysis. Freed from the hype and fashion, it emerges as a great film, if not the one we thought we were seeing at the time. This was at the 1998 Virginia Festival of American Film in Charlottesville, which had "Cool" as its theme. The festival began with the emergence of the Beat Generation and advanced through Cassavetes to *Blowup*—after which the

virus of Cool leaped from its nurturing subculture into millions of willing new hosts, and colored our society ever since, right down to and manifestly including *South Park*.

Watching *Blowup* once again, I took a few minutes to acclimate myself to the loopy psychedelic colors and the tendency of the hero to use words like "fab" (*Austin Powers* brilliantly lampoons the era). Then I found the spell of the movie settling around me. Antonioni uses the materials of a suspense thriller without the payoff. He places them within a London of heartless fashion photography, groupies, bored rock audiences, languid pot parties, and a hero whose dead soul is roused briefly by a challenge to his craftsmanship.

The movie stars David Hemmings, who became a 1960s icon after this performance as Thomas, a hot young photographer with a Beatles haircut, a Rolls convertible, and "birds" hammering on his studio door for a chance to pose and put out for him. The depth of his spiritual hunger is suggested in three brief scenes involving a neighbor (Sarah Miles), who lives with a painter across the way. He looks at her as if she alone could heal his soul (and may have once done so), but she's not available. He spends his days in tightly scheduled photo shoots (the model Verushka plays herself, and there's a group shoot involving grotesque mod fashions) and his nights visiting flophouses to take pictures that might provide a nice contrast in his book of fashion photography.

Thomas wanders into a park and sees, at a distance, a man and a woman. Are they struggling? Playing? Flirting? He snaps a lot of photos. The woman (Vanessa Redgrave) runs after him. She desperately wants the film back. He refuses her. She tracks him to his studio, takes off her shirt, wants to seduce him and steal the film. He sends her away with the wrong roll. Then he blows up his photos, and in the film's brilliantly edited centerpiece, he discovers that he may have photographed a murder.

Antonioni cuts back and forth between the photos and the photographer, using closer shots and larger blowups, until we see arrangements of light and shadow, dots and blurs, that may show—what? Thomas is interrupted by two girls who have been pestering him all day and engages in wild sex play as they roll around in crumpled backdrop paper. Then his eyes return to his blowups, he curtly sends the girls away, he makes more prints, and in the grainy, almost abstract blowups it appears that the woman is looking toward some bushes, there is a gunman there, and perhaps in one photo we see the man lying on the ground. Perhaps not.

Thomas returns to the park and does actually see the man lying dead on the ground. Curiously, many writers say the photographer is not sure if he sees a body, but he clearly does. What's unclear is whether he witnessed a murder. The audience understandably shares his interpretation of the photos, but another scenario is plausible: Redgrave wanted the photos because she was having an adulterous affair, her gray-haired lover dropped dead, she fled the park in a panic, and his body by the next morning had simply been discovered and removed. (The possibility of a scandalous affair plays off the Profumo scandal, in which a cabinet minister was linked to a call girl; the analysis of the photographs recalls the obsession with the Zapruder assassination film.)

Whether there was a murder isn't the point. The film is about a character mired in ennui and distaste, who is roused by his photographs into something approaching passion. As Thomas moves between his darkroom and the blowups, we recognize the bliss of an artist lost in the creative zone; he is not thinking now about money, ambition, or his own nasty personality defects, but is lost in his craft. His mind, hands, and imagination work in rhythmic sync. He is happy.

Later, all his gains are taken back. The body and the photographs disappear. So does Redgrave. (There is an uncanny scene where he sees her standing outside a club, and then she turns and takes a few steps and simply disappears into thin air. At Virginia, we ran the sequence a frame at a time and could not discover the method of her disappearance; presumably she steps into a doorway, but we watched her legs, and they seemed somehow to attach themselves to another body.)

In the final sequence, back in the park, Thomas encounters university students who were in the film's first scene. (These figures were described as "white-faced clowns" in one pan of the film, but a British audience would have known they were participating in the ritual known as Rag Week, in which students dress up and roar around town raising money for charity.) They play tennis with an imaginary ball. The photographer pretends he can see the ball. We hear the sounds of tennis on the sound track.

Then the photographer wanders away across the grass and, from one frame to the next, disappears—like the corpse.

Antonioni has described the disappearance of his hero as his "signature." It reminds us, too, of Shakespeare's Prospero, whose actors "were all spirits, and are melted into air." *Blowup* audaciously involves us in a plot that promises the solution to a mystery and leaves us lacking even its players.

There were, of course, obvious reasons for the film's great initial success. It became notorious for the orgy scene involving the groupies; it was whispered that one could actually see pubic hair (this was only seven years after similar breathless rumors about Janet Leigh's breasts in *Psycho*). The decadent milieu was enormously attractive at the time. Parts of the film have flip-flopped in meaning. Much was made of the nudity in 1966, but the photographer's cruelty toward his models was not commented on; today the sex seems tame, and what makes the audience gasp is the hero's contempt for women.

What remains is a hypnotic conjuring act, in which a character is awakened briefly from a deep sleep of bored alienation and then drifts away again. That is the arc of the film. Not "swinging London." Not existential mystery. Not the parallels between what Hemmings does with his photos and what Antonioni does with Hemmings. But simply the observation that we are happy when we are doing what we do well, and unhappy seeking pleasure elsewhere. I imagine Antonioni was happy while he was making this film.

{ B O D Y   H E A T }

Like a tantalizing mirage, film noir haunts modern filmmakers. Noir is the genre of night, guilt, violence, and illicit passion, and no genre is more seductive. But the best noirs were made in the 1940s and 1950s, before directors consciously knew what they were doing ("We called them B movies," said Robert Mitchum).

Once the French named the genre, once a generation of filmmakers came along who had seen noirs at cinematheques instead of in fleapits, noir could never again be naive. One of the joys of a great noir like *Detour* (1945) is the feeling that it was made by people who took the story perfectly seriously. One of the dangers of modern self-conscious noir, as Pauline Kael wrote in her scathing dismissal of *Body Heat*, is that an actress like Kathleen Turner comes across "as if she were following the marks on the floor made by the actresses who preceded her."

And yet if bad modern noir can play like a parody, good noir still has the power to seduce. Yes, Lawrence Kasdan's *Body Heat* (1981) is aware of the films that inspired it—especially Billy Wilder's *Double Indemnity* (1944). But it has a power that transcends its sources. It exploits the personal style of its stars to insinuate itself; Kael is unfair to Turner, who in her debut role played a woman so sexually confident that we can believe her lover (William Hurt) could be dazed into doing almost anything for her. The moment we believe that, the movie stops being an exercise and starts working. (I think the moment occurs in the scene where she leads Hurt by her hand in that manner a man is least inclined to argue with.)

Women are rarely allowed to be bold and devious in the movies; most directors are men, and they see women as goals, prizes, enemies, lovers, and friends, but rarely as protagonists. Turner's entrance in *Body Heat* announces that she is the film's center of power. It is a hot, humid night in Florida. Hurt, playing a cocky but lazy lawyer named Ned Racine, is strolling on a pier where an exhausted band is listlessly playing. He is behind the seated audience. We can see straight down the center aisle to the bandstand. All is dark and red and orange. Suddenly a woman in white stands up, turns around, and walks straight toward him. This is Matty Walker. To see her is to need her.

Turner in her first movie role was an intriguing original. Slender, with hair down to her shoulders, she evoked aspects of Barbara Stanwyck and Lauren Bacall. But the voice, with its elusive hint of a Latin accent, was challenging. She had "angry eyes," the critic David Thomson observed. And a slight overbite (later corrected, I think), which gave a playful edge to her challenging dialogue ("You're not too smart, are you?" she says soon after meeting Racine. "I like that in a man").

Hurt had been in one movie before *Body Heat*, Ken Russell's *Altered States*, in 1980. He was still unfamiliar: a tall, already balding, indolently handsome man with a certain lazy arrogance to his speech, as if amused by his own intelligence. *Body Heat* is a movie about a woman who gets a man to commit murder for her. It is important that the man not be a dummy; he needs to be smart enough to think of the plan himself. One of the brilliant touches of Kasdan's screenplay is the way he makes Ned Racine think he is the initiator of Matty Walker's plans.

Few movies have done a better job of evoking the weather. Heat, body heat, is a convention of pornography, where performers routinely complain about how warm they are (as if lovemaking could cool them off, instead of making them warmer). Although air-conditioning was not unknown in Miami in 1981, the characters here are constantly in heat; there is a scene where Ned comes home, takes off his shirt, and stands in front of the open refrigerator. The film opens with an inn burning in the distance ("Somebody's torched it to clear the lot," Ned says. "Probably one of my

clients"). There are other fires. There is the use of the color red. There is the sense that heat inflames passion and encourages madness.

In this heat, Matty seems cool. Early in the film, there is a justly famous scene where Matty brings Ned home from a bar, allegedly to listen to her wind chimes, and then asks him to leave. He leaves, then returns, and looks through a window next to her front door. She stands inside, dressed in red, calmly returning his gaze. He picks up a chair and throws it through the window, and in the next shot they are embracing. Knowing what we know about Matty, look once again at her expression as she looks back at him. She looks as confident and absorbed as a child who has pushed a button and is waiting for a video game to respond.

Kasdan, born in 1949, worked in ad agencies before moving to Hollywood to write screenplays. His more personal work languished in desk drawers, while his first credits were two of the biggest blockbusters of all time, *The Empire Strikes Back* (1980) and *Raiders of the Lost Ark* (1981). George Lucas acted as executive producer on this directorial debut to reassure Warner Bros. that it would come in on time and be releasable. It was; David Chute wrote in *Film Comment* that it was "perhaps the most stunning debut movie ever" (which raises the question of *Citizen Kane,* but never mind). Kasdan's subsequent career has alternated between action pieces written for others (*Return of the Jedi* [1983], aspects of *The Bodyguard* [1992]) and quirky, smart films directed by himself (*The Accidental Tourist* in 1988, *I Love You to Death* in 1990, the brilliant, overlooked *Grand Canyon* in 1991, and the unjustly neglected *Mumford* in 1999).

In *Body Heat,* Kasdan's original screenplay surrounds the characters with good, well-written performances in supporting roles. He creates a real world of police stations, diners, law offices, and restaurants, away from which Matty has seduced Ned into her own twisted scenario. The best supporting work in the movie is by Mickey Rourke in his breakthrough role as Ned's friend, a professional arsonist. Richard Crenna is Matty's husband. "He's small, and mean, and weak," she tells Ned, but when we see him, he is not small or weak. Ted Danson and J. A. Preston are a D.A. and a cop, Ned's friends, who are drawn reluctantly into suspecting him of murder (Danson's sense of timing and nuance are perfect in a night scene where he essentially briefs his friend Ned on the case against him).

"Kasdan has modern characters talking jive talk as if they'd been boning up on Chandler novels," Kael wrote, "and he doesn't seem to know if he wants laughs or not." But isn't it almost essential for noir characters to talk in a certain heightened style, and isn't it possible for us to smile in recognition? On the night they first make love, Ned tells Matty, "Maybe you shouldn't dress like that." She says, "This is a blouse and skirt. I don't know what you're talking about." And he says, "You shouldn't wear that body." Chandleresque? Yes. Works in this movie? Yes.

And there is some dialogue that unblinkingly confronts the enormity of the crime that Ned and Matty are contemplating. In many movies, the killers use self-justification and rationalization to talk themselves into murder. There is a chilling scene in *Body Heat* where Ned flatly tells Matty: "That man is gonna die for no reason but—we want him to."

The plot and its double crosses are, of course, part of the pleasure, although watching the film again last night, aware of its secrets, I found the final payoff less rewarding than the diabolical setup. The closing scenes are obligatory (and the final beach scene is perfunctory and unconvincing). The last scene that works as drama is the one where Ned suggests to Matty that *she* go get the glasses in the boathouse, and then she pauses on the lawn to tell him, "Ned, whatever you think—I really do love you."

Does she? That's what makes the movie so intriguing. Does he love her, for that matter? Or is he swept away by sexual intoxication—body heat? You watch the movie the first time from his point of view, and the second time from hers. Every scene plays two ways. *Body Heat* is good enough to make film noir play like we hadn't seen it before.

{ BONNIE AND CLYDE }

There is a moment in *Bonnie and Clyde* when Bonnie, frightened and angry, runs away from Clyde through a field of wheat, and as he pursues her, a cloud sweeps across the field and shadows them. Seen in a high, wide-angle shot, it is one of those moments of serendipity given to few movies. Today the cloud could be generated by computers; on the day the scene was filmed in Texas, it was a perfectly timed accident of nature.

The cloud carries foreboding: Bonnie and Clyde are doomed, and uneasily realize it. Not long after that scene, Bonnie has a final reunion with her mother. By then Bonnie Parker (Faye Dunaway) and Clyde Barrow (Warren Beatty) are famous outlaws, celebrated in the press as populist bank robbers in an America gripped by the Depression. Bonnie speaks wistfully of marrying Clyde and moving in next door to her mother. "You live within a mile of me, honey, and you'll be dead," her mother flatly pronounces. They would indeed die, in a hail of bullets that permanently changed the way the movies depicted violence. But their lives provided a template that would be used time and again in later films; as the ads put it, "They're young . . . they're in love . . . and they kill people." From *Bonnie and Clyde* descended *Badlands, Days of Heaven, Thelma and Louise, Drugstore Cowboy, Natural Born Killers,* and countless other movies in which ordinary people were transformed by sudden violence into legend.

Bonnie and Clyde, made in 1967, was called "the first modern

American film" by the critic Patrick Goldstein, in an essay on its thirtieth anniversary. Certainly it felt like that at the time. The movie opened like a slap in the face. American filmgoers had never seen anything like it. In tone and freedom, it descended from the French New Wave, particularly François Truffaut's own film about doomed lovers, *Jules and Jim*. Indeed, it was Truffaut who first embraced the original screenplay by David Newman and Robert Benton and called it to the attention of Warren Beatty, who determined to produce it.

The legend of the film's production has become almost as famous as its heroes. Stories are told about how Beatty knelt at the feet of studio boss Jack Warner, begging for the right to make the film. How Warner saw the original cut and hated it. How the movie premiered at the Montreal Film Festival and was roasted by Bosley Crowther of the *New York Times*. How Warner Bros. determined to dump it in a chain of Texas drive-ins, and how Beatty implored the studio to give it a chance. How it opened and quickly closed in the autumn of 1967, panned by the critics, receiving only one unreservedly ecstatic newspaper review. (Modesty be damned: It was my own, calling it "a milestone in the history of American movies, a work of truth and brilliance," and predicting, "years from now it is quite possible that *Bonnie and Clyde* will be seen as the definitive film of the 1960s.")

The movie closed but would not go away. The sound track, bluegrass by Flatt and Scruggs, went to the top of the charts. Theadora Van Runkle's berets and maxiskirts for Faye Dunaway started a global fashion craze. Newsweek critic Joe Morgenstern wrote that his original negative review had been mistaken. The movie reopened, went on to become one of the astonished Jack Warner's biggest hits, and won ten Academy nominations (with Oscars for supporting actress Estelle Parsons and cinematographer Burnett Guffey).

But that is only the success story. More important was the impact the film had on the American movie industry. Beatty's willingness to play a violent character with sexual dysfunction was unusual for a traditional 1960s leading man. In an *Esquire* profile by Rex Reed, which appeared as the movie was opening, he was dismissed as a has-been pretty boy. *Bonnie and Clyde* put him permanently on the Hollywood map. He and director Arthur

Penn cast the movie mostly with unknown stage actors—so successfully that all the major players (Faye Dunaway, Gene Hackman, Estelle Parsons, Michael J. Pollard, Gene Wilder) became stars on the basis of this film. Behind the camera, the movie launched the careers not only of Van Runkle but of editor Dede Allen (a New Yorker breaking into a closed shop) and production designer Dean Tavoularis, who went on to work on Coppola's *Godfather* and *Apocalypse Now*. And the cinematography of Guffey launched a whole new wave of its own, of films shot and edited in the more impressionistic French style.

Arthur Penn came fresh to the project after a resounding failure (*Mickey One* [1965], a self-conscious but intriguing art film, also made with Beatty). His later credits included *Night Moves* (1975), *Alice's Restaurant* (1969), and *Little Big Man* (1970). The cowriter, Robert Benton, became an important director *(Kramer vs. Kramer, Places in the Heart, Sophie's Choice)*. It's as if that one film sent all those careers cascading down through the decades to come.

It was a film in which all of the unlikely pieces were assembled at the right time. And more than anything else, it was a masterpiece of tone, in which the actors and filmmakers were all in sync as they moved the material back and forth between comedy and tragedy.

The opening scenes are lighthearted, starting with Clyde's bravado after Bonnie catches him trying to steal her mother's car. She senses in him, instantly, the means of her escape from a boring West Texas town. What he essentially supplies—for her, for the hero-worshiping gang member C. W. Moss (Pollard), and for the hungry newspaper readers—is the possibility of glamour in lives of drab poverty. "We're the Barrow Gang," Clyde says, introducing them at the beginning of a bank robbery so they'll be sure to get credit. And one of the movie's great moments comes as Clyde lends his gun to a dispossessed black sharecropper, to shoot at a bank's foreclosure sign.

If Clyde offers glamour, Bonnie offers publicity. She writes "The Ballad of Bonnie and Clyde" and sends it to a newspaper, and she poses for photos holding a machine gun and a cigar. Clyde's brother, Buck (Hackman), is more levelheaded, more concerned with bank jobs than newspaper headlines; he comes attached to Blanche (Estelle Parsons), whose whiny complaints get on Bonnie's nerves (when agents surround one of their hide-outs, she runs screaming across the lawn, still holding the spatula she was using to cook supper).

Penn directs the film as a series of set pieces, which remain in the memory, focused and clear. The Okie camp where homeless farmers, tractored off their lands by the banks, hunch over campfires. Bonnie's sad, overcast, foggy family reunion. The bank robbery that goes all wrong when C.W. stupidly parks the getaway car. The way laughter turns blindingly to violence, as when a stickup ends with a meat cleaver and a sack of flour, or when a getaway ends with a bullet in a bank man's face. The run-in with a state trooper (Denver Pyle) who is made to pose with Bonnie and Clyde and then unwisely released. The scene where C.W., a gas station attendant, leaves his job and runs off with the gang that's just robbed him. The scene where C.W.'s father effortlessly browbeats his wimpy son for getting a tattoo. And then the slow-motion ballet of the final execution.

Today the freshness of *Bonnie and Clyde* has been absorbed in countless other films, and it's hard to see how radical and original it felt in 1967—just as the impact of *Citizen Kane* in 1941 or *Breathless* in 1960 may not be obvious to those raised in the shadow of its influence. When I saw it, I had been a film critic for less than six months, and it was the first masterpiece I had seen on the job. I felt an exhilaration beyond describing. I did not suspect how long it would be between such experiences, but at least I learned that they were possible.

{ BRIDE OF FRANKENSTEIN }

To a new world of gods and monsters!

So intones Dr. Pretorius to Dr. Henry Frankenstein, toasting their new friendship with a glass of gin ("my only weakness") before proposing a partnership. He unveils a series of miniature living humans, each in its own bell jar: homunculi, he says, which point the way to full-scale experiments in the creation of life. "Alone," he tells Frankenstein, "you have created a man. Now, together, we will create his mate."

Their quest forms the inspiration for James Whale's *Bride of Frankenstein* (1935), the best of the Frankenstein movies—a sly, subversive work that smuggled shocking material past the censors by disguising it in the trappings of horror. Some movies age; others ripen. Seen today, Whale's masterpiece is more surprising than when it was made, because today's audiences are more alert to its buried hints of homosexuality, necrophilia, and sacrilege. But you don't have to deconstruct it to enjoy it; it's satirical, exciting, funny, and an influential masterpiece of art direction.

Whale has long been valued by admirers of 1930s horror films, but in 1998, with the release of Bill Condon's biopic *Gods and Monsters*, based on the novel *Father of Frankenstein*, by Christopher Bram, his life was credited with a new significance. In an era when Hollywood was filled with homosexuals who stayed adamantly in the closet, he was portrayed as openly gay—not only in his life but in his work. This view may have involved wishful thinking; biographers such as Anthony Slide say Whale was "a very private man who kept his personal life to himself," but that doesn't fit the thesis of critics such as Gary Morris, who interpret *Bride* as a bold gay parable. Morris's reading is sometimes torturous (are the monster and the blind hermit a model for a "blissful married couple"?), but he may be right to see Pretorius and Frankenstein as the Monster's same-sex parents ("Henry the father in giving it life, Pretorius a mother-figure who nurtures it"). Pretorius (played by Ernest Thesiger in high-camp overdrive) indeed sometimes seems to relate to the Monster as rough trade. Parable or not, the movie is more fun when its insinuations are allowed to glide beneath the surface as an unspoken subtext.

The film works perfectly well on its own terms, as a sequel to Whale's *Frankenstein* (1931), recasting the Monster as an outcast yearning for friendship. The credits for *Frankenstein* said it was inspired by a novel by "Mrs. Percy B. Shelley." *Bride* improves the billing of the feminist heroine, calling her "Mary Wollstonecraft Shelley" and adding a prologue in which Mary, her husband, Percy, and their friend Lord Byron imagine a sequel to the first story: The Monster survives being burned in a mill and staggers forth, alive and misunderstood.

Elsa Lanchester plays Mary Shelley and also has the unbilled role of the Bride—where she provides one of the immortal images of the cinema with lightninglike streaks of silver in her weirdly towering hair. Whale based the film's look on the stark shadows and jagged tilt shots of German expressionism, and 1930s horror films like his in turn influenced the look of film noir in the 1940s. His inspiration for the Bride was Maria, the artificial woman from Fritz Lang's *Metropolis* (1927), from which he also borrowed ideas for Pretorius's laboratory, with its platform that lifts the Bride up to the heavens to be penetrated by lightning bolts. (Mel Brooks's laboratory for Pretorius in the 1974 *Young Frankenstein* is not merely similar—it uses the same props, which he discovered in storage.)

The central figure of the film is, of course, the Monster (which is not named Frankenstein, despite the movie's title). He is played by Boris Karloff, who in *Frankenstein* got only this credit:

Monster . . . . ?

but in the sequel is billed in bold capitals above the title: KARLOFF. Despite the broadness of the character, Karloff finds room for subtlety and small gestures; although he opposed it, he benefits enormously from the decision to allow the Monster to speak. In *Frankenstein,* he only bleats piteously, but in *Bride*, he stumbles into the forest hut of a blind violinist, who teaches him words ("Wine . . . wine!") that later evolve into his poignant statement to Pretorius: "I want friend like me."

The 1931 film was famous for a scene in which the Monster happens upon a little girl who is floating daisies upon a pond. The Monster joins her in throwing flowers into the water; when the flowers are gone, he takes the next logical step and throws her in. She drowns. The sequel begins with the girl's parents searching the ruins of the burned mill, to be sure the Monster is dead. The father dies, and the mother clutches a hand in the wreckage, discovering it is not her husband's, but the Monster's. Such cold-blooded scenes are in a way more shocking than the forthright violence in the films, but it is interesting how Whale allows his sympathy for the Monster to soften the second story. (This time the Monster saves a drowning girl, although his heroism is misinterpreted as an attack.)

The scene in which the Monster dines with the hermit (O. P. Heggie) is quiet and touching (the hermit thanks God for sending him a visitor to break his loneliness). That first meal is poignant, the second one farcical, as the Monster stumbles into a crypt where Pretorius has interrupted his search for spare parts to sit down to a candlelit dinner. Pretorius invites him to join in, and the Monster puffs contentedly on a cigar.

Bride belongs largely to Pretorius and the Monster, despite the subplot involving Frankenstein (Colin Clive) and his fiancée (whose wedding date is postponed by the doctor's distractions in the laboratory). The climax comes in Pretorius's gothic tower, with the bizarre apparatus that uses lightning to animate the cobbled-together body parts of the Bride. The scene makes such an unforgettable impression that it's easy to forget how little of the movie the Bride actually appears in.

Whale and his screenwriter, William Hurlbut, add wry humor wherever it will fit. They have fun with the character of Minnie (Una

O'Connor), Frankenstein's housekeeper, whose scream could break glass. And they enjoy moments like the one where the Monster saves the shepherdess who has fallen into the water, and muses, "Yes, a woman. Now that's real interesting."

One advantage of horror movies is that they permit extremes and flavors of behavior that would be out of tone in realistic material. From the silent vampire in *Nosferatu* (1922) to the cheerful excesses of Christopher Lee and Peter Cushing in the Hammer horror films of the 1960s, the genre has encouraged actors to crank it up with bizarre mannerisms and elaborate posturings. The characters often use speech patterns so arch that parody is impossible.

The genre also encourages visual experimentation. From *The Cabinet of Dr. Caligari* (1919) onward, horror has been a cue for unexpected camera angles, hallucinatory architecture, and frankly artificial sets. As mainstream movies have grown steadily more unimaginative and realistic in their visuals, horror has provided a lifeline back to the greater design freedom of the silent era. To see sensational "real" things is not the same as seeing the bizarre, the grotesque, the distorted, and the fanciful. There is more sheer shock in a clawed hand unexpectedly emerging from the shadows than in all the effects of *Armageddon* (1998), because *Armageddon* looks realistic, and horror films taunt us that reality is an illusion.

Many biographical details about James Whale (1893–1957) can be glimpsed in *Gods and Monsters,* which mentions his early romance with a friend killed in battle and his great Hollywood movies of the 1930s (not only *Frankenstein* but such titles as *The Old Dark House* and *The Invisible Man*). Whale stopped making films in 1941 and lived quietly and luxuriously, painting and socializing. In the film, he is seen at the end of his life, portrayed by Ian McKellen as a civilized, still hopeful gay man who in his new gardener (Brendan Fraser) sees a last opportunity for seduction. Giving Fraser a flattop haircut, however, is perhaps insisting too much on the parallel between directors as Gods, and the Monsters they create.

{ BROKEN BLOSSOMS }

Lillian Gish told D. W. Griffith she was too old to play the girl in *Broken Blossoms,* and perhaps she was. Born in 1896, she was twenty-three as Griffith prepared the production in 1919, and not as waiflike as audiences remembered her from *The Birth of a Nation,* filmed five years earlier. But Griffith wanted a star, and Gish was that: Incredibly, in an age when silent actors never stopped working, this was her sixty-fourth film.

It is not as important as *The Birth of a Nation,* but neither is it as flawed. Stung by criticism that the second half of his masterpiece was racist in its glorification of the Ku Klux Klan and its brutal images of blacks, Griffith tried to make amends in *Intolerance* (1916), which criticized prejudice. And in *Broken Blossoms,* he told perhaps the first interracial love story in the movies—even though, to be sure, it's an idealized love with no touching.

Gish plays Lucy, the daughter of a brutal London prizefighter named Battling Burrows (Donald Crisp); the titles tell us she was "thrust into his hands by one of his girls." A drunken "gorilla," he lives in a hovel in Limehouse, and when his manager berates him for drinking and carousing, he takes it out on Lucy. Their story is intercut with the story of Cheng Huan (Richard Barthelmess), called "The Yellow Man" in the titles, a Buddhist who journeys from China to bring "a message of peace to the barbarous Anglo-Saxons." Instead, he turns to opium, and "Limehouse knows him only as the Chink store keeper."

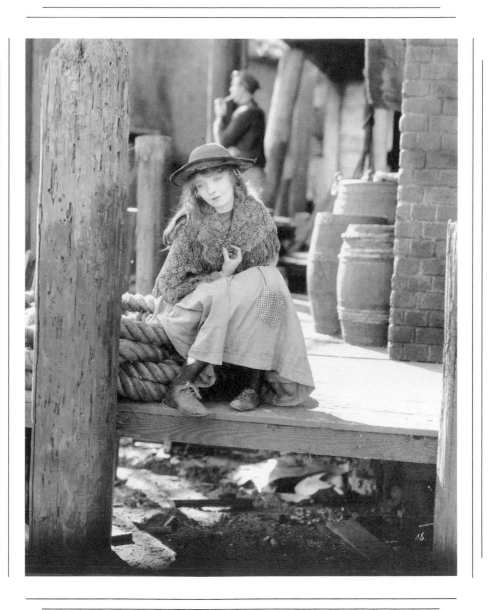

Griffith shot the movie almost entirely on sets, creating a foggy river-side atmosphere to suggest hidden lives. Cheng's room is a refuge upstairs over his shop. Lucy and Battling live in a room without windows, where he sits at a table, wolfing his meals and drinking, while she cowers in a corner. When he orders her to smile, she uses her fingers to push up the corners of her mouth. He gives Lucy money for groceries and goes out to drink more, and she timidly ventures out to do the shopping, clutching a precious hoard of tinfoil which she hopes she can trade for a flower to brighten her grim existence. On the streets, weary housewives warn her against matrimony, and women of the night against prostitution; thus her only two possible escapes seem closed. Through the window of his shop, the Yellow Man sees her, and "the beauty which all Limehouse missed smote him to the heart."

That evening, Lucy spills hot food on Battling's hand, and he whips her almost to death before going out to drink. She stumbles into the Chinese man's store, and he gives her refuge, with "the first gentleness she has ever known." She is able to smile at him without using her fingers. When Battling Burrows finds out where she is, there's a violent showdown, including a striking shot where Lucy, locked in a room with Battling splintering the door with an ax, turns in a helpless circle, screaming.

Gish was one of the great vulnerable screamers of the silent era, although she also had a good line in pluck and independence, and in a long career that ended with *The Whales of August* (1987), she played many strong women. Here she is essentially the passive object of male fantasy—of Battling, who sees her as servant and victim, and Cheng, who idealizes her as his "White Blossom." Griffith emphasizes both her angelic face and her weakness by often lighting and photographing her from above, and many years later, on the set of Robert Altman's *A Wedding* (1978), I heard her rebuke a photographer who was trying for a low-angle shot: "Get up from there! Get up! If God had wanted you to shoot me from that angle, he would have given you a camera in your belly button. Mr. Griffith always said, 'Shoot from above for an angel; shoot from below for a devil.' "

If the attitudes about race in *Broken Blossoms* are more well-meaning and positive than in *The Birth of a Nation*, they are nevertheless painfully dated for today's eyes. But, of course, they are. Marriage between the races was a crime in 1919, and so we see Cheng's face in close-up, looming closer to Lucy as if he wishes to kiss her and then pulling away as the subtitles assure us of his pure intentions. Battling, of course, thinks the Yellow Man has had his way, but the girl cries out, "'Tain't nothing wrong!" Griffith intrigues his audience with the possibility of exotic sex and then cuts to moralizing titles.

The stereotyping of the Chinese character begins with the choice of a Caucasian to play him. There were many Asian actors in silent films, but only one, Sessue Hayakawa, played leading roles, and the most famous of the early Asian characters, like Charlie Chan and Fu Manchu, were played by whites. The character of Cheng is an anthology of stereotypes: He is peaceful Buddhist, opium addict, shopkeeper. But Griffith's film was nevertheless open-minded and even liberal in the context of his time and audiences, and we sense the good intentions behind patronizing titles like this one describing the advice Cheng gets from a Buddhist priest before his journey: "word for word, such as a fond parent of our own land might give."

Although the best silent comedy remains timeless and many silent films remain undated, melodrama like *Broken Blossoms* seems old-fashioned to many viewers. Watching it involves an act of cooperation with the film— even active sympathy. You have to imagine how exotic such stories once seemed, how the foggy streets of Limehouse and the broadly drawn characters once held audiences enthralled. In trying to imagine the film's original impact, it might help to look at Fellini's *La Strada* (1954). Pauline Kael finds many of Fellini's inspirations in *Broken Blossoms*, including Zampano the strongman (Anthony Quinn), whose costume even resembles Battling Burrows's. Gelsomina (Giulietta Masina), his much-abused companion, is obviously drawn from Lucy, and Richard Basehart's Matto, who gives her shelter from the brute, fills the same function as the Yellow Man.

Griffith in 1919 was the unchallenged king of serious American movies (only C. B. DeMille rivaled him in fame), and *Broken Blossoms* was seen as brave and controversial. What remains today is the artistry of the production, the ethereal quality of Lillian Gish, the broad appeal of the melodrama, and the atmosphere of the elaborate sets (the film's budget was actually larger than that of *The Birth of a Nation*). And its social impact. Films like this, naive as they seem today, helped nudge a xenophobic nation toward racial tolerance.

There is all of that, and then there is Lillian Gish's face. Was she the greatest actress of silent films? Perhaps; her face and Louise Brooks's are the first I think of among the silent actresses, just as Chaplin and Keaton stand side by side among the men. When she was filming *The Whales of August* in 1987, her costar was another legend, Bette Davis. The film's director, Lindsay Anderson, told me this story. One day after finishing a shot, he said, "Miss Gish, you have just given me the most marvelous close-up!" "She should," Bette Davis observed dryly. "She invented them."

{ CASABLANCA }

If we identify strongly with the characters in some movies, then it is no mystery that *Casablanca* is one of the most popular films ever made. It is about a man and a woman who are in love and who sacrifice love for a higher purpose. This is immensely appealing; the viewer is able to imagine not only winning the love of Humphrey Bogart or Ingrid Bergman but unselfishly renouncing it, as a contribution to the great cause of defeating the Nazis.

No one making *Casablanca* thought they were making a great movie. It was simply another Warner Bros. release. It was an "A-list" picture, to be sure (Bogart, Bergman, and Paul Henreid were stars, and no better cast of supporting actors could have been assembled on the Warner lot than Peter Lorre, Sydney Greenstreet, Claude Rains, and Dooley Wilson). But it was made on a tight budget and released with small expectations. Everyone involved in the film had been and would be in dozens of other films made under similar circumstances, and the greatness of *Casablanca* was largely the result of happy chance. The screenplay was adapted from a play of no great consequence; memoirs tell of scraps of dialogue jotted down and rushed over to the set. What must have helped is that the characters were firmly established in the minds of the writers, and they were characters so close to the screen personas of the actors that it was hard to write dialogue in the wrong tone.

Humphrey Bogart played strong heroic leads in his career, but he was usually better as the disappointed, wounded, resentful hero. Remember him in *The Treasure of the Sierra Madre* (1948), convinced the others were plotting to steal his gold. In *Casablanca* (1943), he plays Rick Blaine, the hard-drinking American running a nightclub in Casablanca when Morocco was a crossroads for spies, traitors, Nazis, and the French Resistance.

The opening scenes dance with comedy; the dialogue combines the cynical with the weary; wisecracks with epigrams. We see that Rick moves easily in a corrupt world. "What is your nationality?" the German Strasser asks him, and he replies, "I'm a drunkard." His personal code: "I stick my neck out for nobody."

Then "of all the gin joints in all the towns in all the world, she walks into mine." It is Ilsa Lund (Bergman), the woman Rick loved years earlier in Paris. Under the shadow of the German occupation, he arranged their escape and believes she abandoned him—left him waiting in the rain at a train station with their tickets to freedom. Now she is with Victor Laszlo (Henreid), a legendary hero of the French Resistance.

All this is handled with great economy in a handful of shots that still, after many viewings, have the power to move me emotionally as few scenes ever have. The bar's piano player, Sam (Wilson), a friend of theirs in Paris, is startled to see her. She asks him to play the song that she and Rick made their own, "As Time Goes By." He is reluctant, but he does, and Rick comes striding angrily out of the back room ("I thought I told you never to play that song!"). Then he sees Ilsa, a dramatic musical chord marks their close-ups, and the scene plays out in resentment, regret, and the memory of a love that was real. (This scene is not as strong on a first viewing as on subsequent viewings because the first time you see the movie you don't yet know the story of Rick and Ilsa in Paris; indeed, the more you see it, the more the whole film gains resonance.)

The plot, a trifle to hang the emotions on, involves letters of passage that will allow two people to leave Casablanca for Portugal and freedom. Rick obtained the letters from the wheedling little black marketeer Ugarte (Lorre). The sudden reappearance of Ilsa reopens all of his old wounds and breaks his carefully cultivated veneer of neutrality and indifference. When he hears her story, he realizes she has always loved him. But now she is with Laszlo. Rick wants to use the letters to escape with Ilsa, but then, in a sustained sequence that combines suspense, romance, and comedy as they have rarely been

brought together on the screen, he contrives a situation in which Ilsa and Laszlo escape together, while he and his friend the police chief (Rains) get away with murder ("Round up the usual suspects").

What is intriguing is that none of the major characters are bad. Some are cynical, some lie, some kill, but all are redeemed. If you think it was easy for Rick to renounce his love for Ilsa—to place a higher value on Laszlo's fight against Nazism—remember E. M. Forster's comment "If I were forced to choose between my country and my friend, I hope I would be brave enough to choose my friend."

From a modern perspective, the film reveals interesting assumptions. Ilsa Lund's role is basically that of a lover and helpmate to a great man; the movie's real question is, which great man should she be sleeping with?

There is actually no reason why Laszlo cannot get on the plane alone, leaving Ilsa in Casablanca with Rick, and indeed that is one of the endings that were briefly considered. But that would be all wrong. The "happy" ending would be tarnished by self-interest, while the ending we have allows Rick to be larger, to approach nobility ("it doesn't take much to see that the problems of three little people don't amount to a hill of beans in this crazy world"). And it allows us, vicariously experiencing all of these things in the theater, to warm in the glow of his heroism.

In her close-ups during this scene, Bergman's face reflects confusing emotions. And well she might have been confused, since neither she nor anyone else on the film knew for sure until the final day who would get on the plane. Bergman played the whole movie without knowing how it would end, and this had the subtle effect of making all of her scenes more emotionally convincing; she could not tilt in the direction she knew the wind was blowing.

Stylistically the film is not so much brilliant as absolutely sound, rock-solid in its use of Hollywood studio craftsmanship. The director, Michael Curtiz, and the writers (Julius J. Epstein, Philip G. Epstein, and Howard Koch) all won Oscars. One of their key contributions was to show us that Rick, Ilsa, and the others lived in a complex time and place. The richness of the supporting characters (Greenstreet as the corrupt club owner, Lorre as the sniveling cheat, Rains as the perhaps subtly bisexual police chief, and minor characters like the young girl who will do anything to help her husband) sets the moral stage for the decisions of the major characters. When this plot was remade in 1990 as *Havana,* Hollywood practices required all the big scenes to feature the big stars (Robert Redford and Lena Olin) and the film suffered as a result; out of context, they were more lovers than heroes.

Seeing the film over and over again, year after year, I find it never grows overfamiliar. It plays like a favorite musical album; the more I know it, the more I like it. The black-and-white cinematography has not aged as color would. The dialogue is so spare and cynical it has not grown old-fashioned. Much of the emotional effect of *Casablanca* is achieved by indirection. As we leave the theater, we are absolutely convinced that the only thing keeping the world from going crazy is that the problems of three little people do, after all, amount to more than a hill of beans.

"Are you alone?" the private eye is asked in Roman Polanski's *Chinatown*. "Isn't everybody?" he replies. That loneliness is central to a lot of noir heroes, who plunder other people's secrets while running from their own. The tone was set by Dashiell Hammett, and its greatest practitioner was Raymond Chandler. To observe Humphrey Bogart in Hammett's *The Maltese Falcon* (1941) and Chandler's *The Big Sleep* (1946) is to see a fundamental type of movie character being born—a kind of man who processes human tragedy for a living. Yet the Bogart character is never merely cold. His detachment masks romanticism, which is why he's able to idealize bad women. His characters have more education and sensitivity than they need for their line of work. He wrote the rules; later actors were able to slip into the role of noir detective like pulling on a comfortable sweater. But great actors don't follow rules, they illustrate them. Jack Nicholson's character J. J. Gittes, who is in every scene of *Chinatown* (1974), takes the Bogart line and gentles it down. He plays a nice, sad man.

We remember the bandage plastered on Nicholson's nose (after the Polanski character slices him) and think of him as a hard-boiled tough guy. Not at all. In one scene, he beats a man almost to death, but during his working day he projects a courtly passivity. "I'm in matrimonial work," he says, and adds, "It's my métier." His métier? What's he doing with a word like that? And why does he answer the telephone so politely, instead of

barking "Gittes!" into it? He can be raw, he can tell dirty jokes, he can accuse people of base motives, but all the time there's a certain detached underlevel that makes his character sympathetic: Like all private eyes, he wrestles with pigs, but unlike most of them, he doesn't like it.

Nicholson can be sharp-edged, menacing, aggressive. He knows how to go over the top (see *One Flew over the Cuckoo's Nest* [1975] and his Joker in *Batman* [1989]). His performance is key in keeping *Chinatown* from becoming just a genre crime picture—that, and a Robert Towne screenplay that evokes an older Los Angeles, a small city in a large desert. The crimes in *Chinatown* include incest and murder, but the biggest crime is against the city's own future, by men who see that to control the water is to control the wealth. At one point, Gittes asks the millionaire Noah Cross (John Huston) why he needs to be richer: "How much better can you eat? What can you buy that you can't already afford?" Cross replies, "The future, Mr. Gitts, the future." (He never does get Gittes's name right.)

Gittes's involvement begins with an adultery case. He's visited by a woman who claims to be the wife of a man named Mulwray. She says her husband is cheating on her. Gittes's investigation leads him to Mulwray (Darrell Zwerling), to city hearings, to dried riverbeds, and eventually to Mulwray's drowned body and to the real Mrs. Mulwray (Faye Dunaway). Stumbling across murders, lies, and adulteries, he senses some larger reality beneath everything, some conspiracy involving people and motives unknown.

This crime is eventually revealed as an attempt to buy up the San Fernando Valley cheaply by diverting water so that its orange growers go broke. Then that water and more water, obtained through bribery and corruption, will turn the Valley green and create wealth. The Valley has long been seen as a key to California fortunes. I remember Joel McCrea telling me that on his first day as a movie actor, he was greeted by Will Rogers with brief words of advice: "Buy land in the Valley."

The original valley grab was the Owens River Valley scandal of 1908, mirrored in the 1930s by Towne. In the preface to his Oscar-winning screenplay, he recalls, "My wife Julie returned to the hotel one afternoon with two quilts and a public library copy of Carey McWilliams' *Southern California Country, an Island on the Land*—and with it the crime that formed the basis of *Chinatown*." McWilliams, for decades the editor of the *Nation*, not only presented Towne with information about the original land and water grab but also evoked the old Los Angeles, a city born in a desert where no city should logically be found. The screenplay explains, "Either you bring the water to L.A. or you bring L.A. to the water." John A. Alonzo's cinematography, which got one of the movie's eleven Oscar nominations, evokes the L.A. you can glimpse in the backgrounds of old movies, where the sun beats down on streets that are too wide, and buildings seem more defiant than proud. (Notice the shot where the bright sun falls on the fedoras of Gittes and two cops, casting their eyes into shadows like black masks.)

Gittes becomes a man who just wants to get to the bottom of things. He's tired of people's lies. And where does he stand with Evelyn Mulwray, played by Dunaway as a cool, elegant woman who sometimes—especially when her father is mentioned—seems fragile as china? First he's deceived by the fake Evelyn Mulwray and then by the real one. Then he thinks he loves her. Then he thinks he's deceived again. Then he thinks she's hiding her husband's mistress. Then she says it's her sister. Then she says it's her daughter. He doesn't like being jerked around.

Her father the millionaire is played by Huston with treacly charm and mean little eyes. There is a luncheon where he serves Gittes a fish with the head still on, the eyes regarding the man about to eat it. "Just as long as you don't serve the chicken that way," Gittes says. In life and on the screen, Huston (who directed *The Maltese Falcon*) could turn on disarming charm by admitting to his failings: "Of course I'm respectable. I'm old. Politicians, ugly buildings, and whores all get respectable if they last long enough."

Like most noir stories, *Chinatown* ends in a flurry of revelation. All is explained, relationships are redefined, and justice is done—or not. Towne writes of "my eventual conflict with Roman and enduring disappointment over the literal and ghoulishly bleak climax" of the movie. Certainly the wrong people are alive (and dead) at the end of the film, but I am not sure Polanski was wrong. He made the movie just five years after his wife, Sharon Tate, was one of the victims of the Manson gang, and can be excused for tilting toward despair. If the film had been made ten years later, the studio might have insisted on an upbeat ending, but it was produced during that brief window when Robert Evans oversaw a series of Paramount's best films, including *The Godfather*.

For Polanski, born in 1933 in Paris, raised in Poland, *Chinatown* was intended as a fresh start in Hollywood. After a series of brilliant thrillers made in Europe in the early 1960s *(Knife in the Water, Repulsion)*, he came to California and had an enormous success (*Rosemary's Baby*, 1968). Then came the Manson murders, and he fled to Europe, making the curious *Macbeth* (1971) with its parallels to the cult killings. After *Chinatown*, however, came charges of sex with an underage girl, and exile in Europe. *Chinatown* shows he might have developed into a major Hollywood player, instead of scurrying to finance such bizarre projects as *Pirates* (1986).

For Nicholson, the role had enormous importance. After a decade's slumming in exploitation films, he made an indelible impression in *Easy Rider* (1969) and followed it with strong performances in *Five Easy Pieces* (1970), *Carnal Knowledge* (1971), and *The Last Detail* (1973). But with Jake Gittes he stepped into Bogart's shoes as a man attractive to audiences because he suggests both comfort and danger. Men see him as a pal; wise women find weary experience more attractive than untrained lust. From Gittes forward, Nicholson created the persona of a man who had seen it all and was still capable of being wickedly amused. He could sit in the front row at a basketball game and grin at the TV camera as if he expected the players to commit lascivious deeds right there on the floor.

Chinatown was seen as a neonoir when it was released—an update on an old genre. Now years have passed and film history blurs a little, and it seems to settle easily beside the original noirs. That is a compliment.

{ CITIZEN KANE }

"I don't think any word can explain a man's life," says one of the searchers through the warehouse of treasures left behind by Charles Foster Kane. Then we get the famous series of shots leading to the close-up of the word "Rosebud" on a sled that has been tossed into a furnace, its paint curling in the flames. We remember that this was Kane's childhood sled, taken from him as he was torn from his family and sent East to boarding school. Rosebud is the emblem of the security, hope, and innocence of childhood, which a man can spend his life seeking to regain. It is the green light at the end of Gatsby's pier; the leopard atop Kilimanjaro, seeking nobody knows what; the bone tossed into the air in *2001*. It is that yearning after transience that adults learn to suppress. "Maybe Rosebud was something he couldn't get, or something he lost," says Thompson, the reporter assigned to the puzzle of Kane's dying word. "Anyway, it wouldn't have explained anything."

True, it explains nothing, but it is remarkably satisfactory as a demonstration that nothing can be explained. *Citizen Kane* likes playful paradoxes like that. Its surface is as much fun as any movie ever made. Its depths surpass understanding. I have analyzed it a shot at a time with more than thirty groups, and together we have found, I believe, pretty much everything that is there on the screen. The more clearly I can see its physical manifestation, the more I am stirred by its mystery.

It is one of the miracles of cinema that in 1941 a first-time director, a cynical, hard-drinking writer, an innovative cinematographer, and a group of New York stage and radio actors were given the keys to a studio and total control, and made a masterpiece. *Citizen Kane* is more than a great movie; it is a gathering of all the lessons of the emerging era of sound, just as *The Birth of a Nation* (1915) assembled everything learned at the summit of the silent era, and *2001* (1968) pointed the way beyond narrative. These peaks stand above the others.

The origins of *Citizen Kane* are well known. Orson Welles, the boy wonder of radio and stage, was given freedom by RKO Radio Pictures to make any picture he wished. Herman Mankiewicz, an experienced screen-writer, collaborated with him on a screenplay originally called *The American.* Its inspiration was the life of William Randolph Hearst, who had put to-gether an empire of newspapers, radio stations, magazines, and news ser-vices, and then built to himself the flamboyant monument of San Simeon, a castle furnished by rummaging the remains of nations. Hearst was Ted Turner, Rupert Murdoch, and Bill Gates rolled up into an enigma with emptiness at the center.

Arriving in Hollywood at the age of twenty-five, Welles brought a subtle knowledge of sound and dialogue along with him; on his *The Mer-cury Theatre on the Air,* he'd experimented with audio styles more lithe and suggestive than those usually heard in the movies. As his cinematographer he hired Gregg Toland, who on John Ford's *The Long Voyage Home* (1940) had experimented with deep-focus photography—with shots where every-thing was in focus, from the front to the back, so that composition and movement determined where the eye looked first.

For his cast, Welles assembled his New York colleagues, including Joseph Cotten as Jed Leland, the hero's best friend; Everett Sloane as Mr. Bernstein, the mogul's business wizard; Ray Collins as Gettys, the corrupt po-litical boss; and Agnes Morehead as the boy's forbidding mother. The only out-sider was Dorothy Comingore as Susan Alexander, the young woman Kane thought he could make into an opera star. Welles himself played Kane from age twenty-five until his deathbed, using makeup and body language to trace the progress of a man increasingly captive inside his needs. "All he really wanted out of life was love," Leland says. "That's Charlie's story—how he lost it."

The structure of *Citizen Kane* is circular, adding more depth every

time it passes over the life. The movie opens with newsreel obituary footage that briefs us on the life and times of Charles Foster Kane; this footage, with its portentous narration, is Welles's bemused nod in the direction of the *March of Time* newsreels then being produced by another media mogul, Henry Luce. They provide a map of Kane's trajectory, and it will keep us oriented as the screenplay skips around in time, piecing together the memories of those who knew him.

Curious about Kane's dying word, "rosebud," the newsreel editor assigns Thompson, a reporter, to find out what it meant. Thompson is played by William Alland in a thankless performance; he triggers every flashback, yet his face is never seen. As he questions Kane's alcoholic mistress, his ailing old friend, his rich associate, and the other witnesses, the movie loops through time. As often as I've seen *Citizen Kane*, I've never been able to firmly fix the order of the scenes in my mind. I look at a scene and tease myself with what will come next. But it remains elusive: By flashing back through the eyes of many witnesses, Welles and Mankiewicz created an emotional chronology set free from time.

The movie is filled with bravura visual moments: the towers of Xanadu; candidate Kane addressing a political rally; the doorway of his mistress dissolving into a front-page photo in a rival newspaper; the camera swooping down through a skylight toward the pathetic Susan in a nightclub; the many Kanes reflected through parallel mirrors; the boy playing in the snow in the background as his parents determine his future; the great shot as the camera rises straight up from Susan's opera debut to a stagehand holding his nose; and the subsequent shot of Kane, his face hidden in shadow, defiantly applauding in the silent hall.

Along with the personal story is the history of a period. *Citizen Kane* covers the rise of the penny press (here Joseph Pulitzer is the model), the Hearst-promoted Spanish-American War, the birth of radio, the power of political machines, the rise of fascism, the growth of celebrity journalism. A newsreel subtitle reads: "1895 to 1941. All of these years he covered, many of these he was." The screenplay by Mankiewicz and Welles (which got an Oscar, the only one Welles ever won) is densely constructed and covers an amazing amount of ground, including a sequence showing Kane inventing the popular press; a record of his marriage, from early bliss to the montage of increasingly chilly breakfasts; the story of his courtship of Susan Alexander and her disastrous opera career; and his decline into the remote master of Xanadu ("I think if you look carefully in the west wing, Susan, you'll find about a dozen vacationists still in residence").

Citizen Kane knows the sled is not the answer. It explains what Rosebud is, but not what Rosebud means. The film's construction shows how our lives, after we are gone, survive only in the memories of others, and those memories butt up against the walls we erect and the roles we play. There is the Kane who made shadow figures with his fingers, and the Kane who hated the traction trust; the Kane who chose his mistress over his marriage and political career, the Kane who entertained millions, the Kane who died alone.

There is a master image in *Citizen Kane* you might easily miss. The tycoon has overextended himself and is losing control of his empire. After he signs the papers of his surrender, he turns and walks into the back of the shot. Deep focus allows Welles to play a trick of perspective. Behind Kane on the wall is a window that seems to be of ordinary size. But as he walks toward it, we see it is farther away and much higher than we thought. Eventually he stands beneath its lower sill, shrunken and diminished. Then as he walks toward us, his stature grows again. A man always seems the same size to himself, because he does not stand where we stand when we look at him.

A Viewer's Companion to Citizen Kane

■ "ROSEBUD." The most famous word in the history of cinema. It explains everything and nothing. Who, for that matter, actually heard Charles Foster Kane say it before he died? The butler says, late in the film, that he did. But Kane seems to be alone when he dies, and the reflection on the shard of glass from the broken paperweight shows the nurse entering the room. Gossip has it that the screenwriter, Herman Mankiewicz, used "rosebud" as an inside joke, because as a friend of Hearst's mistress Marion

Davies, he knew "rosebud" was the old man's pet name for the most intimate part of her anatomy.

■ DEEP FOCUS. Everyone knows that Orson Welles and his cinematographer, Gregg Toland, used deep focus in *Kane*. But what is deep focus, and were they using it for the first time? The term refers to a strategy of lighting, composition, and lens choice that allows everything in the frame, from the front to the back, to be in focus at the same time. With the lighting and lenses available in 1941, this was just becoming possible, and Toland had experimented with the technique in John Ford's *The Long Voyage Home* a year earlier. In most movies, the key elements in the frame are in focus, and those closer or farther away may not be. When everything is in focus, the filmmakers must give a lot more thought to how they direct the viewer's attention, first here and then there. What the French call mise-en-scène—the arrangement within the frame—becomes more important.

■ OPTICAL ILLUSIONS. Deep focus is especially tricky because movies are two-dimensional, and so you need visual guideposts to determine the true scale of a scene. Toland used this fact as a way to fool the audience's eye on two delightful occasions in the film. One comes when Kane is signing away control of his empire in Thatcher's office. Behind him on the wall are windows that look of normal size and height. Then Kane starts to walk into the background of the shot, and we realize with surprise that the windows are huge, and their lower sills are more than six feet above the floor. As Kane stands under them, he is dwarfed—which is the intent, since he has just lost great power. Later in the film, Kane walks over to stand in front of the great fireplace in Xanadu, and we realize it, too, is much larger than it first seemed.

■ VISIBLE CEILINGS. In almost all movies before *Citizen Kane*, you couldn't see the ceilings in rooms because there weren't any. That's where they put the lights and microphones. Welles wanted to use a lot of low-angle shots that would look up toward ceilings, and so Toland devised a strategy of cloth ceilings that looked real but were not. The microphones were hidden immediately above the ceilings, which in many shots are noticeably low.

■ MATTE DRAWINGS. These are drawings by artists that are used to create elements that aren't really there. Often they are combined with "real" foregrounds. The opening and closing shots of Kane's great castle, Xanadu, are examples. No exterior set was ever built for the structure. Instead, artists drew it and used lights behind it to suggest Kane's bedroom window. "Real" foreground details such as Kane's lagoon and private zoo were added.

- INVISIBLE WIPES. A "wipe" is a visual effect that wipes one image off the screen while wiping another into view. Invisible wipes disguise themselves as something else on the screen that seems to be moving, so you aren't aware of the effect. They are useful in "wiping" from full-scale sets to miniature sets. For example: One of the most famous shots in *Kane* shows Susan Alexander's opera debut, when, as she starts to sing, the camera moves straight up to a catwalk high above the stage, and one stagehand turns to another and eloquently reviews her performance by holding his nose. Only the stage and the stagehands on the catwalk are real. The middle portion of this seemingly unbroken shot is a miniature, built in the RKO model workshop. The model is invisibly wiped in by the stage curtains, as we move up past them, and wiped out by a wooden beam right below the catwalk. Another example: In Walter Thatcher's library, the statue of Thatcher is a drawing, and as the camera pans down, it wipes out the drawing as it wipes in the set of the library.

- INVISIBLE FURNITURE MOVING. In the early scene in the Kanes' cabin in Colorado, the camera tracks back from a window to a table where Kane's mother is being asked to sign a paper. The camera tracks right through where the table would be, after which it is slipped into place before we can see it. But a hat on the table is still trembling from the move. After she signs the paper, the camera pulls up and follows her as she walks back toward the window. If you look sharply, you can see that she's walking right through where the table was a moment before. Later, Mr. Bernstein sits at his desk, then walks away—and when he returns to stand beneath Kane's portrait, the desk has disappeared.

- THE LONGEST FLASH-FORWARD in *Kane*. Between Thatcher's words "Merry Christmas" and "a very Happy New Year," two decades pass.

- FROM MODEL TO REALITY. As the camera swoops above the nightclub and through the skylight to discover Susan Alexander Kane sitting forlornly at a table, it goes from a model of the nightclub roof to a real set. The switch is concealed, the first time, by a lightning flash. The second time we go to the nightclub, it's done with a dissolve.

- CROWD SCENES. There aren't any in *Citizen Kane*. It only looks like there are. In the opening newsreel, stock footage of a political rally is intercut with a low-angle shot showing one man speaking on behalf of Kane. Sound effects make it sound like he's at a big outdoor rally. Later, Kane himself addresses a gigantic indoor rally. Kane and the other actors on the stage are real. The audience is a miniature, with flickering lights to suggest movement.

- SLIGHT FACTUAL DISCREPANCIES. In the opening newsreel, Xanadu is described as being "on the desert coast of Florida." But Florida does not have a desert coast, as you can plainly see during the picnic scene, where footage from an earlier RKO prehistoric adventure was back-projected behind the actors, and if you look closely, that seems to be a pterodactyl flapping its wings.

- THE LUCE CONNECTION. Although *Citizen Kane* was widely seen as an attack on William Randolph Hearst, it was also aimed at Henry R. Luce and his concept of faceless group journalism, as then practiced at his *Time* magazine and *March of Time* newsreels. The opening "News on the March" segment is a deliberate parody of the Luce newsreel, and the reason you can never see the faces of any of the journalists is that Welles and Mankiewicz were kidding the anonymity of Luce's writers and editors.

- AN EXTRA WITH A FUTURE. Alan Ladd can be glimpsed in the opening newsreel sequence and again in the closing warehouse scene. Also visible in the newsreel meeting—Joseph Cotten and Erskine Sanford, playing extras and hoping we don't recognize them.

- MOST THANKLESS JOB on the movie. It went to William Alland, who plays Mr. Thompson, the journalist assigned to track down the meaning of "rosebud." He is always seen from behind or in backlit profile. You can never see his face. At the movie's world premiere, Alland told the audience he would turn his back so they could recognize him more easily. Ironically, it is his voice that supplies the newsreel's booming narration.

- THE BROTHEL SCENE. It couldn't be filmed. In the original screenplay, after Kane hires away the staff of the *Chronicle*, he takes them to a brothel. The Production Code office wouldn't allow that. So the scene, slightly changed, takes place in the *Inquirer* newsroom, still with the dancing girls.

- THE EYELESS COCKATOO. Yes, you can see right through the eyeball of the shrieking cockatoo, in the scene before the big fight between Kane and Susan. It's a mistake.
- THE MOST EVOCATIVE SHOT in the movie. There are many candidates. My choice is the shot showing an infinity of Kanes reflected in mirrors as he walks past.
- THE BEST SPEECH in *Kane*. My favorite is delivered by Mr. Bernstein (Everett Sloane) when he is talking about the magic of memory with the inquiring reporter:

> "A fellow will remember a lot of things you wouldn't think he'd remember. You take me. One day, back in 1896, I was crossing over to Jersey on the ferry, and as we pulled out, there was another ferry pulling in, and on it there was a girl waiting to get off. A white dress she had on. She was carrying a white parasol. I only saw her for one second. She didn't see me at all, but I'll bet a month hasn't gone by since, that I haven't thought of that girl."

- GENUINE MODESTY. In the movie's credits, Welles allowed his director's credit and Toland's cinematography credit to appear on the same card—an unprecedented gesture that indicated how grateful Welles was.
- FALSE MODESTY. In the unique end credits, the members of the Mercury Company are introduced and seen in brief moments from the movie. Then smaller parts are handled with a single card containing many names. The final credit down at the bottom, in small type, says simply:

Kane . . . . Orson Welles

{ CITY LIGHTS }

If only one of Charles Chaplin's films could be preserved, *City Lights* (1931) would come the closest to representing all the different notes of his genius. It contains the slapstick, the pathos, the pantomime, the effortless physical coordination, the melodrama, the bawdiness, the grace, and, of course, the Little Tramp—the character said at one time to be the most famous image on earth.

When he made it, three years into the era of sound, Chaplin must have known that *City Lights* might be his last silent film; he considered making a talkie but decided against it, and although the film has a full musical score (composed by Chaplin) and sound effects, it doesn't use dialogue. Audiences at the time would have appreciated his opening in-joke: The film begins with political speeches, but what emerges from the mouths of the speakers are unintelligible squawks—Chaplin's dig at talkies. When he made *Modern Times* five years later, Chaplin allowed speech onto the sound track, but even then the Tramp remained silent except for some gibberish.

There was perfect logic here. Speech was not how the Tramp expressed himself. In most silent films, there's the illusion that the characters are speaking, even though we can't hear them. Buster Keaton's characters, for example, are clearly talkative. But the Tramp is a mime to his core, a person for whom body language serves as speech. He exists somehow on a different plane from the other characters; he stands outside their lives and

realities, is judged on his appearance, is homeless and without true friends or family, and interacts with the world mostly through his actions. Although he can sometimes be seen to speak, he doesn't need to; unlike most of the characters in silent films, he could have existed comfortably in a silent world.

In *Modern Times,* as Walter Kerr points out in his invaluable book *The Silent Clowns,* the Tramp is constantly trying to get back into jail, where he feels safe and secure. His most frequent refuge is a paddy wagon. In *City Lights,* his only friendships are with people who don't or can't really see him: with a drunken millionaire who sobers up and doesn't recognize him, and with a blind flower girl. His shabby appearance sets him apart and cues people to avoid and stereotype him; a tramp is not . . . one of us. Unlike the Keaton characters, who have jobs and participate eagerly in society, the Tramp is an outcast, an onlooker, a loner.

That's what makes his relationship with the flower girl (Virginia Cherrill) so poignant; does she accept and treasure him only because she can't see what he looks like? (Her grandmother, who would no doubt warn her away from him, is never at home when the Tramp calls.) The last scene of *City Lights* is justly famous as one of the great emotional moments in the movies. The girl, whose sight has been restored by an operation paid for by the Tramp, now sees him as a bum—but smiles at him anyway and gives him a rose and some money, and then, touching his hands, recognizes them. "You?" she asks on the title card. He nods, tries to smile, and asks, "You can see now?" "Yes," she says, "I can see now." She sees, and yet still smiles at him and accepts him. The Tramp guessed correctly: She has a good heart and is able to accept him as himself.

Chaplin and the other silent filmmakers knew no national boundaries. Their films went everywhere without regard for language, and talkies were like the Tower of Babel, building walls between nations. I witnessed the universality of Chaplin's art in one of my most treasured experiences as a moviegoer, in 1972, in Venice, where all of Chaplin's films were shown at the film festival. One night the Piazza San Marco was darkened, and *City Lights* was shown on a vast screen. When the flower girl recognized the Tramp, I heard much snuffling and blowing of noses around me; there wasn't a dry eye in the piazza. Then complete darkness fell, and a spotlight singled out a balcony overlooking the square. Charlie Chaplin walked forward and bowed. I have seldom heard such cheering.

He had by then for many decades been hailed as one of the screen's great creators. In *City Lights*, we can see the invention and humanity that coexist in his films. The movie contains some of Chaplin's great comic sequences, including the famous prizefight in which the Tramp uses his nimble footwork to keep the referee between himself and his opponent. There's the opening scene, where a statue is unveiled to find the Tramp asleep in the lap of a heroic Greco-Roman stone figure (trying to climb down, he gets his pants hooked through the statue's sword and tries to stand at attention during "The Star-Spangled Banner" although his feet can't find a footing). There's the sequence where he tries to save the millionaire from drowning and ends up with the rock tied to his own neck; the scene where he swallows a whistle and gathers a following of dogs; the scene where the millionaire and the Tramp encounter burglars; the scene in the nightclub where Charlie sees Apache dancers and defends the woman dancer against her partner. And there are the bawdy moments, as when the Tramp, working as a street sweeper, avoids a parade of horses only to encounter a parade of elephants; and when the millionaire pours bottles of champagne down the Tramp's pants.

Chaplin was a master of the small touch, the delayed reaction. Consider the moment when he goes to the blind girl's house to give her the money for an eye operation. He has prudently stashed a hundred dollars in his pocket for his own needs, but after she kisses his hand he shrugs, reaches in his pocket, and gives her the final bill.

Chaplin and Keaton are the giants of silent comedy, and in recent years the pendulum of fashion has swung between them. Chaplin ruled supreme for years, but by the 1960s he looked dated and sentimental to some viewers, and Keaton seemed fresher and more contemporary. In the polls taken every ten years by *Sight & Sound*, the British film magazine, Chaplin placed high in 1952 and was gone by 1962; Keaton placed high in 1972 and 1982; and Chaplin replaced him again in 1992. The only thing such polls prove for sure is that a lot of film lovers think the work of both men belongs on a list of the greatest films ever made.

Both filmmakers focused their work on their fictional personalities but took opposite approaches. Keaton plays a different character every time; Chaplin usually plays a version of the Tramp. Keaton's characters desire acceptance, recognition, romance, and stature in the real world, and try to adapt to conditions; Chaplin's characters are perpetual outsiders who rigidly repeat the same strategies and reactions (often the gags come from how inappropriately the Tramp behaves). Keaton's movements are smooth and effortless; Chaplin's odd little lopsided gait looks almost arthritic. They appeared together only once, in Chaplin's *Limelight* (1952). Keaton steals the scene—but, as Kerr observes, Chaplin, who could have reedited it to give himself the upper hand, was content to let Keaton prevail.

There was a time when Chaplin was hailed as the greatest popular artist of the twentieth century, and his films were known to everyone. Today, how many people watch them? Are they shown in schools? I think not. On TV? Not very often. Silent film, the medium that gave Chaplin his worldwide canvas, has now robbed him of his mass audience. His films will live forever, but only for those who seek them out.

Having just viewed *City Lights* and *Modern Times* again, I am still under their spell. Chaplin's gift was truly magical. Silent films create a reverie state; there is no dialogue, no obtrusive superrealism, to interrupt the flow. They stay with you. They are not simply a work but a place. Most of Chaplin's films are available on video. Children who see them at a certain age don't notice they're "silent" but notice only that every frame speaks clearly to them, without all those mysterious words that clutter other films. Then children grow up and forget this wisdom, but the films wait patiently and are willing to teach us again.

{ DAYS OF HEAVEN }

Terrence Malick's *Days of Heaven* has been praised for its painterly images and evocative score, but criticized for its muted emotions. Although passions erupt in a deadly love triangle, all the feelings are somehow held at arm's length. This observation is true enough if you think only about the actions of the adults in the story. But watching this 1978 film again, I was struck more than ever with the conviction that this is the story of a young teenage girl, told by her, and its subject is the way that hope and cheer have been beaten down in her heart. We do not feel the full passion of the adults, because it is not her passion: It is seen at a distance, as a phenomenon, like the weather, or the plague of grasshoppers that signals the beginning of the end.

The film takes place during the years before World War I. Outside Chicago, Bill (Richard Gere) gets in a fight with a steel mill foreman and kills him. With his lover, Abby (Brooke Adams), and his kid sister, Linda (Linda Manz), he hops a train to Texas, where the harvest is in progress, and they all three get jobs as laborers on the vast wheat field of a farmer (Sam Shepard). Bill tells everyone Abby is his sister and gets in a fight with a field hand who suggests otherwise.

The farmer falls in love with Abby and asks her to stay after the harvest is over. Bill overhears a conversation between the farmer and a doctor and learns that the farmer has perhaps a year to live. In a strategy familiar from Henry James's novel *The Wings of the Dove,* he suggests that Abby marry the farmer—and then, when he dies, he and Abby will at last have money enough to live happily. "He was tired of livin' like the rest of 'em, nosing around like a pig in a gutter," Linda confides on the sound track. But later she observes of the farmer: "Instead of getting sicker, he just stayed the same; the doctor must of give him some pills or something."

The farmer sees Bill and Abby in tender moments together, feels that is not the way a brother and sister should behave, and challenges Bill. Bill leaves, hitching a ride with an aerial circus that has descended out of the sky. Abby, the farmer, and Linda live happily for a year, and then Bill returns at harvest time. All of the buried issues boil up to the surface again, against a backdrop of biblical misfortune: a plague of grasshoppers, fields in flame, murder, loss, exile.

Days of Heaven is above all one of the most beautiful films ever made. Malick's purpose is not to tell a story of melodrama, but one of loss. His tone is elegy. He evokes the loneliness and beauty of the limitless Texas prairie. In the first hour of the film, there is scarcely a scene set indoors. The farmworkers camp under the stars and work in the fields, and even the farmer is so besotted by the weather that he tinkers with wind instruments on the roof of his gothic mansion. The film places its humans in a large frame filled with natural details: the sky, rivers, fields, horses, pheasants, rabbits. Malick set many of its shots at the "golden hours" near dawn and dusk, when shadows are muted and the sky is all the same tone. These images are underlined by the famous score of Ennio Morricone, who quotes Saint-Saëns's *Carnival of the Animals.* The music is wistful, filled with loss and regret: in mood, like *The Godfather* theme but not so lush and more remembered than experienced. Voices are often distant, and there is far-off thunder.

Against this backdrop, the story is told in a curious way. We do see key emotional moments between the three adult characters (Bill advises Abby to take the farmer's offer, the farmer and Abby share moments together in which she realizes she is beginning to love him, and Bill and the farmer have their elliptical exchanges in which neither quite states the obvious). But all of their words together, if summed up, do not equal the total of the words in the voice-over spoken so hauntingly by Linda Manz.

She was sixteen when the film was made, playing younger, with a face that sometimes looks angular and plain, but at other times (especially in a shot where she is illuminated by firelight and surrounded by darkness) has a startling beauty. Her voice tells us everything we need to know about her character (and is so particular and unique we almost think it tells us about the actress too). It is flat, resigned, emotionless, with some kind of quirky eastern accent.

The whole story is told by her. But her words are not a narration so much as a parallel commentary, with asides and footnotes. We get the sense that she is speaking some years after the events have happened, trying to reconstruct times that were seen through naive eyes. She is there in almost the first words of the film ("My brother used to tell everyone they were brother and sister," a statement that is more complex than it seems). And still there in the last words of the film, as she walks down the tracks with her new "best friend." She is there after the others are gone. She is the teller of the tale.

This child, we gather, has survived in hard times. She has armored herself. She is not surprised by the worst. Her voice sounds utterly authentic; it seems beyond performance. I remember seeing the film for the first time and being blindsided by the power of a couple of sentences she speaks near the end. The three of them are in a boat on a river. Things have not worked out well. The days of heaven are over. She says, "You could see people on the shore, but it was far off and you couldn't see what they were doing. They were probably calling for help or something—or they were trying to bury somebody or something."

That is the voice of the person who tells the story, and that is why *Days of Heaven* is correct to present its romantic triangle obliquely, as if seen through an emotional filter. Children know that adults can be seized with sudden passions for one another, but children are concerned primarily with how these passions impact upon themselves: Am I more or less secure, more or less loved, because there has been this emotional realignment among the adults who form my world?

Since it was first released, *Days of Heaven* has gathered legends to itself. Terrence Malick, born in 1943, made *Badlands* with newcomers Sissy Spacek and Martin Sheen in 1973, made this film five years later, and then disappeared from view. Because the film made such an impression, the fact of his disappearance took on mythic, Salingerian proportions. He was, one heard, living in Paris. Or San Francisco. Or Montana. Or Austin. He was dying. Or working on another film. Or on a novel, or a play. In the late 1990s, Malick finally returned to work, making *The Thin Red Line,* which with its narration, its close attention to details of nature, its sadness in the face of death, picks up where he left off.

Days of Heaven's great photography has also generated a mystery. The credit for cinematography goes to the Cuban Nestor Almendros, who won an Oscar for the film; *Days of Heaven* established him in America, where he went on to great success. Then there is a small credit at the film's end: "Additional photography by Haskell Wexler." Wexler, too, is one of the greatest of all cinematographers. That credit has always rankled him, and he once sent me a letter in which he described sitting in a theater with a stopwatch to prove that more than half of the film's footage was shot by him. The reason he didn't get top billing is a story of personal and studio politics, but the fact remains that between them these two great cinematographers created a film whose look remains unmistakably in the memory.

What is the point of *Days of Heaven*—the payoff, the message? This is a movie made by a man who knew how something felt, and found a way to evoke it in us. That feeling is how a child feels when it lives precariously, and then is delivered into security and joy, and then has it all taken away again—and blinks away the tears and says it doesn't hurt.

{ The Decalogue }

Ten commandments, ten films. Krzysztof Kieslowski sat for months in his small, smoke-filled room in Warsaw writing the scripts with a lawyer he'd met in the early 1980s, during the Solidarity trials. Krzysztof Piesiewicz didn't know how to write, the director remembered, but he could talk. For hours they talked about Poland in turmoil, and together they wrote the screenplay for *No End* (1985), which told three stories of life under martial law. The government found it unsympathetic, the opposition found it compromised, and the Catholic Church found it immoral. During the controversy, the collaborators ran into each other in the rain, and Piesiewicz, maybe looking for more trouble, shouted, "Someone should make a film about the Ten Commandments."

They made ten films, each an hour long, for Polish television. The series ran in the late 1980s, played at the Venice and other film festivals, and gathered extraordinary praise. But the form was ungainly for theatrical showing (do you ask audiences to sit for ten hours, or come for five two-hour sessions?), and *The Decalogue* never had an ordinary U.S. theatrical run, nor was it available here on video. In 2000, at last, it was released in North America on tapes and DVD.

I taught a class on *The Decalogue* a few years ago, using tapes from England, and found we lost a lot of time trying to match up the films and the Commandments. There isn't a one-to-one correlation; some films touch

on more than one commandment, and others involve the whole ethical system suggested by the Commandments. These are not simplistic illustrations of the rules, but stories that involve real people in the complexities of real problems.

All the stories involve characters who live in the same high-rise Warsaw apartment complex. We grow familiar with the layout and even glimpse characters from one story in the backgrounds of others—sharing the lift, for example. There is a young man who appears in eight of them, a solemn onlooker who never says anything but sometimes makes sad eye contact. I thought perhaps he represented Christ, but Kieslowski, in an essay about the series, says, "I don't know who he is; just a guy who comes and watches us, our lives. He's not very pleased with us." Directors are notorious for not pinning down the meanings of their images. I like the theory of Annette Insdorf, in her valuable book about Kieslowski, *Double Lives, Second Chances;* she compares the watcher to the angels in Wim Wenders's *Wings of Desire* (1987), who are "pure gaze"—able to "record human folly and suffering but unable to alter the course of the lives they witness."

The ten films are not philosophical abstractions, but personal stories that involve us immediately; I hardly stirred during some of them. After seeing the series, Stanley Kubrick observed that Kieslowski and Piesiewicz "have the very rare ability to *dramatize* their ideas rather than just talking about them." Quite so. There is not a moment when the characters talk about specific commandments or moral issues. Instead, they are absorbed in trying to deal with real-life ethical challenges.

Consider the heroine of *Decalogue: Two,* who wants a doctor to tell her whether her sick husband will live or die. The doctor, a gruff and solitary being, is almost cruelly distant with her; he resists being asked to play God. The woman explains why she must know: She is pregnant with another man's child. Her husband is not fertile. If he is going to live, she will have an abortion. If he is going to die, she will have the baby.

The stuff of soap opera. But here it becomes a moral puzzle, solved finally only through a flashback to the doctor's own painful past—and even then the solution is indirect, since events do not turn out as anyone anticipates. Kieslowski roots the issues in very specific performances by the doctor and the woman (Aleksander Bardini and Krystyna Janda), and a beautiful, subtle thing happens: The film is about their *separate* moral challenges, and not about the two of them locked together by one problem.

Or look at the moral switch in *Decalogue: Six*, which is about a lonely teenage boy who uses a telescope to spy on the sex life of a morally careless, lonely woman who lives across the way. He decides he loves her. They see each other because he is a clerk in the post office. He takes a morning milk route so he can see her then too. Almost inevitably, she finds out he is a Peeping Tom (and also an anonymous phone caller and a prankster), but we can hardly anticipate what she does then.

In one of the sharp but plausible dramatic twists that Kieslowski likes in all of his films, the woman invites the teenager to her apartment and uses his sexual inexperience to humiliate him. And that is still only the halfway point in their moral duel; what happens next, to him, to her, to them, shows right and wrong shifting back and forth between them as sinner and victim exchange roles. Their relationship shows "situational ethics" becoming fluid and confusing.

Kieslowski deliberately avoided everyday facts of life in Poland, because he thought they were a distraction—the rules, the laws, the shortages, the bureaucracy. He deals with those parts of life that are universal. In *Decalogue: One*, for me the saddest of all his stories, he tells about the love between a smart father and a genius son. Together they use computers to calculate the freezing rate of a nearby pond so they will know when the ice is thick enough to skate safely. But ponds and currents cannot always be studied so simply, and perhaps the computer is a false god.

None of these films are simple demonstrations of black and white moral issues. *Decalogue: Five* is about a murderer who seems completely amoral. To understand him is not to forgive him. But the story also focuses on his defense attorney, a young man trying his first case and passionately opposed to the death penalty. *Decalogue: Nine* is about a man who discovers his wife is having an affair. He hides himself to spy on them and eavesdrops as she breaks up forever with her lover—and then she discovers her husband in hiding. She did the wrong thing (adultery) and the right one (ending it); his spying was a violation of her trust—and then there is an outcome where pure chance almost leads to a death, which was avoidable if either had been more honest.

At the end, you see that the Commandments work not like science, but like art; they are instructions for how to paint a worthy portrait with our lives.

Kieslowski (1941–96) and Piesiewicz wrote the screenplays intending that each would be filmed by a different director. But Kieslowski was unwilling to give them up, and he directed all ten, each one with a different cinematographer so that the visual styles would not become repetitious. The settings are much the same: gray exteriors, in winter for the most part, small apartments, offices. The faces are where the life of the films resides.

These are not characters involved in the simpleminded struggles of Hollywood plots. They are adults, for the most part outside organized religion, faced with situations in their own lives that require them to make moral choices. You shouldn't watch the films all in one sitting, but one at a time. Then if you are lucky and have someone to talk with, you discuss them and learn about yourself. Or if you are alone, you discuss them with yourself, as so many of Kieslowski's characters do.

{ DETOUR }

Detour is a movie so filled with imperfections that it would not earn the director a passing grade in film school. This movie from Hollywood's poverty row, shot in six days, filled with technical errors and ham-handed narrative, starring a man who can only pout and a woman who can only sneer, should have faded from sight soon after it was released in 1945. And yet it lives on, haunting and creepy, an embodiment of the guilty soul of film noir. No one who has seen it has easily forgotten it.

Detour tells the story of Al Roberts, played by Tom Neal as a petulant loser with haunted eyes and a weak mouth, who plays piano in a nightclub and is in love, or says he is, with a singer named Sue. Their song, significantly, is "I Can't Believe You Fell in Love with Me." He wants to get married, she leaves for the West Coast, he continues to play piano, but then: "When this drunk gave me a ten-spot, I couldn't get very excited. What was it? A piece of paper crawling with germs."

So he hitchhikes to California, getting a lift in Arizona from a man named Haskell, who tells him about a woman hitchhiker who left deep scratches on his hand: "There oughta be a law against dames with claws." Haskell dies of a heart attack. Al buries the body and takes Haskell's car, clothes, money, and identification; he claims to have no choice because the police will in any event assume he murdered the man. He picks up a hitchhiker named Vera (Ann Savage), who "looked like she'd just been thrown off the crummiest freight train in the world." She seems to doze, then sits bolt upright and makes a sudden verbal attack: "Where'd you leave his body? Where did you leave the owner of this car? Your name's not Haskell!" Al realizes he has picked up the dame with the claws.

Haskell had told them both the same unlikely story, about running away from home at fifteen after putting a friend's eye out in a duel ("My dad had a couple of Franco-Prussian sabers"). In Los Angeles, Vera reads that Haskell's rich father is dying, and dreams up a con for Al to impersonate the long-lost son and inherit the estate. Waiting for the old man to die, they sit in a rented room, drinking, playing cards, and fighting, until Al finds himself with another corpse on his hands, once again in a situation that makes him look guilty of murder.

Roberts is played by Tom Neal as a sad sack who seems relieved to surrender to Vera ("My favorite sport is being kept prisoner"). Ann Savage plays Vera as a venomous castrator. Her lines are acid and angry; in an era before four-letter words, she lashes Al with "sucker" and "sap." Of course Al could simply escape from her. Sure, she has the key to the room, but any woman who kills a bottle of booze in a night can be dodged fairly easily. Al stays because he wants to stay. He wallows in mistreatment.

The movie was shot on the cheap with B-minus actors, but it was directed by a man of qualities: Edgar G. Ulmer (1904–72), a refugee from Hitler, who was an assistant to the great F. W. Murnau on *The Last Laugh* (1924) and *Sunrise* (1927) and provided one of the links between German expressionism, with its exaggerated lighting, camera angles, and dramaturgy, and the American film noir, which added jazz and guilt.

The difference between a crime film and a noir film is that the bad guys in crime movies know they're bad and want to be, while a noir hero thinks he's a good guy who has been ambushed by life. Al Roberts complains to us, "Whichever way you turn, fate sticks out a foot to trip you." Most noir heroes are defeated through their weaknesses. Few have been weaker than Roberts. He narrates the movie by speaking directly to the audience, mostly in a self-pitying whine. He's pleading his case, complaining that life hasn't given him a fair break.

Most critics of *Detour* have taken Al's story at face value: He was unlucky in love; he lost the good girl and was savaged by the bad girl; he was

an innocent bystander who looked guilty even to himself. But the critic Andrew Britton argues a more intriguing theory in Ian Cameron's *Book of Film Noir*. He emphasizes that the narration is addressed directly to us. We're not hearing what happened, but what Al Roberts wants us to believe happened. It's a "spurious but flattering account," he writes, pointing out that Sue the singer hardly fits Al's description of her, that Al is less in love than in need of her paycheck, and that his cover-up of Haskell's death is a rationalization for an easy theft. For Britton, Al's version illustrates Freud's theory that traumatic experiences can be reworked into fantasies that are easier to live with.

Maybe that's why *Detour* insinuates itself so well—why audiences respond so strongly. The jumps and inconsistencies of the narrative are nightmare psychology. Al's not telling a story, but scurrying through the raw materials, assembling an alibi. Consider the sequence where Al buries Haskell's body and takes his identity. Immediately after, Al checks into a motel, goes to sleep, and dreams of the very same events. It's a flashback side by side with the events it flashes back to, as if his dream mind is doing a quick rewrite.

Tom Neal makes Al flaccid, passive, and self-pitying. That's perfect for the material. (In real life, Neal was as unlucky as Al; he was convicted of manslaughter in the death of his third wife.) Ann Savage's work is extraordinary. There is not a single fleeting shred of tenderness or humanity in her performance as Vera, as she snaps out her pulp dialogue ("What'd you do—kiss him with a wrench?"). These are two pure types: the submissive man and the female hellion.

The movie's low budget is obvious. During one early scene, Ulmer uses thick fog to substitute for New York streets. He shoots as many scenes as possible in the front seats of cars, with shabby rear projection (the only meal Al and Vera have together is in a drive-in). For a flashback, he simply zooms in on Neal's face, cuts the lights in the background, and shines a light in his eyes. Sometimes you can see him stretching to make ends meet. When Al calls long-distance to Sue, for example, Ulmer pads his running time by editing in stock footage of telephone wires and switchboard operators, but can't spring for any footage of Sue actually speaking into the phone. Al does all the talking, and then Ulmer cuts to her lamely holding the receiver to her ear.

And it's strange that the first vehicles to give lifts to the hitchhiking Al seem to have right-hand drives. He gets in on what would be the driver's side in America, and the cars drive off on the "wrong" side of the road. Was the movie shot in England? Not at all. My guess is that the negative was flipped. Ulmer possibly shot the scenes with the cars going from left to right, then reflected that for a journey from the East to the West Coasts, right to left would be more conventional film grammar. Placing style above common sense is completely consistent with Ulmer's approach throughout the film. A movie like this provides a persuasive argument against the theory that a film must be well made to be successful.

Do these limitations and stylistic transgressions hurt the film? No. They *are* the film. *Detour* is an example of material finding the appropriate form. Two bottom-feeders from the swamps of pulp swim through the murk of low-budget noir and are caught gasping in Ulmer's net. They deserve one another. At the end, Al is still complaining: "Fate, for some mysterious force, can put the finger on you or me, for no good reason at all." Oh, it has a reason.

{ DO THE RIGHT THING }

I have only been given a few filmgoing experiences in my life to equal the first time I saw *Do the Right Thing*. Most movies remain up there on the screen. Only a few penetrate your soul. In May 1989, I walked out of the screening at the Cannes Film Festival with tears in my eyes. Spike Lee had done an almost impossible thing. He'd made a movie about race in America that empathized with all the participants. He didn't draw lines or take sides, but simply looked with sadness at one racial flashpoint that stood for many others.

Not everybody thought the film was evenhanded. I sat behind a woman at the press conference who was convinced the film would cause race riots. Some critics agreed. On the Criterion DVD of the film, Lee reads from his reviews, noting that Joe Klein, in *New York* magazine, laments the burning of Sal's Pizzeria but fails to even note that it follows the death of a young black man at the hands of the police.

Many audiences are shocked that the destruction of Sal's begins with a trash can thrown through the window by Mookie (Lee), the employee Sal refers to as "like a son to me." Mookie is a character we're meant to like. Lee says he has been asked many times over the years if Mookie did the right thing. Then he observes, "Not one person of color has ever asked me that question." But the movie in any event is not just about how the cops kill a black man and a mob burns down a pizzeria. That would be too sim-

ple, and this is not a simplistic film. It covers a day in the life of a Brooklyn street, so that we get to know the neighbors and see by what small steps the tragedy is approached.

The victim, Radio Raheem (Bill Nunn), is not blameless; he plays his boom box at deafening volume and the noise drives not only Sal (Danny Aiello) crazy but also the three old black guys who sit and talk at the corner. He wears steel knuckles that spell out "Love" and "Hate" (that's an echo of Mitchum's preacher in *The Night of the Hunter*), and although we know Radio is harmless, and we've seen that "Love" wins when he stages an imaginary bout for Mookie, to the cops the knuckles look bad. Not that the cops look closely, because they are white, and when they pull Radio off Sal in the middle of a fight, it doesn't occur to them that Radio might have been provoked (Sal has just pounded his boom box to pieces with a baseball bat).

There are really no heroes or villains in the film. There is even a responsible cop, who screams, "That's enough!" as another cop chokes Radio with his nightstick. And perhaps the other cop is terrified because he is surrounded by a mob and the pizzeria is on fire. On and on, around and around, black and white, fear and suspicion breed and grow. Because we know all of the people and have spent all day on the street, we feel as much grief as anger. Radio Raheem is dead. And Sal, who has watched the neighborhood's kids grow up for twenty-five years and fed them with his pizza, stands in the ruins of his store. A pizzeria does not equal a human life, but its loss is great to Sal, because it represents a rejection of the meaning of his own life, and Spike Lee knows that—feels bad for Sal and gives him a touching final scene with Mookie in which the unspoken subtext might be: Why can't we eat pizza, and raise our families, and run our businesses, and work at our jobs, and not let racism colonize our minds with suspicion?

The riot starts because Buggin' Out (Giancarlo Esposito) is offended that Sal has only photos of Italians on the wall of his pizzeria: Sinatra, DiMaggio, Pacino. He wonders why there isn't a black face up there. Sal tells him to open his own store and put up anyone he wants. One answer to Sal is that he's kept in business by the black people who buy his pizza. An answer to *that* is that we see no black-owned business on the street, and if it were not for Sal and the Koreans who run the corner grocery, the residents would have no place to buy food. And the answer to *that* is that economic discrimination against blacks has been institutionalized for years in America. And around and around.

The thing is, there are no answers. There may be heroes and villains, but on this ordinary street in Brooklyn, they don't conveniently turn up wearing labels. You can anticipate, step by step, during a long summer day, that trash can approaching Sal's window, propelled by misunderstandings, suspicions, insecurities, stereotyping, and simple bad luck. Racism is so deeply ingrained in our society that the disease itself creates mischief, while most blacks and whites alike are only onlookers.

Seeing the film again today, I was reminded of what a stylistic achievement it is. Spike Lee was thirty-two when he made it, assured, confident, in the full joy of his power. He takes this story, which sounds like grim social realism, and tells it with music, humor, color, and exuberant invention. A lot of it is just plain fun. He breaks completely away from realism in many places—in the close-ups of blacks, whites, and Koreans chanting a montage of racial descriptions, for example, or in the patter of the local disc jockey (Samuel L. Jackson), who surveys the street from his window and seems like the neighborhood's sound track. At other times, Lee makes points with deadpan understatement. There are two slow-motion sequences involving the way that people look at each other. One shows two cops and the three old black guys exchanging level gazes of mutual contempt. Another takes place when Sal speaks tenderly to Jade (Joie Lee), and the camera pans slowly across the narrowed eyes of both Mookie and Pino (John Turturro), one of Sal's sons. Neither one likes that tone in Sal's voice.

It is clear that Sal has feelings for Jade, which he will probably always express simply by making her a special slice of pizza. He tells her what big brown eyes she has. Sal is sincere when he says he likes his customers, and he holds his head in his hands when Pino calls them "niggers" and berates a simpleminded street person. But in his rage Sal is also capable of using "nigger," and for that matter the blacks are not innocent of racism either and come within an inch of burning out the Koreans just on general principles.

Lee paints the people with love for detail. Notice the sweet scene between Mookie and Tina (Rosie Perez), the mother of his child. How he takes ice cubes and runs them over her brow, eyes, ankles, thighs, and then the close-up of their lips as they talk softly to one another. And see the affection which he shows Da Mayor (Ossie Davis), an old man who tries to cool everyone's tempers. Da Mayor's scenes with Mother Sister (Ruby Dee) show love at the other end of the timeline.

None of these people are perfect. But Lee makes it possible for us to understand their feelings; his empathy is crucial to the film, because if you can't try to understand how the other person feels, you're a captive inside the box of yourself. Thoughtless people have accused Lee over the years of being an angry filmmaker. He has much to be angry about, but I don't find it in his work. The wonder of *Do the Right Thing* is that he is so fair. Those who found this film an incitement to violence are saying much about themselves and nothing useful about the movie. Its predominant emotion is sadness. Lee ends with two quotations, one from Martin Luther King, advocating nonviolence, and the other from Malcolm X, advocating violence "if necessary." A third, from Rodney King, ran through my mind.

{ DOUBLE INDEMNITY }

"No, I never loved you, Walter—not you, or anybody else. I'm rotten to the heart. I used you, just as you said. That's all you ever meant to me. Until a minute ago, when I couldn't fire that second shot."

Is she kidding? Walter thinks so: "Sorry, baby. I'm not buying." The puzzle of Billy Wilder's *Double Indemnity*, the enigma that keeps it new, is what these two people *really* think of one another. They strut through the routine of a noir murder plot, with the tough talk and the cold sex play. But they never seem to really like each other all that much, and they don't seem that crazy about the money either. What are they after?

Walter (Fred MacMurray) is Walter Neff ("two *f*'s—like in Philadelphia"). He's an insurance salesman, successful but bored. The woman is Phyllis Dietrichson (Barbara Stanwyck), a lazy blonde who met her current husband by nursing his wife—to death, according to her stepdaughter. Neff pays a call one day to renew her husband's automobile insurance. He's not at home, but she is, wrapped in a towel and standing at the top of a staircase. "I wanted to see her again," Neff tells us. "Close, and without that silly staircase."

The story was written in the 1930s by James M. Cain, the hardboiled author of *The Postman Always Rings Twice*. A screenplay kicked around Hollywood, but the Hays Office nixed it for "hardening audience attitudes toward crime." By 1944, Wilder thought he could film it. Cain wasn't available, so he hired Raymond Chandler to do the screenplay. Chandler, whose novel *The Big Sleep* Wilder loved, turned up drunk, smoked a smelly pipe, didn't know anything about screenplay construction, but could put a nasty spin on dialogue. Together they eliminated Cain's complicated endgame and deepened the relationship between Neff and Keyes (Edward G. Robinson), the claims manager at the insurance company. They told the movie in flashback, narrated by Neff, who arrives at his office late at night, dripping blood, and recites into a Dictaphone. The voice-over worked so well that Wilder used it again in *Sunset Boulevard* (1950), which was narrated by a character who is already dead the first time he speaks. No problem. *Double Indemnity* originally ended with Neff in the gas chamber, but that scene was cut because an earlier one turned out to be the perfect way to close the film.

To describe the story is to miss the nuances that make it tantalizing. Phyllis wants Walter to sell her husband a $50,000 double indemnity policy and then arrange the husband's "accidental" death. Walter is willing, ostensibly because he's fallen under her sexual spell. They perform a clever substitution. The husband, on crutches with a broken leg, is choked to death before a train ride. Taking his place, Neff gets on the train and jumps off. They leave the husband's body on the tracks. Perfect. But later that night, going to the drugstore to establish an alibi, Neff remembers, "I couldn't hear my own footsteps. It was the walk of a dead man."

A clever crime. But why did they do it? Phyllis was bored and her husband had lost a lot of money in the oil business, so she had a motive. But it's as if the idea of murder materialized only because Neff did—right there in her living room, talking about insurance. On their third meeting, after a lot of aggressive wordplay, they agree to kill the husband and collect the money. I guess they also make love; in 1944 movies, you can't be sure, but if they do, it's only the once.

Why? Is Neff blinded by lust and greed? That's the traditional reading of the film: weak man, strong woman. But he's aloof, cold, hard, terse. He always calls her "baby," as if she's a brand, not a woman. His eyes are guarded and his posture reserved. He's not moonstruck. And Phyllis? Cold too. But later in the film, she says she cares more about "them" than about the money. We can believe the husband died for money if they both

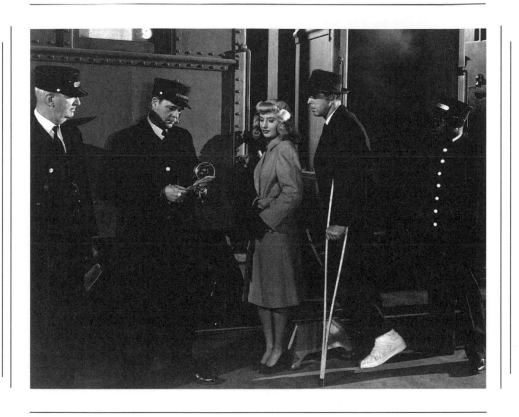

seem driven by greed, but they're not. We can believe he died because of their passion, but it seems more like a pretense and fades away after the murder.

Standing back from the film and what it expects us to think, I see them engaged not in romance or theft, but in behavior. They're intoxicated by their personal styles. Styles learned in the movies and from radio and the detective magazines. It's as if they were invented by Ben Hecht through his extraordinary influence on Hollywood crime dialogue in the previous decade. Walter and Phyllis are pulp characters with little psychological depth, and that's the way Billy Wilder wants it. His best films are sardonic comedies, and in this one, Phyllis and Walter play a bad joke on themselves.

More genuine emotion is centered elsewhere. It involves Neff's fear of discovery and his feelings for Keyes. Edward G. Robinson plays the inspector as a nonconformist who loosens his tie, reclines on the office couch, smokes cheap cigars, and wants to make Neff his assistant. He's a father figure, or more. He's also smart, and eventually he figures out that a crime was committed—and exactly how it was committed. His investigation leads to two scenes of queasy tension. One is when Keyes invites Neff to his office and then calls in a witness who saw Neff on the train. Another is when Keyes calls unexpectedly at Neff's apartment, when Neff expects Phyllis to arrive momentarily—and incriminatingly. Does Keyes suspect Neff? You can't really say. He arranges situations in which Neff's guilt might be discovered, but they're part of his routine techniques; perhaps only his subconscious, "the little man who lives in my stomach," suspects Neff.

The end of the film is curious (it's the beginning too, so I'm not giving it away). Why does the wounded Neff go to the office and dictate a confession if he still presumably hopes to escape? Because he *wants* to be discovered by Keyes? Neff tells him, "You know why you couldn't figure this one, Keyes? I'll tell you. Because the guy you were looking for was too close—right across the desk from you." Keyes says, "Closer than that, Walter," and then Neff says, "I love you too." Neff has been lighting Keyes's smokes all during the movie, and now Keyes lights Neff's. You see why a gas chamber would have been superfluous.

Wilder's *Double Indemnity* was one of the earlier film noirs. The photography by John Seitz helped develop the noir style of sharp-edged shadows and shots, strange angles, and lonely Edward Hopper settings. It's the right fit for the hard urban atmosphere and dialogue created by Cain, Chandler, and the other writers Edmund Wilson called "the boys in the back room."

Double Indemnity has one of the most familiar noir themes: The hero is not a criminal, but a weak man who is tempted and succumbs. In this "double" story, the woman and man tempt one another; neither would have acted alone. Both are attracted not so much by the crime as by the thrill of committing it with the other person. Love and money are pretenses. The husband's death turns out to be their one-night stand.

Wilder, born in Austria in 1906, in America since 1933, still a Hollywood landmark, has an angle on stories like this. He doesn't go for the obvious arc. He isn't interested in the same things the characters are interested in. He wants to know what happens to them after they do what they think is so important. He doesn't want truth, but consequences.

Few other directors have made so many films that were so taut, savvy, cynical, and, in many different ways and tones, funny. After a start as a screenwriter, his directorial credits include *The Lost Weekend* (1945), *Sunset Boulevard* (1950), *Ace in the Hole* (1951), *Stalag 17* (1953), *Sabrina* (1954), *The Seven Year Itch* (1955), *Witness for the Prosecution* (1957), *Some Like It Hot* (1959), *The Apartment* (1960), and *The Fortune Cookie* (1966). I don't like lists but I can't stop typing. *Double Indemnity* was his third film as a director. That early in his career, he was already cocky enough to *begin* a thriller with the lines "I killed him for money—and for a woman. I didn't get the money. And I didn't get the woman." And end it with the hero saying "I love you too" to Edward G. Robinson.

{ D R A C U L A }

Movie lore has it that Bela Lugosi could barely speak English when he was chosen by Universal Pictures to star in *Dracula* (1931). Lon Chaney had been scheduled to play the role, a wise casting decision after his success in the silent classics *The Hunchback of Notre Dame* (1923) and *The Phantom of the Opera* (1925). But he died as *Dracula* was going into production, and the mysterious forty-nine-year-old Hungarian, who starred in a 1927 Broadway production of *Dracula,* was cast. Legend must exaggerate, because the Hungarian émigré Lugosi had lived and worked in America for a decade when the film was made, and yet there is something about his line readings that suggests a man who comes sideways to English—perhaps because in his lonely Transylvanian castle, Dracula has had centuries to study it but few opportunities to practice it.

Certainly it is Lugosi's performance, and the cinematography of Karl Freund, that make Tod Browning's 1931 film such an influential Hollywood picture. The greatest of all the vampire films is F. W. Murnau's silent *Nosferatu* (1922), but Murnau's work was almost a dead end, complete and self-contained, a masterpiece that stood alone. (When Werner Herzog made his version of *Nosferatu* with Klaus Kinski in 1979, he was so in awe of the original that he shot on some of the same locations, "for the voodoo.") The look of Browning's *Dracula* was inspired by Murnau's gloomy gothic

visuals, well known to the German cameraman Freund, who worked with Murnau on *The Last Laugh* (1924). It was Freund who was instrumental in creating the startling impact of the arrival at Castle Dracula, the entrance to the castle's forbidding interior spaces, and such *Nosferatu*-inspired shots as the hand snaking from a coffin and rats snuffling in a crypt.

What was new about the film was sound. It was the first talking picture based on Bram Stoker's novel, and somehow Count Dracula was more fearsome when you could hear him—not an inhuman monster, but a human one, whose painfully articulated sentences mocked the conventions of drawing room society. And here Lugosi's accent and his stiffness in English were an advantage.

Lugosi was by all accounts a strange, deliberately theatrical man, who drew attention to himself by stylized behavior. He made his foreignness an asset, and in Hollywood and New York used his sinister, self-mocking accent to advantage. After the success of *Dracula*, he often appeared in public dressed formally, with a flowing cape, as if still playing the role. In later life, addicted to drugs, he was reduced to self-parody, and a glimpse of his final years can be found represented in *Ed Wood* (1994), which is set during his last picture.

The vampire Dracula has been the subject of dozens of films; something deep within the legend is suited to cinema. Perhaps it is the joining of eroticism with terror. The vampire's attack is not specifically sexual, but in drinking the blood of his victims, he is engaged in the most intimate of embraces, and no doubt there is an instinctive connection between losing one's virginity (and one's soul) and becoming one of the undead. Vampirism is like elegant, slow-motion rape, done politely by a creature who charms you into surrender.

The Dracula myth has been filmed so often, in so many different ways (most recently by Francis Ford Coppola in his *Bram Stoker's Dracula* [1992]), that its material has become like an opera libretto or a play by Shakespeare: We know the story and all the beats, and are concerned mostly with the style and production. All of the serious movie Draculas draw from Lugosi's performance. Max Schreck, who starred in *Nosferatu*, was more inhuman and distant, a skeletal wraith, but Lugosi, with his deep eyes (made eerie by Freund with pinpoint lights) and his glossy black hair, created one of the most influential of all movie performances, making distinctive impressions that influenced movie Draculas for years to come—especially Hammer Films star Christopher Lee, who played the character at least seven times.

If the film's look and star performance were influential, so was its dialogue. Many of the movie's great lines have entered into folklore:

I never drink . . . wine.

For one who has not lived even a single lifetime, you are a wise man, Van Helsing.

Listen to them. Children of the night. What music they make.

The story is familiar to every moviegoer. Renfield (Dwight Frye), an English real estate agent, visits Transylvania to sell a London property to the count. He really wants to make that sale; he takes no warning from the fear of the villagers when Dracula's name is mentioned. He survives a terrifying ride in a coach with no driver. And then he plunges into his doom. The establishing shots of the fearsome interiors of Castle Dracula owe everything to the tradition of German expressionism. There is the sinister politeness with which Dracula greets his guest and offers him food and . . . wine. Then the overpowering of Renfield. The return to England on the ship with its deadly cargo of coffins (another sequence that owes much to *Nosferatu*). The ghost ship that drifts into port, everyone on board apparently dead except for Renfield, who is stark staring mad.

In London, the vampire feasts on the blood of strangers encountered in the night, in scenes owing something to the legend of Jack the Ripper. Then he introduces himself into high society by insinuating himself into the box at the opera occupied by Dr. Seward (Herbert Bunston). The doctor owns Carfax Abbey, which is next door to the sanitarium where the unfortunate Renfield has been imprisoned (giggling and eating spiders for their blood). He meets Seward's daughter, Mina (Helen Chandler), her fiancé, Jonathan Harker (David Manners), and her friend Lucy (Frances

Dade). They are joined eventually by the vampire hunter Dr. Van Helsing (Edward Van Sloan), who explains vampirism in more detail than the drama probably requires.

The scenes in Carfax Abbey are an anticlimax after the expressionist terrors of the scenes set in Transylvania and aboard the ship. They're based on the same Broadway play in which Lugosi first played Dracula and owe more to the tradition of drawing room drama (and, it must be said, comedy) than to the underlying appeal of vampirism. Yet even here Browning is able to add unsettling touches, as in the way he suggests Dracula's presence in the visits of bats and in the drifting of fog.

Tod Browning (1882–1962) is a director whose name is central to any study of the horror genre, and yet most of his best work is overshadowed by his collaborators. Lon Chaney, "the man of a thousand faces," seems to be the key creative force behind Browning's landmarks *The Unholy Three* (1925) and *West of Zanzibar* (1928). Lugosi, Freund, and the subject matter are the creative engines behind *Dracula*. One Browning picture that stands alone as his personal vision is *Freaks* (1932), set in a circus sideshow, and so shocking it has been banned here and there ever since.

Dracula had no musical score when it was first released, apart from some fugitive strains of *Swan Lake*. That left an opportunity. I saw a restored version of the film in September 1999 at the Telluride Film Festival, with the Kronos Quartet performing Philip Glass's newly composed score. That version is now available on video. Purists argue that Browning's original decision was the best one—to enhance the horror by eerie sound effects instead of underlining it with music. But *Dracula* has been pushed and pulled in so many different directions by so many different artists that Glass is only following the tradition in adding his own contribution. The Glass score is effective in the way it suggests not just moody creepiness but the urgency and need behind Dracula's vampirism. It evokes a blood thirst.

Is the 1931 *Dracula* still a terrifying film, or has it become a period piece? The "most chilling, genuinely frightening film ever made," vows the reference series Cinebooks. Perhaps that was true in 1931, but today I think the movie is interesting mostly for technical reasons—for the stylized performances, the photography, the sets. There is a moment, though, when Lugosi draws close to the sleeping Lucy, and all of the elements of the material draw together. We consider the dreadful trade-off: immortality, but as a vampire. From our point of view, Dracula is committing an unspeakable crime. From his, offering an unspeakable gift.

{ DR. STRANGELOVE }

Every time you see a great film, you find new things in it. Viewing Stanley Kubrick's *Dr. Strangelove* for perhaps the tenth time, I focused on what George C. Scott does with his face. His performance is the funniest thing in the movie—better even than the inspired triple performance by Peter Sellers or the nutjob general played by Sterling Hayden—but this time I found myself paying special attention to the tics and twitches, the grimaces and eyebrow archings, the sardonic smiles and gum-chewing, and I enjoyed the way Scott approached the role as a duet for voice and facial expression.

That can be dangerous for an actor. Directors often ask actors to underplay closer shots, because too much facial movement translates into mugging or overacting. Billy Wilder once asked Jack Lemmon for "a little less" so many takes in a row that Lemmon finally exploded: "Whaddya want! Nothing?" Lemmon recalls that Wilder raised his eyes to heaven: "Please, God!" Kubrick, whose attention to the smallest detail in every frame was obsessive, would have been aware of George C. Scott's facial gymnastics, and yet he endorsed them, and when you watch *Strangelove,* you can see why.

Scott's work is hidden in plain view. His face here is so plastic and mobile it reminds you of Jerry Lewis or Jim Carrey. Yet you don't consciously notice his expressions, because Scott sells them with the energy and conviction of his performance. He *means* what he says so urgently that the

expressions seem generated by his very sincerity; his voice speaks, his face mimes the words. Consider the scene where his character, General Buck Turgidson, is informing the president that it is quite likely a B-52 bomber will be able to fly under Russian radar and deliver its payload even though the entire Soviet Air Force knows where the plane is headed. "He can barrel in that baby so low!" Scott says, with his arms spread wide like wings and his head shaking in admiration at how good his pilots are—so good one of them is about to bring an end to civilization.

Another actor waving his arms around might simply look absurd. Scott absorbs the body language so completely into the moment that it simply plays as drama (and comedy). In another scene in the movie, scurrying around the war room, he slips, falls to a knee, rights himself, and carries on. Kubrick the perfectionist left the unplanned slip in the film, because Scott made it seem convincing and not an accident.

Dr. Strangelove (1964) is filled with great comic performances, and just as well, because there's so little else in the movie apart from faces, bodies, and words. Kubrick shot it on four principal locations (an office and the perimeter of an air force base, the "war room," and the interior of a B-52 bomber). His special effects are competent but not dazzling (we are obviously looking at model planes flying over Russia). The war room itself, one of the most memorable of all movie interiors, was created out of a big circular desk, a ring of lights, some back-projected maps, and darkness. The headquarters of General Jack D. Ripper, the haywire air force general, is just a room with some office furniture in it.

Yet out of these rudimentary physical props and a brilliant screenplay (which Kubrick and Terry Southern based on a novel by Peter George), Kubrick made what is arguably the best political satire of the century, a film that pulled the rug out from under the cold war by arguing that if a "nuclear deterrent" destroys all life on earth, it is hard to say exactly what it has deterred.

Dr. Strangelove's humor is generated by a basic comic principle: People trying to be funny are never as funny as people trying to be serious and failing. The laughs have to seem *forced* on unwilling characters by the logic of events. A man wearing a funny hat is not funny. But if the man doesn't know he's wearing a funny hat—now you've got something.

The characters in *Dr. Strangelove* do not know their hats are funny. The film begins with General Ripper (Sterling Hayden) fondling a phallic cigar while launching an unauthorized nuclear strike against Russia. He has become convinced that the commies are poisoning "the purity and essence of our natural fluids" by adding fluoride to the water supply (in the 1950s, this was a cherished right-wing belief). Ripper's nuclear strike, his cigar technique, and his concern for his "precious bodily fluids" are so entwined that they inspire unmistakable masturbatory associations.

The only man standing between Ripper and nuclear holocaust is a British liaison, Group Captain Mandrake (Sellers), who listens with disbelief to Ripper's rantings. Meanwhile, Ripper's coded message goes out to airborne B-52s to launch an attack against Russia. A horrified President Muffley (Sellers again) convenes his advisers in the war room and is informed by Turgidson, bit by reluctant bit, of the enormity of the situation: The bombers are on the way, they cannot be recalled, General Ripper cannot be reached, and so on. Eventually, Muffley calls the Russian premier to confess everything ("Dimitri, we have a little problem . . .").

Other major players include the sinister strategist Dr. Strangelove (Sellers a third time), a character whose German accent now evokes Henry Kissinger, although in 1964, nuclear think-tanker Herman Kahn was the likely inspiration. Strangelove's black-gloved right hand is an unruly weapon with a will of its own, springing into Nazi salutes and trying to throttle him to death. Action in the war room and on the air force base is intercut with the B-52 cockpit, ruled by Major T. J. "King" Kong (Slim Pickens); when he's told by his radioman that the order to attack has come through, he tells them, "No horsin' around on the airplane!"

Major Kong was originally intended to be Sellers's fourth role in the movie, but he was uncertain about the cowboy accent. Pickens, a character actor from Westerns, was brought in by Kubrick, who reportedly didn't tell him the film was a comedy. Pickens's patriotic speeches to his crew (and his promises of promotion and medals) are counterpoint to the desperate American efforts to recall the flight.

I've always thought the movie ends on an unsure note. After the first nuclear blast, Kubrick cuts back to the war room, where Strangelove muses that deep mines could be used to shelter survivors, whose descendants could return to the surface in ninety years (Turgidson is intrigued by the ten-to-one ratio of women to men). Then the film abruptly ends in its famous montage of many mushroom clouds while Vera Lynn sings "We'll Meet Again." It seems to me there should be no more dialogue after the first blast; Strangelove's survival strategy could be moved up to just before Slim Pickens's bareback ride to oblivion. I realize there would be a time lapse while Russian missiles responded to the attack, but I think the film would be more effective if the original blast brought an end to all further story developments. (Kubrick originally planned to end the film with a pie fight, and a table laden with pies can be seen in the background of the war room. He filmed the scene but wisely realized that his purpose was satire, not slapstick.)

Dr. Strangelove and *2001: A Space Odyssey* (1968) are Kubrick's unquestioned masterpieces. His two great films share a common theme: Man designs machinery that functions with perfect logic to bring about a disastrous outcome. The U.S. nuclear deterrent and the Russian "doomsday machine" function exactly as they are intended, and destroy life on earth. The computer HAL 9000 serves the space mission by attacking the astronauts.

Stanley Kubrick (1928–99) was a perfectionist who went to obsessive lengths in order to get everything in his films to work just right. He owned his own cameras and sound and editing equipment. He often made dozens of takes of the same shot. He was known to telephone projectionists to complain about out-of-focus screenings. Are his two best films a nudge in his own ribs?

{ DUCK SOUP }

My father loved the Marx Brothers above all other comedians or, indeed, all other movie stars. The first movie he ever took me to was *A Day at the Races* (1937). All I remember about that experience was my father's laughter. But there was something else, too, that I understood only much later: the sound of his voice as he described the brothers. He used the tone that people employ when they are talking about how someone got away with something.

That is the same tone I have heard, and used, in discussing such subjects as *Some Like It Hot, The Producers, Blazing Saddles, Airplane!*, Monty Python, Andy Kaufman, *Saturday Night Live, South Park,* Howard Stern, *There's Something About Mary,* or *Being John Malkovich*—or even movies that are only indirectly comedies, like *Pulp Fiction.* There is a kind of admiration for material that dares something against the rules and yet is obviously and irresistibly funny. How much more anarchic the Marx Brothers must have seemed in their time than we can understand today. They were among the first to evoke that tone; you can see whom the Marx Brothers inspired, but not whom they were inspired by, except indirectly by the rich tradition of music hall, vaudeville, and Yiddish comedy that nurtured them.

Movies gave them a mass audience, and they were the instrument that translated what was once essentially a Jewish style of humor into the dominant note of American comedy. Although they were not taken as seriously, they were as surrealist as Dalí, as shocking as Stravinsky, as verbally playful as Gertrude Stein, as alienated as Kafka. Because they worked in the genres of slapstick and screwball, they did not get the same kind of attention, but their effect on the popular mind was probably more influential. "As an absurdist essay on politics and warfare," wrote the British critic Patrick McCray, "*Duck Soup* can stand alongside (or even above) the works of Beckett and Ionesco."

The Marx Brothers created a body of work in which individual films are like slices from the whole, but *Duck Soup* (1933) is probably the best. It represents a turning point in their movie work; it was their last film for Paramount and the last in which all of the scenes directly involved the brothers. When it was a box office disappointment, they moved over to MGM, where production chief Irving Thalberg ordered their plots to find room for conventional romantic couples, as if audiences could only take so much Marx before they demanded something mediocre (Buster Keaton's sound comedies for MGM suffered from the same meddling and dilution).

A Night at the Opera (1935), their first MGM film, contains some of their best work, yes, but in watching it, I fast-forward over the sappy interludes involving Kitty Carlisle and Allan Jones. In *Duck Soup*, there are no sequences I can skip; the movie is funny from beginning to end.

To describe the plot would be an exercise in futility, since a Marx Brothers movie exists in moments, bits, sequences, business, and dialogue, not in comprehensible stories. Very briefly, *Duck Soup* stars Groucho as Rufus T. Firefly, who becomes dictator of Fredonia under the sponsorship of the rich Mrs. Teasdale (Margaret Dumont, the brothers' tireless and irreplaceable foil). Neighboring Sylvania and its Ambassador Trentino (Louis Calhern) have designs on the country, and Trentino hires Harpo and Chico as spies. This flimsy premise provides a clothesline for one inspired sequence after another, including sustained examples of Groucho's puns and sneaky double entendres. But it also supports a couple of wordless physical sequences that probably have their roots in the vaudeville acts the brothers performed and saw years earlier.

One of these is the three-hat routine involving Chico and Harpo and the straight man, Edgar Kennedy (who started with Mack Sennett and

Chaplin). Chico, as a spy, inexplicably adopts the cover of a peanut vendor, and Harpo is a passerby. Kennedy has the lemonade cart next to Chico's peanut cart, and the brothers make his life miserable in a routine that involves their three hats changing position as quickly as the cards in a monte game.

The other sequence is one of the gems of the first century of film. Harpo disguises himself as Groucho and, for reasons much too complicated to explain, sneaks into Mrs. Teasdale's, tries to break into a safe, and shatters a mirror. Groucho himself comes downstairs to investigate. Harpo is standing inside the frame of the broken mirror and tries to avoid detection by pretending to be Groucho's reflection. This leads to a sustained pantomime involving flawless timing, as Groucho tries to catch the reflection in an error, and Harpo matches every move. Finally, in a perfect escalation of zaniness, Chico blunders into the frame, also dressed as Groucho.

It is impossible to discuss Groucho's dialogue without quoting it, and pointless to quote it, since Groucho's delivery is essential to the effect. He played an utterly irreverent character whose speech was at the mercy of puns, insults, and bawdy insinuations that tiptoed just this side of the censors (as when Rufus T. Firefly tantalizes Mrs. Teasdale with visions of marriage and then confesses, "All I can offer you is a Rufus over your head"). Many gifted comedy writers, including S. J. Perelman, labored over the Marx Brothers movie scripts, but all their dialogue had its origins in Groucho's own speaking style, perfected over the years.

In 1972, I was able to spend some time with Groucho, for a profile for *Esquire*. He was then eighty-one and still unmistakably occupying the persona he had made famous. (Who he was in private remains a mystery to me; in public he was always onstage.) His first words to me could have been said in more or less the same way by Rufus T. Firefly: "*Esquire* isn't my favorite magazine, you know. Interviews are really murder. They keep asking you questions. I could be brought up on a rape charge. I don't mind a hatchet job, if it's truthful. *Could* you pin a rape charge on me? Could you try? I'd appreciate it. You don't do any dental work, do you? I have to go to the dentist before I go to France."

In two sessions separated by a couple of weeks, I heard him talk for hours at a time, always in the same way, circling his material looking for loopholes. I began to think of him as a soloist, with speech as his instrument. Like a good musician, he no longer had to think of the notes; he worked in terms of timing and the through-line, and questions did not inspire answers, but improvisations.

Groucho as a comedian, of course, would have been impossible in the silent era, just as Chaplin and Keaton adapted only uncertainly to sound. And yet in appearance the three essential brothers (Zeppo seemed superfluous) were like caricatures from the silent era. Harpo, of course, was always silent anyway. Chico had the Italian persona, with the curly hair and Pinocchio hat. And Groucho was such an artificial creation, with his bold slash of a greasepaint mustache, his eyebrows, and his cigar. His look was so bizarre it wasn't makeup so much as a mask; there are times during the mirror sequence in *Duck Soup* when we have to ask ourselves which one is the real Groucho.

Dated as *Duck Soup* inevitably is in some respects, it has moments that seem startlingly modern, as when Groucho calls for help during the closing battle sequence, and the response is stock footage edited out of newsreel shots of fire engines, elephants, motorcycles, you name it. There is an odd moment when Harpo shows Groucho a doghouse tattooed on his stomach, and a real dog emerges from it and barks at him. The brothers broke the classical structure of movie comedy and glued it back again haphazardly, and nothing was ever the same.

Why the title? The critic Tim Dirks explains, "It is claimed that Groucho provided the following recipe: 'Take two turkeys, one goose, four cabbages, but no duck, and mix them together. After one taste, you'll duck soup the rest of your life.' "

{ E.T. }

Dear Raven and Emil,

Sunday we sat on the big green couch and watched *E.T.* [1982] together with your mom and dad. It was the first time either of you had seen it, although you knew a little of what to expect because we took the *E.T.* ride together at the Universal tour. I had seen the movie lots of times before, so I kept one eye on the screen and the other on the two of you. I wanted to see how a boy on his fourth birthday and a girl who had just turned seven a week ago would respond to the movie.

Well, it "worked" for both of you, as we say in Grandpa Roger's business. Raven, you never took your eyes off the screen—not even when it looked like E.T. was dying and you had to scoot over next to me because you were afraid. Emil, you had to go sit on your dad's knee a couple of times, but you never stopped watching, either. No trips to the bathroom or looking for lost toys. You were watching that movie with all of your attention.

The early scenes show a spaceship landing, and they suggest that a little creature has been left behind. The ship escapes quickly after men in pickup trucks come looking for it. Their headlights and flashlights make visible beams through the foggy night, and you remembered the same effect during the ride at Universal. And the keys hanging from their belts jangle on the sound track. It's how a lost little extraterrestrial would experience it.

Then there are shots of a suburban house, sort of like the one you

live in, with a wide driveway and a big backyard. A little boy named Elliot (Henry Thomas) is in the yard when he thinks he sees or hears something. We already know, of course, that it's E.T.

The camera watches Elliot moving around. And Raven, that's when you asked me, "Is this E.T.'s vision?" And I said, yes, we were seeing everything now from E.T.'s point of view. And I thought you'd asked a very good question, because most kids your age wouldn't have noticed that the camera *had* a point of view—that we were seeing everything from low to the ground, as a short little creature would view it, and experiencing what he (or she) would see after wandering out of the woods on a strange planet.

As we continued to watch the movie, I realized how right you were to ask that question. The whole movie is based on what moviemakers call point of view. Almost every single important shot is seen either as E.T. would see it or as Elliot would see it. And things are understood as they would understand them. There aren't any crucial moments where the camera pulls back and seems to be a grown-up. We're usually looking at things through a child's eye—or an alien's.

When Elliot and E.T. see each other for the first time, they both jump back in fright and surprise, and let out yelps. We see each of them from the other's point of view. When the camera stands back to show a whole scene, it avoids showing it through adult eyes. There's a moment, for example, when Elliot's mom (Dee Wallace) is moving around doing some housework and never realizes that E.T. is scurrying around the room just out of her line of sight. The camera stays back away from her. We don't see her looking this way and that, because it's not about which way she's looking.

Later, we do get one great shot that shows what she sees. She's looking in Elliot's closet at all of his stuffed toys lined up and doesn't real- ize one of the "toys" is actually E.T. We all laughed at that shot, but it was an exception; basically we looked out through little eyes, not big ones (for example, in the scene where they take E.T. trick-or-treating with a sheet over his head, and we can see out like he can through the holes in the sheet).

In the scenes that really worried you, Raven, the men in the trucks come back. They know E.T. is in Elliot's house, and they're scientists who want to examine the alien creature. But there isn't a single moment when they use grown-up talk and explain what they're doing. We only hear small pieces of their dialogue, as Elliot might overhear it.

By then, of course, we know Elliot and E.T. are linked mentally, so Elliot can sense that E.T. is dying. Elliot cries out to the adults to leave E.T. alone, but the adults don't take him seriously. A kid knows what that feels like. And then, when Elliot gets his bigger brother to drive the getaway car, and the brother says, "I've never driven in forward before!" you could identify with that. Kids are always watching their parents drive and never getting to do it themselves.

We loved the scene where the bicycles fly. We suspected it was coming, because E.T. had taken Elliot on a private bike flight earlier, so we knew he could do it. I was thinking that the chase scene before the bikes fly was a little too long, as if Steven Spielberg (who made the film) was trying to build up too much unnecessary suspense. But when those bikes took off, what a terrific moment! I remember when I saw the movie at Cannes: Even the audience there, people who had seen thousands of movies, let out a whoop at that moment.

Then there's the scene at the end. E.T. has phoned home, and the spaceship has come to get him. He's in the woods with Elliot. The gangplank on the ship comes down, and in the doorway we can see another creature like E.T. standing with the light behind.

Emil, you said, "That's E.T.'s mommy!" And then you paused a second and said, "Now, how did I know that?"

We all laughed, because you made it sound funny, as you often do— you're a natural comedian. But remembering it now, I asked myself how *did* Emil know that? It could have been E.T.'s daddy or sister or the pilot of the ship. But I agree with you it probably was his mommy, because she sounded just like a mommy as she made the noise of calling E.T.

And then I thought, the fact that you knew was a sign of how well Steven Spielberg made his movie. At four, you are a little young to understand "point of view," but you are definitely old enough to react to one. For the whole movie, you'd been seeing almost everything through the eyes of E.T. or Elliot. By the last moments, you were identifying with E.T. And whom did he miss the most? Whom did he want to see standing in the spaceship door for him? His mommy.

Of course maybe Steven Spielberg didn't see it the same way, and thought E.T. only seemed like a kid and was really five hundred years old. That doesn't matter, because Spielberg left it open for all of us. That's the sign of a great filmmaker. He only explains what he has to explain, and with a great movie, the longer it runs, the less has to be explained. Some other filmmaker who wasn't so good might have had subtitles saying, "E.T.? Are you out there? It's mommy!" But that would have been dumb. And it would have deprived you, Emil, of the joy of *knowing* it was E.T.'s mommy and the delight of being able to tell the rest of us.

Well, that's it for this letter. We had a great weekend. I was proud of how brave you both were during your first pony rides. And proud of what good movie critics you are too.

Love,
Grandpa Roger

THE EXTERMINATING ANGEL

The dinner guests arrive twice. They ascend the stairs and walk through the wide doorway, and then they arrive again—the same guests, seen from a higher camera angle. This is a joke, and soon we will understand the punch line: The guests, having so thoroughly arrived, are incapable of leaving. Luis Buñuel's *The Exterminating Angel* (1962) is a macabre comedy, a mordant view of human nature that suggests we harbor savage instincts and unspeakable secrets. Take a group of prosperous dinner guests and pen them up long enough, he suggests, and they'll turn on one another like rats in an overpopulation study.

Buñuel begins with small alarming portents. The cook and the servants suddenly put on their coats and escape from the house just as the dinner guests are arriving. The hostess is furious: She planned an after-dinner entertainment involving a bear and two sheep. Now it will have to be canceled. It is typical of Buñuel that such surrealistic touches are dropped in without comment.

The dinner party is a success. The guests whisper slanders about each other, their eyes playing across the faces of their fellow guests with greed, lust, and envy. After dinner, they stroll into the drawing room, where we glimpse a woman's purse, filled with chicken feathers and rooster claws. A doctor predicts that one of the women will be bald within a week. But the broader outlines of the gathering seem normal enough: Drinks are passed, the piano is played, everyone looks elegant in dinner dress. Then, in a series of subtle developments, it becomes apparent that no one can leave. They make preliminary gestures. They drift toward the hallway. There is nothing to stop them. But they cannot leave. They never exactly state that fact; there is an unspoken rueful acceptance of the situation, as they make themselves comfortable on sofas and rugs.

This is a brilliant opening for an insidious movie. The tone is low-key, but so many sinister details have accumulated that by the time the guests settle down for the night, Buñuel has us wrapped in his spell.

He was the most iconoclastic and individual of directors, a Spaniard who drifted into the orbit of the surrealists in Paris. For many years, he directed the Spanish dubs for Hollywood films, and his greatest work was done between the ages of sixty and seventy-seven. His first film, *Un Chien Andalou* (1928), cowritten with Salvador Dalí, caused an uproar (he filled his pockets with stones, he wrote in his autobiography, so he would have something to throw if the audience attacked him). It contained one of the most famous images in cinema, of a cloud cutting across the face of the moon, paired with a razor blade slicing an eyeball.

After that film, he made the scandalous and long-repressed *L'Age d'Or* (1930) and the scabrous documentary *Land Without Bread* (1932), shot in the poorest corner of Spain. Buñuel didn't direct another film until he became an exile in Mexico in the late 1940s. There he made both commercial and personal projects, almost all of them displaying his obsessions. An enemy of Franco's Spain, he was antifascist, anticlerical, and antibourgeois. He also had a sly streak of foot fetishism ("That was a wonderful afternoon little Luis spent on the floor of his mother's closet when he was twelve," Pauline Kael once said, "and he's been sharing it with us ever since").

His firmest conviction was that most people were hypocrites—the sanctimonious and comfortable most of all. He also had a streak of nihilism. In one film, a Christ figure, saddened by the sight of a dog tied to a wagon axle and too tired to keep up, buys the dog to free it. As he does, another dog tied to another wagon limps past unnoticed in the background.

By the time he came to make *The Exterminating Angel*, Buñuel's career was on its delayed upswing. He had made a great international hit, *Viridiana,* in 1960; it won many festival prizes and represented his return to

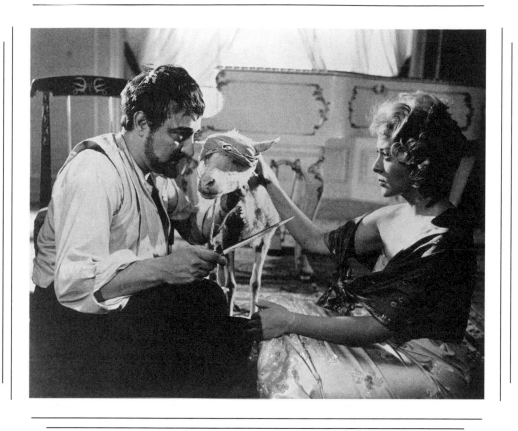

Spain after decades overseas. But its central image—a scandalous tableau re-creating the Last Supper—displeased the Spanish censors, and he was back in Mexico again and primed for bitter satire when he made *The Exterminating Angel.*

The way I read it, the dinner guests represent the ruling class in Franco's Spain. Having set a banquet table for themselves by defeating the workers in the Spanish civil war, they sit down for a feast, only to find it never ends. They're trapped in their own bourgeois cul-de-sac, shunned by the world. Increasingly resentful at being shut off from the world outside, they grow mean and restless; their worst tendencies are revealed. Of course Buñuel never made his political symbolism that blatant. *The Exterminating Angel* plays as a deadpan comedy about the unusual adventures of his dinner guests. Hours lengthen into days, and their dilemma takes on a ritualistic quality—it seems like the natural state of things. The characters pace in front of the open door. There is an invisible line they cannot cross. One guest says to another, "Wouldn't it be a good joke if I sneaked up and pushed you out?" The other says, "Try it, and I'll kill you." Soldiers are ordered to enter the house but cannot. A child runs boldly toward the house and scampers away again. Whatever inhibits the guests inhibits their rescuers.

Conditions deteriorate. Guests snatch an ax from the wall and break through plaster to open a pipe for drinking water. Two lovers kill themselves. The bodies are stacked in a closet. There are whiffs of black magic. The sheep wander into the room, are killed and cooked on a fire made from broken furniture; so close to civilization is the cave.

Buñuel belongs to a group of great directors who obsessively reworked the themes that haunted them. There is little stylistically to link Ozu, Hitchcock, Herzog, Bergman, Fassbinder, and Buñuel, except for this common thread: Some deep wound or hunger was imprinted on them early in life, and they worked all of their careers to heal or cherish it.

Buñuel was born in 1900, so the dates of his films reflect the years of his life. He had the most remarkable late flowering in the history of the movies. His Mexican films of the 1940s and 1950s are often inspired—especially *Los Olvidados* (1950), *Él* (1952), and *The Criminal Life of Archibaldo de la Cruz* (1955). *Viridiana* was his international comeback, and then came *The Exterminating Angel,* which he said might be his last film—but the curtain was just rising on the great days of his career. His most famous film, *Belle de Jour* (1967), won the grand prize at Venice. It starred Catherine Deneuve as a respectable Parisian housewife who becomes fascinated by a famous bordello and finds herself working there two or three afternoons a week. At the prize ceremony at Venice, Buñuel again announced his retirement. Not quite. In 1970, he starred Deneuve again, in *Tristana*, a morbid romance between an aging pederast and the woman he adopts, mistreats, and loses. After her leg is amputated, she returns to him for support, and revenge.

Then came three great films in which Buñuel's talent flowed in a great liberated stream of wicked satire and cheerful obsession. *The Discreet Charm of the Bourgeoisie* (1972), which won the Oscar as best foreign film, is a reversal of *Exterminating Angel*. This time dinner guests are forever sitting down to a feast but are repeatedly frustrated in their desire to eat. Then came *The Phantom of Liberty* (1974), a free-form film that began with one group of characters, then followed another, and another. His last film was *That Obscure Object of Desire* (1977), about an aging man who believes one woman and no other can satisfy his desires; Buñuel had the woman played interchangeably by two different actresses.

Buñuel died in 1983, leaving behind a wonderful autobiography in which he said the worst thing about death was that he would not be able to read tomorrow's newspaper. He created a world so particular it is impossible to watch any Buñuel film for very long without knowing who its director was. *The Exterminating Angel* begins with the statement "The best explanation of this film is that, from the standpoint of pure reason, there is no explanation." For a man who could make a film like that, reading the newspaper must have been hilarious.

{ FARGO }

The telephone rings at 3 A.M. and a pregnant woman puts on her police uniform to go out into the Minnesota winter and investigate a homicide. "Eggs," her sleepy husband says. He'll make her eggs. We see them eating at a Formica table in the kitchen; steps lead down to the back door. He stays at the table as she goes outside. Then she returns, his head tilting as he hears her. "Hon," she says, "prowler needs a jump."

This is the scene where *Fargo* shows how it is going to take a story about pathetic criminals and make it into a great movie. Our first shot of Chief Marge Gunderson (Frances McDormand) comes deep into the film. The crime elements are already in place. We've met Jerry Lundegaard (William H. Macy), the auto sales executive with an absurd plan to have his wife kidnapped so he can steal most of the ransom. We've met Carl Showalter (Steve Buscemi) and his silent, implacable partner (Peter Stormare), who have agreed to kidnap her for $40,000, plus a new car Jerry will steal off the lot. These are quirky, skewed, priceless characters, but when things go wrong and Marge and her husband, Norm (John Carroll Lynch), are introduced, the movie finds its center.

Marge Gunderson is one of a handful of characters whose names remain in our memories, like Travis Bickle, HAL 9000, Fred C. Dobbs. They are completely, defiantly themselves, in movies that depend on precisely who they are. Marge is the chief in Brainerd, Minnesota, has bouts of

morning sickness, eats all the junk food she can get her hands on, speaks in a "you betcha" Minnesota accent where "yeah," pronounced *ya,* is volleyed like a refrain. She's a natural police officer, very smart; at the crime scene, she quickly and correctly reconstructs what happened and determines there were two killers, one big, one small. Her male partner, not so swift, fails to realize that "DLR" indicates a dealer plate; that inspires one of the movie's famous lines: "I'm not sure I agree with you 100 percent on your police work there, Irv."

Fargo (1996) was directed by Joel Coen, produced by Ethan Coen, cowritten by the brothers, and set in the Scandinavian-American upper Midwest where they grew up. It begins with the information that it is "based on a true story" and ends with a disclaimer that its "persons and events" are fictitious. It's fiction; "true story" is an ironic stylistic device.

But *Fargo* is true to the rhythms of small-town life. When Marge Gunderson stands at the first crime scene and counts three dead bodies, she correctly intuits that the perpetrators are not from Brainerd. Venturing to the big city on her investigation, she asks a friend for a tip on a good place to eat and is steered to the buffet at the Radisson. Jerry Lundegaard is as trapped by his sales manager's job and his implacable father-in-law (Harve Presnell) as any character in Sinclair Lewis; he's juggling a stolen car and a double fraud (he will tell the kidnappers they're splitting an $80,000 ransom but tell his father-in-law the ransom is $1 million). His son bolts away from the dinner table to meet his friends at McDonald's. His wife, Jean (Kristin Rudrüd), works furiously at every household task, chopping, stirring, and knitting as fast as she can.

Against these domestic details, the crimes stand out as amoral and violent. There are ugly moments. Everyone remembers the scene where Stormare (who once played Hamlet for Bergman) pushes his partner's leg into the wood-chipper. More heartless is the scene where poor Jean, blind-folded and barefoot, tries to run away in the snow, and Buscemi laughs at her. There are also the shootings, sudden and merciless ("Oh, Daddy!" says Buscemi, shocked by the first one). Against this, Chief Marge uses folksy small-town cheerfulness as a tool for prying criminals loose from their secrets.

Not everyone liked the way the movie juxtaposed violence and humor. Stanley Kauffmann said of the Coens, "Their jumbling of tones makes the grim parts harder to credit and makes the funny parts seem like old-fashioned comic relief." I disagree. As a teenager I was a newspaper reporter sometimes assigned to crime stories; a friend's father was the coroner and took me along to death scenes. I remember how the small-city cops talked in the presence of death, and Marge Gunderson has the right notes. Much of the humor may serve as comic relief, but that is not a bad thing; comic relief is, after all, intended as relief, and the Coens get their laughs through a close observation of human nature. Notice the scene where the killers shack up in a motel room with two hookers. A brief long shot of energetic pumping cuts directly to a shot where the hookers and their clients are all flat on their backs, watching *The Tonight Show*.

William H. Macy's performance is an implosion of fear and frustration. Here is a man who wants a simple thing: a $750,000 loan from his rich father-in-law so he can buy parking lots and make some money of his own. Yes, Jerry's portrait-studio photo is on the auto agency's Wall of Fame, but so are dozens of others. His office's vertical blinds are handled visually like prison bars. If he can steal $920,000, he can buy the lots. True, his wife will have to be kidnapped, but he can live with that.

His plan is pathetic. He finds the kidnappers at third hand. He knows nothing about them. The GMAC lawyers are badgering him daily for information that would expose the missing "tan Sierra" (actually, we learn, burnt umber). The father-in-law insists on personally delivering the ransom, which means Jerry can't cut out the $920,000. And there's Marge, sitting across his desk, chipper, asking him questions he cannot answer. Macy sweats, his smile a grimace, his self-control like a death grip, and things pile up, and up, and up.

There is a scene many viewers find inexplicable. On the evening between her first and second interviews with Jerry, Marge has dinner with a high school classmate, Mike Yanagita (Steve Park). The critic Jonathan Rosenbaum says it's "a disturbing interlude that strikes many others as wrong or dubious," but he finds it a key: "in terms of theme—a lonely individual lying compulsively, trying without success to hide his desperation—it registers as central." I agree. I think that Mike works as a mirror of Jerry and that the dinner scene acts as the link between Marge's first and second interviews with him. The next morning, she is preparing to return to Brainerd when a high school girlfriend tells her that everything Mike said was a lie. That's the wake-up call that leads back to Jerry's desk at the dealership. The Mike interlude not only provides a delicate study of Marge coping with an embarrassing situation but is infinitely better than the alternative—a single interview with Jerry that simply grinds him down.

The snow and cold provide the Coens with visual punctuation and a pervasive sense of place. The opening shot fades into Jerry's lonely journey to deliver the Sierra. High-angle shots show two frozen parking lots, where the Buscemi character inexplicably chooses to steal license plates and make a ransom transfer (he doesn't catch on that the parking-fee collectors are eyewitnesses, and that leads to two more murders). He buries the loot beside a barbed-wire fence that stretches into infinity and uses a plastic windshield scraper as a pathetic marker. When Jerry duels with an unhappy customer (Gary Houston), the man and his wife have their goose-down coats piled in their laps.

The dark and cold weigh down everything, and in the middle, in their warm cocoon, are Chief Marge and her hubby, Norm, the painter of ducks. Without them, *Fargo* might have been *In Cold Blood* laced with unseemly humor. The Coens sometimes seem to scorn their characters, but their love for Marge redeems *Fargo*. Marge is the catalyst, and her speech at the end is Shakespearean in the way it heals wounds and restores order: "There's more to life than a little money, you know. Don't you know that? And here you are. And it's a beautiful day."

{ FLOATING WEEDS }

Sooner or later, everyone who loves movies comes to Ozu. He is the quietest and gentlest of directors, the most humanistic, the most serene. But the emotions that flow through his films are strong and deep, because they reflect the things we care about the most: parents and children, marriage or a life lived alone, illness and death, and taking care of one another.

Yasujiro Ozu was born in 1903 and died in 1963, but his films were not widely seen outside Japan until the early 1970s because he was thought to be "too Japanese." He is universal; I have never heard more weeping in the audience during any movie than during his *Tokyo Story* (1953), which is about children who in a subtle way are too busy to pay proper attention during a visit from their parents.

It is impossible to select Ozu's best film because his work is so much of a piece, and almost always to the same high standard. His stories usually involve two generations. They are family dramas, without violence. There are few scenes where the characters vent their emotions, and some of the most important decisions are implied, not said. He is wise about the ways we balance our selfishness with the needs of others.

For me, *Floating Weeds* (1959) is like a familiar piece of music that I can turn to for reassurance and consolation. It is so atmospheric—so evocative of a quiet fishing village during a hot and muggy summer—that it envelops me. Its characters are like neighbors. It isn't a sad story. The central character is an actor with a healthy ego who has tried to arrange his life according to his own liking and finds to his amazement that other people have wills of their own. He is funny, wrongheaded, and finally touching.

His name is Komajuro (Ganjiro Nakamura). He leads a traveling acting troupe that performs cut-rate kabuki in the provinces ("floating weeds" is a Japanese term for itinerent actors). His mistress Sumiko, played by the pretty and wise Machiko Kyo, is loyal to him, as are the other veteran actors, but it's clear that the troupe is failing. As the film opens, we hear the offscreen putter of an exhausted boat engine. Then we see the troupe on the boat deck, collapsed in the shade, fanning themselves, smoking. Onshore, the troupe members fan out through the town, putting up posters and staging a ragtag parade (a little boy grows so excited he must dash away and pee against a wall). The theater owner gives them cramped living quarters upstairs.

Komajuro goes to visit a woman who runs a saki bar. Her name is Oyoshi (Haruko Sugimura), and years earlier she bore the actor's son. He is now a handsome young man named Kiyoshi (Hiroshi Kawaguchi), who works in the post office and has been told that Komajuro is his uncle. The old actor is proud of his son but embarrassed to admit his parentage; he wants to keep the secret. His mistress discovers the secret, is enraged, and sets a trap: She pays a pretty young actress (Ayako Wakao) to seduce the youth. The old actor, of course, doesn't want his son involved with a woman of (he well knows) easy virtue. His dilemma grows thornier when the two young people fall in love: How can he exercise authority without revealing the truth?

This material could be told in many ways. It could be a soap opera, a musical, a tragedy. Ozu tells it in a series of everyday events. He loves his characters too much to crank up the drama into artificial highs and lows. Above all, we get a sense of the physical existence of these people, especially old Komajuro's physical weariness as he settles down gratefully in the saki shop and lights a cigarette and looks around, pleased to have a moment for himself.

Ozu's scenes mirror the rhythms of ordinary life. He shows minor characters in desultory conversations; we learn much about the troupe from the gossip of the supporting actors. We see a performance before a sparse

audience; the actors peer out through the curtain, counting the house and looking for cute girls. The performance desperately needs to be restaged with a fresh eye and perhaps a more interested cast.

Ozu doesn't dart from one plot point to another. He uses his famous visual style to allow us to contemplate and inhabit the action. The camera is always a little lower than the characters; when they are seated on tatamis, it is only a few feet from the floor. This brings a kind of stature to their ordinariness. Between scenes, he often cuts to "pillow shots"—two or three quiet compositions, showing an architectural detail, a banner in the wind, a tree, or the sky.

His camera never moves. No pans. No tracking shots. There are not even any dissolves; just cuts between one composition and the next. This is very contemplative. We are prompted to look and involve ourselves, instead of simply reacting.

Ozu is known for violating the traditional rules of visual composition. He often composes a conversation so that the characters don't seem to be looking at each other. I think I know why. With alternating over-the-shoulder shots, the audience is required to identify with the point of view of one character and then the other. When Ozu shoots them both looking in the same direction, we are kept outside the conversation; we can regard both objectively and leave them their privacy.

His shots are direct, but often beautiful. Notice the way he handles an argument between the old actor and his mistress. The camera does not move. They are on opposite sides of a narrow street. It is raining in between them. She walks back and forth with a red umbrella. Break this up into dramatic close-ups, and you'd shatter it. The space and rain between them is the visual counterpoint to their feelings (and perhaps, passionate as they are, neither one wants to get wet).

The movie's music, by Kojun Saito, is lilting and nostalgic. For some reason, it always reminds me of the music in *Mr. Hulot's Holiday*. Both sound tracks evoke the feeling of summer in a village near the sea, where the heat and the quiet have created a kind of dreamy suspension of the rules.

Ozu made fifty-four films, starting with silents in 1927 and continuing until *An Autumn Afternoon*, the year before he died. He worked with the same actors and technicians again and again. In *Tokyo-Ga*, Wim Wenders's 1985 documentary, both his cameraman Kazuo Miyagawa and the veteran actor Chishu Ryu weep when they remember him. He was a small, quiet, chain-smoking man who never aimed for an international audience and who was content to tell domestic stories with small variations. Fewer than a dozen of his films are available in the West on video. But films like *Tokyo Story, Late Spring* (1949), *Early Spring* (1956), *Late Autumn* (1960), and *An Autumn Afternoon* (1962) are available, and to look at any Ozu film is to glimpse the whole.

"I have formulated my own directing style in my head," he once said, "proceeding without any unnecessary imitation of others." By "others" he did not mean his contemporaries. He meant the entire cinematic language going back to D. W. Griffith. He fearlessly "crosses the line," moving his camera through 360 degrees so that props on one side of the screen seem to leap to the other side. He violates all the rules about matching eyeline shots. He once had a young assistant who suggested that perhaps he should shoot conversations so that it seemed to the audience that the characters were looking at one another. Ozu agreed to a test. They shot a scene both ways and compared them. "You see?" said Ozu. "No difference!"

Ozu was most Japanese in taking similar materials and working them again and again in subtly different ways, always in his own style. Like the Japanese printmakers of earlier centuries, he disliked novelty and preferred variations on a theme. When you see his films, you feel in the arms of a serenely confident and caring master. In his stories about people who live far away, you recognize, in one way or another, everyone you know.

{ GATES OF HEAVEN }

There's your dog; your dog's dead. But
where's the thing that made it move? It had to
be something, didn't it?

The above words, spoken by a woman who has just buried her dog, express the central mystery of *Gates of Heaven* and of life. No philosopher has stated it better. They form the truth at the center of Errol Morris's 1978 documentary, which is surrounded by layer upon layer of comedy, pathos, irony, and human nature. I have seen this film perhaps thirty times and am still not anywhere near the bottom of it. All I know is, it's about a lot more than pet cemeteries.

In the mid-1970s, Morris, who had never made a film, read newspaper articles about the financial collapse of the Foothill Pet Cemetery in Los Altos, California. After much legal unpleasantness, dead animals were dug up and relocated in the Bubbling Well Pet Memorial Park, in the Napa Valley. Thinking there might be a film in these events, Morris went with cinematographer Ned Burgess to interview Floyd McClure, the paraplegic operator of the first cemetery, and the Calvin Harberts family, of Bubbling Well.

The film they made has become an underground legend, a litmus

test for audiences, who cannot decide if it is serious or satirical, funny or sad, sympathetic or mocking. Morris went on to become one of America's best-known documentarians, with such credits as *The Thin Blue Line* (1988), *A Brief History of Time* (1992), *Fast, Cheap and Out of Control* (1997), and *Mr. Death* (1999). But *Gates of Heaven* remains in a category by itself, unclassifiable, provocative, tantalizing. When I put it on my list of the ten greatest films ever made, some readers refused to take me seriously, but I was not joking. This eighty-five-minute film about pet cemeteries has given me more to think about over the past twenty years than most of the other films I've seen. It has also given me vast amusement. Sometimes the same moments seem funny on one viewing, sad on the next.

The film is told without narration, by the people involved. It falls into two parts, separated by a remarkable monologue. The first half belongs to Floyd McClure, who recalls his "Kismet idea" of locating a pet cemetery on a site that had "great visual ability." He remembers with ferocity a childhood experience when he helped a friend bury a pet before the garbage trucks could haul it away, and his bottom teeth are bared in anger as he talks about his great enemy—rendering plants. When he first visited one, as a 4-H kid, he recalls thinking, "I'm sitting on the floors of hell right now."

His words, and the words of everyone in the film, are heard with great intensity. They express themselves in an American idiom that approaches poetry, and even their mistakes are eloquent, as when McClure talks about performing "pacific tasks." But Morris also has an ear for irony, and we suspect his wicked grin behind the camera as McClure expands on the problem of living near a rendering plant: "The only thing that hit your nostrils wasn't that good piece of meat you bought to eat . . . you first had to grab the wineglass off the table, and take a whiff of that, to get the smell of the rendering company out of your nose before you could eat."

His scenes are intercut with the sad recollections of some of his investors, in particular a man who apologetically says he lost $30,000 on the scheme, and then sighs in a way that lets you know he will never see that much money again. And there is comic relief in the form of the archenemy, the owner of a rendering plant, who reports that people just don't want to know what happens to dead animals: "Every once in a while they'll lose a giraffe at the zoo, or they'll lose Big Bertha, or Joe the Bear." And to avoid offending the sensibilities of animal lovers, "we actually have to deny we have that animal."

The centerpiece of the film is an extended monologue spoken by a woman named Florence Rasmussen, who sits in the doorway of her home, overlooking the first pet cemetery. William Faulkner or Mark Twain would have wept with joy to have created such words as fall from her mouth, as she tells the camera the story of her life. She paints the details in quick, vivid sketches and then contradicts every single thing she says. Morris recalls that he photographed her just where and as he found her.

Then the film journeys to the Napa Valley, where the Cal Harberts family operates the Bubbling Well Pet Memorial Park. He's also founded a church which teaches that God loves animals as well as men. Much of his bombast is undercut by his tart-tongued wife, Scottie, but she best expresses the church's philosophy: "Surely at the gates of heaven an all-compassionate God is not going to say, well, you're walking in on two legs—you can go in. You're walking on four legs—we can't take you."

We meet the Harberts' two sons. Danny is a sad romantic with a wispy mustache who started out well in college but then started partying all night. He lost his girlfriend and now knows "a broken heart is something that everyone should experience." His older brother, Philip, sold insurance in Salt Lake City but has now returned to Napa, where he analyzes his tasks (digging graves, combing dead dogs) in terms of the success principles of W. Clement Stone. Danny is more pragmatic, analyzing the challenge of digging a grave: "You don't want to make it too large because you don't want to waste space, and you don't want to make it too small because you can't get the thing in there."

In one remarkable unbroken shot, a grieving pet owner delivers a long speech about the death of her dog and the measures she recommends to other pet owners, and when she gets to the very last word, her husband interrupts to pronounce it with bleak finality: "Neutered." This is the kind of perfect moment that cannot be written and cannot be anticipated; it can only be filmed as it happens.

There is an undertone to the Harberts family that is hard to put a finger on. The parents seem prosperous and live in a comfortable home, but Danny is being gnawed by loneliness, and Philip, having "relocated his little family," has undergone severe retrenchment. In the insurance game, he says, "I went from a sales*man* to a sales *man*ager" (he likes plays on words), and would impress employees by arranging his office "to display the maximum trophies." But now he admits to "real fear" as he attempts to memorize the routes he must drive to pick up dead animals from veterinarian offices.

Danny's life is poignant too. After getting his degree in business, he didn't find a job and returned home to live in a cabin where he grows marijuana on the windowsill and lays down tracks on his sound system. In the afternoons, when the guests have gone, he places his hundred-watt speakers on a hilltop and plays his guitar, which can be heard "all over the valley." He is like the last of a species, repeating a mournful call for another of his own kind.

The signs on the pet markers are eloquent in their way. "I knew love; I knew this dog." "Dog is God spelled backwards." "For saving my life." At the end of the film, having laughed earlier, we find ourselves silent. These animal lovers are expressing the deepest of human needs, for love and companionship. "When I turn my back," says Floyd McClure, "I don't know you, not truly. But I can turn my back on my little dog, and I know that he's not going to jump on me or bite me; but human beings can't be that way."

When I am asked to lecture and show a film, I often bring *Gates of Heaven*. Afterward, the discussions invariably rage without end: Is he making fun of those people? Are people ridiculous for caring so much about animals? The film is a put-on, right? It can't really be true?

Cal Harberts promises in the film that his park will still be in existence in thirty, fifty, or one hundred years. Many years have passed. I searched for the Bubbling Well Pet Memorial Park on the World Wide Web and found it *(www.bubbling-well.com/)*. There is information about its Garden of Companionship, Kitty Curve, and Pre-Need Plans, but no mention of this film. Or of the Harberts.

{ THE GENERAL }

Buster Keaton was not the Great Stone Face so much as a man who kept his composure in the midst of chaos. Other silent actors might mug to get a point across, but Keaton remained observant and collected. That's one reason his best movies have aged better than those of his rival, Chaplin. He seems not dated, but like a modern visitor to the world of the silent clowns.

Consider an opening sequence in *The General* (1927), his masterpiece about a Southern railway engineer who has "only two loves in his life"—his locomotive and the beautiful Annabelle Lee. Early in the film, Keaton, dressed in his Sunday best, walks to his girl's house. He is unaware that two small boys are following him, marching in lockstep—and that following them is Annabelle Lee herself (Marion Mack).

He arrives at her door. She watches unobserved. He polishes his shoes on the back of his pants legs and then knocks, pauses, looks about, and sees her standing right behind him. This moment would have inspired an overacted double take from many other silent comedians. Keaton plays it with his face registering merely heightened interest. They go inside. He sits next to her on the sofa. He becomes aware that the small boys have followed them in. His face reflects slight unhappiness. He rises, puts on his hat as if to leave, and opens the door, displaying such courtesy you would think the boys were his guests. The boys walk out and he closes the door on them.

He is not a man playing for laughs, but a man absorbed in a call on the most important person in his life. That's why it's funny. That's also why the movie's most famous shot works—the one where, rejected by his girl, he sits disconsolately on the drive rod of the big engine. As it begins to move, it lifts him up and down, but he does not notice because he thinks only of Annabelle Lee. This series of shots establishes his character as a man who takes himself seriously, and that is the note he will sound all through the film. We don't laugh at Keaton, but identify with him.

The General is an epic of silent comedy, one of the most expensive films of its time, including an accurate historical re-creation of a Civil War episode, hundreds of extras, dangerous stunt sequences, and an actual locomotive falling from a burning bridge into a gorge far below. It was inspired by a real event, "the Great Locomotive Chase," and William Pittenger, the engineer who was involved, collaborated on the screenplay.

As the film opens, war has been declared and Johnny Gray (Keaton) has been turned down by a rebel enlisting officer (he is more valuable as an engineer, although nobody explains that to him). "I don't want you to speak to me again until you are in uniform," Annabelle declares. Time passes. Johnny is the engineer of the General, a Southern locomotive. The train is stolen by Union spies, and Johnny chases it on foot, by sidecar, by bicycle, and finally with another locomotive, the Texas. Then the two sides switch trains, and the chase continues in reverse. Annabelle Lee was a passenger on the stolen train, becomes a prisoner of the Union troops, is rescued by Johnny, and rides with him during the climactic chase scenes that end with the famous shot of the Texas falling into the gorge (where, it is said, its rusted hulk remains to this day).

It would seem logically difficult to have much of a chase involving trains, since they must remain on tracks, and so one must forever be behind the other one—right? Keaton defies logic with one ingenious silent comic sequence after another, and it is important to note that he never used a double and did all of his own stunts, even very dangerous ones, with a calm acrobatic grace.

The train's obvious limitations provide him with ideas. An entire Southern retreat and Northern advance take place unnoticed behind him, while he chops wood. Two sight gags involve his puzzlement when railcars he thought were behind him somehow reappear in front of him. He sets up

the locations along the way so that he can exploit them differently on the way back. One famous sequence involves a cannon on a flatcar, which Keaton wants to fire at the other train. He lights the fuse and runs back to the locomotive, only to see that the cannon has slowly reversed itself and is now pointed straight at him.

One inspiration builds into another. To shield himself from the cannonball, he runs forward and sits on the cowcatcher of the speeding Texas, with no one at the controls and a big railroad tie in his arms. The Union men throw another tie onto the tracks, and Keaton, with perfect aim and timing, knocks the second off by throwing the first. It's flawless and perfect, but consider how risky it is to sit on the front of a locomotive hoping one tie will knock another out of the way without either one smashing your brains out.

Between chase scenes, he blunders into a house where the Northern generals are planning their strategy, and rescues Annabelle Lee—but not before Keaton creates a perfect little cinematic joke.

He is hiding under the dining table as the Northerners confer. One of them burns a hole in the tablecloth with his cigar. Annabelle Lee is brought into the room, and we see Keaton's eye peering through the hole, and then there's a reverse shot of the girl, with Keaton using the hole in the cloth to create a "found" iris shot—one of those shots so beloved of Griffith, in which a circle is drawn around a key element on the screen.

The General was voted one of the ten greatest films of all time in the authoritative *Sight & Sound* poll. Who knows if it is even Keaton's greatest? Others might choose *Steamboat Bill, Jr.* (1928). His other classics include *Our Hospitality* (1923), *The Navigator* (1924), *Go West* (1925), and *The Cameraman* (1928), where he played a would-be newsreel photographer who lucks into his career.

Born in 1895, the same year as the cinema, he was raised in a vaudeville family. As part of the act, he was literally thrown around the stage; like W. C. Fields, he learned his physical skills in a painful childhood apprenticeship. He started in films with Fatty Arbuckle in 1917 and directed his first shorts in 1920. In less than a decade, from 1920 to 1928, he created a body of work that stands beside Chaplin's (some would say above it), and he did it with fewer resources, because he was never as popular or as well funded as the Little Tramp.

When the talkies came in, he made an ill-advised deal with MGM that ended his artistic independence, and the rest of his life was a long second act—so long that in the 1940s he was reduced to doing a live half-hour TV show in Los Angeles, but also long enough that his genius was rediscovered and he made a crucial late work, Samuel Beckett's *Film* (1965), and was hailed with a retrospective at Venice shortly before his death in 1966.

Today I look at Keaton's works more often than any other silent films. They show such a graceful perfection, such a meshing of story, character, and episode, that they unfold like music. Although they're filled with gags, you can rarely catch Keaton writing a scene around a gag; instead, the laughs emerge from the situation; he was "the still, small, suffering center of the hysteria of slapstick," wrote the critic Karen Jaehne. And in an age when special effects were in their infancy, and a "stunt" often meant actually doing on the screen what you appeared to be doing, Keaton was ambitious and fearless. He had a house collapse around him. He swung over a waterfall to rescue a woman he loved. He fell from trains. And always he did it in character, playing a solemn and thoughtful man who trusts in his own ingenuity.

"Charlie's tramp was a bum with a bum's philosophy," he once said. "Lovable as he was, he would steal if he got the chance. My little fellow was a working man, and honest." That describes his characters, and it reflects their creator.

{ THE GODFATHER }

The Godfather (1972) is told entirely within a closed world. That's why we sympathize with characters who are essentially evil. The story by Mario Puzo and Francis Ford Coppola is a brilliant conjuring act, inviting us to consider the Mafia entirely on its own terms. Don Vito Corleone (Marlon Brando) emerges as a sympathetic and even admirable character; during the entire film, this lifelong professional criminal does nothing that, in context, we can really disapprove of. We see not a single actual civilian victim of organized crime. No women trapped into prostitution. No lives wrecked by gambling. No victims of theft, fraud, or protection rackets. The only police officer with a significant speaking role is corrupt.

The story views the Mafia from the inside. That is its secret, its charm, its spell; in a way it has shaped the public perception of the Mafia ever since. The real world is replaced by an authoritarian patriarchy where power and justice flow from the Godfather, and the only villains are traitors. There is one commandment, spoken by Michael (Al Pacino): "Don't ever take sides against the family."

It is significant that the first shot is inside a dark, shuttered room. It is the wedding day of Vito Corleone's daughter, and on such a day a Sicilian must grant any reasonable request. A man has come to ask for punishment for his daughter's rapist. Don Vito asks why he did not come to him immediately.

"I went to the police, like a good American," the man says. The Godfather's reply will underpin the entire movie: "Why did you go to the police? Why didn't you come to me first? What have I ever done to make you treat me so disrespectfully? If you'd come to me in friendship, then this scum that ruined your daughter would be suffering this very day. And, if by chance, an honest man like yourself should make enemies . . . then they would become my enemies. And then they would fear you."

As the day continues, there are two more séances in the Godfather's darkened study, intercut with scenes from the wedding outside. By the end of the wedding sequence, most of the main characters will have been introduced, and we will know essential things about their personalities. It is a virtuoso stretch of filmmaking: Coppola brings his large cast onstage so artfully that we are drawn at once into the Godfather's world.

The screenplay of *The Godfather* follows no formulas except for the classic structure in which power passes between the generations. The writing is subtly constructed to set up events later in the film. Notice how the request by Johnny Fontane, the failing singer, pays off in the Hollywood scenes; how his tears set up the shocking moment when a mogul wakes up in bed with what is left of his racehorse. Notice how the undertaker is told "some day, and that day may never come, I will ask a favor of you" and how when the day comes, the favor is not violence (as in a conventional movie), but Don Vito's desire to spare his wife the sight of his son's maimed body. And notice how a woman's "mistaken" phone call sets up the trap in which Sonny (James Caan) is murdered. It's done so neatly that you have to think back through the events to figure it out.

Now here is a trivia question: What is the name of Vito's wife? She exists in the movie as an insignificant shadow, a plump Sicilian grandmother who poses with her husband in wedding pictures, but plays no role in the events that take place in his study. There is little room for women in *The Godfather*. Sonny uses and discards them, and ignores his wife. Connie (Talia Shire), the don's daughter, is so disregarded her husband is not allowed into the family business. He is thrown a bone—"a living"—and later, when he is killed, Michael coldly lies to his sister about what happened.

The irony of the title is that it eventually comes to refer to the son, not the father. As the film opens, Michael is not part of the family business and plans to marry a WASP, Kay Adams (Diane Keaton). His turning point comes when he saves his father's life by moving his hospital bed and whispers to the unconscious man, "I'm with you now."

After he shoots the corrupt cop, Michael hides in Sicily, where he falls in love and marries Apollonia (Simonetta Stefanelli). They do not speak the same language; small handicap for a Mafia wife. He undoubtedly loves Apollonia, as he loved Kay, but what is he thinking here? That he can no longer marry Kay because he has chosen a Mafia life? After Apollonia's death and his return to America, he seeks out Kay and eventually they marry. Did he tell her about Apollonia? Such details are unimportant to the story.

What is important is loyalty to the family. Much is said in the movie about trusting a man's word, but honesty is nothing compared to loyalty. Michael doesn't even trust Tom Hagen (Robert Duvall) with the secret that he plans to murder the heads of the other families. The famous "baptism massacre" is tough, virtuoso filmmaking. The baptism provides him with an airtight alibi, and he becomes a godfather in both senses at the same time.

Vito Corleone is the moral center of the film. He is old, wise, and opposed to dealing in drugs. He understands that society is not alarmed by "liquor, gambling . . . even women." But drugs are a dirty business to Don Vito, and one of the movie's best scenes is the Mafia summit in which he argues his point. The implication is that in the Godfather's world there would be no drugs, only "victimless crimes," and justice would be dispatched evenly and swiftly.

My argument is taking this form because I want to point out how cleverly Coppola structures his film to create sympathy for his heroes. The Mafia is not a benevolent and protective organization, and the Corleone family is only marginally better than the others. Yet when the old man falls dead among his tomato plants, we feel that a giant has passed.

Gordon Willis's cinematography is celebrated for its atmospheric, expressive shadows; his style earned him the nickname "the Prince of Darkness." You cannot fully appreciate his work on video because the picture is artificially brightened. Coppola populates his dark interior spaces with remarkable faces. Those in the front line—Brando, Pacino, Caan, Duvall—are attractive in one way or another, but the actors who play their associates are chosen for their fleshy, thickly lined faces—for huge jaws and deeply set eyes. Look at Abe Vigoda as Tessio, the fearsome enforcer. The first time we see him, he's dancing with a child at the wedding, her satin pumps balanced on his shoes. The sun shines that day, but never again. He is developed as a hulking presence who implies the possibility of violent revenge. Only at the end is he brightly lit again, to make him look vulnerable as he begs for his life.

The Brando performance is justly famous and often imitated. We know all about his puffy cheeks and his use of props like the kitten in the opening scene. Those are actors' devices. Brando uses them but does not depend on them. He embodies the character so convincingly that at the end, when he warns his son two or three times that "the man who comes to you to set up a meeting—that's the traitor," we are not thinking of acting at all. We are thinking that the don is growing old and repeating himself, but we are also thinking that he is probably absolutely right.

Pacino plays Michael close to his vest; he has learned from his father never to talk in front of outsiders, never to trust anyone unnecessarily, to take advice but keep his own counsel. All of the other roles are so successfully filled that a strange thing happened as I watched the restored 1997 version: Familiar as I am with Robert Duvall, when he first appeared on the screen I found myself thinking, "There's Tom Hagen."

Coppola went to Italy to find Nino Rota, composer of many Fellini films, to score the picture. Hearing the sadness and nostalgia of the movie's main theme, I realized what the music was telling us: Things would have turned out better if we had only listened to the Godfather.

GONE WITH THE WIND

Gone with the Wind (1939) presents a sentimental view of the Civil War, in which the "Old South" takes the place of Camelot and the war was fought not so much to defeat the Confederacy and free the slaves as to give Miss Scarlett O'Hara her comeuppance. We've known that for years; the tainted nostalgia comes with the territory. Yet after all these years, *GWTW* remains a towering landmark of film, because it tells a good story, and tells it wonderfully well.

For the story it wanted to tell, it was the right film at the right time. Scarlett O'Hara is not a creature of the 1860s, but of the 1930s: a free-spirited, willful modern woman. The way was prepared for her by the flappers of Fitzgerald's jazz age, by the bold movie actresses of the period, and by the economic reality of the Depression, which for the first time put lots of women to work outside their homes. Scarlett's lusts and headstrong passions have little to do with myths of delicate Southern flowers, and everything to do with the sex symbols of the movies that shaped her creator, Margaret Mitchell: actresses like Clara Bow, Jean Harlow, Louise Brooks, and Mae West. She was a woman who wanted to control her own sexual adventures, and that is the key element in her appeal. She also sought to control her economic destiny, in the years after the South's collapse, first by planting cotton and later by running a successful lumber business. She was the symbol the nation needed as it headed into World War II: the spiritual sister of Rosie the Riveter.

Of course she could not quite be allowed to get away with marrying three times, coveting sweet Melanie's husband, Ashley, shooting a plundering Yankee, and banning her third husband from the marital bed in order to protect her petite waistline from the toll of childbearing. It fascinated audiences (it fascinates us still) to see her high-wire defiance in a male chauvinist world, but eventually such behavior had to be punished, and that is what "Frankly, my dear, I don't give a damn" is all about. If *GWTW* had ended with Scarlett's unquestioned triumph, it might not have been nearly as successful. Its original audiences (women, I suspect, even more than men) wanted to see her swatted down—even though, of course, tomorrow would be another day.

Rhett Butler was just the man to do it. As he tells Scarlett in a key early scene, "You need kissing badly. That's what's wrong with you. You should be kissed, and often, and by someone who knows how." For "kissed," substitute the word you're thinking of. Dialogue like that reaches something deep and fundamental in most people; it stirs their fantasies about being brought to sexual pleasure despite themselves. ("Know why women love the Horse Whisperer?" I was asked by a woman friend. "They figure, if that's what he can do with a horse, think what he could do with me.") Scarlett's confusion is between her sentimental fixation on a tepid "Southern gentleman" (Ashley Wilkes) and her unladylike lust for a bold man (Rhett Butler). The most thrilling struggle in *GWTW* is not between North and South, but between Scarlett's lust and her vanity.

Clark Gable and Vivien Leigh were well matched in the two most coveted movie roles of the era. Both were served by a studio system that pumped out idealized profiles and biographies, but we now know what outlaws they were: Gable, the hard-drinking playboy whose studio covered up his scandals; Leigh, the neurotic, drug-abusing beauty who was the despair of every man who loved her. They brought experience, well-formed tastes, and strong egos to their roles, and the camera, which often shows more than the story intends, caught the flash of an eye and the readiness of body language that suggested sexual challenge. Consider the early scene where they first lay eyes on one another during the barbecue at Twelve Oaks. Rhett "exchanges a cool, challenging stare with Scarlett," observes the critic Tim Dirks. "She notices him undressing her with his eyes: 'He looks as if . . . as if he knows what I look like without my shimmy.'"

If the central drama of *Gone with the Wind* is the rise and fall of a sexual adventuress, the counterpoint is a slanted but passionate view of the Old South. Unlike most historical epics, *GWTW* has a genuine sweep, a convincing feel for the passage of time. It shows the South before, during, and after the war, all seen through Scarlett's eyes. And Scarlett is a Southerner. So was Margaret Mitchell. The movie signals its values in the printed narration that opens the film, in language that seems astonishing in its bland, unquestioned assumptions:

> *There was a land of Cavaliers and Cotton Fields called the Old South. Here in this pretty world, Gallantry took its last bow. Here was the last ever to be seen of Knights and their Ladies Fair, of Master and of Slave. Look for it only in books, for it is no more than a dream remembered, a Civilization gone with the wind.*

Yes, with the capital letters and all. One does not have to ask if the slaves saw it the same way. The movie sidesteps the inconvenient fact that plantation gentility was purchased with the sweat of forced labor (there is more sympathy for Scarlett getting calluses on her pretty little hands than for all the crimes of slavery). But to its major African American characters it does at least grant humanity and complexity. Hattie McDaniel, as Mammy, is the most sensible and clear-sighted person in the entire story (she won one of the film's eight Oscars), and although Butterfly McQueen, as Prissy, will always be associated with the line "I don't know nothin' about birthin' babies," the character is engaging and subtly subversive.

Remember that when *GWTW* was made, segregation was still the law in the South and the reality in the North. The Ku Klux Klan was written out of one scene for fear of giving offense to elected officials who belonged to it. The movie comes from a world with values and assumptions fundamentally different from our own—and yet, of course, so does all great classic fiction, including Homer and Shakespeare. A politically correct *GWTW* would not be worth making, and might largely be a lie.

As an example of filmmaking craft, *GWTW* is still astonishing. Several directors worked on the film. George Cukor incurred Clark Gable's dislike and was replaced by Victor Fleming, who collapsed from nervous exhaustion and was relieved by Sam Wood and Cameron Menzies. The real auteur was the producer, David O. Selznick, the Spielberg of his day, who understood that the key to mass appeal was the linking of melodrama with state-of-the-art production values. Some of the individual shots in *GWTW* still have the power to leave us breathless, including, of course, the burning of Atlanta, the flight to Tara, and the "street of dying men," shot as Scarlett wanders into the street and the camera pulls back until the whole Confederacy seems to lie broken and bleeding as far as the eye can see.

There is a joyous flamboyance in the visual style that is appealing in these days when so many directors have trained on the blandness of television. Consider an early shot where Scarlett and her father look out over the land, and the camera pulls back, the two figures and a tree held in black silhouette with the landscape behind them. Or the way the flames of Atlanta are framed to backdrop Scarlett's flight in the carriage.

I've seen *Gone with the Wind* in five of its major theatrical revivals—1954, 1961, 1967 (the abortive "wide-screen" version), 1989, and the 1998 restoration. It will be around for years to come, a superb example of Hollywood's art and a time capsule of weathering sentimentality for a Civilization gone with the wind, all right—gone but not forgotten.

{ GRAND ILLUSION }

Apart from its other achievements, Jean Renoir's *Grand Illusion* influenced two famous later movie sequences: the digging of the escape tunnel in *The Great Escape* and the singing of the "Marseillaise" to enrage the Germans in *Casablanca*. Even the details of the tunnel dig are the same—the way the prisoners hide the excavated dirt in their pants and shake it out on the parade ground during exercise.

But if *Grand Illusion* (1937) had been merely a source of later inspiration, it wouldn't be on so many lists of great films. It's not a movie about a prison escape, nor is it jingoistic in its politics; it's a meditation on the collapse of the old order of European civilization. Perhaps that was always a sentimental upper-class illusion, the notion that gentlemen on both sides of the line subscribed to the same code of behavior. Whatever it was, it died in the trenches of World War I.

"Neither you nor I can stop the march of time," the captured French aristocrat, Captain de Boieldieu, tells the German prison camp commandant, von Rauffenstein. A little later, distracting the guards during an escape of others from the high-security German fortress, the Frenchman forces the German to shoot him, reluctantly, and they have a final deathbed exchange. "I didn't know a bullet in the stomach hurt so much," he tells the German. "I aimed at your legs," says the German, near tears. And a little later, he says, "For a commoner, dying in a war is a tragedy. But for you and I—it's a good way out."

What the Frenchman knows and the German won't admit is that the new world belongs to commoners. It changed hands when the gentlemen of Europe declared war. And the "grand illusion" of Renoir's title is the notion that the upper classes somehow stand above war. The German cannot believe that his prisoners, whom he treats almost as guests, would try to escape. After all, they have given their word not to.

The commandant is played by Erich von Stroheim, in one of the most famous of movie performances. Even many who have not seen the movie can identify stills of the wounded ace pilot von Rauffenstein, his body held rigid by a neck and back brace, his eye squinting through a monocle. De Boieldieu (Pierre Fresnay), from an old aristocratic family, is a pilot von Rauffenstein personally shot down earlier in the war. The other two major characters are also French prisoners: Maréchal (Jean Gabin), a workingman, a member of the emerging proletariat; and Rosenthal (Marcel Dalio), a Jewish banker who has ironically purchased the chateau that de Boieldieu's family can no longer afford. The movie, filmed as the clouds of World War II were gathering, uses these characters to illustrate how the themes of the first war would tragically worsen in the second.

So pointed was Renoir's message that when the Germans occupied France, *Grand Illusion* was one of the first things they seized. It was "Cinematic Public Enemy Number One," Propaganda Minister Joseph Goebbels announced, ordering the original negative seized. Its history since then would make a movie like *The Red Violin*, as the print moved across borders in shadowy ways. For many years, it was assumed that the negative was destroyed in a 1942 Allied air raid. But as Stuart Klawens reported in the *Nation*, it had already been singled out by a German film archivist named Frank Hensel, then a Nazi officer in Paris, who had it shipped to Berlin. When Renoir supervised the assembly of a "restored" print in the 1960s, nothing was known of this negative. He worked from the best available surviving theatrical prints. The result, the version that has been seen all over the world until now, was a little scratched and murky, and encumbered by clumsy subtitles.

The original negative meanwhile was captured by Russians as they occupied Berlin, and was shipped to an archive in Moscow. In the mid-1960s, according to Klawens, a Russian film archive and one in Toulouse,

France, exchanged some titles, including the priceless *Grand Illusion*. But since many prints of the film existed and no one thought the original negative had survived, the negative waited for thirty years before being identified as a treasure. What that means is that the restored print of *Grand Illusion* now available on video is the best seen since the movie's premiere. And new subtitles by Lenny Borger are much improved—"cleaner and more pointed," says critic Stanley Kauffmann.

This print looks and feels like a brand-new film. Here is a crisp print that underlines Renoir's visual style, his mastery of a subtly moving camera that allowed him to film extended passages without cutting. In the paintings of his father, Auguste Renoir, our eyes are led gently through the composition. In the films of the son, there is a quiet voluptuousness; the camera doesn't point or intrude, but glides.

As *Grand Illusion* opens, we meet von Rauffenstein in the German officers' mess. Having shot down two French fliers, he issues orders: "If they are officers, invite them for lunch." Maréchal and de Boieldieu are later sent to a POW camp, where they meet Rosenthal, already a prisoner, and benefit from the boxes of food his family sends him; often they eat better than their captors. Here are the tunnel-digging sequences, and the famous talent show scene, where total silence falls as they regard a man costumed as a woman, for it has been so long since they've seen a real one.

The tunnel digging is interrupted when all the prisoners are transferred. A few years pass, and now the three principal characters have been sent to Wintersborn, a fortress with high, unscalable walls. After a back wound ended his flying days, von Rauffenstein volunteered to be commandant here as a way of remaining in service. He is strict but fair, still deceived by notions of class loyalty.

In these scenes, von Stroheim makes an indelible impression, as a man deluded by romantic notions of chivalry and friendship. It is a touching performance, a collaboration between the great silent director and Renoir, then emerging as a master of sound. The performance is better even than it seems: Audiences assume Erich von Stroheim was a German, but mystery clouds his origins. Born in Vienna in 1885, by 1914 he was working with D. W. Griffith in Hollywood, but when did he immigrate to America (and add the "von" to his name)? Renoir writes in his memoirs:

"Stroheim spoke hardly any German. He had to study his lines like a schoolboy learning a foreign language."

The break from the fortress prison produces the touching deathbed farewell between de Boieldieu and von Rauffenstein, which is the film's most emotional scene, and then we join the workingman Maréchal and the banker Rosenthal as they try to escape by walking cross-country through German territory. They're given shelter by a farm widow who sees security in Maréchal, and perhaps Renoir is whispering that the true class connection across enemy lines is between the workers, not the rulers.

Jean Renoir, born in 1894, is on any list of the half-dozen greatest filmmakers, and his *Rules of the Game* (1939) is even more highly considered than *Grand Illusion*. He fought in World War I, then quickly returned to Paris and entered the movie business. In his best films, observation and sympathy for the characters define every shot; there is hardly a camera decision made for pure effect, without thinking first of where best to stand to see the characters.

Renoir moved to America in 1940 and made several Hollywood films, notably *The Southerner* (1945), with a screenplay by Faulkner, before going independent in the 1950s with *The River* (1951), based on Rumer Godden's Calcutta story. In a long retirement, he was sought out by younger filmmakers and critics, who found him as sunny as a grandfather in one of his father's impressionist paintings. He died in 1979. He would have been much cheered to know that even then the pristine negative of *Grand Illusion* was waiting in Toulouse to be discovered.

{ GREED }

Erich von Stroheim's *Greed* (1925), like the Venus de Milo, is acclaimed as
a classic despite missing several parts deemed essential by its creator. Its unhappy history is well known. Von Stroheim's original film was more than
nine hours long. After it was cut, cut, and cut again, it was released at about
140 minutes, in a version that he disowned—and that inspired a fistfight
with Louis B. Mayer. It is this version that is often voted one of the greatest films of all time.

The inspiration for *Greed* was *McTeague,* a novel by Frank Norris
about the rough, simple son of a drunken miner, who learns dentistry from
a quack, moves to San Francisco, marries a woman who is a miser, and ends
up in Death Valley next to the body of his rival for both the woman and her
lottery winnings. It was a bleak and sardonic story for the Roaring Twenties, and neither Mayer nor his new MGM partner, Irving Thalberg,
thought the public wanted it—not at nine-plus hours, certainly.

For von Stroheim, a martinet who affected the dress, bearing, and
monocle of a Prussian officer, their opposition was like a curse that followed
him. At Universal in 1922, where Thalberg was then employed, von Stroheim's *Foolish Wives* was cut by a third, and then Thalberg fired him from
his next film, *Merry-Go-Round.* He fled to MGM to make *Greed,* which
cost $750,000 and took a year to shoot, only to have Thalberg catch up with
him there and demand more cuts.

No one now alive has seen the original version, but a San Francisco drama critic named Idwal Jones was present at its first studio screening, which began at 10 A.M. and continued without breaks for lunch or anything else, von Stroheim sitting ramrod straight through the whole thing as an example to the others. Jones was a friend of the director's, but his account of that experience does not inspire our envy. He liked the individual parts well enough; it was just that there were so many of them: "Every episode is developed to the full, every comma of the book put in, as it were." He noted that von Stroheim "worships realism like an abstract ideal; worships it more, and suffers more in its achievement, than other men do for wealth or fame."

Indeed the film is realistic. Opening scenes were shot in the very gold mine that Norris wrote about; it was reopened for the movie. The San Francisco dentist office was not a set, but a real second-floor office, which still exists. Von Stroheim could have shot his desert scenes outside Palm Springs, but insisted on shooting in the 120-degree heat of Death Valley itself; the camera had to be cooled with iced towels. Some of his crew mutinied and others complained. Von Stroheim slept with his pistol, and as his two actors engaged in their death struggle, he screamed, "Fight! Fight! Try to hate each other as you hate me!"

These memories and others are recalled in a book about von Stroheim by Thomas Quinn Curtis, a longtime friend of the director's, who until fairly recent years was the *Paris Herald-Tribune*'s film critic. He recalls lunching one day in Paris with Louis B. Mayer, who told him the story of his fight with von Stroheim. That evening, Curtis had dinner with the director, who said, "That's entirely accurate." Their fight began when von Stroheim picked up his gloves to stalk out of the mogul's office. "I suppose you consider me rabble," Mayer said. "Not even that," said von Stroheim. Mayer struck him so hard that von Stroheim fell out through the office door and onto the floor, still clutching gloves and cane. "You see, my hands were occupied," he told Mayer's secretary.

Why were their tempers so inflamed? Partly because in Mayer's view a fortune had been squandered on an unreleasable picture; he found the film's view of human nature sour, cynical, and uncommercial. McTeague (Gibson Gowland) is a quack who first falls in love with Trina (Zasu Pitts) after chloroforming her in his chair, then leaning over her to inhale the per-

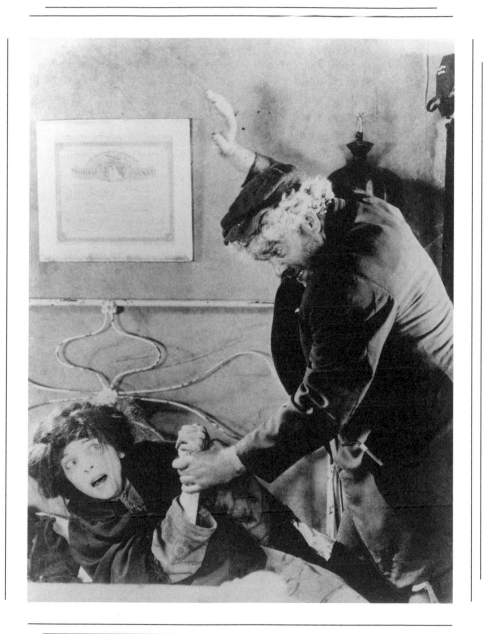

fume of her hair. Trina is a miser who begrudges her man a five-cent bus fare on a rainy day and polishes her coins until they glisten. Trina's original suitor, Marcus (Jean Hersholt, of the Humanitarian Award), essentially gives her to McTeague, then wants her back after she wins a lottery. And there is a good possibility that McTeague and Trina engage in premarital sex, which was scandalous in 1925. (Much depends on a title card that says "Please! Oh, please!" Does she mean please do or please don't?)

The missing seven hours of *Greed* have been called the Holy Grail of the cinema. Apparently they were destroyed to extract the silver nitrate used in their manufacture. The movie that remained had a decent run in the 1920s and was later restored by silent film historian Kevin Brownlow; it is that version that is considered a masterpiece. In the 1990s, an ambitious new approach was made to the material by the film restorer Rick Schmidlin, who discovered a trove of original production stills and a copy of von Stroheim's long-lost 330-page original shooting script. He has taken that material and edited it together with the surviving footage to produce a four-hour version that is available on video.

Comparing the two versions, we can see how not only length but prudish sensibilities went into MGM's chop-job. Early in their relationship, McTeague and Trina take the interurban train out into the countryside. As they're standing at the station, Trina's title card in the shortened MGM version reads, "This is the first day it hasn't rained in weeks. I thought it would be nice to go for a walk." In Schmidlin's reconstruction from the shooting script, it reads, "Let's go over and sit on the sewer," and so they do, perching on a manhole cover.

The original version of *Greed* is perhaps a masterpiece more lamented than missed; there is a point after which an audience will simply not sit still. Even von Stroheim's friend Jones wondered if it could be shown "on the installment plan," and muses about how "German professors sit for years before they develop *Sitzfleisch*," loosely translated as "iron rumps." My own feeling, having seen both versions, is that movie lovers will want to begin with the familiar 140-minute film (which after all is a great experience) and then, if their curiosity is aroused, look at Schmidlin's version to get an idea of all they have missed.

The surviving *Greed* is an uncompromising exercise in naturalism, capturing the rough working-class lives of the new American cities, where saloons doubled as living rooms. And there is a real poignancy in the plight of McTeague, who may by the end be a double murderer but is essentially a gentle, simpleminded soul. One of the scenes cut out by MGM is reconstructed by Schmidlin; it shows McTeague buying theater tickets for his engagement party. He wants the tickets on the right side of the theater. "As you face the stage, or the audience?" asks the ticket seller. "The side away from the drums," says McTeague, confused, and after he becomes convinced the man is toying with him, he explodes.

Here is a man who only wants to be a dentist and inhale Trina's lovely fragrance, and his bones end up in Death Valley. His last act is to set free his pet canary, which flutters a little and dies. No wonder Mayer and Thalberg thought the jazz age wasn't ready for this film.

{ A HARD DAY'S NIGHT }

When it opened in 1964, *A Hard Day's Night* was a problematic entry in a disreputable form, the rock and roll musical. The Beatles were already a publicity phenomenon (70 million viewers watched them on *The Ed Sullivan Show*), but they were not yet cultural icons. Many critics attended the movie prepared to condescend, but the movie could not be dismissed: It was so joyous and original that even the early reviews acknowledged it as something special. After more than three decades, it has not aged and is not dated; it stands outside its time, its genre, and even rock and roll. It is one of the great life-affirming landmarks of the movies.

In 1964, what we think of as "the sixties" had not yet really emerged from the embers of the 1950s. Perhaps this is the movie that sounded the first note of the new decade—the opening chord on George Harrison's new twelve-string guitar. The film was so influential in its liberating, androgynous imagery that untold thousands of young men walked into the theater with short haircuts and their hair started growing during the movie and didn't get cut again until the 1970s.

It was clear from the outset that *A Hard Day's Night* was in a different category from the rock musicals that had starred Elvis and his imitators. It was smart, it was irreverent, it didn't take itself seriously, and it was shot and edited by Richard Lester in an electrifying black-and-white, semi-documentary style that seemed to follow the boys during a day in their lives.

It was charged with the personalities of the Beatles, whose one-liners dismissed the very process of stardom they were undergoing. "Are you a mod or a rocker?" Ringo is asked at a press conference. "I'm a mocker," he says.

Musically the Beatles represented a liberating breakthrough just when the original rock impetus from the 1950s was growing thin. The film is wall-to-wall with great songs, including "I Should Have Known Better," "Can't Buy Me Love," "I Wanna Be Your Man," "All My Loving," "Happy Just to Dance with You," "She Loves You," and others, including the title song, inspired by a remark dropped by Starr and written overnight by Lennon and McCartney.

The Beatles were obviously not housebroken. The American rock stars who preceded them had been trained by their managers; Presley dutifully answered interview questions like a good boy. The Beatles had a clone look—matching hair and clothes—but they belied it with the individuality of their dialogue, and there was no doubt which one was John, Paul, George, or Ringo. The original version of Alun Owen's Oscar-nominated screenplay supplied them with short one-liners (in case they couldn't act), but they were naturals, and new material was written to exploit that. They were the real thing.

The most powerful quality evoked by *A Hard Day's Night* is liberation. The long hair was just the superficial sign of that. An underlying theme is the difficulty establishment types have in getting the Beatles to follow orders. Although their manager (Norman Rossington) tries to control them and their TV director (Victor Spinetti) goes berserk because of their improvisations during a live TV broadcast, they act according to the way they feel. When Ringo grows thoughtful, he wanders away from the studio, and a recording session has to wait until he returns. When the boys are liberated from their "job," they run like children in an open field, and it is possible that this scene (during "Can't Buy Me Love") snowballed into all the love-ins, be-ins, and happenings in the park of the later 1960s. The notion of doing your own thing lurks within every scene in the film.

When a film is strikingly original, its influence shapes so many other films that you sometimes can't see the newness in the first one. Godard's jump cuts in *Breathless* (1960) turned up in every TV ad. Truffaut's freeze-frame at the end of *The 400 Blows* (1959) became a cliché. Richard

Lester's innovations in *A Hard Day's Night* have become familiar, but because the style, the subject, and the stars are so suited to one another, the movie hasn't dated; it's filled with the exhilaration of four musicians who were having fun and creating at the top of their form and knew it.

Movies were tamer in 1964. Big Hollywood productions used crews of a hundred and Mitchell cameras the size of motorcycles. Directors used the traditional grammar of master shot, alternating close-ups, insert shots, reestablishing shots, dissolves and fades. Actors were placed in careful compositions. But the cat was already out of the bag; directors like John Cassavetes had started making movies that played like dramas but looked like documentaries. They used light 16mm cameras, handheld shots, messy compositions that looked like they might have been snatched during moments of real life.

That was the tradition Lester drew on. In 1959, he'd directed *The Running, Jumping and Standing Still Film*, starring Peter Sellers and Spike Milligan among others. It was handheld, anarchic, goofy, and contains the same spirit that infects *A Hard Day's Night*. Lester had shot documentaries and TV commercials, could work quick and dirty, and knew he had to, because his budget was $500,000.

In his opening sequence, which shows the Beatles mobbed at a station as they try to board a train, Lester achieves an incredible energy level. We feel the hysteria of the fans and the excitement of the Beatles, intercut with the title song (the first time movie titles had done that), implying that the songs and the adulation were sides of the same coin. Other scenes borrow the same documentary look; a lot feels improvised, although only a few scenes actually were.

Lester did not invent the techniques used in *A Hard Day's Night*, but he brought them together into a grammar so persuasive that he influenced many other films. Today when we watch TV and see quick cutting, handheld cameras, interviews conducted on the run with moving targets, quickly intercut snatches of dialogue, music under documentary action, and all the other trademarks of the modern style, we are looking at the children of *A Hard Day's Night*.

The film is so tightly cut there's hardly a down moment, but even with so many riches it's easy to pick the best scene: the concert footage as the Beatles sing "She Loves You." This is one of the most sustained orgasmic sequences in the movies. As the Beatles perform, Lester shows them clearly having a lot of fun—grinning as they sing—and then intercuts them with quick shots of the audience, mostly girls, who scream without pause for the entire length of the song, cry, jump up and down, call out the names of their favorites, and create a frenzy so passionate that it still, after all these years, has the power to excite. (My favorite audience member is the tearful young blonde, beside herself with ecstasy, tears running down her cheeks, crying out "George!")

The innocence of the Beatles and *A Hard Day's Night* was, of course, not to last. Ahead was the crushing pressure of being the most popular musical group of all time, and the dalliance with the mystic East, and the breakup, and the druggy fallout from the sixties, and the death of John Lennon. The Beatles would go through a long summer, a disillusioned fall, a tragic winter. But oh, what a lovely springtime. And it's all in a movie.

{ HOOP DREAMS }

There is a point in *Hoop Dreams* where the story, about two inner-city kids who dream of playing pro basketball, comes to a standstill while the mother of one of them addresses herself directly to the camera.

"Do you all wonder sometime how I am living?" asks Sheila Agee. "How my children survive, and how they're living? It's enough to really make people want to go out there and just lash out and hurt somebody."

Yes, we have wondered. Her family is living on $268 a month in aid; when her son Arthur turned eighteen, his $100 payment was cut off, although he was still in high school. Their gas and electricity have been turned off in the winter. The family uses a camp lantern for light.

Arthur cannot graduate from Marshall, his Chicago high school, without transfer credits from St. Joseph's in suburban Westchester—the school that recruited him, dropped him, and won't release the transcripts until $1,300 in back tuition is paid. Since this debt would not exist if scouts had not found Arthur on a playground and offered him a scholarship, there is irony there. The rich school reaches into the city not to help worthy students, but to find good basketball players. If they don't make the grade, they're thrown back in the pond. But then it's payback time. Arthur becomes a star at Marshall and helps them finish third in the state. St. Joseph's is eliminated earlier in the play-offs. And William Gates, the other eighth grader recruited by the school, has missed months of playing time because of injuries. When Arthur plays in the state semifinals at the University of Illinois, both Gates and his coach, Gene Pingatore, have to sit in the crowd.

No screenwriter would dare write this story; it is drama and melodrama, packaged with outrage and moments that make you want to cry. *Hoop Dreams* (1994) has the form of a sports documentary, but along the way it becomes a revealing and heartbreaking story about life in America. When the filmmakers began, they planned to make a thirty-minute film about eighth graders being recruited from inner-city playgrounds to play for suburban schools. Their film eventually encompassed six years, involved 250 hours of footage, and found a reversal of fortunes they could not possibly have anticipated.

Early in the film, we see the young men get up at 5:30 A.M. for the ninety-minute commute to the suburbs. One of them talks about St. Joseph's with its "carpets and flowers." From the beginning, William Gates is more naturally gifted than Arthur Agee. He stars on the varsity as a freshman, while Arthur plays for the freshman team. William is quick, brilliant, confident; Pingatore compares him with his great discovery Isiah Thomas, the NBA star who was also recruited by St. Joseph's. Both students arrive at the school reading at a fourth-grade level, but Gates quickly makes up the lost time, suggesting that his neighborhood schools were to blame. Arthur makes slower progress, in classrooms and on the court. "Coach keeps asking me, 'When you gonna grow?'" He smiles. He is eventually dropped from the squad, loses his scholarship, and after two months out of school enrolls at Marshall.

Gates seems headed for stardom, but injuries strike him. A ligament is repaired in his junior year. Torn cartilage is removed. Maybe he returns to the court too soon. He injures himself again. He loses confidence. Meanwhile, at Marshall, Arthur grows into his game and leads the team to a brilliant season. But the spotlight is still on Gates. He attends the Nike All-American Summer Camp at Princeton, where promising prep stars are scrutinized by famous coaches (Joey Meyer, Bobby Knight) and lectured by Dick Vitale (a showboat) and Spike Lee (a harsh realist). Arthur spends that summer working at Pizza Hut at $3.35 an hour. Then comes the senior year where Arthur leads his team to the state finals.

Both young men are recruited by colleges. Gates, despite his in-

juries, gets an offer from Marquette that promises him a four-year scholarship even if he can never play. He takes it. Agee, whose grades are marginal, ends up at Mineral Area Junior College in Missouri. There are eight black students on the campus. Seven of them are basketball players and live in the same house. If his grades are good enough, he can use this as a springboard to a four-year school (and he does).

The sports stories develop headlong suspense, but the real heart of the film involves the scenes filmed in homes, playgrounds, and churches in the inner city. There are parallel dramas involving fathers: Arthur's leaves the family after twenty years, gets involved with drugs, spends time in jail, returns, testifies in song at a Sunday service, but does not quite regain his son's trust. William's father has been out of the picture for years; he runs an auto garage, is friendly when he sees his son occasionally. The mothers are the key players in both families—and we also glimpse an extended family network that lends encouragement and support.

Every time I see *Hoop Dreams,* I end up thinking of Arthur's mother, Sheila, as the film's heroine. During the course of the film, her husband leaves and gets into trouble, she suffers chronic back pain, she loses a job and goes on welfare, Arthur is dropped by St. Joseph's—and then, in the film's most astonishing revelation, we discover she has graduated as a nurse's assistant, with the top grades in her class.

There are moments in the film where the camera simply watches, impassively, as we arrive at our own conclusions. One is when Arthur and his parents visit St. Joseph's to get his transcripts and are told they need to come up with a payment plan. "Tuition provides 90 percent of our income," a school official says. Yes, but the school was not looking for tuition when it recruited Arthur; it was looking for a basketball player, and when it didn't get the player it expected, it should have had the grace to forgive him his debts.

Coach Pingatore and the school were parties to a suit to prevent the film from being released theatrically. The school comes off looking pragmatic and cold, but then *Hoop Dreams* reflects a reality that is true all over America, and not just at St. Joseph's. As for Pingatore, I think he comes across pretty well. He has his dream too, of finding another Isiah Thomas. He wants to win. His record shows he is a good coach. He gives William sound advice, although perhaps he's too eager to see him return after his injury. William tells the filmmakers that the coach thinks sports are all-important, but I covered high school sports for two years and never met a coach who didn't. After saying farewell to William, Pingatore observes, "One goes out the door, and another one comes in the door. That's what it's all about." There is sad poetry there.

The movie was produced by the team of director Steve James, cinematographer Peter Gilbert, and editor Frederick Marx. They benefited by a remarkable intersection of opportunity and luck. They could not have known when they started how perfectly the experiences of Agee and Gates would generate the story they ended up telling. Over the years, there have been updates on their progress. William played for Marquette for four years and graduated; he did social work while supporting his wife's college education, then planned to return to law school. Arthur got into Arkansas State, played two years, has done some movie acting, has formed a foundation to help inner-city kids get to college. Neither one played for the NBA. Of the 500,000 kids playing high school basketball in any given year, only 25 do. But their hoop dreams did come true.

{ IKIRU }

The old man knows he is dying of cancer. In a bar, he tells a stranger he has money to spend on a "really good time" but doesn't know how to spend it. The stranger takes him out on the town, to gambling parlors, dance halls, and the red-light district, and finally to a bar where the piano player calls for requests and the old man, still wearing his overcoat and hat, asks for "Life Is Short—Fall in Love, Dear Maiden."

"Oh, yeah, one of those old twenties songs," the piano man says, but he plays it, and then the old man starts to sing. His voice is soft and he scarcely moves his lips, but the bar falls silent, the party girls and the drunken salary men drawn for a moment into a reverie about the shortness of their own lives.

This moment comes near the center point of *Ikiru,* Akira Kurosawa's 1952 film about a bureaucrat who works for thirty years at the Tokyo City Hall and never accomplishes anything. Mr. Watanabe has become the chief of his section and sits with a pile of papers on either side of his desk, in front of shelves filled with countless more documents. Down a long table on either side of him, his assistants shuffle these papers back and forth. Nothing is ever decided. His job is to deal with citizen complaints, but his real job is to take a small rubber stamp and press it against each one of the documents, to show that he has handled it.

The opening shot of the film is an X ray of Watanabe's chest. "He has gastric cancer, but doesn't yet know it," says a narrator. "He just drifts

through life. In fact, he's barely alive." The X ray dissolves into his face—into the sad, tired, utterly common face of the actor Takashi Shimura, who, in eleven films by Kurosawa and many by others, played an everyman who embodied his characters by not seeming to embody anything at all.

There is a frightening scene in his doctor's office, where another patient chatters mindlessly; he is a messenger of doom, describing Watanabe's precise symptoms and attributing them to stomach cancer. "If they say you can eat anything you want," he says, "that means you have less than a year." When the doctor uses the very words that were predicted, the old bureaucrat turns away from the room, so that only the camera can see him, and he looks utterly forlorn.

Kurosawa opens his story with a deliberate, low-key pacing, although at the end there is rage against the dying of the light. In a scene that never fails to shake me, Watanabe goes home and cries himself to sleep under his blanket, while the camera pans up to a commendation he was awarded after twenty-five years at his post.

It is not so bad that he must die. What is worse is that he has never lived. "I just can't die—I don't know what I've been living for all these years," he says to the stranger in the bar. He never drinks, but now he is drinking: "This expensive saki is a protest against my life up to now."

His leave of absence from the office continues, day after day. Finally a young woman who wants to resign tracks him down to get his stamp on her papers. He asks her to spend the day with him, and they go to pachinko parlors and the movies. She tells him her nicknames for everyone in the office. His nickname is "the Mummy." She is afraid she has offended him, but no: "I became a mummy for the sake of my son, but he doesn't appreciate me."

She encourages him to go see his son. But when he tries to tell him about his illness, the son cuts him off—insists on getting the property due him before the old man squanders it on women. Later, on a final outing with the young woman, he tells her about a time when he was young and thought he was drowning. He says, "My son's far away somewhere—just as my parents were far away when I was drowning."

The word *ikiru* has been translated as "to live," and at some point on his long descent into despair, Mr. Watanabe determines to accomplish at least one worthwhile thing before he dies. He arrives at this decision in a restaurant, talking to the young woman while in a room behind them there is a celebration going on. As he leaves, girls in the other room sing "Happy Birthday" to a friend—but in a way they sing for Watanabe's rebirth.

A group of women has been shuttled from one office to another, protesting against a pool of stagnant water in their neighborhood. Watanabe becomes a madman, personally escorting the case from one bureaucrat to another, determined to see that a children's park is built on the wasteland before he dies. And all leads up to Watanabe's final triumph, seen in one of the greatest closing shots in the cinema.

The scenes of his efforts do not come in chronological order, but are flashbacks from his funeral service. Watanabe's family and associates gather to remember him, drinking too much and finally talking too much, trying to unravel the mystery of his death and the behavior that led up to it. And here we see the real heart of the movie, in the way one man's effort to do the right thing can inspire, or confuse, or anger, or frustrate those who see it only from the outside, through the lens of their own unexamined lives.

We who have followed Watanabe on his last journey are now brought forcibly back to the land of the living, to cynicism and gossip. Mentally we urge the survivors to think differently, to arrive at our conclusions. And that is how Kurosawa achieves his final effect: He makes us not witnesses to Watanabe's decision, but evangelists for it. I think this is one of the few movies that might actually be able to inspire someone to lead his or her life a little differently.

Kurosawa made it in 1952, when he was forty-two (and Shimura was only forty-seven). It came right after *Rashomon* (1950) and *The Idiot* (1951), which also starred Shimura. Ahead was his popular classic *The Seven Samurai* (1954) and other samurai films like *The Hidden Fortress* (1958), the film that inspired the characters R2D2 and C-3PO in *Star Wars*. The film was not released internationally until 1960, maybe because it was thought "too Japanese," but in fact it is universal.

I saw *Ikiru* first in 1960 or 1961. I went to the movie because it was playing in a campus film series and cost only a quarter. I sat enveloped in the story of Watanabe for two and a half hours, and wrote about it in a class where the essay topic was Plato's statement "the unexamined life is not worth living." Over the years I have seen *Ikiru* every five years or so, and each time it has moved me and made me think. And the older I get, the less Watanabe seems like a pathetic old man and the more he seems like every one of us.

{ It's a Wonderful Life }

The best thing that ever happened to *It's a Wonderful Life* (1946) is that it fell out of copyright protection and into the shadowy no-man's-land of the public domain. Because the movie was no longer under copyright, any television station that could get its hands on a print of the movie could air it, at no cost, as often as it wanted to. And that led to the rediscovery of Frank Capra's once-forgotten film, and its elevation into a Christmas tradition. PBS stations were the first to jump on the bandwagon, in the early 1970s, using the saga of the small-town hero George Bailey as counterprogramming against expensive network holiday specials. To the amazement of TV program directors, the audience for the film grew and grew over the years, until now many families make it an annual ritual.

What is remarkable about *It's a Wonderful Life* is how well it holds up over the years; it's one of those ageless movies, like *Casablanca* or *The Third Man,* that improve with time. Some movies, even good ones, should be seen only once. When we know how they turn out, they've surrendered their mystery and appeal. Other movies can be viewed an indefinite number of times. Like great music, they improve with familiarity. *It's a Wonderful Life* falls in the second category. Both director Capra and his star, James Stewart, considered it their favorite film.

The movie works like a strong and fundamental parable, "A Christmas Carol" in reverse: Instead of a mean old man being shown scenes of happiness, we have a good man who plunges into despair. The hero is George Bailey (Stewart), a man who never quite makes it out of his quiet birthplace of Bedford Falls. As a young man he dreams of shaking the dust from his shoes and traveling to far-off lands, but one thing and then another keeps him at home—especially his responsibility to the family savings and loan association, which is the only thing standing between Bedford Falls and the greed of Mr. Potter (Lionel Barrymore), the avaricious local banker.

George marries his high school sweetheart (Donna Reed, in her first starring role), settles down to raise a family, and helps half the poor folks in town buy homes where they can raise their own. Then, when George's absentminded uncle (Thomas Mitchell) misplaces some bank funds during the Christmas season, it looks as if the evil Potter will have his way, after all. George loses hope and turns mean (even his face seems to darken). He despairs, and is standing on a bridge contemplating suicide when an Angel 2nd Class named Clarence (Henry Travers) saves him and shows him, in a series of depressing tableaux, what life in Bedford Falls would have been like without him.

Frank Capra never intended *It's a Wonderful Life* to be pigeonholed as a "Christmas picture." This was the first movie he made after returning from service in World War II, and he wanted it to be special—a celebration of the lives and dreams of America's ordinary citizens, who tried the best they could to do the right thing by themselves and their neighbors. After becoming Hollywood's poet of the common man in the 1930s with a series of populist parables *(It Happened One Night, Mr. Deeds Goes to Town, Mr. Smith Goes to Washington, You Can't Take It with You),* Capra found the idea for *It's a Wonderful Life* in a story by Philip Van Doren Stern that had been gathering dust on studio shelves.

For Stewart, also recently back in civilian clothes, the movie was a chance to work again with Capra, for whom he had played Mr. Smith. The movie they made was dark and unconventional by Capra standards, replacing the optimism of his prewar work with the observation that things can sometimes work out badly. It is a truism that Hollywood trailers advertise not the movie that has been made, but the movie that the studio *wishes* had been made. The trailer for *It's a Wonderful Life* played up the love angle between Stewart and Donna Reed, played down the message, and sidestepped

the gloom—but the movie was not a box office hit and was all but forgotten before the public domain prints began to make their rounds.

The central gloom of the film makes such an impact that some of the lighthearted scenes may be overlooked—such as the slapstick comedy of the high school hop, where the dance floor opens over a swimming pool, and Stewart and Reed accidentally jitterbug right into the water (this covered pool was not a set; it actually existed at Hollywood High School). There's also the drama of George rescuing his younger brother from a fall through the ice, and the scene where Donna Reed loses her bathrobe and Stewart ends up talking to the shrubbery. The telephone scene—where an angry Stewart and Reed find themselves helplessly drawn toward each other—is wonderfully romantically charged.

The darker later passages have an elemental power, as the drunken George Bailey staggers through a town he wants to hate, and then revisits it through the help of a gentle angel. Stewart here first reveals a face that moviegoers would see again in such Hitchcock pictures as *Vertigo* (1958) and such Anthony Mann westerns as *The Naked Spur* (1953). If he was, as Andrew Sarris wrote, "the most complete actor-personality in the American cinema," it was this film that was his turning point toward completeness, revealing a dark side that had been hard to see before the war. The lanky, cheerful leading man of such prewar comedies as *The Philadelphia Story* and *The Shop Around the Corner* (both 1940) was unshaven, bitter, reeling from bar to bar, contemplating suicide.

Stewart's active service as an army air force pilot no doubt contributed. While other stars stayed at home or entertained the troops, Stewart enlisted as a private, rose to colonel, flew dozens of combat missions, and won the Distinguished Flying Cross. He was a legitimate war hero, and what he saw in the war is no doubt reflected in George Bailey's face as he stands on that Bedford Falls bridge.

Stewart would go on in the next years to play murderers and bounty hunters, the sexually obsessed and the morally bankrupt, abandoning his upbeat prewar image. It was apart from anything else a canny career move, adding longevity and linking him with directors—especially Hitchcock, Mann, and John Ford—who were among the most creative in town. The Capra picture can be seen as transitional. George Bailey stares into the depths of despair and loses faith in his fellow citizens, but pulls back from the brink. The picture concedes that evil exists and that the world can be a sad and lonely place, but at the end all is back in place and Bedford Falls's traditional values have been reaffirmed.

Capra's approach, here as elsewhere, is to depend on the underlying parable to provide the movie's arc. We sense all along, even at the gloomiest moments, that we are on a journey to hope. Capra was not a complex film-maker, and one reason for his postwar decline may be his own failure to adjust, as Stewart did, to the way the war shook the fundamental American optimism. In *It's a Wonderful Life,* however, the tension between Stewart's dark side and Capra's hope is what gives the film life. It redeems even the corniest moments in the movie—those galaxies that wink while the heavens consult on George's fate. There is a certain boldness in those galaxies, which are so disarmingly simple. A more sophisticated entry point to George's life story might have seemed labored.

It's a Wonderful Life did little for Frank Capra's postwar career, and indeed he never regained the box office magic that he had during the 1930s. Such later films as *State of the Union* (1948) and *Pocketful of Miracles* (1961) have the Capra touch but not the magic, and the director did not make another feature after 1961. But he remained an active public figure and Hollywood citizen until a stroke slowed him in the late 1980s; he died in 1991. At a seminar with film students in the 1970s, he was asked if there was still a way to make movies about the kinds of values and ideals found in the Capra films.

"Well, if there isn't," he said, "we might as well give up."

{ JFK }

I don't have the slightest idea whether Oliver Stone knows who killed Kennedy. I have many doubts about the factual accuracy of his 1991 film *JFK*. I don't think that's the point. This is not a film about the facts of the assassination, but about the feelings. *JFK* accurately reflects our national state of mind since November 22, 1963. We feel that the whole truth has not been told, that more than one shooter was involved, that somehow maybe the CIA, the FBI, Castro, the anti-Castro Cubans, the Mafia, or the Russians, or all of the above, were involved. We don't know how. That's just how we feel.

Shortly after the film was released, I ran into Walter Cronkite and received a tongue-lashing, aimed at myself and my colleagues who had praised *JFK*. There was not, he said, a shred of truth in it. It was a mish-mash of fabrications and paranoid fantasies. It did not reflect the most elementary principles of good journalism. We should all be ashamed of ourselves. I have no doubt Cronkite was correct, from his point of view. But I am a film critic and my assignment is different than his. He wants facts. I want moods, tones, fears, imaginings, whims, speculations, nightmares. As a general principle, I believe films are the wrong medium for fact. Fact belongs in print. Films are about emotions. My notion is that *JFK* is no more or less factual than Stone's *Nixon*—or *Gandhi, Lawrence of Arabia, Gladiator, Amistad, Out of Africa, My Dog Skip*, or any other movie based on "real

life." All we can reasonably ask is that it be skillfully made, and seem to approach some kind of *emotional* truth.

Given that standard, *JFK* is a masterpiece. It's like a collage of all the books and articles, documentaries and TV shows, scholarly debates and conspiracy theories since 1963. We know the litany by heart: the grassy knoll, the hobos in dress shoes, the parade route, the Bay of Pigs, Oswald in Russia, the two Oswalds, Clay Shaw, Allen Dulles, three shots in 2.6 seconds, the eyewitness testimony, the man with the umbrella, the gunpowder tests, the palm print, Jack Ruby, the military-industrial complex, the wrong shadows on the photograph, the Zapruder film, and on and on. These items are like pegs on a child's workbench: We pound one down, and another one springs up.

Oliver Stone was born to make this movie. He is a filmmaker of feverish energy and limitless technical skills, able to assemble a bewildering array of facts and fancies and compose them into a film without getting bogged down. His secret is that he doesn't intend us to remember all his pieces and fit them together and arrive at logical conclusions. His film is not about the case assembled by his hero, New Orleans State's Attorney Jim Garrison (Kevin Costner). It is about Garrison's obsession. The film's thrust is not toward truth, but toward frustration and anger. Too many lies have been told and too much evidence tainted for the truth to *ever* be known. All Garrison can reasonably hope to prove is that the official version is unlikely or impossible and that tantalizing clues and connections suggest a hidden level on which the dots connect differently.

Stone was much criticized for choosing Garrison as his hero. Whom should he have chosen? Earl Warren? Allen Dulles? Walter Cronkite? As a filmmaker it is his assignment to find a protagonist who reflects his feelings. Jim Garrison may not have been on the right track, but he was a perfect surrogate for our national doubts. He asked questions that have never been satisfactorily answered—questions that can *have* no answers, and indeed cannot even be questions, if the Warren Report orthodoxy is correct. Jim Garrison was the obvious hero for any film about a conspiracy to assassinate Kennedy.

Stone found the right visual style too. We've been bombarded by incoming information. It's come for decades in films, in print, on the TV news, in documentaries, in photographs analyzed down to their constituent molecules. None of this stuff fits together. A film with a smooth and consistent visual style would have felt false. Stone and his expert cinematographer, Robert Richardson (who won the Oscar), work in every relevant visual medium: 35mm, 16mm, Super 8, 8mm, video, still photos, color, black and white. His editors, Joe Hutshing and Pietro Scalia, also Oscar winners, assemble this material like the pieces of a jigsaw. It's not linear; there's a sense of parallel events moving forward on more than one front at a time. Consider the scene with Garrison and his investigators in a restaurant, which is intercut with shots of the alleged fabrication of the photo of Oswald and the rifle. As the group breaks up in frustration, the trajectory of the other sequence lands the photo on the cover of *Life* magazine. Was the photo fabricated? Who knows? The shadows sure don't seem to match.

Of course it was also the Time-Life empire that supplied conspiracy theorists with their most valuable weapon, the Zapruder film. The conspirators, whoever they may have been, "didn't figure on Zapruder," the film says. Without his grainy home movie, we would have no way of knowing that the shots were so closely spaced that it seems unlikely Oswald could have fired all of them. Yes, I know about Gerald Posner's book *Case Closed*, which argues everything could have happened more or less as the Warren Commission concluded. *JFK* argues, and most of us still agree, that Oswald's high-speed accuracy is hard to believe. It reflects our gut feelings. It speaks for our dark suspicions.

Stone uses a huge cast. To help us follow all those characters through the thicket of evidence, reconstructions, flashbacks, hypothetical meetings, and fleeting glimpses, he makes use of typecasting and the star system. Actors like Gary Oldman are chosen not just because they are very skilled but because they look like the characters they play (Oswald, in his case). Stars like Jack Lemmon, Ed Asner, Walter Matthau, Kevin Bacon, Donald Sutherland, and Sissy Spacek are used to create instant emotional zones around their characters. Less recognizable stars like Michael Rooker are cast in satellite roles; he plays a key Garrison investigator. We recognize him every time he turns up on the screen, but he doesn't upstage the boss.

And Kevin Costner, in the central role, brings all of his believability and likability and dogged determination to the character of Garrison: He's not a hotshot or a genius, but a stubborn man who gets mad when he's lied to.

There's a lot of exposition in the film. There are times when Stone essentially asks us to listen while a character explains things. These scenes could have been deadly. He makes them exciting by using persuasive actors, by cutting between many different points of view, and by reconstructing the events being described. The key narrator is "Mr. X," the high-level Pentagon official played by Sutherland (said to be based on the conspiracy advocate Colonel L. Fletcher Prouty). Does what he tells Garrison reflect thinking inside the military establishment in the early 1960s? It sounds likely—more likely, certainly, than the pious platitudes of the official version.

The assassination of John F. Kennedy will obsess history as it has obsessed those whose lives were directly touched. The facts, such as they are, will continue to be elusive and debatable. Any factual film would be quickly dated. But *JFK* will stand indefinitely as a record of how we *felt*. How the American people suspect there was more to it than was ever revealed. How we suspect Oswald did not act entirely alone. That there was some kind of a conspiracy. *JFK* is a brilliant reflection of our unease and paranoia, our restless dissatisfaction. On that level, it is completely factual.

{ LA DOLCE VITA }

have heard theories that Federico Fellini's *La Dolce Vita* catalogs the seven deadly sins, takes place on the seven hills of Rome, and involves seven nights and seven dawns, but I have never looked into them, because that would reduce the movie to a crossword puzzle. I prefer it as an allegory, a cautionary tale of a man without a center.

Fellini shot the movie in 1959 on the Via Veneto, the Roman street of nightclubs, sidewalk cafés, and the parade of the night. His hero is a gossip columnist, Marcello, who chronicles "the sweet life" of fading aristocrats, second-rate movie stars, aging playboys, and women of commerce. The role was played by Marcello Mastroianni, and now that his life has ended, we can see that it was his most representative. The two Marcellos—character and actor—flowed together into a handsome, weary, desperate man, who dreams of someday doing something good, but is trapped in a life of empty nights and lonely dawns.

The movie leaps from one visual extravaganza to another, following Marcello as he chases down stories and women. He has a suicidal fiancée (Yvonne Furneaux) at home. In a nightclub, he picks up a promiscuous society beauty (Anouk Aimée), and together they visit the basement lair of a prostitute. The episode ends not in decadence, but in sleep; we can never be sure that Marcello has had sex with anyone.

Another dawn. And we begin to understand the film's structure: a series of nights and dawns, descents and ascents. Marcello goes down into subterranean nightclubs, hospital parking lots, the hooker's hovel, and an ancient crypt. And he ascends St. Peter's dome, climbs to a choir loft, and to the high-rise apartment of Steiner (Alain Cuny), the intellectual who is his hero. He will even fly over Rome.

The famous opening scene, as a statue of Christ is carried above Rome by a helicopter, is matched with the close, in which fishermen on the beach find a sea monster in their nets. Two Christ symbols: the statue "beautiful" but false, the fish "ugly" but real. During both scenes, there are failures of communication. The helicopter circles as Marcello tries to get the phone numbers of three sunbathing beauties. At the end, across a beach, he sees the shy girl he met one day when he went to the country in search of peace to write his novel. She makes typing motions to remind him, but he does not remember, shrugs, and turns away.

If the opening and closing scenes are symmetrical, so are many others, matching the sacred and profane and casting doubts on both. An early sequence finds Marcello covering the arrival in Rome of an improbably buxom movie star (Anita Ekberg), and consumed with desire. He follows her to the top of St. Peter's, into the bowels of a nightclub, and into the Roman night, where wild dogs howl and she howls back. His pursuit ends at dawn when she wades into the Trevi Fountain and he wades after her, idealizing her into all women, into The Woman; she remains forever just out of reach.

This sequence can be paired with a later one where children report a vision of the Virgin. Marcello races to the site, which is surrounded by TV cameras and a crowd of the devout. Again, we have an idealized woman and the hope that she can solve every problem. But the children lead the faithful on a chase, just as the Ekberg led Marcello around Rome. They see the Virgin here, and then there, as the lame and the blind hobble after them and their grandfather cadges for tips. Once again everything collapses in an exhausted dawn.

The central episodes in *La Dolce Vita* involve Steiner, who represents all that Marcello envies. Steiner lives in an apartment filled with art. He presides over a salon of poets, folksingers, intellectuals. He has a beautiful wife and two perfect children. When Marcello sees him entering a

church, they ascend to the organ loft and Steiner plays Bach while urging Marcello to have more faith in himself and finish that book. Then follows the night of Steiner's party, and the moment (more or less the exact center of the film) where Marcello takes his typewriter to a country trattoria and tries to write. Then comes the terrible second Steiner scene, when Marcello discovers that Steiner's serenity was made from a tissue of lies.

To mention these scenes is to be reminded of how many other great moments this rich film contains. The echo chamber. The Mass at dawn. The final desperate orgy. And, of course, the touching sequence with Marcello's father (Annibale Ninchi), a traveling salesman who joins Marcello on a tour of the night. In a club, they see a sad-faced clown (Polidor) lead a lonely balloon out of the room with his trumpet. And Marcello's father, filled with the courage of champagne, grows bold with a young woman who owes Marcello a favor—only to fall ill and leave, gray and ashen, again at dawn.

The movie is made with boundless energy. Fellini stood here at the dividing point between the neorealism of his earlier films (like *La Strada* [1956]) and the carnival visuals of his extravagant later ones (*Juliet of the Spirits* [1965], *Amarcord* [1974]). His autobiographical *8½*, made three years after *La Dolce Vita,* is a companion piece, but more knowing: There the hero is already a filmmaker, but here he is a young newspaperman on the make.

The music by Nino Rota is of a perfect piece with the material. It is sometimes quasi-liturgical, sometimes jazz, sometimes rock; lurking beneath is the irreverence of tuba and accordions, and snatches of pop songs ("Stormy Weather" and even "Jingle Bells"). The characters are forever in motion, and Rota gives them music for their processions and parades.

The casting is all typecasting. Anita Ekberg might not have been much of an actress, but she was the only person who could play herself. Lex Barker, a onetime movie Tarzan, is droll as her alcoholic boyfriend. Alain Cuny's severe self-confidence as Steiner is convincing, which is why his end is a shock. And remember Anouk Aimée, her dark glasses concealing a black eye; the practical, commonsensical Adriana Moneta as the streetwalker; Alain Dijon as the satanic ringleader at the nightclub; and always Mastroianni, his eyes squinting against a headache or a deeper ache of the soul. He was always a passive actor, and here that quality is needed. Seeking happiness but unable to take the steps to find it, he spends his nights in endless aimless searching, trying to please everyone, the juggler with more balls than skills.

Movies do not change, but their viewers do. When I saw *La Dolce Vita* in 1961, I was an adolescent for whom "the sweet life" represented everything I dreamed of: sin, exotic European glamour, the weary romance of the cynical newspaperman. When I saw it again, around 1970, I was living in a version of Marcello's world; Chicago's North Avenue was not the Via Veneto, but at 3 A.M. the denizens were just as colorful, and I was about Marcello's age.

When I saw the movie around 1980, Marcello was the same age, but I was ten years older, had stopped drinking, and saw him not as a role model, but as a victim, condemned to an endless search for happiness that could never be found, not that way. By 1991, when I analyzed the film a frame at a time at the University of Colorado, Marcello seemed younger still, and while I had once admired and then criticized him, now I pitied and loved him. And when I saw the movie right after Mastroianni died, I thought that Fellini and Marcello had taken a moment of discovery and made it immortal. There may be no such thing as the sweet life. But it is necessary to find that out for yourself.

{ THE LADY EVE }

If I were asked to name the single scene in all of romantic comedy that was sexiest and funniest both at the same time, I would advise beginning at six seconds past the twenty-minute mark in Preston Sturges's *The Lady Eve* and watching as Barbara Stanwyck toys with Henry Fonda's hair in an unbroken shot that lasts three minutes and fifty-one seconds.

Stanwyck plays an adventuress who has lured a rich but unworldly young bachelor to her cabin on an ocean liner and is skillfully tantalizing him. She reclines on a chaise. He has landed on the floor next to her. "Hold me tight!" she says, holding him tight—allegedly because she has been frightened by a snake. Now begins the unbroken shot. Her right arm cradles his head, and as she talks, she toys with his earlobe and runs her fingers through his hair. She teases, kids, and flirts with him, and he remains almost paralyzed with shyness and self-consciousness. And at some point during this process, she falls for him.

That isn't part of her plan. Stanwyck plays Jean Harrington, a con woman who travels first-class with her father and their valet, fleecing rich travelers in card games and whatever else comes along. She sets her sights on Charles Pike (Fonda), heir to a brewery fortune, as he comes aboard after a snake-hunting expedition in South America. She drops an apple on his pith helmet as he climbs the rope ladder to the ship, and is reprimanded by her father: "Don't be vulgar, Jean. Let us be crooked, but never common."

What is delightful about Stanwyck's performance is how she has it both ways. She is a crook, and yet can be trusted. A seductress, and yet a pushover for romance. A gold digger, and yet she wants nothing from him. And he is a naive innocent who knows only that her perfume smells mighty good to someone who has been "up the Amazon" for a year. She falls for him so quickly and so thoroughly that she's even frank about her methods; just before he kisses her in the moonlight in the ship's bow, she tells him, "They say a moonlit deck's a woman's business office."

Howard Hawks once said that the flaw in his *Bringing Up Baby*, one of the great screwball comedies, is that everyone in it is a screwball; there's no baseline of sanity to measure the characters against. *The Lady Eve* (1941), which in its way is just as preposterous as the Hawks picture, doesn't make that mistake. Fonda is the rock. He remains vulnerable and sincere throughout the picture because, like all young men who are truly and badly in love, his consciousness is focused on one thing: the void in his heart that only she can fill.

That frees Stanwyck for one of her greatest performances, a flight of romance and comedy so graceful and effortless that she is somehow able to play different notes at the same time. The movie establishes Jean Harrington in an inspired early scene, as she joins her father, a phony colonel, in the ship's lounge. Using the mirror in her compact, she spies on Charlie Pike as he sits alone and reads a book (its title, *Are Snakes Necessary?*, is a sly addition to the movie's phallic imagery). Sturges cuts to the view reflected in the mirror, and Jean provides a tart voice-over narration for her father, describing the attempts of every woman in the room to catch the handsome bachelor's eye. Then, as Charlie leaves the room, she simply sticks out a foot and trips him; as he picks himself up, she blames him for breaking off the heel of her shoe.

He escorts her to her stateroom, and she tells him to pick out a new pair of shoes and put them on her feet. "You'll have to kneel down," she says, and swings her nyloned leg almost in his face. His vision blurs with passion, and Sturges comes within an inch of violating the Production Code, the way her toe swings dangerously close. Poor Charlie falls for her, soon finds himself playing poker with Jean and her father, wins six hundred dollars as part of their setup, and then undergoes the exquisite torment of her ear-and-hair caress.

The plot unfolds as screwball invention, except that after boy meets girl and boy loses girl, boy wins what he only thinks is another girl. Jean, hurt by the way he has not trusted her, gets herself invited to a dinner at his father's palatial mansion by posing as "Lady Eve Sidwich." Charlie is struck by how much Eve resembles Jean. "It's the same dame!" says his faithful valet Muggsy (William Demarest). But Charlie can't believe it and follows her moon-eyed through a series of pratfalls.

Sturges says in his memoirs that the studios were always trying to get him to limit his pratfalls, and at the sneak previews he crossed his fingers as Demarest fell into the bushes and Fonda tripped over a couch and a curtain before getting a roast beef in his lap. But they all worked. "That couch has been there fifteen years and nobody ever fell over it before!" exclaims Charlie's father. Lady Eve: "Oh, well—now the ice is broken!"

Barbara Stanwyck (1907–90) was known primarily as a gifted dramatic actress *(Golden Boy, Stella Dallas, Double Indemnity)*. Preston Sturges (1898–1959), who in the early 1940s made one inspired comedy after another *(Sullivan's Travels, The Palm Beach Story)* and scarcely seemed able to step wrong, had promised her a comic role and gave her one for the ages.

Although the movie would be inconceivable without Fonda, *The Lady Eve* is all Stanwyck's. The love, the hurt, and the anger of her character provide the motivation for nearly every scene, and what is surprising is how much genuine feeling she finds in the comedy. Watch her eyes as she regards Fonda, in all of their quiet scenes together, and you will see a woman who is amused by a man's boyish shyness and yet aroused by his physical presence. At first she loves the game of seduction, and you can sense her enjoyment of her own powers. Then she is somehow caught up in her own seduction. There has rarely been a woman in a movie who more convincingly desired a man.

Her father is played by Charles Coburn (1877–1961), a valuable character actor from the 1930s through the 1950s, who was sort of a road-company Charles Laughton. Here Coburn and Sturges make a crucial right decision: "Colonel" Harrington is not blustering and broad, but a smart and perceptive man, not loud, who loves his daughter. Their relationship is established in a quiet scene the morning after Jean first meets Charlie. She is in her stateroom, still in bed. Her father enters in dressing gown, sits on her bed, and plays with a deck of cards while questioning her. At this point in the movie, we have a good notion, but no hard evidence, that he is a fraud. "What are you doing?" she asks. "Dealing fives," he says. She wants to see. He shows her four aces, puts them on top of the deck, and then deals four hands without dealing a single ace—dealing the fifth card every time. (It's hard to be sure, but here and elsewhere it looks as if Coburn himself is handling the cards.)

The scene establishes him as a shark, makes it clear they're confederates, and underlines, by the way she calls him "Harry," that they're two adults and not locked into a narrow daddy-daughter relationship. The scene also sets up the hilarious scene that night, where the colonel tries to cheat Charlie at cards, and Jean outcheats him to rescue the man she loves.

A movie like *The Lady Eve* is so hard to make that you can't make it at all unless you find a way to make it seem effortless. Preston Sturges does a kind of breathless balancing act here, involving romance, deception, and physical comedy. Consider the scenes where Jean masquerades as the Lady Eve. She throws Charlie off the scent by her very lack of a disguise: Brazenly entering his house looking exactly like herself, she adds a British accent and dares him to call her bluff. She knows he cannot, and the masquerade sets up the two final lines of the film, which I will not mention here—except to say that for my money, either one is equal to "Nobody's perfect!" at the end of *Some Like It Hot*.

LAST YEAR
AT MARIENBAD

How clearly I recall standing in the rain outside the Co-Ed theater near the campus of the University of Illinois, waiting to see *Last Year at Marienbad*. On those lonely sidewalks, in that endless night, how long did we wait there? And was it the first time we waited in that line, to enter the old theater with its columns, its aisles, its rows of seats—or did we see the same film here last year?

Yes, it's easy to smile at Alain Resnais's 1961 film, which inspired so much satire and yet made such a lasting impression. Incredible to think that students actually did stand in the rain to be baffled by it, and then to argue for hours about its meaning—even though the director claimed it had none. I hadn't seen *Marienbad* in years, and when I saw the new DVD edition in a video store, I reached out automatically: I wanted to see it again, to see if it was silly or profound, and perhaps even to recapture an earlier self—a nineteen-year-old who hoped Truth could be found in Art.

Viewing the film again, I expected to have a cerebral experience, to see a film more fun to talk about than to watch. What I was not prepared for was the voluptuous quality of *Marienbad,* its command of tone and mood, its hypnotic way of drawing us into its puzzle, its austere visual beauty. Yes, it involves a story that remains a mystery, even to the characters themselves. But one would not want to know the answer to this mystery. Storybooks with happy endings are for children. Adults know that stories keep on unfolding, repeating, turning back on themselves, on and on until that end which no story can evade.

The film takes place in an elegant chateau, one with ornate ceilings, vast drawing rooms, enormous mirrors and paintings, endless corridors, and grounds in which shrubbery has been tortured into geometric shapes and patterns. In this chateau are many guests—elegant, expensively dressed, impassive. We are concerned with three of them: "A" (Delphine Seyrig), a beautiful woman; "X" (Giorgio Albertazzi), with movie-idol good looks, who insists they met last year and arranged to meet again this year; and "M" (Sascha Pitoëff), who may be A's husband or lover, but certainly exercises authority over her. He has a striking appearance, with his sunken triangular face, high cheekbones, deep-set eyes, and subtle vampirish overbite.

The film is narrated by X. The others have a few lines of dialogue here and there. On the sound track is disturbing music by Francis Seyrig, mostly performed on an organ—gothic, liturgical, like a requiem. X tells A they met last year. He reminds her of the moments they shared. Their conversations. Their plans to meet in her bedroom while M was at the gaming tables. Her plea that he delay his demands for one year. Her promise to meet him again next summer.

A does not remember. She entreats X, unconvincingly, to leave her alone. He presses on with his memories. He speaks mostly in the second person: You told me . . . you said . . . you begged me . . . It is a narrative he is constructing for her, a story he is telling her about herself. It may be true. We cannot tell. Resnais said that as the cowriter of the story he did not believe it, but as the director he did. The narrative presses on. The insistent, persuasive X recalls a shooting, a death. No—he corrects himself. It did not happen that way. It must have happened this way, instead . . .

We see her in white, in black. Dead, alive. The film, photographed in b&w by Sacha Vierny, is in wide screen. The extreme width allows Resnais to create compositions in which X, A, and M seem to occupy different planes, even different states of being. (The DVD is letterboxed; to see this film panned-and-scanned would be pointless.) The camera travels sinuously; the characters usually move in a slow and formal way, so that any sudden movement is a shock (when A stumbles on a gravel walk and X steadies her, it is like a sudden breath of reality).

The men play a game. It has been proposed by M. It involves setting out several rows of matchsticks (or cards, or anything). Two players take turns removing matchsticks, as many as they want, but only from one row at a time. The player who is left with the last matchstick loses. M always wins. On the sound track, we hear theories: "The one who starts first wins . . . the one who goes second wins . . . you must take only one stick at a time . . . you must know when to . . ." The theories are not helpful because M always wins anyway. The characters analyzing the stick game are like viewers analyzing the movie: You can say anything you want about it, and it makes no difference.

"I'll explain it all for you," promised Gunther Marx, a professor of German at Illinois. We were sitting over coffee in the student union, late on that rainy night in Urbana. (He would die young; his son Frederick would be one of the makers of *Hoop Dreams*.) "It is a working out of the anthropological archetypes of Claude Lévi-Strauss. You have the lover, the loved one, and the authority figure. The movie proposes that the lovers had an affair, that they didn't, that they met before, that they didn't, that the authority figure knew it, that he didn't, that he killed her, that he didn't. Any questions?"

I sipped my coffee and nodded thoughtfully. This was deep. I never subsequently read a single word by Lévi-Strauss, but you see I have not forgotten the name. I have no idea if Marx was right. The idea, I think, is that life is like this movie: No matter how many theories you apply to it, life presses on indifferently toward its own inscrutable ends. The fun is in asking questions. Answers are a form of defeat.

It is possible, I realize, to grow impatient with *Last Year at Marienbad*. To find it affected and insufferable. It doesn't hurtle through its story like today's hits—it's not a narrative pinball machine. It is a deliberate, artificial artistic construction. I watched it with a pleasure so intense I was surprised. I knew to begin with there would be no solution. That the three characters would move forever through their dance of desire and denial, and that their clothing and the elegant architecture of the chateau was as real as the bedroom at the end of *2001*—in other words, simply a setting in which human behavior could be observed.

There is one other way to regard the movie. Consider the narration.

X tells A this, and then he tells her that. M behaves as X says he does—discovering them together, not discovering them, firing a pistol, not firing it. A remembers nothing, but acts as if she cares. She thinks she hasn't met X before, and yet in some scenes they appear to be lovers.

Can it be that X is the artist—the author, the director? That when he speaks in the second person ("You asked me to come to your room"), he is speaking to his characters, creating their story? That first he has M fire a pistol, but that when he doesn't like that and changes his mind, M obediently reflects his desires? Isn't this how writers work? Creating characters out of thin air and then ordering them around? Of course even if X is the artist, he seems quite involved in the story. He desperately wants to believe he met A last year at Marienbad, and that she gave him hope—asked him to meet her again this year. That is why writers create characters: to be able to order them around and to be loved by them. Of course sometimes characters have wills of their own. And there is always the problem of M.

{ L'ATALANTE }

To live happily ever after with the one you love, you must be able to live with him or her at all. Little problems must be worked out. She does not like cats on the table while she is eating. He has a closet filled with a year's dirty laundry. She treasures their private moments together. He treasures his best friend, who is bearded and garrulous and arrives at meals in an under-shirt. She wants to see Paris. He worries about his work. You see how it is.

Jean Vigo's *L'Atalante* (1934) tells such a love story. It is on many lists of the greatest films, a distinction that obscures how down-to-earth it is, how direct in its story of a new marriage off to a shaky start. The French director François Truffaut fell in love with it one Saturday afternoon in 1946, when he was fourteen: "When I entered the theater, I didn't even know who Jean Vigo was. I was immediately overwhelmed with wild en-thusiasm for his work." Hearing a critic attack another movie because "it smells like dirty feet," Truffaut considered that a compliment, and thought of Vigo and the pungent life he evoked on a French canal barge.

Truffaut saw Vigo's life work that afternoon in Paris; it added up to less than two hundred minutes. Legends swirled around the director, who died of tuberculosis at twenty-nine, just a few months after the premiere. Already famous for *Zero for Conduct* (1933), he was so ill when he made *L'Atalante*, during an unusually cold winter, that sometimes he directed from a stretcher: "It is easy to conclude that he was in a kind of fever while

he worked," Truffaut wrote, and when a friend advised him to guard his health, Vigo replied that "he lacked the time and had to give everything right away."

The film premiered to polite responses in Paris and at the Venice Film Festival. London critics were its first great champions. It was seen for years in a butchered version, chopped down from eighty-nine to sixty-five minutes, and only in 1990 was it restored. That version is now available on video.

In outline, *L'Atalante* seems a simple story. It begins with the marriage of a young barge captain named Jean and a village girl named Juliette, "who always had to do things differently." There is no wedding feast. Still wearing her wedding dress, she holds to a boom and swings on board the barge, to begin life not only with her husband but also with his massive and shambling friend Jules, a sailor who has been to Yokohama and Singapore but now plies the waterways between Le Havre and Paris. The barge is further crowded by a cabin boy and at least six cats.

Juliette makes the best of her situation. When a cat has kittens in her bed, she strips the sheets over the objections of Jules, who sees no need for such fastidiousness. One night on the radio she hears the magic words "This is Paris!" She has never been to Paris, or anywhere else. When the barge arrives in the city, Jean tells her to get dressed up for a night on the town—but Jules goes in search of fleshy pleasures, and they must stay with the boat. Eventually she slips off alone to the city, planning to be back before she is missed. Jean finds her gone and angrily resumes the journey. The barge is missing when she returns . . .

These details fail to evoke the enchanted quality of *L'Atalante*, which is not about what lovers do, but about how they feel—how tender they are, how sensitive and foolish. The film is shot in a poetic way that sees them as the figures in a myth; Atalante is not only the barge name but the name of a Greek goddess who, says *Brewer's Dictionary*, "being very swift of foot, refused to marry unless the suitor should first defeat her in a race." Can it be that Jean and Juliette were racing away from one another, and he did a better job of it?

The movie's effect comes through the way it evokes specific moments in the life of the young couple, rather than tying them to a plot. They will be the moments that memory illuminates fifty years from now, when everything else has grown vague. Consider their first morning, as the waking couple is serenaded by an accordion and a bargeman's song. The argument over the laundry. An extraordinary moment when old Jules and Juliette are alone in the cabin, and he seems almost ready to assault her, but she distracts him with the dress she is making, and gets him to model it. And how her unexpected cheerfulness (did she even sense any danger?) inspires him to show her the treasures of his life, climaxing with a jar that contains the hands of his best friend ("all that is left of him").

There is a sequence in a canalside bistro where a magician flirts with her, tempts her with pretty scarves, dances with her, and enrages Jules. The man paints word pictures of Paris which echo in her imagination until she *must* go see the city for herself—not to be disloyal to Jean, but because she is like a little girl who cannot help herself.

Their separation is painful for them both. Her early joy turns into fear; her purse is stolen, hawk-faced men make lewd suggestions, the city is no longer magical. Jean holds his head in anguish. And then Vigo releases all the pent-up loneliness with a bold gesture. Earlier, Juliette told Jean that when she put her face into water and opened her eyes, she could see her true love: "I saw you before I met you." Now in desperation Jean plunges into the icy canal, and Juliette's smiling presence swims up before him. "This must count as one of the most dazzling images of a loving woman in the history of the cinema," wrote the novelist Marina Warner. After Jean climbs back on board, the old man and the cabin boy try to cheer him with music, but he wanders off and, in a heartbreaking shot, embraces a block of ice as if it is his love.

Juliette is played by Dita Parlo, a legendary Berlin-born actress who made twenty-five films between 1928 and 1940, and one more each in 1950 and 1965. Her other famous role was as the farm woman who takes in the escaped convicts in Renoir's *Grand Illusion* (1937). Madonna's book *Sex* was inspired, she said, by Parlo in *L'Atalante*. Garboesque in the pale refinement of her face, she seems too elegant to be an untraveled country girl, but that quality works when it is set beside Michel Simon's crusty old Jules.

Simon, not yet forty when the film was made, looks sixty, weathered by salt air and pickled in seaport saloons. Inspired by the sight of the two young lovers kissing, he has his best moment when he demonstrates how he can wrestle too—and grapples with himself on the deck, while Vigo dissolves between exposures to make him into two lonely ghosts fighting for possession of the same body.

Jean Dasté, who plays Jean, conveys the helplessness of a young man who knows he is in love but knows nothing about the practical side of a relationship—how he must see Juliette's needs and intuit what wounds her. Although the film ends with everyone joyously back on board, we doubt, somehow, that we have seen their last fight.

The movie's look is softly poetic. Vigo and his cinematographer, Boris Kaufman, who years later labored for Otto Preminger in Hollywood, shot mostly on location, capturing the cold winter canal landscapes, the smoky bistros, the cramped living quarters, the magnificence of the muscular old barge as water pours into locks to lift it up to Paris. This is the kind of movie you return to like a favorite song, remembering where you were when you first saw it, and how it made you feel, and how its feet smelled.

{ L'Avventura }

Tell me that you love me.
I love you.
Tell me once more.
I don't love you.

By the time the above exchange takes place, deep inside Michelangelo Antonioni's *L'Avventura*, the conversation has nothing to do with love. It is more like an attempt to pass the time—like a game of solitaire or flipping a coin. There is not even the possibility that the characters are in love, can love, have loved, will love. "Too shallow to be truly lonely," Pauline Kael wrote, "they are people trying to escape their boredom by reaching out to one another and finding only boredom once again."

L'Avventura created a stir in 1960, when Kael picked it as the best film of the year. It was seen as the flip side of Fellini's *La Dolce Vita* (1960). Both directors were Italian; both depicted their characters in a fruitless search for sensual pleasure; both films ended at dawn with emptiness and soul-sickness. But Fellini's characters, who were middle-class and had lusty appetites, at least were hopeful on their way to despair. For Antonioni's idle and decadent rich people, pleasure is anything that momentarily distracts them from the lethal ennui of their existence. Kael again: "The characters are active only in trying to discharge their anxiety: sex is their sole means of contact."

The plot of *L'Avventura* became famous because, it was said, nothing happened in the movie. What we saw was a search without a conclusion, a disappearance without a solution. The title in English means "The Adventure," and it was not hard to imagine Antonioni's dry smile as he penned those words on the first page of his screenplay.

A group of wealthy friends is cruising the sea near Sicily on a yacht. They anchor near an island, swim ashore, and begin to explore. Anna (Lea Massari) has quarreled with her lover, Sandro (Gabriele Ferzetti), and has been overheard saying she wanted to be left alone. They both go ashore, along with her friend Claudia (Monica Vitti) and others. After a time, Anna cannot be found. The others search the island for her; it is mostly rocks and scrubby trees, and there seem few places to hide, but she cannot be found.

And she is never seen again. If *L'Avventura* were a conventional movie, you would be furious with me for revealing this information because you would assume the movie was about the search for Anna. It is not. It is about the sense in which all of the characters are on the brink of disappearance; their lives are so unreal and their relationships so tenuous they can barely be said to exist. They are like bookmarks in life: holding places, but not involved in the story.

The yacht is sent to bring help. As Anna's friends comb the island, Aldo Scavarda's cinematography is haunting: Humans are placed off-center in compositions, as if the rocks have been there forever and these visitors are likely to slip off into the sea—or the sky, or shadows. They hear a boat, far away. There is a teasing shot in which we see it—or almost see it. Did Anna leave on it? Later, perhaps they hear another boat.

These phantom boats are like the dead body that was or wasn't on the park grass in Antonioni's *Blowup* (1966). The 1975 Australian film *Picnic at Hanging Rock* is also about a person consumed by a landscape. The effect of Anna's disappearance is disquieting; we want to know there either was a boat or wasn't a boat, and Anna either did or didn't leave on it. The film remains slippery. Eventually the yacht returns with the police and Anna's father (who seems unhappy to be called away from his responsibilities for something insignificant like the disappearance of a child).

Then there is a scene that is shocking in two ways: first because it occurs at all, and second because it hardly seems to occur—it's like the ghost

boat we're not sure we saw. The party has returned to the yacht, and Sandro, Anna's lover, grabs Claudia, her friend, and kisses her. Claudia pulls away. The moment passes. What is she thinking? Is she disgusted that he would so soon betray Anna? It is impossible to know.

Onshore, Sandro makes a report at police headquarters and follows Claudia onto a train. He says he loves her. Later, they are joined by other friends, including Gloria (Dorothy De Poliolo), a sexy writer who walks oblivious through working-class streets where the men and boys boldly ogle her; she accepts their attention as if it is the weather. There is an interesting point being made here: She is at pains to present herself as sexy but has forgotten why she does that. She dresses and moves out of a memory of a time when she cared what men thought of her. They still think, but she has burned out her ability to care.

Claudia accepts Sandro as her lover. Anna is forgotten. Neither mourns her. She served a function (lover, friend), and now that she is gone, that function must be filled by another. They check into a hotel room together, and while the bellboy is watching, Sandro tries to kiss Claudia, but when the bellboy has gone, Sandro doesn't try again. He goes down to a party in the hotel. Claudia sleeps, wakes, runs down the corridor, hoping (or afraid) that Anna has returned. She finds Sandro downstairs, sprawled on a sofa with a prostitute. She runs outside. As Sandro rises, the hooker asks for a *souvenir*—French for a memory—and he throws bills down at her body. Outside, the empty dawn.

When *L'Avventura* was released, it became a joke to refer to "Antoniennui." At its premiere at the Cannes festival, the audience booed, but it won the Jury Prize and became a box office success all over the world. It was the most pure and stark of several films about characters who drifted in existential limbo. In America, it came at a time when beatniks cultivated detachment, when modern jazz kept an ironic distance from melody, when it was hip to be cool. That whole time came crashing down later in the 1960s, but while it lasted, *L'Avventura* was its anthem.

I did not much connect with the film when I saw it first—how could I, at eighteen? These people were bored by a lifestyle beyond my wildest dreams. When I taught the film in a class fifteen years later, it seemed affected and contrived, a feature-length idea but not a movie. Only recently, seeing it again, did I realize how much clarity and passion Antonioni brought to the film's silent cry of despair.

His characters were parasites whose money allowed them to clear away the distractions of work, responsibility, goals and purposes, and exposed the utter emptiness within. It is possible to be rich and happy, of course, but for that you need a mind, and interests. It is impossible to be happy simply because one is ceaselessly entertained. *L'Avventura* becomes a place in our imagination—a melancholy moral desert.

Why don't we have movies like *L'Avventura* anymore? Because we don't ask the same kinds of questions anymore. We have replaced the "purpose of life" with the "choice of lifestyle." I used to think Peggy Lee's "Is That All There Is?" was the saddest song. Antonioni can think of a sadder one: "More."

{ LAWRENCE OF ARABIA }

What a bold, mad act of genius it was, to make *Lawrence of Arabia,* or even think that it could be made. In the words years later of one of its stars, Omar Sharif: "If you are the man with the money and somebody comes to you and says he wants to make a film that's four hours long, with no stars, and no women, and no love story, and not much action either, and he wants to spend a huge amount of money to go film it in the desert—what would you say?"

The impulse to make this movie was based, above all, on imagination. The story of *Lawrence* is not founded on violent battle scenes or cheap melodrama, but on David Lean's ability to imagine what it would look like to see a speck appear on the horizon of the desert and slowly grow into a human being. He had to know how that would feel before he could convince himself that the project had a chance of being successful.

There is a moment in the film when the hero, the British eccentric soldier and author T. E. Lawrence, has survived a suicidal trek across the desert and is within reach of shelter and water—and he turns around and goes back, to find a friend who has fallen behind. This sequence builds up to the shot in which the shimmering heat of the desert reluctantly yields the speck that becomes a man—a shot that is held for a long time before we can even begin to see the tiny figure. On television, this shot doesn't work at all—nothing can be seen. In a movie theater, looking at the stark clarity of

a 70mm print, we lean forward and strain to bring a detail out of the waves of heat, and for a moment we experience some of the actual vastness of the desert and its unforgiving harshness.

By being able to imagine that sequence, Lean was able to imagine why the movie would work. *Lawrence of Arabia* is not a simple biography or an adventure movie—although it contains both elements—but a movie that uses the desert as a stage for the flamboyance of a driven, quirky man. Although it is true that Lawrence was instrumental in enlisting the desert tribes on the British side in the 1914–17 campaign against the Turks, the movie suggests that he acted less out of patriotism than out of a need to reject conventional British society, choosing to identify with the wildness and theatricality of the Arabs. There was also a sexual component, involving his masochism.

T. E. Lawrence must be the strangest hero to ever stand at the center of an epic. To play him, Lean cast one of the strangest of actors, Peter O'Toole, a lanky, almost clumsy man with a beautiful sculptured face and a speaking manner that hesitates between amusement and insolence. O'Toole's assignment was a delicate one. Although it was widely believed that Lawrence was a homosexual, a multimillion-dollar epic filmed in 1962 could not be frank about that. And yet Lean and his writer, Robert Bolt, didn't simply cave in and rewrite Lawrence into a routine action hero. Everything is here for those willing to look for it.

Using O'Toole's peculiar speech and manner as their instrument, they created a character who combined charisma and craziness, who was so different from conventional military heroes that he could inspire the Arabs to follow him in a mad march across the desert. There is a moment in the movie when O'Toole, dressed in the flowing white robes of a desert sheik, does a victory dance on top of a captured Turkish train, and he almost seems to be posing for fashion photos. This is a curious scene because it seems to flaunt gay stereotypes, and yet none of the other characters in the movie seem to notice—nor do they take much notice of the two young desert urchins that Lawrence takes under his protection.

What Lean, Bolt, and O'Toole create is a sexually and socially unconventional man who is simply presented as what he is, without labels or comment. Could such a man rally the splintered desert tribes and win a war against the Turks? Lawrence did. But he did it partially with mirrors, the movie suggests. One of the key characters is an American journalist (Arthur Kennedy), obviously inspired by Lowell Thomas, who single-handedly laundered and retailed the Lawrence myth to the English-language press. The journalist admits he is looking for a hero to write about. Lawrence is happy to play the role. And only role-playing would have done the job; an ordinary military hero would have been too small for this canvas.

For a movie that runs 216 minutes, plus intermission, *Lawrence of Arabia* is not dense with plot details. It is a spare movie in clean, uncluttered lines, and there is never a moment when we're in doubt about the logistical details of the various campaigns. Lawrence is able to unite various desert factions, the movie argues, (1) because he is so obviously an outsider that he cannot even understand, let alone take sides with, the various ancient rivalries, and (2) because he is able to show the Arabs that it is in their own self-interest to join the war against the Turks. Along the way he makes allies of such desert leaders as Sherif Ali (Omar Sharif), Prince Feisal (Alec Guinness), and Auda abu Tayi (Anthony Quinn), both by winning their respect and by appealing to their logic. The dialogue in these scenes is not complex, and sometimes Bolt makes it so spare it sounds like poetry.

I've noticed that when people remember *Lawrence of Arabia*, they don't talk about the details of the plot. They get a certain look in their eye, as if they are remembering the whole experience and have never quite been able to put it into words. Although it seems to be a traditional narrative film—like *The Bridge on the River Kwai* (1957), which Lean made just before it, or *Doctor Zhivago* (1965), which he made just after—it actually has more in common with such essentially visual epics as Kubrick's *2001* and Eisenstein's *Aleksandr Nevsky*. It is spectacle and experience, and its ideas are about things you can see or feel, not things you can say. Much of its appeal is based on the fact that it does not contain a complex story with a lot of dialogue; we remember the quiet, empty passages, the sun rising across the desert, the intricate lines traced by the wind in the sand.

Although it won the Academy Award as the year's best picture in 1962, *Lawrence of Arabia* might have been lost if it hadn't been for the film restorers Robert A. Harris and Jim Painten. They discovered the original negative in Columbia's vaults, inside crushed and rusting film cans, and also about thirty-five minutes of footage that had been trimmed by distributors from Lean's final cut. They put it together again, sometimes by one crumbling frame at a time. (Harris sent me one of the smashed cans as a demonstration of Hollywood's carelessness with its heritage.)

To see it in a movie theater is to appreciate the subtlety of F. A. "Freddie" Young's desert cinematography—achieved despite blinding heat, and the blowing sand that worked its way into every camera. *Lawrence of Arabia* was one of the last films to actually be photographed in 70mm (as opposed to being blown up to 70 from a 35mm negative). There was a hunger within filmmakers like Lean (and Kubrick, Coppola, Tarkovsky, Kurosawa, Stone) to break through the boundaries, to dare a big idea and have the effrontery to impose it on timid studio executives. The word "epic" in recent years has become synonymous with "big-budget B picture." What you realize watching *Lawrence of Arabia* is that the word "epic" refers not to the cost or the elaborate production, but to the size of the ideas and vision. Werner Herzog's *Aguirre, the Wrath of God* didn't cost as much as the catering in *Pearl Harbor,* but it is an epic and *Pearl Harbor* is not.

As for *Lawrence,* after its glorious rerelease in 70mm in 1989, it has returned again to video, where it crouches inside its box like a tall man in a low room. You can view it on video and get an idea of its story and a hint of its majesty, but to get the *feeling* of Lean's masterpiece, you need to somehow, somewhere, see it in 70mm on a big screen. This experience is on the short list of things that must be done during the lifetime of every lover of film.

{ LE SAMOURAI }

An empty room. No, not empty. In the shadows we can barely see a man on the bed. He lights a cigarette, and smoke coils up toward a wisp of light from the window. After a time the man gets up, fully dressed, and moves to a hatstand near the door. He puts on his fedora, adjusting the brim with delicate precision, and goes out into the street.

Like a painter or a musician, a filmmaker can suggest complete mastery with just a few strokes. Jean-Pierre Melville involves us in the spell of *Le Samourai* (1967) before a word is spoken. He does it with light: a cold light, like dawn on an ugly day. And color: grays and blues. And actions that speak in place of words.

The man hot-wires a car and drives it down a forlorn street to a garage, where the door gapes open. He wheels it inside. A mechanic is waiting, and changes the license plates on the car. The driver waits and smokes. The mechanic opens a drawer and hands him papers. The driver extends his hand. For a handshake? No, for a gun. He pockets it. He hands the mechanic cash. Then he drives away. Not a word spoken.

The man, named Jef Costello, is played by Alain Delon, the tough pretty boy of French movies. He was thirty-two when this movie was made, an actor so improbably handsome that his best strategy for dealing with his looks was to use a poker face. He seems utterly unaware here of his appearance; at times he seems to be playing himself in a dream. A "beautiful de-structive angel of the dark street," David Thomson called him.

Costello is a killer for hire. The movie follows him with meticulous attention to detail while he establishes an alibi, kills a nightclub owner, survives a police lineup, is betrayed by those who hired him, and becomes the subject of a police manhunt that involves a cat-and-mouse chase through the Paris Métro. During all of this time, he barely betrays an emotion.

Two women help supply his alibis. A woman named Jane loves him, we guess, although she has a rich lover and Jef knows it (she is played by Nathalie Delon, his real-life wife). The other woman, a black musician named Valerie (Caty Rosier) who plays the piano in the nightclub, lies at the lineup and says she has never seen him. But she knows she has. Is she lying to help him? Or because she knows the men who hired him, and knows they do not want him caught? This question weighs on Costello's mind after he is betrayed by his employers, and he goes to see the piano player, who is utterly fearless even though he might kill her. Costello's women seem to reflect his own existential detachment: He does his job, he functions at the top of his ability, he has no values, he is a professional, there is no room for sentiment in how he lives.

"There is no solitude greater than a samurai's," says a quotation at the beginning of the film. "Unless perhaps it is that of a tiger in the jungle." The quotation is attributed to the *Book of Bushido*, which I was disappointed to find out is fictional—a creation of Melville's. The quotation and the whole pose of the Costello character are meant to suggest a man who operates according to a rigid code. But as Stanley Kauffmann points out in his review, "a samurai did not accept commissions to kill merely for money: honor and ethics were involved."

Here the honor and ethics seem to be Jef Costello's loyalty to himself; a samurai was prepared to die for his employer, and Costello is self-employed. Perhaps he should have taken his text from a real book, *The Code of the Samurai*, from Japan's sixteenth century. It begins with words Melville might well have quoted: "One who is a samurai must before all things keep constantly in mind, by day and by night . . . the fact that he has to die. That is his chief business."

The film is masterful in its control of acting and visual style.

Against Delon's detachment and cold objectivity, Melville sets the character of the police inspector (François Périer), who barks commands over police radio while masterminding the manhunt. He knows Jef is lying, but can't prove it, and there is a slimy scene where he tries to blackmail Jane into betraying Jef. Meanwhile, Jef tries to find the men who hired him, so he can get revenge.

One of the pleasures of *Le Samourai* is to realize how complicated the plot has grown, in its flat, deadpan way. With little dialogue and spare scenes of pure action (most of it unsensational), the movie devises a situation in which Jef is being sought all over Paris by both the police and the underworld, while he simultaneously puts his own plan into effect and deals with both women.

The movie teaches us how action is the enemy of suspense—how action releases tension instead of building it. Better to wait for a whole movie for something to happen (assuming we really care whether it happens) than to sit through a film where things we don't care about are happening constantly.

Melville uses character, not action, to build suspense. Consider a scene where one of the underworld hirelings calls on Costello, to apologize and hire him for another job, and Jef stares at him with utterly blank, empty eyes.

"Nothing to say?" the goon says.

"Not with a gun on me."

"Is that a principle?"

"A habit."

Melville is in love with the processes of things in the movie. The sequence when Jef is tailed by cops on the underground has inspired several other films. Police are stationed on every platform, but Costello hops in and out of cars, switches platforms and trains, and toys with them. There is also a lovingly directed sequence where two flatfoots plant a wire in Costello's apartment. And a final scene where Costello returns to the nightclub where the murder took place, and is able to resolve all the plot strands and make his own statement—all while essentially remaining passive.

David Thomson wrote that this film is "so tough that its impassive romanticism is not just fascinating, but nearly comic." Some of the comic details are so quiet they could be missed. Consider the bird in Costello's drab hotel room. It is a gray, shabby bird (of course), with an unpleasant chirp. Why would this man have a bird? Is it even his? Did it come with the room? The bird's chirp provides an amusing payoff after the cops wire the room and set up a tape recorder that records only chirps for a while. Apart from the bird, the room contains the following personal possessions of Costello: his trench coat, his fedora, his pack of cigarettes, and a bottle of mineral water. At one point, he walks over to an armoire, and on top of it, I was delighted to see, were rows of water bottles and neatly arranged packs of cigarettes. You smile because such details are a very quiet wink from Melville, telling you he knows what he's up to.

Jean-Pierre Melville (1917–73) was born Grumbach but renamed himself after the American novelist. He was a hero of the French Resistance. After the war, by starting his own studio and making independent films on very small budgets, he essentially pointed the way for the French New Wave. "I'm incapable of doing anything but rough drafts," he once said, but in fact *Le Samourai* is as finished and polished as a film can be.

The elements of the film—the killer, the cops, the underworld, the women, the code—are as familiar as the movies themselves. Melville loved 1930s Hollywood crime movies and in his own work helped develop modern film noir. There is nothing absolutely original in *Le Samourai* except for the handling of the material. Melville pares down and leaves out. He disdains artificial action sequences and manufactured payoffs. He drains the color from his screen and the dialogue from his characters. At the end, there is a scene that cries out (in Hollywood terms anyway) for a last dramatic enigmatic statement, but Melville gives us banalities and then silence. He has been able to keep constantly in mind his hero's chief business.

{ M }

The horror of the faces: That is the overwhelming image that remains from a recent viewing of the restored version of *M,* Fritz Lang's 1931 film about a child murderer in Germany. In my memory, it was a film that centered on the killer, the creepy little Hans Beckert, played by Peter Lorre. But Beckert has relatively limited screen time, and only one consequential speech— although it's a haunting one. Most of the film is devoted to the search for Beckert, by both the police and the underworld, and many of these scenes are played in close-up. In searching for words to describe the faces of the actors, I fall hopelessly upon "piglike."

What was Lang up to? He was a famous director, his silent films like *Metropolis* (1927) worldwide successes. He lived in a Berlin where the left-wing plays of Brecht coexisted with the decadent milieu re-created in movies like *Cabaret* (1972). By 1931, the Nazi Party was on the march in Germany, although not yet in full control. His own wife would later become a party member. He made a film that has been credited with forming two genres: the serial killer movie and the police procedural. And he filled it with grotesques. Was there something beneath the surface, some visceral feeling about his society that this story allowed him to express?

When you watch *M,* you see a hatred for the Germany of the early 1930s that is visible and palpable. Apart from a few perfunctory shots of everyday bourgeoisie life (such as the pathetic scene of the mother waiting

275

for her little girl to return from school), the entire movie consists of men seen in shadows, in smoke-filled dens, in disgusting dives, in conspiratorial conferences. And the faces of these men are cruel caricatures: fleshy, twisted, beetle-browed, dark-jowled, out of proportion. One is reminded of the stark faces of the accusing judges in Carl Theodor Dreyer's *The Passion of Joan of Arc* (1928), but those are more forbidding than ugly.

What I sense is that Lang hated the people around him, hated Nazism, and hated Germany for permitting it. His next film, *The Testament of Dr. Mabuse* (1933), had villains who were unmistakably Nazis. It was banned by the censors, but Joseph Goebbels, so the story goes, offered Lang control of the nation's film industry if he would come on board with the Nazis. He fled, he claimed, on a midnight train—although Patrick McGilligan's book *Fritz Lang: The Nature of the Beast* is dubious about many of Lang's grandiose claims.

Certainly *M* is a portrait of a diseased society, one that seems even more decadent than the other portraits of Berlin in the 1930s. Its characters have no virtues and lack even attractive vices. In other stories of the time, we see nightclubs, champagne, sex, and perversion. When *M* visits a bar, it is to show close-ups of greasy sausages, spilled beer, rotten cheese, and stale cigar butts.

The film's story was inspired by the career of a serial killer in Düsseldorf. In *M*, Hans Beckert preys on children—offering them candy and friendship and then killing them. The murders are all offscreen, and Lang suggests the first one with a classic montage that includes the little victim's empty dinner plate, her mother calling frantically down an empty spiral staircase, and her balloon—bought for her by the killer—caught in electric wires.

There is no suspense about the murderer's identity. Early in the film, we see Beckert looking at himself in a mirror. Peter Lorre at the time was twenty-six, plump, baby-faced, clean-shaven, and as he looks at his reflected image, he pulls down the corners of his mouth and tries to make hideous faces, to see in himself the monster others see in him. His presence in the movie is often implied rather than seen; he compulsively whistles the same tune, from *Peer Gynt,* over and over, until the notes stand in for the murders.

The city is in turmoil. The killer must be caught. The police put all their men on the case, making life unbearable for the criminal element ("There are more cops on the streets than girls," a pimp complains). To reduce the heat, the city's criminals team up to find the killer, and as Lang intercuts between two summit conferences—the cops and the criminals—we are struck by how similar the two groups are, visually. Both sit around tables in gloomy rooms, smoking so voluminously that at times their very faces are invisible. In their fat fingers their cigars look fecal. (As the criminals agree that murdering children violates their code, I was reminded of the summit on drugs in *The Godfather*.)

M was Lang's first sound picture, and he was wise to use dialogue so sparingly. Many early talkies felt they had to talk all the time, but Lang allows his camera to prowl through the streets and dives, providing a rat's-eye view. One of the film's most spectacular shots is utterly silent, as the captured killer is dragged into a basement to be confronted by the city's assembled criminals, and the camera shows their faces: hard, cold, closed, implacable.

It is at this inquisition that Lorre delivers his famous speech in defense, or explanation. Sweating with terror, his face a fright mask, he cries out, "I can't help myself! I haven't any control over this evil thing that's inside of me! The fire, the voices, the torment!" He tries to describe how the compulsion follows him through the streets, and ends, "Who knows what it's like to be me?"

This is always said to be Lorre's first screen performance, although McGilligan establishes that it was his third. It was certainly the performance that fixed his image forever, during a long Hollywood career in which he became one of Warner Bros.'s most famous character actors (*Casablanca, The Maltese Falcon, The Mask of Dimitrios*). He was also a comedian and a song-and-dance man, and although you can see him opposite Fred Astaire in *Silk Stockings* (1957), it was by playing psychopaths that he supported himself. He died in 1964.

Fritz Lang (1890–1976) became, in America, a famous director of film noir. His credits include *You Only Live Once* (1937, based on the Bonnie and Clyde story), Graham Greene's *Ministry of Fear* (1944), *The Big Heat* (1953, with Lee Marvin hurling hot coffee in Gloria Grahame's face), and *While the City Sleeps* (1956, another story about a manhunt). He was often accused of sadism toward his actors; he had Lorre thrown down the stairs into the criminal lair a dozen times, and Peter Bogdanovich describes a scene in Lang's *Western Union* (1941) where Randolph Scott tries to burn the ropes off his bound wrists. John Ford, watching the movie, said, "Those are Randy's wrists, that is real rope, that is a real fire."

For years *M* was available only in scratchy, dim prints. Even my earlier laser disc is only marginally watchable. The new version, restored by the Munich Film Archive, is not only better to look at but easier to follow, since more of the German dialogue has been subtitled. (Lorre also recorded a sound track in English, which should be made available as an option on the eventual DVD version.) Watching the new print of *M*, I found the film more powerful than I remembered, because I was not watching it through a haze of disintegration.

And what a haunting film it is. It doesn't ask for sympathy for the killer, Hans Beckert, but it asks for understanding. As he says in his own defense, he cannot escape or control the evil compulsions that overtake him. Elsewhere in the film, an innocent old man, suspected of being the killer, is attacked by a mob that forms on the spot. Each of the mob members was presumably capable of telling right from wrong and controlling his actions (as Beckert was not), and yet as a mob they moved with the same compulsion to kill. There is a message there somewhere. Not "somewhere," really, but right up front, where it's a wonder it escaped the attention of the Nazi censors.

THE MALTESE FALCON

Among the movies we not only love but treasure, *The Maltese Falcon* stands as a great divide. Consider what was true after its release in 1941 and was not true before:

(1) The movie defined Humphrey Bogart's performances for the rest of his life; his hard-boiled Sam Spade rescued him from a decade of middling roles in B gangster movies and positioned him for *Casablanca* (1943), *The Treasure of the Sierra Madre* (1948), *The African Queen* (1951), and his other classics. (2) It was the first film directed by John Huston, who for more than forty years would be a prolific maker of movies that were muscular, stylish, and daring. (3) It contained the first screen appearance of Sydney Greenstreet, who went on, in *Casablanca* and many other films, to become one of the most striking character actors in movie history. (4) It was the first pairing of Greenstreet and Peter Lorre, and so well did they work together that they made nine other movies, including *Casablanca*—and *The Mask of Dimitrios* (1944), in which they were not supporting actors, but actually the stars. (5) And some film histories consider *The Maltese Falcon* the first film noir. It put down the foundations for that native American genre of mean streets, knife-edged heroes, dark shadows, and tough dames.

Of course film noir was waiting to be born. It was already there in the novels of Dashiell Hammett, who wrote *The Maltese Falcon,* and the work of Raymond Chandler, James M. Cain, John O'Hara, and the other boys in the back room. "Down these mean streets a man must go who is not himself mean," wrote Chandler, and that was true of his hero, Philip Marlowe (whom Bogart would play). But it wasn't true of Hammett's Sam Spade, who *was* mean and who set the stage for a decade in which unsentimental heroes talked tough and cracked wise.

The moment everyone remembers from *The Maltese Falcon* comes near the end, when Brigid O'Shaughnessy (Mary Astor) has been collared for murdering Spade's partner. She says she loves Spade. She asks if Sam loves her. She pleads for him to spare her from the law. And he replies, in a speech some people can quote by heart, "I hope they don't hang you, precious, for that sweet neck . . . The chances are you'll get off with life. That means if you're a good girl, you'll be out in twenty years. I'll be waiting for you. If they hang you, I'll always remember you."

Cold. Spade is cold and hard, like his name. When he gets the news that his partner has been murdered, he doesn't blink an eye. Didn't like the guy. Kisses his widow the moment they're alone together. Beats up Joel Cairo (Lorre) not just because he has to but because Cairo carries a perfumed handkerchief, and you know what that meant in a 1941 movie. Turns the rough stuff on and off. Loses patience with Greenstreet, throws his cigar into the fire, smashes his glass, barks out a threat, slams the door, and then grins to himself in the hallway, amused by his own act.

If he didn't like his partner, Spade nevertheless observes a sort of code involving his death. "When a man's partner is killed," he tells Brigid, "he's supposed to do something about it." He doesn't like the cops, either; the only person he really seems to like is his secretary, Effie (Lee Patrick), who sits on his desk, lights his cigarettes, knows his sins and accepts them. How do Bogart and Huston get away with making such a dark guy the hero of a film? Because he does his job according to the rules he lives by, and because we sense (as we always would with Bogart after this role) that the toughness conceals old wounds and broken dreams.

John Huston (1906–87) had worked as a writer at Warner Bros. before convincing the studio to let him direct. *The Maltese Falcon* was his first choice, even though it had been filmed twice before by Warner's (in 1931 under the same title, and in 1936 as *Satan Met a Lady*). "They were such wretched pictures," Huston told his biographer, Lawrence Grobel. He saw

Hammett's vision more clearly, saw that the story was not about plot but about character, saw that to soften Sam Spade would be deadly, fought the tendency (even then) for the studio to pine for a happy ending.

When he finished his screenplay, he set to work storyboarding it, sketching every shot. That was the famous method of Hitchcock, whose *Rebecca* won the Oscar as the best picture of 1940. Like Orson Welles, who was directing *Citizen Kane* across town, Huston was excited by new stylistic possibilities; he gave great thought to composition and camera movement. To view the film in a stop-action analysis, as I have, is to appreciate complex shots that work so well they seem simple. Huston and his cinematographer, Arthur Edeson, accomplished things that in their way were as impressive as what Welles and Gregg Toland were doing on *Kane*.

Consider an astonishing unbroken seven-minute take. Grobel's book *The Hustons* quotes Meta Wilde, Huston's longtime script supervisor:

> It was an incredible camera setup. We rehearsed two days. The camera followed Greenstreet and Bogart from one room into another, then down a long hallway, and finally into a living room; there the camera moved up and down in what is referred to as a boom-up and boom-down shot, then panned from left to right and back to Bogart's drunken face; the next pan shot was to Greenstreet's massive stomach from Bogart's point of view . . . One miss and we had to begin all over again.

Was the shot just a stunt? Not at all; most viewers don't notice it, because they're swept along by its flow. And consider another shot, where Greenstreet chatters about the falcon while waiting for a drugged drink to knock out Bogart. Huston's strategy is crafty. Earlier, Greenstreet has set it up by making a point: "I distrust a man who says 'when.' If he's got to be careful not to drink too much, it's because he's not to be trusted when he does." Now he offers Bogart a drink, but Bogart doesn't sip from it. Greenstreet talks on, and tops up Bogart's glass. He still doesn't drink. Greenstreet watches him narrowly. They discuss the value of the missing black bird. Finally Bogart drinks and passes out. The timing is everything; Huston doesn't give us close-ups of the glass to underline the possibility that it's drugged. He depends on the situation to generate the suspicion in our minds. (This was, by the way, Greenstreet's first scene in the movies.)

The plot is the last thing you think of about *The Maltese Falcon*. The black bird (said to be made of gold and encrusted with jewels) has been stolen, men have been killed for it, and now Gutman (Greenstreet) has arrived with his lackeys (Lorre and Elisha Cook, Jr.) to get it back. Spade gets involved because the Mary Astor character hires him to—but the plot goes around and around, and eventually we realize that the black bird is an example of Hitchcock's "MacGuffin"—it doesn't matter what it is so long as everyone in the story wants or fears it.

To describe the plot in a linear and logical fashion is almost impossible. That doesn't matter. The movie is essentially a series of conversations punctuated by brief, violent interludes. It's all style. It isn't violence or chases, but the way the actors look, move, speak, and embody their characters. Under the style is attitude: Hard men, in a hard season, in a society emerging from Depression and heading for war, are motivated by greed and capable of murder. For an hourly fee, Sam Spade will negotiate this terrain. Everything there is to know about Sam Spade is contained in the scene where Brigid asks for his help and he criticizes her performance: "You're good. It's chiefly your eyes, I think—and that throb you get in your voice when you say things like, 'Be generous, Mr. Spade.'" He always stands outside, sizing things up. Few Hollywood heroes before 1941 kept such a distance from the conventional pieties of the plot.

I had forgotten what perfect pitch Woody Allen brought to *Manhattan*—how its tone and timing slip so gracefully between comedy and romance. I hadn't seen it in years, and remembered mostly the broad outlines, the one-liners, the romance between a middle-aged man and a high school girl. Seeing it again, I realize it's more subtle, more complex, and not about love, but loss. There are a lot of songs on the sound track, but the one that speaks for the hero says "they're playing songs of love, but not for me."

The movie's May–November romance was criticized because Isaac (Woody Allen) and Tracy (Mariel Hemingway) seem to have so little in common. But she at least has what lovers need, an ability to idealize the other person, and that's his fatal lack in the relationship: He doesn't feel she's special enough, and he doesn't see a future for them. Urging her to go to London on a scholarship, he consoles her, "You'll think of me as a fond memory." He spends half of their time together trying to break up, and finally succeeds, taking her to a soda fountain after school—a location with perfect irony, given her age—to tell her he loves another woman, which is not exactly true. "Now I don't feel so good," she says, in one of several lines that Hemingway makes both simple and heartbreaking.

Only later, too much later, does Isaac confess to a friend, "I think I really missed a good bet when I let Tracy go." Well, maybe he did, or maybe he was right and there was no plausible future between a forty-two-year-old

(however immature) and a seventeen-year-old. The movie isn't about that. It's about the cynicism and superficiality of the modern mating dance, and how all Isaac's glib sophistication can't save him from true feelings, when they come.

His character is surrounded by other adults who inhabit the wreckage of relationships. Isaac's former wife (Meryl Streep) left him to live with a woman and writes a best-seller ridiculing their marriage and love life; we doubt her new relationship is sound if it leaves her so obsessed with the previous one. Yale (Michael Murphy) has been happily married for years but is having an affair with Mary (Diane Keaton). Both men have the tactic of trying to escape from relationships by telling the woman it's for her own good. Allen has Mary tell Yale they have no future, right after Isaac has told Tracy the same thing. Yale even more or less gives Mary to Isaac, to get her off his hands ("You'd be great for her"), and they have a little fling before Yale realizes he loves her, after all.

Neither man can deal with affection. Both hide behind words but are powerless in the face of emotional truth. The movie is not really about love in the present, but love in the past—about the wistful pain when we realize we had a beautiful thing and screwed it up. In a more conventional movie, Yale and Mary would be the central couple, and Isaac and Tracy would be their best friends; authors since Shakespeare have mirrored their heroic lovers with comedic counterpoints, but Allen's whole career is based on making the secondary characters heroic. The relationship of Isaac and Mary is not a romantic comedy, then, but complex and tricky, and unforgiving in the way it sees Isaac running in place because he doesn't know whether to run toward Mary or away from her.

It is at the same time a breathtaking hymn to the idea of being in love in Manhattan, a city Allen loves. The opening shot is a stunner, looking west across Central Park at dawn while Gershwin's "Rhapsody in Blue" does what it always does—makes us feel transcendent. The locations are like an anthology of Manhattan shrines: The characters visit the Guggenheim, Elaine's, Zabar's deli. They sit on a park bench at dawn beneath a towering bridge, and ride a carriage through Central Park, and row boats in the lagoon. They go to art movies and concerts and eat Chinese food in bed and play racquetball. Allen knows that songs are the sound tracks of our lives and gives us not only "But Not for Me" but "Sweet and Lowdown," "I Got a Crush on You," "Do Do Do," "Lady Be Good," "Embraceable You," "Someone to Watch over Me," and, when Isaac runs and runs to the girl he finally realizes he loves, "Strike Up the Band."

All of these locations and all of these songs would not have the effect they do without the wide-screen black-and-white cinematography of Gordon Willis. This is one of the best-photographed movies ever made, and a compelling argument for letterboxing on home video, since many of the compositions exploit the full width of the screen. Consider, for example, the sweet little conversation Isaac and Tracy have in his apartment, in a pool of light in the lower left corner of the screen, while the empty apartment stretches out toward a spiral staircase on the right: How better to show Tracy bringing life into this vast but lonely home?

Some of the scenes are famous just because of Willis's lighting. For example, the way Isaac and Mary walk through the observatory as if they're strolling among the stars or on the surface of the moon. Later, as their conversation gets a little lost, Willis daringly lets them disappear into darkness and then finds them again with just a sliver of sidelighting.

Keaton, of course, was famous after *The Godfather* (1972), but she became a star and won an Oscar in Allen's *Annie Hall* (1977). *Manhattan*, made two years later, has echoes of Annie in Mary, but they're more a case of Keaton's personal mannerisms than of a similarity in the characters. Mary is less flighty, less a deliberate eccentric, more a woman who uses her bright intelligence as a shield against loneliness. She's too smart to cause trouble and too careless to stay out of it; she tells the married Yale she doesn't want him to leave his wife, she doesn't want to be a home breaker, yet she loves him—and she's stuck on Sunday afternoons with no one to talk to or play with. "It's just bad timing," she finally says. Her fling with Isaac is really based on their mutual isolation; they don't have anyone else to call.

This was Mariel Hemingway's first substantial role, and it won her an Oscar nomination. Like her character, she was just turning eighteen. Her performance is so direct, so artless, so without affect, that it goes straight to the heart of the matter. And her size plays an interesting role in the movie. She is, of course, taller than Allen, but the meaning of that difference is not as simple as the tall girl/short guy syndrome. Seeing them together on the screen, I was struck by how unconcealable she is, how her presence is such an inescapable fact; in social situations, Isaac tends to take cover, to hide behind his wit, to make guerrilla raids on conversations, and this girl at his side makes him so visible. She attracts enemy fire. Watch Isaac's face when Mary asks, "And what do you do, Tracy?" and she replies, "I go to high school."

Woody Allen, it is said, always plays the same character in his movies. This is unfair. He often has the same verbal facility, yes, and some of the same mannerisms, but Isaac here is seen very specifically as a man whose yearnings and insecurities are founded on a deep immaturity. He wants, but doesn't know what he wants. He quits his job in an attack of ethics but has no backup plan. Look at Allen's face in Isaac's final scene with Tracy, as he pleads with her to stay with him, to not go to London, even while he realizes he is simply being selfish. A lesser actor would have gone over the top in the pleading and then overdone the disappointment. Allen finds the difficult, precise tone of a man who desires and regrets and yet actually does like this young woman enough to know she's doing the right thing. He had her but he lost her, and now they both know their time has passed. He isn't planning the future, but trying to rewrite the past. She'll think of him as a fond memory.

{ McCabe & Mrs. Miller }

It is not often given to a director to make a perfect film. Some spend their lives trying, but always fall short. Robert Altman has made a dozen films that can be called great in one way or another, but one of them is perfect, and that one is *McCabe & Mrs. Miller* (1971). This is one of the saddest films I have ever seen, filled with a yearning for love and home that will not ever come—not for McCabe, not with Mrs. Miller, not in the town of Presbyterian Church, which cowers under a gray sky always heavy with rain or snow. The film is a poem—an elegy for the dead.

Few films have such an overwhelming sense of location. Presbyterian Church is a town thrown together out of raw lumber, hewn from the forests that threaten to reclaim it. The earth is either mud or frozen ice. The days are short and there is little light inside, just enough from a gas lamp to make a gold tooth sparkle, a teardrop glisten. This is not the kind of movie where the characters are introduced. They are all already here. They have been here for a long time. They know all about one another.

A man rides into town through the rain. He walks into a saloon, makes sure he knows where the back door is, goes out to his horse again, comes in with a cloth, and covers a table. The men are pulling up chairs before he has settled down. He is a gambler named McCabe (Warren Beatty). Somebody thinks he heard that McCabe once shot a man. In the background, somebody is vaguely heard asking, "Laura, what's for dinner?"

This is the classic Altman style, which emerged full-blown in *MASH* (1970) and can be seen in *3 Women* (1977), *Thieves Like Us* (1974), *Nashville* (1975), *California Split* (1974), *The Long Goodbye* (1973), *The Player* (1992), *Cookie's Fortune* (1999), and all the others. It begins with one fundamental assumption: All of the characters know each other, and the camera will not stare at first one and then another, like an earnest dog, but is at home in their company. Nor do the people line up and talk one after another, like characters in a play. They talk when and as they will, and we understand it's not important to hear every word; sometimes all that matters is the tone of a room.

The town of Presbyterian Church is almost all male, and most of the men are involved in building the town. It looks like a construction site, holes half-dug, lumber piled up waiting to be used, an old painted door joined to a raw new frame. Apart from work, there is nothing to do but drink, gamble, and hire the pleasures of women. McCabe takes his winnings and purchases three fancy women—not as entertainment, as an investment. They're not too fancy; one is fat, one has no teeth, they all look scrubbed with too much cheap soap. His plan is to open a whorehouse and saloon, with a bathhouse in the back.

Mrs. Miller (Julie Christie) arrives in town and wants to become his partner. She is a Cockney who has long since ceased to be interested in her own beauty, except for what it will earn her. She explains to McCabe that he knows nothing of women, cannot see through their excuses, cannot quiet their fears or see them through female troubles, does not even know enough to keep the whole town from being clapped out within a week. She will import some classier women from San Francisco. They will do better than he can do on his own. He has to agree.

We get to know them in half-seen, half-heard moments. There is a time when he gets into bed with her, and we realize with a start that the movie has not established that they are sleeping together. Later, it doubles back to reveal that she charges him, just like all the others. She gets five dollars, top price. McCabe spends a lot of time talking to himself, muttering criticisms and vows. He says to himself what he would like to say to her: "If just one time you could be sweet without money to it." And, "I got poetry in me!" His soliloquies are meandering, rueful, oblique. His most sustained

burst of conversational energy is a joke he tells about a frog; he does it in dialect, and I think it's a private joke, since he sounds uncannily like Gene Hackman's character Buck in *Bonnie and Clyde*.

There is always money involved. One day a man named Bart dies, and they bury him. At the funeral, Mrs. Miller and Bart's widow (Shelley Duvall) make eye contact. That night they are talking. The widow will have to become a whore. She knows it, Mrs. Miller knows it, the whole town knows it. How else can she support herself? "It's what you were doing before with Bart," Mrs. Miller explains, "only now you can keep some of the money for yourself."

Men arrive from a big mining company to make McCabe an offer for his holdings. Full of beans, he rejects their offer and names his price, much too high. That night he brags to Mrs. Miller, whose face shows what a mistake he has made. The men are gone by breakfast time. Miller rides into town to try to accept their offer, but is too late to find them. He knows the company will send someone to kill him.

All of this unfolds mostly indoors, in dark rooms lit by lanterns and log fires. Episodes are punctuated by Leonard Cohen songs, sad frontier laments. The cinematographer, Vilmos Zsigmond, embraces the freedom of the wide-screen Panavision image (this was before screens got narrower again to accommodate home video). He drowns the characters in nature. It is dark, wet, cold, and then it snows. These are simple people. There is a moment when two couples are dancing to a music box in the whorehouse parlor. It comes to the end of a tune, and all four cluster around the box, bending low, peering at its mechanism, poised in suspense. The next tune begins and they spring up, relieved, to dance again.

Life is cheap here. The film shows one of the most heartbreaking deaths in the history of the western. A goofy kid (Keith Carradine) has ridden into town and visited all the girls in the house. Now he has started across a suspension bridge. A young gunslinger approaches from the other side and cold-bloodedly talks him into being shot to death. The kid knows he is going to get shot. He tries to be friendly and ingratiating, but the time has come. The town looks on, impassive. You don't want to be caught on a bridge facing a guy like that. We realize at the end of the film that this episode on the bridge is the whole story in microcosm: Some people are just incapable of not getting themselves killed.

Snows falls steadily all through the closing passages of the film. There is no musical sound track, apart from the Cohen songs. McCabe is tracked through the town by three hired killers, including the young gunslinger. The snow falls so heavily, blowing at a slant, it is like unheard music. In some movies, the hero gets killed, and then there is a shot of his woman, looking sad. Here we see Mrs. Miller looking sad even before McCabe meets his fate. She is in the opium den down in the Chinatown end of Presbyterian Church. Her attention is focused on pretty colors and surfaces. This time and place are so dead for her that she simply shuts down her mind.

Study the title. *McCabe & Mrs. Miller.* Not "and," as in a couple, but "&," as in a corporation. It is a business arrangement. Everything is business with her. What sorrows she knew before she arrived in Presbyterian Church are behind her now. Everything else is behind her now too, the opium promises. Poor McCabe. He had poetry in him. Too bad he rode into a town where nobody knew what poetry was but one, and she already lost to it.

{ METROPOLIS }

Stirred by the visionary images of *Dark City,* I revisited Fritz Lang's *Metropolis* and once again fell under its eerie spell. The movie has a plot that defies common sense, but its very discontinuity is a strength. It makes *Metropolis* hallucinatory—a nightmare without the reassurance of a steadying story line. Few films have ever been more visually exhilarating.

Generally considered the first great science fiction film, *Metropolis* (1927) fixed for the rest of the century the image of a futuristic city as a hell of scientific progress and human despair. From this film, in various ways, descended not only *Dark City* but *Blade Runner, The Fifth Element, Alphaville, Escape from L.A., Gattaca,* and Batman's Gotham City. The laboratory of its evil genius, Rotwang, created the visual look of mad scientists for decades to come, especially after it was mirrored in *Bride of Frankenstein* (1935). And the device of the "false Maria," the robot who looks like a human being, inspired the "replicants" of *Blade Runner.* Even Rotwang's artificial hand was given homage in *Dr. Strangelove.*

What many of these movies have in common is a loner hero who discovers the inner workings of the future society, penetrating the system that would control the population. Even Batman's villains are the descendants of Rotwang, giggling as they pull the levers that will enforce their will. The buried message is powerful: Science and industry will become the weapons of demagogues.

Metropolis employed vast sets, 25,000 extras, and astonishing special effects to create two worlds: the great city of Metropolis, with its stadiums, skyscrapers, and expressways in the sky, and the subterranean workers' city, where the clockface shows ten hours to cram another day into the workweek. Lang's film is the summit of German expressionism, the combination of stylized sets, dramatic camera angles, bold shadows, and frankly artificial theatrics.

The production itself made even Stanley Kubrick's mania for control look benign. According to Patrick McGilligan's book *Fritz Lang: The Nature of the Beast*, the extras were hurled into violent mob scenes, made to stand for hours in cold water, and handled more like props than human beings. The heroine was made to jump from high places, and when she was burned at a stake, Lang used real flames. The irony was that Lang's directorial style was not unlike the approach of the villain in his film.

The story tells of a great city whose two halves—the pampered citizens of the surface and the slaves of the depths—are ignorant of one another. The city is run by the ruthless Joh Fredersen (Alfred Abel), a businessman-dictator. His son, Freder (Gustav Fröhlich), is in the Pleasure Gardens one day when Maria (Brigitte Helm), a woman from the subterranean city, brings a group of workers' children to the surface. Freder, struck by Maria's beauty and astonished to learn of the life led by the workers, seeks out the demented genius Rotwang (Rudolf Klein-Rogge), who knows the secrets of the lower world.

What follows is Freder's descent into the depths and his attempts to help the workers, who are rallied by the revolutionary Maria. Meanwhile, Rotwang devises a robot, captures the real Maria, and transfers her face to the robot—so that the workers, still following Maria, can be fooled and controlled. (The electrical arcs, bubbling beakers, glowing rings of light, and mad-scientist props in the transformation sequence have influenced a thousand films.)

Lang develops this story with scenes of astonishing originality. Consider the first glimpse of the underground power plant, with workers straining to move heavy dial hands back and forth. What they're doing makes no logical sense, but visually the connection is obvious: They are controlled like hands on a clock. And when the machinery explodes, Freder has a vision in which the machinery turns into an obscene devouring monster.

Other dramatic visual sequences: A chase scene in the darkened catacombs, with the real Maria pursued by Rotwang (the beam of his light is like a club to bludgeon her). The image of the Tower of Babel as Maria addresses the workers. Their faces, arrayed in darkness from the top to the bottom of the screen. The doors in Rotwang's house, opening and closing on their own. The lascivious dance of the false Maria, as the workers look on and the screen fills with large, wet, staring eyeballs. The flood of the lower city, and the undulating arms of the children flocking to Maria to be saved.

The gaps and logical puzzles of the story (some caused by clumsy reediting after the film left Lang's hands) are swept away by this torrent of images. "To enjoy the film the viewer must observe but never think," the critic Arthur Lenning said, and Pauline Kael contrasted its "moments of almost incredible beauty and power" with "absurd ineptitudes." Even when the plot seems adrift, however, the movie itself never lacks confidence: The city and system are so overpowering they dwarf any merely logical problems. Although Lang saw his movie as antiauthoritarian, the Nazis liked it enough to offer him control of their film industry (he fled to America instead). Some of the ideas in *Metropolis* seem echoed in Leni Riefenstahl's pro-Hitler *Triumph of the Will* (1935)—where, of course, they have lost their irony.

Much of what we see in *Metropolis* doesn't exist except in visual trickery. The visual effects were the work of Eugen Schüfftan, who later worked in 1960s Hollywood as the cinematographer of *Lilith* and *The Hustler*. According to *Magill's Survey of Cinema*, "his photographic system allowed people and miniature sets to be combined in a single shot, through the use of mirrors, rather than laboratory work." Other effects were created in the camera by cinematographer Karl Freund.

The result was astonishing for its time. Without all of the digital tricks of today, *Metropolis* fills the imagination. Today the effects look like effects, but that's their appeal. Looking at the original *King Kong* not long ago, I found that its effects, primitive by modern standards, gained a certain weird effectiveness. Because they looked strange and unworldly compared to the slick, utterly convincing effects that are now possible, they were *more* evocative: The effects in movies like *Jurassic Park* and *Titanic* are done so well, by comparison, that we simply think we are looking at real things, which is not quite the same kind of fun.

Metropolis has not existed for years in the version that Lang completed. It was chopped by distributors, censors, and exhibitors, key footage was lost, and only by referring to the novelization of the story by Thea von Harbou can various story gaps be explained. In 1984, a reconstructed version was released, adding footage gathered from Germany and Australia to existing prints, and that version, produced by Giorgio Moroder, was then color-tinted "according to Lang's original intentions" and given an MTV-style musical score. This is the version most often seen today. Purists quite reasonably object to it, but one can turn off the sound and dial down the color to create a silent b&w print. I am not crazy about the sound track, but in watching the Moroder version I enjoyed the tinting and felt that Lang's vision was so powerful it swept aside the quibbles: Best to see this well-restored print with all the available footage than to stand entirely on principle.

Metropolis does what many great films do, creating a time, place, and characters so striking that they become part of our arsenal of images for imagining the world. The ideas of *Metropolis* have been so often absorbed into popular culture that its horrific future city is almost a given (when Albert Brooks dared to create a utopian future in *Defending Your Life,* it seemed wrong, somehow, without satanic urban hellscapes). Lang filmed for nearly a year, driven by obsession, often cruel to his colleagues, a perfectionist madman, and the result is one of those seminal films without which the others cannot be fully appreciated.

{ MR. HULOT'S HOLIDAY }

The first time I saw Jacques Tati's *Mr. Hulot's Holiday*, I didn't laugh as much as I thought I was supposed to. But I didn't forget the film, and I saw it again in a film class, and then bought the laser disc and saw it a third and fourth time, and by then it had become part of my treasure. But I still didn't laugh as much as I thought I was supposed to, and now I think I understand why. It is not a comedy of hilarity, but a comedy of memory, nostalgia, fondness, and good cheer. There are some real laughs in it, but *Mr. Hulot's Holiday* gives us something rarer: an amused affection for human nature—so odd, so valuable, so particular.

The movie was released in 1953 and played for months, even years, in art cinemas. *Mr. Hulot* was as big a hit in its time as *Like Water for Chocolate*, *The Gods Must Be Crazy*, and other small films that people recommend to each other. There was a time when any art theater could do a week's good business just by booking *Hulot*. Jacques Tati (1909–82) made only four more features in the next twenty years, much labored over, much admired, but this is the film he will be remembered for.

The movie tells the story of Mr. Hulot's holiday by the sea, in Brittany. As played by Tati, Hulot is a tall man, all angles, "a creature of silhouettes," as Stanley Kauffmann observed: "There is never a close-up of him, and his facial expressions count for little." He arrives at the seaside in his improbable little car, which looks like it was made for a soap box derby and rides on bicycle wheels. (I always assumed this vehicle was built for the movie, but no: It is a 1924 Amilcar and must have given its original owners many perplexing moments.)

Hulot, decked out in holiday gear and smoking a pipe, is friendly to a fault, but he is the man nobody quite sees. The holidaymakers are distracted by their own worlds, companions, and plans, and notice Hulot only when something goes wrong, as it often does. The lobby of his seaside hotel, for example, is an island of calm until he leaves the door open, so that the wind can create a series of small but amusing annoyances which must have taken days to set up.

Tati doesn't make a big point of establishing characters, but gradually we recognize faces. There is a pretty blonde (Nathalie Pascaud) who is on holiday by herself, and is always cheerful, in a detached sort of way. Hulot the eligible bachelor walks out with her, takes her for a ride, and even attempts unsuccessfully to go horseback riding with her, but she keeps him at a distance with her smile; she remains an elusive vision, like the blonde in the convertible in *American Graffiti*. Others are busy beavering away at being themselves. There is a waiter who cannot believe the trouble people put him to. An old couple who think they have been assigned to inspect everything in their path. A retired general, easily offended. Small children who are protected by the god of children, so their ice cream cone seems certain to spill but never quite does.

Mr. Hulot's Holiday is a French film, with hardly any words in it. It plays as a silent film with music (a lilting, repetitive melody), a lot of sound effects, and half-heard voices. Tati was a silent clown; he worked as a mime as a young man, and his Hulot seems to lack the knack of getting into a conversation.

The movie is constructed with the meticulous attention to detail of a Keaton or Chaplin. Sight gags are set up with such patience that they seem to expose hidden functions in the clockwork of the universe. Consider the scene where Hulot is painting his kayak, and the tide carries the paint can out to sea and then floats it in again, perfectly timed, when his brush is ready for it again. How was this scene done? Is it a trick, or did Tati actually experiment with tides and cans until he got it right? Is it "funny"? No, it is miraculous. The sea is indifferent to painters, but nevertheless provides the can when it is needed, and life goes on, and the boat gets painted.

And then consider Tati when he goes out paddling in his tiny

kayak, which like his car is the wrong size for him. It capsizes. In another comedy, that would mean the hero gets wet, and we're supposed to laugh. Not here; the boat folds up in just such a way that it looks like a shark, and there is a panic on the beach. Hulot remains oblivious. There is an almost spiritual acceptance in his behavior; nothing goes as planned, but nothing surprises him.

Not only sights but sounds have a will of their own in Tati's universe. Listen to the thwanking sound made by the door in the hotel dining room. Does it annoy Hulot, who has been placed at the Lonely Guy table near to it? Probably, but it is in the nature of the door to thwank, and we sense that it has thwanked for a generation, and will thwank until the day the little clapboard hotel is torn down to put up a beachfront gargantoplex.

Let me try to explain my relationship with *Hulot*. The first time I saw it, I expected something along the lines of a Hollywood screwball comedy. Instead, the movie opens with its sweet little melody, which is quite pleased that life goes on. Hulot arrives (inconveniencing a dog that wants to sleep in the road) and tries his best to be a well-behaved holidaymaker. He is so polite that when the announcer on the hotel's radio says, "Good night, everybody!" he bows and doffs his hat. Because there were no close-ups, because the movie did not insist on exactly who Hulot was, he became the audience—he was me.

I met all the people Hulot met, I became accustomed to their daily perambulations as he did, and I accompanied him as he blundered into a funeral and was mistaken as a mourner, and when he was accosted by a rug, and when a towrope boinged him into the sea. And then the holiday was over, and everyone began to pack and leave, and there was the hint of how lonely this coastal village would be until next summer, when exactly the same people would return to do exactly the same things.

When I saw the film a second time, the wonderful thing was, it was like returning to the hotel. It wasn't like I was seeing the film again; it was like I was recognizing the people from last year. There's the old couple again (good, they made it through another year), the waiter (where does he work in the winter?), and the blond girl (still no man in her life; maybe this is the summer that . . .).

When has a film so subtly and yet so completely captured nostalgia for past happiness? The movie is about the simplest of human pleasures: the desire to get away for a few days, to play instead of work, to breathe in the sea air, and maybe meet someone nice. It is about the hope that under-lies all vacations and the sadness that ends them. And it is amused, too, that we go about our days so intently while the sea and the sky go about theirs.

{ MY DARLING CLEMENTINE }

"What kind of town *is* this?" Wyatt Earp asks on his first night in Tombstone. "A man can't get a shave without gettin' his head blowed off." He gets up out of the newfangled barber's chair at the Bon Ton Tonsorial Parlor and climbs through the second-story window of a saloon, his face still half-lathered, to konk a gun-toting drunk on the head and drag him out by the heels.

Earp (Henry Fonda) already knows what kind of town it is. In the opening scenes of John Ford's greatest western, *My Darling Clementine* (1946), he and his brothers are driving cattle east to Kansas. Wyatt, Virgil, and Morgan leave the herd in charge of their kid brother, James, and go into town for a shave and a beer. As they ride down the main street of Tombstone, under a vast and lowering evening sky, gunshots and raucous laughter are heard in the saloons, and we don't have to ask why the town has the biggest graveyard west of the Rockies.

Ford's story reenacts the central morality play of the western. Wyatt Earp becomes the town's new marshal, there's a showdown between law and anarchy, the law wins, and the last shot features the new schoolmarm—who represents the arrival of civilization. Most westerns put the emphasis on the showdown. *My Darling Clementine* builds up to the legendary gunfight at the OK Corral, but it is more about everyday things—haircuts, romance, friendship, poker, and illness.

At the center of the film is Henry Fonda's performance as Wyatt Earp. He's usually shown as a man of action, but Fonda makes him the new-style westerner, who stands up when a woman comes into the room, and knows how to carve a chicken and dance a reel. Like a teenager, he sits in a chair on the veranda of his office, tilts back to balance on the back legs, and pushes off against a railing with one boot and then the other. He's thinking of Clementine, and Fonda shows his happiness with body language.

Earp has accepted the marshal's badge because when he and his brothers returned to their herd, they found the cattle rustled and James dead. There is every reason to believe the crime was committed by Old Man Clanton (Walter Brennan) and his "boys" (grown, bearded, and mean). An early scene ends with Clanton baring his teeth like an animal showing its fangs. Earp buries James in a touching scene ("You didn't get much of a chance, did you, James?"). Then, instead of riding into town and shooting the Clantons, he tells the mayor he'll become the new marshal. He wants his revenge, but legally.

The most important relationship in the movie is between Earp and Doc Holliday (Victor Mature), the professional gambler who runs Tombstone but is dying of TB. They are natural enemies, but a quiet, unspoken regard grows up between the two men, maybe because Earp senses the sadness at Holliday's core. Holliday's rented room has his medical diploma on the wall and his doctor's bag beneath it, but he doesn't practice anymore. Something went wrong back East, and now he gambles for a living and drinks himself into oblivion. His lover is a prostitute, Chihuahua (Linda Darnell), and he talks about leaving for Mexico with her. But as he coughs up blood, he knows what his prognosis is.

The marshal's first showdown with Holliday is a classic Ford scene. The saloon grows quiet when Doc walks in, and the bar clears when he stands at it. He walks up to Earp at the bar and tells him, "Draw!" Earp says he can't—doesn't have a gun. Doc calls for a gun, and a man down the bar slides him one. Earp looks at the gun and says, "Brother Morg's gun. The other one, the good-lookin' fellow—that's my brother Virg." Doc registers this information and returns his own gun to its holster. He realizes Earp's brothers have the drop on him. "Howdy," says Doc. "Have a drink."

Twice Doc tells someone to get out of town, and twice Earp reminds him that's the marshal's job. Although the Clantons are the first order of business, Doc and Earp seem headed for a showdown. Yet they have a scene together that is one of the strangest and most beautiful in all of John Ford's work. A British actor (Alan Mowbray) has come to town to put on a play, and when he doesn't show up at the theater, Earp and Holliday find him in the saloon, on top of a table, being tormented by the Clantons. The actor begins Hamlet's famous soliloquy but is too drunk and frightened to continue. Doc Holliday, from memory, completes the speech, and could be speaking of himself: "but that the dread of something after death, the undiscovered country from whose bourn no traveller returns, puzzles the will."

The gentlest moments in the movie involve Earp's feelings for Clementine (Cathy Downs), who arrives on the stage from the east, looking for "Dr. John Holliday." She is the girl Doc left behind. Earp, sitting outside the hotel, rises quickly to his feet as she gets out of the stage, and his movements show that he's in awe of this graceful vision. Clementine has been seeking Doc all over the West, we learn, and wants to bring him home. Doc tells her to get out of town. And Chihuahua monitors the situation jealously.

Clementine is packed to go the next morning when the marshal, all awkward and shy, asks her to join him at the church service and dance. They walk in stately procession down the covered boardwalk while Ford's favorite hymn plays: "Shall We Gather at the River?" When the fiddler strikes up, Wyatt and Clementine dance—he clumsy but enthusiastic and with great joy. This dance is the turning point of the movie and marks the end of the Old West. There are still shots to be fired, but civilization has arrived in Tombstone.

The legendary gunfight at the OK Corral has been the subject of many films, including *Frontier Marshal* (1939), *Gunfight at the O.K. Corral* (1957), *Tombstone* (1993, with Val Kilmer's brilliant performance as Doc), and *Wyatt Earp* (1994). Usually the gunfight is the centerpiece of the film. Here it plays more like the dispatch of unfinished business; Ford doesn't linger over the violence.

There is the quiet tenseness in the marshal's office as Earp prepares to face the Clantons, who've shouted their challenge that they'd be waiting for him at the corral. Earp's brothers are with him because this is "family business." Earp turns down other volunteers, but when Doc turns up, he lets him take part because Doc has family business too (one of the Clanton boys has killed Chihuahua). Under the merciless clear sky of a desert dawn, in silence except for far-off horse whinnies and dog barks, the men walk down the street and take care of business.

John Ford (1894–1973) was, many believe, the greatest of all American directors. He is a little out of fashion now, and you no longer hear, as you once did, *The Grapes of Wrath* (1940) described as the best American film. Certainly he did more than any other director to document the passages of American history. He filmed *My Darling Clementine* in his beloved Monument Valley, on the Arizona-Utah border, where towering outcroppings make stark sculptures on the horizon.

For Ford, a western was not quite such a "period film" as it would be for later directors. He shot on location in the desert and prairie, his cast and crew living as if they were on a cattle drive, eating out of the chuck wagon, sleeping in tents. He made dozens of silent westerns, met the real Wyatt Earp on the set of a movie, and heard the story of the OK Corral directly from him (even so, history tells a much different story than this film). Ford worked repeatedly with the same actors (his "stock company"), and it is interesting that he chose Fonda rather than John Wayne, his other favorite, for Wyatt Earp. Maybe he saw Wayne as the embodiment of the Old West, and the gentler Fonda as one of the new men who would tame the wilderness.

My Darling Clementine must be one of the sweetest and most good-hearted of all westerns. The giveaway is the title, which is not about Wyatt or Doc or the gunfight, but about Clementine, who was certainly the most important thing to happen to Marshal Earp during the course of the story. There is a moment, soon after she arrives in town, when Earp gets a haircut and a quick spray of perfume at the Bon Ton Tonsorial Parlor. Clem stands close to him and says she loves "the scent of the desert flowers." "That's me," says Earp. "Barber."

{ My Life to Live }

Godard. We all went to Jean-Luc Godard in the 1960s. We stood in the rain outside the Three Penny Cinema, waiting for the next showing of *Week End* (1967). One year the New York Film Festival showed two of his movies, or was it three? One year at the Toronto festival Godard said, "The cinema is not the station. The cinema is the train." Or perhaps it was the other way around. We nodded. We loved his films. As much as we talked about Tarantino after *Pulp Fiction*, we talked about Godard in those days. I remember a sentence that became part of my verbal repertory: "His camera rotates 360 degrees, twice, and then stops and moves back in the other direction just a little—to show that it knows what it's doing!"

And now the name Godard inspires a blank face from most filmgoers. Subtitled films are out. Art films are out. Self-conscious films are out. Films that test the edges of the cinema are out. Now it is all about the mass audience: It must be congratulated for its narrow tastes and catered to. Some few in every generation, however, tire of the mob's taste and go poking in the corners, and for them Godard is waiting—implacable, oblique, tantalizing.

I originally considered choosing *Breathless* (1960), which fired an opening salvo of the French New Wave, had us all talking about "jump cuts," and made Jean-Paul Belmondo a star. But there is a new DVD of *My Life to Live (Vivre Sa Vie)*, from 1962. I slip it into the machine, and within five minutes I am so fascinated that I do not move, I do not stir, until it is over. This is a great movie, and I am not surprised to find Susan Sontag describing it as "one of the most extraordinary, beautiful, and original works of art that I know of."

It tells the story of Nana, played by Anna Karina, who was Godard's wife at the time. With her porcelain skin, her wary eyes, her helmet of shiny black hair, her chic outfits, always smoking, hiding her feelings, she is a young woman of Paris. The title shots show her in profile and full face, like mug shots, and we will be looking at her for the whole movie, trying to read her, for she reveals nothing willingly. Each shot begins with Michel Legrand music, which stops abruptly, to begin again with the next shot—as if to say, the music will try to explain, but fail. In the next shots, we see her from behind, in a café, as she talks to a man, Paul. We learn he is her husband, that she has left him and their child, that she has vague plans to go into the movies.

Raoul Coutard, the cinematographer who worked side by side with Godard during this period, has his camera track back and forth, first behind Nana's head, then Paul's, their faces glimpsed in the mirror. "The film was made by sort of a second presence," Godard said. The camera is not just a recording device but a *looking* device, which by its movements makes us aware that it sees her, wonders about her, glances first here and then there, exploring the space she occupies, speculating.

The movie is in twelve sections, each one with titles like an old-fashioned novel. She plays pinball. She works in a record store. She needs money. She tries to steal her flat key from the office of her concierge, but is caught and frog-marched to the street, her arm twisted behind her. She has no home and no money. Is this her fault, or fate? Why did she leave Paul? Has she no feelings for her child? The movie does not say. She is impassive. She goes to see a movie (Dreyer's *The Passion of Joan of Arc*, about a woman judged by men). She ditches the guy who bought her the ticket and meets a guy in a bar who wants to take some pictures of her. She's picked up by the cops—a dispute about a "dropped" thousand-franc note. She goes to a street where prostitutes work. She lets a guy pick her up. She won't let him kiss her.

The camera is right there. In the record store, it pans back and forth

with Nana and a customer, then turns and looks out a window. In a bar, the camera starts to pan to the left and then glances back again. On the street with the hookers, the camera looks first down one side and then the other, slowing at a woman it finds intriguing. She meets Raoul, a pimp. "Give me a smile," he says as the camera holds them both in two-shot. She refuses, then smiles and exhales at the same time, and the camera turns away from Raoul and approaches her, suddenly interested, as she does. We are implicated. We are the camera, watching, wondering. The camera is not expressing a "style," but the way people look at other people.

Famous shots. She smokes while a client embraces her, looking over his shoulder, eyes empty. Later, Raoul inhales and kisses her, and she blows out his smoke. What is there to do in this Paris but hang out in bars, smoke, wish you had more money? Prostitution for her isn't much more interesting than pinball. In France, prostitution is called "the life," which gives another meaning to the title. There is a monotone Q&A conversation in which Raoul explains the rules of her new trade. Then the movie devolves into a crime story, and we are reminded that *Breathless* also ended in a violent shooting in the street, although in *My Life to Live*, the camera sees the violent moment and then—looks down! Down at the street, or at its feet. The film looks away from its own ending.

There is a scene in a café a little earlier, with Nana in conversation with the man at the next table, a philosopher (Brice Parain, apparently playing himself). He tells her the story of a man who runs away from danger and then stops, paralyzed by the thought of how to put one foot in front of another. "The first time he thought," observes the philosopher, "it killed him."

If she thinks, will it kill her? We notice her openness, her curiosity, in talking to the old man. This from a woman who has been reluctant to reveal any thoughts or feelings, who has been all surface. We are reminded of a story Paul told earlier in the film, about a child who explained that if you take away the outside of a chicken, you have the inside, and if you take away the inside, you have the soul. Nana is all outside.

The film has no extra gestures. It regards with a level, interested gaze. The camera by its discipline discourages us from interpreting Nana's life in a melodramatic way. There is that dry French logic, the way every statement seems prefaced by an inaudible "of course." Curious, then, how moving Anna Karina makes Nana. She waits, she drinks, she smokes, she walks the streets, she makes some money, she turns herself over to the first pimp she meets, she gives up control of her life. There is one scene where she dances to a jukebox and laughs, and we can glimpse the young girl that may be inside, that may be her soul. The rest is all outside.

Godard said he shot the film in sequence. "All I had to do was put the shots end to end. What the crew saw at the rushes is more or less what the public sees." He tried to use first takes. "If retakes were necessary, it was no good." So Coutard's camera was seeing for the first time, and that is why it is so involved and curious. And we see as it sees and as Nana lives, without rehearsal, the first time through. The effect of the film is astonishing. It is clear, astringent, unsentimental, abrupt. Then it is over. It was her life to live.

{ NASHVILLE }

Taking down Pauline Kael's 1976 collection *Reeling* to reread her review of *Nashville* (1975), I find a yellow legal sheet marking the page: my notes for a class I taught on the film. "What is this story *about*?" I wrote. The film may be great because you can't really answer that question.

It is a musical; Robert Altman observes in his commentary on the new DVD release that it contains more than an hour of music. It is a docudrama about the Nashville scene. It is a political parable, written and directed in the immediate aftermath of Watergate (the scenes in the Grand Ole Opry were shot on the day Nixon resigned). It tells interlocking stories of love and sex, of hearts broken and mended. And it is a wicked satire of American smarminess ("Welcome to Nashville and to my lovely home," a country star gushes to Elliott Gould).

But more than anything else, it is a tender poem to the wounded and the sad. The most unforgettable characters in the movie are the best ones: Lily Tomlin's housewife, who loves her deaf sons. The lonely soldier who stands guard over the country singer his mother saved from a fire. The old man grieving his wife who has just died. Barbara Harris's runaway wife who rises to the occasion when she is handed the microphone after a shooting. And even that smarmy country singer (Henry Gibson), who when the chips are down acts in the right way. Kael writes: "Who watching the pious Haven Hamilton sing the evangelical 'Keep A'Goin,' his eyes flashing with

a paranoid gleam as he keeps the audience under surveillance, would guess that the song represented his true spirit, and that when injured he would think of the audience before himself?"

The movie takes place over five days in Nashville, during the countdown to a presidential primary. A candidate named Hal Phillip Walker, never seen on-screen, is running for the upstart Replacement Party and has won four earlier primaries. His candidacy was launched, according to the ABC newsman Howard K. Smith, when during a speech to college students he asked such questions as, "Does Christmas smell like oranges to you?" Yes, Smith's commentary concludes, Christmas *has* always smelled a little like oranges to him.

Michael Murphy plays John Triplette, a smooth-talking, polished advance man, setting up an election-eve rally at Nashville's Parthenon. Ned Beatty, who plays Tomlin's husband, is the local lawyer helping him. Triplette wants country legend Barbara Jean (Ronee Blakley) to sing at the rally, but her husband (Allen Garfield) wants no political tie-in. Meanwhile, other drifters and hopefuls converge on the city, hopeful of a break, singing on open-mike nights, peddling songs, making tapes.

One of them is Tom Frank (Keith Carradine), a ladies' man who runs into the Tomlin character at a recording studio (she sings with a gospel choir). He urgently calls her at home, and she hangs up on him. But her marriage with Beatty is not good, and we feel her pain when he doesn't even *try* to communicate with his deaf children. "What's he sayin'?" he wearily asks his wife as his son glows with excitement about a swimming lesson.

Eventually Tomlin does go to meet the folksinger, in a club where many other characters also happen to be hanging out. Robert Altman has always been the most inclusive of directors, a man whose sets are always like a party and whose movies often feel that way. He embraces talent, he is loyal to old friends, he wants to find a place for everyone. (One of the pleasures of listening to his commentary on the new DVD is to hear him describe decades of work with some of the people on-screen—including assistant director Tommy Thompson, who plays a role in this movie, was Altman's best friend, and was still working with him when he died on the set of a movie ten days before the commentary was recorded).

Because Altman, born in 1925, himself effortlessly swims in a sea of friends and associates, he finds it easy to make movies that do the same thing—what's amazing is not how many characters there are in *Nashville* (more than twenty-five significant speaking roles), but how many *major* characters. To get into this movie at all is to be given scenes of weight and depth, so that your character makes an impression. And there are not just many characters but many themes. It is easy to follow the political commentary in the film (Hal Phillip Walker's campaign could stand for all the dissidents since, from Jesse Ventura to Ralph Nader). More subtle is a thread that examines country music lyrics as they apply to the lives of the characters.

Kael is perceptive here. Early in the film, we've heard Haven Hamilton (Gibson) singing the lyric "For the sake of the children, we must say goodbye." Later, when Tomlin gets out of the folksinger's bed to go home to her children, it's "for exactly that reason," Kael says. The singer (Carradine) tries to hurt her with his phone call to another woman, but Tomlin is oblivious. The singer wearily hangs up as Tomlin leaves, and we realize Altman has told a short story of amazing impact in just a few minutes. The singer barely remembers most of the women he beds, Kael observes, but this woman "he'll remember forever."

Almost all of the songs in *Nashville,* and there are a lot of them, were written by the actors who sing them—Blakley, Karen Black, Gibson, Carradine, and others. None of them are terrific singers (Gwen Welles plays a waitress who cannot sing at all, and finally finds a friend honest enough to tell her). Altman says in his commentary that little time was devoted to rehearsal ("we spent more time on the hair"), and the offhand, earnest tone of the songs sounds better than a polished performance would. Likewise the inane ramblings of Geraldine Chaplin, as a BBC reporter who barges in where she's not wanted and sticks her mike under people's noses. As she wanders in a junkyard, free-associating, we wonder if she's really with the BBC at all—she's so loopy, maybe she's an impostor.

Underneath the songs, the romance, and the politics runs a darker current, of political assassination. The stage is set by Barbara Baxley, playing Haven's tough mistress, who has a long monologue about the Kennedys. We begin to focus on two young drifters—the soldiers who spend the night in the singer's hospital room and another young man who has rented a furnished room. When Barbara Jean sings at a riverboat concert, we realize, chillingly, that both of them are in the front row, standing side by side. Is there a threat there? Which one?

Robert Altman's life work has refused to contain itself within the edges of the screen. His famous overlapping dialogue, for which he invented a new sound recording system, is an attempt to deny that only one character talks at a time. His characters have neighbors, friends, secret alliances. They connect in unexpected ways. Their stories are not contained by conventional plots.

From his first great success in *MASH* (1970) to the wonderful *Cookie's Fortune* (1999), there are a lot of interlocking characters in his stories, and almost alone among white American directors he never forgets that a lot of black people live and work in town. In *Nashville* and his back-to-back triumphs *The Player* (1992) and *Short Cuts* (1993), he pointed the way for Paul Thomas Anderson's *Boogie Nights* (1997) and *Magnolia* (1999). The buried message may be that life doesn't proceed in a linear fashion to the neat ending of a story. It's messy and we bump up against others, and we're all in this together. That's the message I get at the end of *Nashville*, and it has never failed to move me.

{ NETWORK }

Strange how Howard Beal, "the mad prophet of the airwaves," dominates our memories of *Network*. We remember him in his soaking-wet raincoat, hair plastered to his forehead, shouting, "I'm mad as hell, and I'm not going to take this anymore." The phrase has entered into the language. But Beal (Peter Finch) is the movie's sideshow. The story centers on Diana Christensen (Faye Dunaway), the ratings-hungry programming executive who is prepared to do anything for better numbers. The mirror to which she plays is Max Schumacher (William Holden), the middle-aged news executive who becomes Diana's victim and lover, in that order.

What is fascinating about Paddy Chayefsky's Oscar-winning screenplay is how smoothly it shifts its gears, from satire to farce to social outrage. The scenes involving Beal and the revolutionary "liberation army" are cheerfully over the top. The scenes involving Diana and Max are quiet, tense, convincing drama. The action at the network executive level aims for behind-the-scenes realism; we may doubt that a Howard Beal could get on the air, but we have no doubt the idea would be discussed as the movie suggests. And then Chayefsky and the director, Sidney Lumet, edge the backstage network material over into satire too—but subtly, so that in the final late-night meeting where the executives decide what to do about Howard Beal, we have entered the madhouse without noticing.

The movie caused a sensation in 1976. It was nominated for ten

Oscars, won four (Finch, Dunaway, supporting actress Beatrice Straight, Chayefsky), and stirred up much debate about the decaying values of television. Seen a quarter century later, it is like prophecy. When Chayefsky created Howard Beal, could he have imagined Jerry Springer, Howard Stern, and the WWF?

Parts of the movie have dated—most noticeably Howard Beal's first news set, a knotty-pine booth that makes it look like he's broadcasting from a sauna. Other parts, including the network strategy meetings, remain timeless. And the set that Beal graduates to, featuring soothsayers and gossip columnists on revolving pedestals, nicely captures the feeling of some of the news/entertainment shows, where it's easier to get airtime if you're a "psychic" than if you have useful information to convey.

Most people remember that Howard Beal got fed up, couldn't take it anymore, and had a meltdown on the air. It wasn't quite like that. Beal is portrayed as an alcoholic doing such a bad job that he's fired by his boss (Holden). Then they get drunk together and joke about him committing suicide on the air. The next day, in a farewell broadcast, Beal announces that he will indeed kill himself because of falling ratings. He's yanked from the air but begs for a chance to say farewell, and *that's* when he says, the next day, "Well, I'll tell you what happened: I just ran out of bullshit." His frankness is great for the ratings, Diana convinces her bosses to overturn Max's decision to fire him, Howard goes back on the air, and he is apparently deep into madness when he utters his famous line.

Lumet and Chayefsky know just when to pull out all the stops. After Beal orders his viewers to "repeat after me," they cut to exterior shots of people leaning out of their windows and screaming that they're mad as hell too. Unlikely, but great drama, and electrifying in theaters at the time. Beal's ratings skyrocket (he is fourth after *The Six Million Dollar Man, All in the Family,* and *Phyllis*), and a new set is constructed on which he rants and raves after his announcer literally introduces him as a "mad prophet."

Counter to this extravagant satire is the affair between Max and Diana. Dunaway gives a seductive performance as the obsessed programming executive; her eyes sparkle and she moistens her lips when she thinks of higher ratings, and in one sequence she kisses Max while telling him how

cheaply she can buy some James Bond reruns. Later, in bed, discussing ratings during sex, she climaxes while gasping about the *Mao Tse-tung Hour.*

That's her idea for a prime-time show based on the exploits of a group obviously inspired by the Symbionese Liberation Army. In a secluded safe house, she negotiates with its armed leader, has a run-in with a Patty Hearst type, and uses an Angela Davis type as her go-between. This material is less convincing, except as an illustration of the lengths to which she will go.

Much more persuasive is Holden's performance as a newsman who was trained by Edward R. Murrow and now sees his beloved news division destroyed by Diana. At the same time, Max is fascinated by her and deliberately begins an affair. For him, it is intoxication with the devil, and maybe love. For her—it is hard to say what it is because, as he accurately tells her at the end, "There's nothing left in you I can live with."

Beatrice Straight's role as Max's wife is small but so powerful it won her the Oscar. It is a convincing portrait of a woman who has put up with an impossible man for so long that, although she feels angry and betrayed, she does not feel surprised. The meaning of Max's decision to cheat is underlined by the art direction; he and his wife live in a tasteful apartment with book-lined walls, and then he moves into Dunaway's tacky duplex. It is clear that although she cares how she dresses (costumes by Theoni V. Aldredge), she doesn't care where she lives, because she is not a homebody; her home is in a boardroom, a corner office, or a control booth.

The film is filled with vivid supporting roles. Ned Beatty has a sharp-edged cameo as a TV executive (he's the one who says, "It's because you're on television, dummy"). Robert Duvall plays an executive who, when murder is suggested, insists he wants to "hear everybody's thoughts on this." Wesley Addy is the handsome, gray-haired executive in the network's display window; he looks good at stockholder meetings.

One of Chayefsky's key insights is that the bosses don't much care what you say on TV, as long as you don't threaten their profits. Howard Beal calls for outrage, he advises viewers to turn off their sets, his fans chant about how fed up they are—but he only gets in trouble when he reveals plans to sell the network's parent company to Saudi Arabians. There's a parallel here with *The Insider,* a 1999 film about CBS News, where *60*

Minutes can do just about anything it wants to, except materially threaten CBS profits.

Sidney Lumet, born in 1924, a product of the golden age of live television, is one of the most consistently intelligent and productive directors of his time. His credits are an honor roll of good films, many of them with a conscience, including *12 Angry Men* (1957), *Long Day's Journey into Night* (1962), *Fail-Safe* (1964), *Serpico* (1973), *Dog Day Afternoon* (1975), *Prince of the City* (1981), *The Verdict* (1982), *Running on Empty* (1988), and *Q&A* (1990).

Because he works in many different genres and depends on story more than style, Lumet is better known inside the business than out, but few directors are better at finding the right way to tell difficult stories; consider the development of Al Pacino's famous telephone call in *Dog Day Afternoon*. His book *Making Movies* has more common sense in it about how movies are actually made than any other I have read. In *Network*, which is rarely thought of as a "director's picture," it is his unobtrusive skill that allows all those different notes and energy levels to exist within the same film. In other hands, the film might have whirled to pieces. In his, it became a touchstone.

THE NIGHT
OF THE HUNTER

Charles Laughton's *The Night of the Hunter* (1955) is one of the greatest of all American films but has never received the attention it deserves because of its lack of the proper trappings. Many "great movies" are by great directors, but Laughton directed only this one film, which was a critical and commercial failure long overshadowed by his acting career. Many great movies use actors who come draped in respectability and prestige, but Robert Mitchum was always a raffish outsider. And many great movies are realistic, but *The Night of the Hunter* is an expressionistic oddity, telling its chilling story through visual fantasy. People don't know how to categorize it, so they leave it off their lists.

Yet what a compelling, frightening, and beautiful film it is! And how well it has survived its period. Many films from the mid-1950s, even the good ones, seem somewhat dated now, but by setting his story in an invented movie world outside conventional realism, Laughton gave it a timelessness. Yes, the movie takes place in a small town on the banks of a river. But the town looks as artificial as a Christmas card scene, the family's house with its strange angles inside and out looks too small to live in, and the river becomes a set so obviously artificial it could have been built for a completely stylized studio film like *Kwaidan*.

Everybody knows the Mitchum character, the sinister "Reverend" Harry Powell. Even those who haven't seen the movie have heard about the

knuckles of his two hands, and how one has the letters *H-A-T-E* tattooed on them and the other the letters *L-O-V-E*.

Many movie lovers know by heart the reverend's explanation to the wide-eyed boy: "Ah, little lad, you're staring at my fingers. Would you like me to tell you the little story of right-hand/left-hand?" And the scene where the reverend stands at the top of the stairs and calls down to the boy and his sister has become the model for a hundred other horror scenes.

But does this familiarity give *The Night of the Hunter* the recognition it deserves? I don't think so, because those famous trademarks distract from its real accomplishment. It is one of the most frightening of movies, with one of the most unforgettable of villains, and on both of those scores it holds up as well after four decades as I expect *The Silence of the Lambs* to do many years from now.

The story, somewhat rearranged: In a prison cell, Harry Powell discovers the secret of a condemned man (Peter Graves), who has hidden $10,000 somewhere around his house. After being released from prison, Powell seeks out the man's widow, Willa Harper (Shelley Winters), and two children, John (Billy Chapin) and the owl-faced Pearl (Sally Jane Bruce). They know where the money is, but don't trust the "preacher." But their mother buys his con game and marries him, leading to a tortured wedding night inside a high-gabled bedroom that looks a cross between a chapel and a crypt.

Soon Willa Harper is dead, seen in an incredible shot at the wheel of a car at the bottom of the river, her hair drifting with the seaweed. And soon the children are fleeing down the dream-river in a small boat while the preacher follows them implacably on the shore. This beautifully stylized sequence uses the logic of nightmares, in which no matter how fast one runs, the slow step of the pursuer keeps the pace. The children are finally taken in by a Bible-fearing old lady (Lillian Gish), who would seem to be helpless to defend them against the single-minded murderer, but is as unyielding as her faith.

The shot of Winters at the bottom of the river is one of several remarkable images in the movie, which was photographed in black and white by Stanley Cortez, who shot Orson Welles's *The Magnificent Ambersons* (1942), and once observed he was "always chosen to shoot weird things." He shot few weirder than here, where one frightening composition shows a streetlamp casting Mitchum's terrifying shadow on the walls of the children's bedroom. The basement sequence combines terror and humor, as when the preacher tries to chase the children up the stairs, only to trip, fall, recover, lunge, and catch his fingers in the door. And the masterful nighttime river sequence uses giant foregrounds of natural details, like frogs and spiderwebs, to underline a kind of biblical progression as the children drift to eventual safety.

The screenplay, based on a novel by Davis Grubb, is credited to James Agee, one of the icons of American film writing and criticism, who was then in the final stages of alcoholism. Laughton's widow, Elsa Lanchester, is adamant in her autobiography: "Charles finally had very little respect for Agee. And he hated the script, but he was inspired by his hatred." She quotes the film's producer, Paul Gregory: "the script that was produced on the screen is no more James Agee's . . . than I'm Marlene Dietrich."

Who wrote the final draft? Perhaps Laughton had a hand. Lanchester and Laughton both remembered that Mitchum was invaluable as a help in working with the two children, whom Laughton could not stand, but the final film is all Laughton's, especially the dreamy Bible-evoking final sequence, with Lillian Gish presiding over events like an avenging elderly angel.

Robert Mitchum (1917–97) was one of the great icons of the second half-century of cinema. Despite his sometimes scandalous offscreen reputation, despite his genial willingness to sign on to half-baked projects, he made a group of films that led David Thomson, in his *Biographical Dictionary of Film,* to ask, "How can I offer this hunk as one of the best actors in the movies?" And answer: "Since the war, no American actor has made more first-class films, in so many different moods." *The Night of the Hunter,* he observes, represents "the only time in his career that Mitchum acted outside himself," by which he means there is little of the Mitchum persona in the preacher.

Mitchum was uncannily right for the role, with his long face, his gravel voice, and the silky tones of a snake-oil salesman. And Shelley Winters, all jitters and repressed sexual hysteria, is somehow convincing as she falls so prematurely into, and out of, his arms. The supporting actors are like a chattering gallery of Norman Rockwell archetypes, their lives centered around bake sales, soda fountains, and gossip. The children, especially the little girl, look more odd than lovable, which helps the film move away from realism and into stylized nightmare. And Lillian Gish and Stanley Cortez quite deliberately, I think, composed that great shot of her that looks like nothing so much as Whistler's mother holding a shotgun.

Charles Laughton (1899–1962) showed here that he had an original eye, and a taste for material that stretched the conventions of the movies. It is risky to combine horror and humor, and foolhardy to approach them through expressionism. Making his first film, Laughton made a film like no other before or since, and with such confidence it seemed to draw on a lifetime of work. Critics were baffled by it, the public rejected it, and the studio had a much more expensive Mitchum picture (*Not as a Stranger* [also 1955]) it wanted to promote instead. But nobody who has seen *The Night of the Hunter* has forgotten it, or Mitchum's voice coiling down those basement stairs: *"Chil . . . dren?"*

{ NOSFERATU }

To watch F. W. Murnau's *Nosferatu* (1922) is to see the vampire movie before it had really seen itself. Here is the story of Dracula before it was buried alive in clichés, jokes, TV skits, cartoons, and more than thirty other films. The film is in awe of its material. It seems to really believe in vampires.

Max Schreck, who plays the vampire, avoids most of the theatrical touches that would distract from all the later performances, from Bela Lugosi to Christopher Lee to Frank Langella to Gary Oldman. The vampire should come across not like a flamboyant actor, but like a man suffering from a dread curse. Schreck plays the count more like an animal than like a human being; the art direction by Murnau's collaborator, Albin Grau, gives him bat ears, clawlike nails, and fangs that are in the middle of his mouth like a rodent's, instead of on the sides like a Halloween mask.

Murnau's silent film was based on the Bram Stoker novel, but the title and character names were changed because Stoker's widow charged, not unreasonably, that her husband's estate was being ripped off. Ironically, in the long run Murnau was the *making* of the Stoker estate because *Nosferatu* inspired dozens of other Dracula films, none of them as artistic or unforgettable, however, although Werner Herzog's 1979 version with Klaus Kinski comes close.

"Nosferatu" is a better title anyway than "Dracula." Say "Dracula" and you smile. Say "Nosferatu" and you've bitten into a lemon. Murnau's story begins in Bremen, with Knock (Alexander Granach), a simian little real estate agent, assigning his employee Hutter (Gustav von Wangenheim) to visit the remote castle of Count Orlok, who wishes to buy a house in town—"a deserted one." A clue to the story can be found in Orlok's letter, which we see over Knock's shoulder. It is written in occult symbols; since Knock can read it, we should not be surprised later when he calls Orlok "Master."

During Hutter's trip to Orlok's lair in the Carpathian Mountains, Murnau's images foretell doom. In an inn, all of the customers fall silent when Hutter mentions Orlok's name. Outside, horses bolt and run, and a hyena snarls before slinking away. At Hutter's bedside, he finds a book that explains vampire lore. They must sleep, he learns, in earth from the graveyards of the Black Death.

Hutter's hired coach refuses to take him onto Orlok's estate. The count sends his own coach, which travels in fast motion, as does his servant, who scurries like a rat. Hutter is still laughing at warnings of vampirism, but his laugh fades at dinner, when he cuts himself with a bread knife and the count seems unhealthily interested in "Blood—your beautiful blood!"

Two of the key sequences in the film now follow; both are montages in which simultaneous events are intercut. That's a routine technique today, but Murnau is credited with helping to introduce the montage, and here we see Orlok advancing on Hutter while, in Bremen, his wife, Ellen, sleepwalks and cries out a warning that causes the vampire to turn away. (He advances and retreats through an archway shaped to frame his batlike head.) Later, after Hutter realizes his danger, he escapes from the castle and races back to Bremen by coach, while Orlok travels by sea, and Murnau intercuts the coach with shipboard events and Ellen restlessly waiting.

The shots on the ship are the ones everyone remembers. The cargo is a stack of coffins, all filled with earth (from the nourishing graveyards of the plague). Crew members sicken and die. A brave mate goes below with a hatchet to open a coffin, and rats tumble out. Then Count Orlok rises straight up, stiff and eerie, from one of the coffins, in a shot that was as frightening and famous in its time as the rotating head in *The Exorcist*. The ship arrives in port with its crew dead, and the hatch opens by itself.

Murnau now inserts scenes with little direct connection to the

story, except symbolically. One involves a scientist who gives a lecture on the
Venus flytrap, the "vampire of the vegetable kingdom." Then Knock, in a jail
cell, watches in close-up as a spider devours its prey. Why cannot man likewise be a vampire? Knock senses his Master has arrived, escapes, and scurries about the town with a coffin on his back. As fear of the plague spreads,
"the town was looking for a scapegoat," the titles say, and Knock creeps
about on rooftops and is stoned, while the street is filled with dark processions of the coffins of the newly dead.

Ellen Hutter learns that the only way to stop a vampire is for a good
woman to distract him so that he stays out past the first cock's crow. Her
sacrifice not only saves the city but also reminds us of the buried sexuality
in the Dracula story. Bram Stoker wrote with ironclad nineteenth-century
Victorian values, inspiring no end of analysis from readers who wonder if
the buried message of *Dracula* might be that unlicensed sex is dangerous to
society. The Victorians feared venereal disease the way we fear AIDS, and
vampirism may be a metaphor: The predator vampire lives without a mate,
stalking his victims or seducing them with promises of bliss—like a rapist
or a pickup artist. The cure for vampirism is obviously not a stake through
the heart, but nuclear families and bourgeois values.

Is Murnau's *Nosferatu* scary in the modern sense? Not for me. I ad-
mire it more for its artistry and ideas, its atmosphere and images, than for
its ability to manipulate my emotions like a skillful modern horror film. It
knows none of the later tricks of the trade, like sudden threats that pop in
from the side of the screen. But *Nosferatu* remains effective: It doesn't scare
us, but it haunts us. It shows not that vampires can jump out of shadows,
but that evil can grow there, nourished on death.

In a sense, Murnau's film is about all of the things we worry about
at three in the morning—cancer, war, disease, madness. It suggests these
dark fears in the very style of its visuals. Much of the film is shot in shadow.
The corners of the screen are used more than is ordinary; characters lurk or
cower there, and it's a rule of composition that tension is created when the
subject of a shot is removed from the center of the frame. Murnau's special
effects add to the disquieting atmosphere: the fast motion of Orlok's servant, the disappearance of the phantom coach, the manifestation of the

count out of thin air, the use of a photographic negative to give us white trees against a black sky.

Murnau (1888–1931) made twenty-two films but is known mostly for four masterpieces: *Nosferatu; The Last Laugh* (1924), with Emil Jannings as a hotel doorman devastated by the loss of his job; *Faust* (1926), with its demon filling the sky over a little village; and *Sunrise* (1927), which won Janet Gaynor an Oscar for her work as a woman whose husband considers murdering her. The worldwide success of *Nosferatu* and *The Last Laugh* won Murnau a Hollywood contract with Fox, and he moved to America in 1926. His last film was *Tabu* (1931); he was killed in a car crash on the Pacific Coast Highway just before its premiere, his promising career cut short at forty-three.

If he had lived, the rest of his career would have been spent making sound films. He probably would have made some great ones. But with a silent like *The Last Laugh,* he did not require a single title card to tell his story. And *Nosferatu* is more effective for being silent. It is commonplace to say that silent films are more "dreamlike," but what does that mean? In *Nosferatu,* it means that the characters are confronted with alarming images and denied the freedom to talk them away. There is no repartee in nightmares. Human speech dissipates the shadows and makes a room seem normal. Those things that live only at night do not need to talk, for their victims are asleep, waiting.

{ NOTORIOUS }

Alfred Hitchcock's *Notorious* is the most elegant expression of the master's visual style, just as *Vertigo* is the fullest expression of his obsessions. It contains some of the most effective camera shots in his—or anyone's—work, and they all lead to the great final passages in which two men find out how very wrong they both were.

This is the film, with *Casablanca* (1943), that assures Ingrid Bergman's immortality. She plays a woman whose notorious reputation encourages U.S. agents to recruit her to spy on Nazis in postwar Rio. And that reputation nearly gets her killed when the man she loves mistrusts her. His misunderstanding is at the center of a plot in which all of the pieces come together with perfect precision, so that two people walk down a staircase to their freedom, and a third person climbs steps to his doom.

Hitchcock made the film in 1946, when World War II was over but the cold war was just beginning. A few months later, he would have made the villains communists, but as he and Ben Hecht worked on the script, Nazis were still uppermost in their minds. (An opening subtitle says, "Miami, Florida, 3:20 p.m., April 20, 1946"—admirably specific, but as unnecessary as the similarly detailed information at the beginning of *Psycho* [1960].)

The story stars Bergman as a patriotic American named Alicia Huberman, whose father is a convicted Nazi spy. Alicia is known for drinking

and apparent promiscuity and is recruited by an agent named Devlin (Cary Grant) to fly to Rio and insinuate herself into the household of a spy ring led by Sebastian (Claude Rains). Sebastian once loved her, and perhaps he still does; Devlin is essentially asking her to share the spy's bed to discover his secrets. And this she is willing to do, because by the time he asks her, she is in love—with Devlin.

All of these sexual arrangements are, of course, handled with the sort of subtle dialogue and innuendo that Hollywood used to get around the Production Code. There is never a moment when improper behavior is actually stated or shown, but the film leaves no doubt. By the time all of the pieces are in place, we actually feel more sympathy for Sebastian than for Devlin. He may be a spy, but he loves Alicia sincerely, while Devlin may be an American agent but has used Alicia's love to force her into the arms of another man.

Hitchcock was known for his attention to visual details. He drew storyboards of every scene before shooting it, and slyly plays against Grant's star power in the scene introducing Devlin to the movie. At a party the night her father has been convicted, Alicia drinks to forget, with a group of casual friends. The camera positions itself behind the seated Devlin, so we see only the back of his head. He anchors the shot as the camera moves left and right, following the morally ambiguous Alicia as she flirts, drinks, and tries to forget.

There are more famous shots the next morning. Alicia awakens with a hangover, and there is a gigantic foreground close-up of a glass of Alka-Seltzer (it will be paired much later in the movie with a huge foreground coffee cup that we know contains arsenic). From her point of view, she sees Devlin in the doorway, backlit and upside down. As she sits up, he seems to rotate 180 degrees. He suggests she become a spy. She refuses, talking of her plans to take a pleasure cruise. He plays a secret recording that proves she is, after all, patriotic—despite her loose image. As the recording begins, she is in shadow. As it continues, she is in bars of light. As it ends, she is in full light. Hitchcock has choreographed the visuals so that they precisely reflect what is happening in the story.

The film is rich with other elegant shots, the most famous beginning with the camera on a landing high above the entrance hall of Sebastian's mansion in Rio. It ends, after one unbroken movement, with a close-up of a key in Alicia's nervously twisting hand. The key will open the wine cellar, where Devlin (posing as a guest) will join Alicia in trying to find Sebastian's secret. One of the bottles contains not wine, but a radioactive substance used in bombs. Of course it could contain anything—maps, codes, diamonds—because it is a MacGuffin (Hitchcock's name for that plot element that everyone is concerned about, although it hardly matters what it is).

The Hecht screenplay is ingenious in playing the two men against one another. Sebastian, played by Rains, is smaller, more elegant, more vulnerable, and dominated by his forbidding mother (Leopoldine Konstantin). Devlin, played by Grant, is tall, physically imposing, crude at times, suspicious where Sebastian is trusting. Both men love Alicia, but the wrong man trusts her, and the plot leads to a moment of inspired ingenuity in which Devlin is able to escort Alicia out of the Nazi mansion in full view of all of the spies, and the circumstances are such that nobody can stop him. (There is a point earlier in the film where Devlin walks all the way up the same staircase, and if you count his steps, you will find that on the way down he and Alicia descend more steps than there actually are—Hitchcock's way of prolonging the suspense.)

Throughout Hitchcock's career, he devised stories in which elegant women, usually blondes, were manipulated into situations of great danger. Hitchcock was the puppet master, with the male actors as his surrogates. *Vertigo* (1958) treats this theme so openly it almost gives the game away. But look how it works in *Notorious,* where Devlin (like the Jimmy Stewart character in *Vertigo*) grooms and trains an innocent woman to be exactly who he desires her to be, and then makes her do his bidding.

The great erotic moment in *Vertigo* is the one where the man kisses the woman of his fantasy while the room whirls around him. There is a parallel scene in *Notorious,* and it was famous at the time as the longest kiss in the history of the movies. It was not, however, a single kiss, as Tim Dirks points out in his essay on the film. The Production Code forbade a kiss lasting longer than three seconds, and so Bergman and Grant alternate kissing with dialogue and eye play while never leaving one another's arms. The sequence begins on a balcony overlooking Rio, encompasses a telephone call and a discussion of the dinner menu, and ends with a parting at the apartment door, taking three minutes in all. The three-second rule, of course, led to a *better* scene; an actual 180-second kiss might look like an exercise in slobbering, and the interplay of dialogue and lip and eye contact is electric.

The choice of Ingrid Bergman for the starring role was ideal; of all the actresses of the time she most subtly combined the noble and the carnal. Consider *Casablanca* (all of the viewers of *Notorious* would have), in which she lives with a Resistance hero but in her heart loves a scruffy bar owner, and yet emerges as an idealistic heroine. In *Notorious*, we never seriously doubt that she is the heroine, but we can understand why the Grant character does. She appears to be a dipsomaniac, and besides, she sleeps with Sebastian. But she does it because she loves Devlin. Devlin has difficulty in loving a woman who would do that; one is reminded of Groucho Marx, who refused to join any club that would have him as a member.

In recent years, so many movies have ended in obligatory chases and shoot-outs that the ability to write a well-crafted third act has almost died out. Among its many achievements, *Notorious* ends well. Like clockwork, the inevitable events of the last ten minutes take place, and they all lead to the final perfect shot, in which another Nazi says to Sebastian, "Alex, will you come in, please? I wish to talk to you." And Alex goes in, knowing he will never come out alive.

{ ON THE WATERFRONT }

Conscience. That stuff can drive you nuts.

So says Terry Malloy, the longshoreman who testifies against his union in *On the Waterfront*. The line, said by Marlon Brando, resonates all through the picture because the story is about conscience—and so is the story behind the story. This was the film made in 1954 by Elia Kazan after he agreed to testify before the House Un-American Activities Committee (HUAC), named former associates who were involved with the Communist Party, and became a pariah in left-wing circles.

On the Waterfront was, among other things, Kazan's justification for his decision to testify. In the film, when a union boss shouts, "You ratted on us, Terry," the Brando character shouts back, "I'm standing over here now. I was rattin' on myself all those years. I didn't even know it." That reflects Kazan's belief that communism was an evil that temporarily seduced him and had to be opposed. Brando's line finds a dramatic echo in *A Life*, Kazan's 1988 autobiography, where he writes of his feelings after the film won eight Oscars, including best picture, actor, actress, and director: "I was tasting vengeance that night and enjoying it. *On the Waterfront* is my own story; every day I worked on that film, I was telling the world where I stood and my critics to go and fuck themselves."

In that statement, you can feel the passion that was ignited by the

HUAC hearings and the defiance of those who named names, or refused to. For some viewers, the buried agenda of *On the Waterfront* tarnishes the picture; the critic Jonathan Rosenbaum told me he could "never forgive" Kazan for using the film to justify himself. But directors make films for all sorts of hidden motives, some noble, some shameful, and at least Kazan was open about his own. And he made a powerful and influential movie, one that continued Brando's immeasurable influence on the general change of tone in American movie acting in the 1950s.

"If there is a better performance by a man in the history of film in America, I don't know what it is," Kazan writes in his book. If you changed "better" to "more influential," there would be one other performance you could suggest, and that would be Brando's work in Kazan's *A Streetcar Named Desire* (1951). In these early films, Brando cut through decades of screen mannerisms and provided a fresh, alert, quirky acting style that was not realism so much as a kind of heightened riff on reality. He became famous for his choices of physical gestures during crucial scenes (and as late as *The Godfather* [1972], he was still finding them—the cat in his lap, the spray gun in the tomato patch).

In *On the Waterfront*, there's a moment when Terry goes for a walk in the park with Edie (Eva Marie Saint), the sister of a man who has been thrown off a roof for talking to crime investigators. She drops a glove. He picks it up, and instead of handing it back, he pulls it on over his own worker's hands. A small piece of business on the edge of the shot, but it provides texture. And look at the scene between Terry and his brother, Charley (Rod Steiger), in the backseat of a taxi. This is the "I coulda been a contender" scene, and it has been quoted and parodied endlessly (most memorably by Robert De Niro in *Raging Bull*). But it still has its power to make us feel Terry's pain, and even the pain of Charley, who has been forced to pull a gun on his brother. Here is Kazan on Brando:

> . . . what was extraordinary about his performance, I feel, is the contrast of the tough-guy front and the extreme delicacy and gentle cast of his behavior. What other actor, when his brother draws a pistol to force him to do something shameful, would put his hand on the gun and push it away with the gentleness of a caress? Who else could read 'Oh, Charley!' in a

tone of reproach that is so loving and so melancholy and suggests the terrific depth of pain?

Kazan's screenplay was by Budd Schulberg, and his producer was Sam Spiegel, one of the great independent buccaneers (his next production after *Waterfront* was *The Bridge on the River Kwai*). Spiegel at first proposed Frank Sinatra for the role of Terry Malloy, and Kazan agreed: "He spoke perfect Hobokenese." The young, wiry Sinatra would have been well cast, but then Spiegel decided that Brando, a much bigger star, could double the budget available for the film. Kazan had already discussed costumes with Sinatra and felt bad about the switch, but Sinatra "let me off easy."

The film was based on the true story of a longshoreman who tried to overthrow a corrupt union. In life, he failed; in the film, he succeeds, and today the ending of *On the Waterfront* feels too stagy and upbeat. The film was shot on location in Hoboken, on and near the docks, with real longshoremen playing themselves as extras (sometimes they're moved around in groups that look artificially blocked). Brando plays a young ex-prizefighter, now a longshoreman given easy jobs because Charley is the right-hand man of the corrupt boss, Johnny Friendly (Lee J. Cobb). After he unwittingly allows himself to be used to set up the death of Edie's brother, he starts to question the basic assumptions of his life—including his loyalty to Charley and Johnny, who, after all, ordered him to take a dive in his big fight in Madison Square Garden.

The other major character is a priest (Karl Malden) who tries to encourage longshoremen to testify against corruption. After one rebel is deliberately crushed in the hold of a ship, the priest makes a speech over his body ("If you don't think Christ is down here on the waterfront, you got another thing coming"). It would have been the high point of another kind of film, but against Brando's more sinuous acting, it feels like a set piece.

Eva Marie Saint makes a perfect foil for Brando, and the two have a famous scene in a bar where he reveals, almost indirectly, that he likes her, and she turns the conversation from romance to conscience. At one point, Kazan and his cinematographer, Boris Kaufman, frame her pale face and hair in the upper right-hand corner of the screen, with Brando in lower center, as if a guardian angel is hovering above him.

The film's best scenes are the most direct ones. Consider the way Brando refuses to cooperate with investigators who seek him out on the docks, early in the film. And the way he walks around on the rooftop where he keeps his beloved pigeons—lithe and catlike. Steiger is invaluable to the film, and in their taxi conversation, he brings a gentleness to match Brando's: The two brothers are in mourning for the lost love between them.

The screenplay by Schulberg straddles two styles—the emerging realism and the stylized gangster picture. To the latter tradition belongs lines like "He could sing, but he couldn't fly," when the squealer is thrown off the roof. To the former: "You know how the union works? You go to a meeting, you make a motion, the lights go out, then you go out." Brando's "contender" speech is so famous it's hard to see anew, but watch the film again and you feel the reality of the sadness between the two men, and the simple words that express it.

On the Waterfront was nominated for twelve Oscars and won eight. Ironically the other three nominations were all for best supporting actor, where Cobb, Malden, and Steiger split the vote. Today the story no longer seems as fresh; both the fight against corruption and the romance fall well within ancient movie conventions. But the acting and the best dialogue passages have an impact that has not dimmed; it is still possible to feel the power of the film and of Brando and Kazan, who changed American movie acting forever.

{ PANDORA'S BOX }

Louise Brooks regards us from the screen as if the screen were not there; she casts away the artifice of film and invites us to play with her. She carries her beauty like a gift she doesn't think much about, and confronts us as a naughty girl. When you meet someone like this in life, you're attracted, but you know in your gut she'll be nothing but trouble.

Life cannot permit such freedom, and so Brooks, in her best films, is ground down—punished for her joy. At the end of *Pandora's Box* (1928) she's killed while in the embrace of Jack the Ripper, and the audience isn't even asked to accept her death as punishment for her wicked ways. It's more a settling of scores: Anyone who looks that great, and lives life on her own terms, has to be swatted down by fate or the rest of us will grow discouraged.

Louise Brooks was swatted down as well. She was "way too wild in a business that was way too tame," said Dr. Paolo Cherchi Usai, curator of the film collection at Eastman House, which preserved her films and sparked her revival. By the late 1990s, according to an article in *Wired* magazine, she was "the most popular dead actress on the Web"—not a status one aspires to, but reflecting growing admiration for two great films she made in Germany, right at the end of the silent era, after she had burned all her bridges in Hollywood.

These films are *Pandora's Box* and *Diary of a Lost Girl* (1929), both

directed by the master of psychosexual melodrama, G. W. Pabst. Now restored and available on video, they glisten with the purity of black and white, and Brooks's face is fixed forever: the bangs cut low over the eyes ("One of the ten haircuts that changed the world," according to *InStyle* magazine); the eyebrows rich and level, parallel to the bangs; the deep, dark eyes; the mouth often caught in a pout or a tease; the porcelain skin; the perfect regularity of features that made her almost a cartoon (she inspired the comic strip *Dixie Dugan*).

She is thin but not skinny, a flapper. Her lovers included Charles Chaplin, CBS president William Paley (who gave her a lifetime stipend), and many others—including the clients of an escort agency she worked for in New York in the 1940s, after all of her rich and famous friends had forgotten her. She was "too wild" (thrown out of the Algonquin Hotel at eighteen for "promiscuity"), but there was another problem: She drank too much. When she drank, she did things like telling Paramount to go to hell when they asked her to come back to Hollywood and dub dialogue into her last silent film.

Her life was as harrowing as Frances Farmer's, but it had a happier ending. After the early fame (she danced with Martha Graham at sixteen), the Hollywood stardom, the German films, and the slow decline (she lusted after John Wayne while they made a B western together), there came the lost years of drinking and "escorting," and then—well, it happened that her New York apartment was across the hall from John Springer's, and he was a publicist. When James Card, then the film curator at Eastman House, asked Springer where Brooks could be found, Springer knocked on her door. Card invited Brooks to visit Rochester for a look at her old films and invited her to stay. Then he fell in love with her, although the nature of their relationship is unclear. He took her to Paris for a retrospective at the Cinémathèque Française, where rumpled old Henri Langlois declared, "There is no Garbo! There is no Dietrich! There is only Louise Brooks!" Brooks must have smiled to hear her name linked with two of her reputed lovers.

In Rochester, she wrote memoirs which were eventually collected into *Lulu in Hollywood,* one of the few film books that can be called indispensable. She remembered Bogart as a kid starting out on the New York stage, and the private lovability of her old friend W. C. Fields. And she was frank about her rise and especially her fall. Many silent stars became boring relics, repeating the same memorized anecdotes. Louise Brooks was saved by the astringent power of her wit.

The other night I looked again at *Pandora's Box*, which was offered to her by Pabst just as Hollywood dumped her. If it were not for her presence and especially her close-ups, would it be a great film? No, but then it isn't without them. The plot, which could be remade today, involves a young woman named Lulu who says she is not a prostitute, while we notice that she behaves exactly like one. She's entertaining the meter reader as the film begins, and then welcomes Schigolch (Carl Goetz), a seedy old man who may be her father, her pimp, or both. He wants her to meet an acrobat who wants her for a trapeze act, but first she gets a visit from her lover and patron, Schön (Fritz Kortner), a newspaper publisher.

Schön is depressed. He is about to be married and wants to break off their relationship. He is more depressed when he finds Schigolch hiding behind the furniture with a bottle. Lulu visits Schön at his office, where she is also an erotic magnet for the publisher's son (Francis Lederer) and for a countess (Alice Roberts), who is one of the first obvious lesbians in the movies. Lulu becomes a dancer in a revue produced by the son. Schön (with fiancée and son) unwisely visits backstage. "I will not dance for that woman," Lulu says, pointing to the fiancée. Attempting to shake her to her senses, Schön grows aroused, is found by his fiancée in a compromising situation, and marries Lulu instead. "For sheer erotic dynamism," Pauline Kael wrote, those backstage scenes "have never been equaled."

Those who love Lulu tend to die violently and unexpectedly. The look on her face during the accidental shooting of one character is fascinating: She seems to be standing outside her own life, watching it happen. There is an episode on a gambling ship where a disreputable marquis attempts to sell her to an Egyptian pimp on the grounds that since she can't return to Germany anyway, she might as well make the best of a bad situation.

There is a flight by rowboat, and then Jack the Ripper materializes from the London fog. At this late stage in the movie, we are asked to believe that Lulu, freezing and starving and concerned for her old pimp (or father), has decided to commit her very first act of sex for cash. When Jack the Ripper explains that he has no money, however, she likes his looks enough to invite him upstairs anyway. Not a good judge of character.

This synopsis could apply equally to a great or a laughable film. Brooks makes it a great one. She seems to stand outside *Pandora's Box*. She looks modern: She doesn't have the dated makeup of many silent stars, but could be a Demi Moore or Winona Ryder, electronically inserted into old scenes by computer. As she careens from one man to another, the only constant factor is her will: She wants to party, she wants to make love, she wants to drink, she wants to tell men what she wants, and she wants to get it. There is no other motive than her desire: not money, not sex, just selfishness. It could get ugly, but she makes it look like fun. You can't get something for nothing, but if you can put off paying the bill long enough, it may begin to feel like you can.

THE PASSION
OF JOAN OF ARC

You cannot know the history of silent film unless you know the face of Renée Maria Falconetti. In a medium without words, where the filmmakers believed that the camera captured the essence of characters through their faces, to see Falconetti in Dreyer's *The Passion of Joan of Arc* (1928) is to look into eyes that will never leave you.

Falconetti (as she is always called) made only this single movie. "It may be the finest performance ever recorded on film," wrote Pauline Kael. She was an actress in Paris when she was seen on the stage of a little boulevard theater by Carl Theodor Dreyer (1889–1968), the Dane who was one of the greatest early directors. It was a light comedy, he recalled, but there was something in her face that struck him: "There was a soul behind that facade." He did screen tests without makeup and found what he sought: a woman who embodied simplicity, character, and suffering.

Dreyer had been given a large budget and a screenplay by his French producers, but he threw out the screenplay and turned instead to the transcripts of Joan's trial. They told the story that has become a legend: Of how a simple country maid from Orléans, dressed as a boy, led the French troops in their defeat of the British occupation forces. How she was captured by French loyal to the British and brought before a church court, where her belief that she had been inspired by heavenly visions led to charges of heresy. There were twenty-nine cross-examinations, combined with torture, before Joan was burned at the stake in 1431. Dreyer combined them into one inquisition, in which the judges, their faces twisted with their fear of her courage, loomed over her with shouts and accusations.

If you go to the Danish Film Museum in Copenhagen, you can see Dreyer's model for the extraordinary set he built for the film. He wanted it all in one piece (with movable walls for the cameras), and he began with towers at four corners, linked with concrete walls so thick they could support the actors and equipment. Inside the enclosure were chapels, houses, and the ecclesiastical court, built according to a weird geometry that put windows and doors out of plumb with one another and created sharp angles and discordant visual harmonies (the film was made at the height of German expressionism and the French avant-garde movement in art).

It is helpful to see the model in Copenhagen, because you will never see the whole set in the movie. There is not one single establishing shot in all of *The Passion of Joan of Arc,* which is filmed mostly in close-ups and medium shots, creating fearful intimacy between Joan and her tormentors. Nor are there easily read visual links between shots. In his rigorous shot-by-shot analysis of the film, David Bordwell of the University of Wisconsin concludes, "Of the film's over 1,500 cuts, fewer than 30 carry a figure or object over from one shot to another; and fewer than 15 constitute genuine matches on action."

What does this mean to the viewer? There is a language of shooting and editing that we subconsciously expect when we go to the movies. We assume that if two people are talking, the cuts will make it seem that they are looking at one another. We assume that if a judge is questioning a defendant, the camera placement and editing will make it clear where they stand in relationship to one another. If we see three people in a room, we expect to be able to say how they are arranged and which is closest to the camera. Almost all such visual cues are missing from *The Passion of Joan of Arc.*

Instead, Dreyer cuts the film into a series of startling images. The prison guards and the ecclesiastics on the court are seen in high contrast, often from a low angle, and although there are often sharp architectural angles behind them, we are not sure exactly what the scale is (are the windows and walls close or far?). Bordwell's book reproduces a shot of three priests,

presumably lined up from front to back, but shot in such a way that their heads seem stacked on top of one another. All of the faces of the inquisitors are shot in bright light, without makeup, so that the crevices and flaws of the skin seem to reflect a diseased inner life.

Falconetti, by contrast, is shot in softer grays rather than blacks and whites. Also without makeup, she seems solemn and consumed by inner conviction. Consider an exchange where a judge asks her whether St. Michael actually spoke to her. Her impassive face seems to suggest that whatever happened between Michael and herself was so beyond the scope of the question that no answer is conceivable.

Why did Dreyer fragment his space, disorient the visual sense, and shoot in close-up? I think he wanted to deliberately avoid the picturesque temptations of a historical drama. There is no scenery here, aside from walls and arches. Nothing was put in to look pretty. You do not leave discussing the costumes (although they are all authentic). The emphasis on the faces insists that these very people did what they did. He strips the church court of its ritual and righteousness and betrays its members as fleshy hypocrites in the pay of the British; their narrow eyes and mean mouths assault Joan's sanctity.

For Falconetti, the performance was an ordeal. Legends from the set tell of Dreyer forcing her to kneel painfully on stone and then wipe all expression from her face—so that the viewer would read suppressed or inner pain. He filmed the same shots again and again, hoping that in the editing room he could find exactly the right nuance in her facial expression. There is an echo in the famous methods of the French director Robert Bresson, who in his own 1962 *The Trial of Joan of Arc* put actors through the same shots again and again, until all apparent emotion was stripped from their performances. In his book on Dreyer, Tom Milne quotes the director: "When a child suddenly sees an onrushing train in front of him, the expression on his face is spontaneous. By this I don't mean the feeling in it (which in this case is sudden fear), but the fact that the face is completely uninhibited." That is the impression he wanted from Falconetti.

That he got it is generally agreed. Perhaps it helps that Falconetti never made another movie (she died in Buenos Aires in 1946). We do not have her face in other roles to compare with her face here, and the movie seems to exist outside time (the French director Jean Cocteau famously said it played like "an historical document from an era in which the cinema didn't exist").

To modern audiences, raised on films where emotion is conveyed by dialogue and action more than by faces, a film like *The Passion of Joan of Arc* is an unsettling experience—so intimate we fear we will discover more secrets than we desire. Our sympathy is engaged so powerfully with Joan that Dreyer's visual methods—his angles, his cutting, his close-ups—don't play like stylistic choices, but like the fragments of Joan's experience. Exhausted, starving, cold, in constant fear, only nineteen when she died, she lives in a nightmare where the faces of her tormentors rise up like spectral demons.

Perhaps the secret of Dreyer's success is that he asked himself, "What is this story really about?" And after he answered that question he made a movie that was about absolutely nothing else.

{ PEEPING TOM }

The movies make us into voyeurs. We sit in the dark, watching other people's lives. It is the bargain the cinema strikes with us, although most films are too well behaved to mention it. Michael Powell's *Peeping Tom,* a 1960 movie about a man who filmed his victims as they died, broke the rules and crossed the line. It was so loathed on its first release that it was pulled from theaters and effectively ended the career of one of Britain's greatest directors. Why did critics and the public hate it so? I think because it didn't allow the audience to lurk anonymously in the dark, but implicated us in the voyeurism of the title character.

Martin Scorsese once said that this movie, and Fellini's *8 ½,* contain all that can be said about directing. The Fellini film is about the world of deals and scripts and showbiz, and the Powell is about the deep psychological process at work when a filmmaker tells his actors to do as he commands, while he stands in the shadows and watches.

Scorsese is Powell's most famous admirer. As a child, he studied the films of "the Archers"—the team of director Powell and writer Emeric Pressburger. Scorsese haunted the late-show screenings of their films, drinking in Powell's bold images and confident, unexpected story development. Powell and Pressburger made some of the best and most successful films of the 1940s and 1950s, including *The Thief of Bagdad* (1940), with its magical special effects; *The Life and Death of Colonel Blimp* (1943), with

Roger Livesey's great performance spanning three wars; *The Red Shoes* (1948), with Moira Shearer as a ballet dancer; *Black Narcissus* (1947), with Deborah Kerr as a nun in the Himalayas; and *Stairway to Heaven* (1946), with David Niven as a dead airman. Then came *Peeping Tom*.

It is a movie about looking. Its central character is a focus puller at a British movie studio; his job is to tend the camera, as an acolyte might assist at the Mass. His secret life involves filming women with a camera that has a knife concealed in its tripod; as they realize their fate, he films their faces and watches the footage over and over in the darkness of his rooms. He is working on a "documentary," he tells people, and only in the film's final shot do we realize it is not only about his crimes but about his death. He does not spare himself the fate of his victims.

This man, named Mark Lewis, has been made into a pitiful monster by his own upbringing. When Helen (Anna Massey), the friendly girl who lives downstairs, shows an interest in his work, he shows her films taken by his own father. Films of Mark as a little boy, awakened in the night by a flashlight in his eyes. Films of his father dropping lizards onto his bedclothes as he slept. Tapes of his frightened cries. Mark's father, a psychologist specializing in the subject of fear, used his son for his experiments. When a police psychologist learns the story, he muses, "He has his father's eyes . . ."

There is more. We see little Mark filmed beside his mother's dead body. Six weeks later, another film, as his father remarries. (Wheels within wheels: The father is played by Michael Powell, Mark's childhood home is the London house where Powell was raised, and Mark as a child is played by Powell's son.) At the wedding, Mark's father gives him a camera as a present. For Mark the areas of sex, pain, fear, and filmmaking are connected. He identifies with his camera so much that when Helen kisses him, he responds by kissing the lens of his camera. When a policeman handles Mark's camera, Mark's hands and eyes restlessly mirror the officer's moves, as if Mark's body yearns for the camera and is governed by it. When Helen tries to decide whether she should wear a piece of jewelry on the shoulder or at the neckline, Mark's hands touch his own body in the same places, as if he is a camera, recording her gestures.

Powell originally thought to cast Laurence Harvey in the lead, but he settled instead on Karlheinz Böhm, an Austrian actor with such a slight accent in English that it sounds more like diffidence. Böhm was blond, handsome, soft, and tentative. Powell was interested to learn that his new star was the son of the famous symphony conductor. He might know something of overbearing fathers. Böhm's performance creates a vicious killer who is shy and wounded. The movie despises him, yet sympathizes with him. He is a very lonely man. He lives upstairs in a rooming house. The first room is conventional, with a table, a bed, a kitchen area. The second room is like a mad scientist's laboratory, with cameras and film equipment, a developing room, a screening area, obscure equipment hanging from the ceiling.

Helen is startled when he reveals that the house is his childhood home, and he is the landlord: "You? But you walk around as if you can't afford the rent." Helen lives with her mother (Maxine Audley), who is alcoholic and blind, and listens to Mark's footsteps. When Helen tells her mother they're going out together, her mother says, "I don't trust a man who walks so softly." Later, Mark surprises the mother inside his inner room, and she cuts right to the heart of his secret: "I visit this room every night. The blind always visit the rooms they live under. What am I seeing, Mark?"

Powell's film was released just months before *Psycho,* another shocking film by a British director. Hitchcock's film arguably had even more depraved subject matter than Powell's, and yet it was a boost for his career, perhaps because audiences expected the macabre from Hitchcock but Powell was more identified with elegant and stylized films. The outraged uproar over *Peeping Tom* essentially finished his career, although he made a few more films. By the late 1970s, however, Scorsese was sponsoring revivals and restorations, and joined Powell on the audio commentary tracks of several videos. Indeed, Powell and Scorsese's editor, Thelma Schoonmaker, fell in love and married, and she assisted him in writing the best directorial autobiographies I have read, *A Life in Movies* and *Million-Dollar Movie.*

There is a major sequence in *Peeping Tom* that Hitchcock might have envied. After hours at the film studio, Mark persuades an extra (Moira Shearer) to stay behind so he can film her dancing. She is almost giddy to have her own solo shots, and dances around a set and even into a big blue trunk. The next day, the body is discovered inside the trunk—while Mark, unseen, films the discovery.

The film's visual strategies implicate the audience in Mark's voyeurism. The opening shot is through Mark's viewfinder. Later, we see the same footage in Mark's screening room, in a remarkable shot from behind Mark's head. As the camera pulls back, the image on the screen moves in for a close-up, so the face of the victim effectively remains the same size as Mark's head shrinks. In one shot, Powell shows us a member of the audience being diminished by the power of the cinematic vision. Other movies let us enjoy voyeurism; this one exacts a price.

Powell (1905–90) was a director who loved rich colors, and *Peeping Tom* is shot in a saturated Technicolor with shots like one where a victim's body under a bright red blanket stands out against the gray street. He was a virtuoso of camera use, and in *Peeping Tom* the basic strategy is to always suggest that we are not just seeing but looking. His film is a masterpiece precisely because it doesn't let us off the hook, like all of those silly teenage slasher movies do. We cannot laugh and keep our distance: We are forced to acknowledge that we watch, horrified but fascinated.

{ PERSONA }

Shakespeare used six words to pose the essential human choice: "To be, or not to be?" Elisabeth, a character in Ingmar Bergman's *Persona*, uses two to answer it: "No, don't!" She is an actress who one night stopped speaking in the middle of the performance and has been silent ever since. Now her nurse, Alma, has in a fit of rage started to throw a pot of boiling water at her. "No, don't!" translates as: I do not want to feel pain, I do not want to be scarred, I do not want to die. She wants to *be*. She admits she exists.

Persona is a film we return to over the years for the beauty of its images and because we hope to understand its mysteries. It is apparently not a difficult film: Everything that happens is perfectly clear, and even the dream sequences are clear—as dreams. But it suggests buried truths, and we despair of finding them. *Persona* was one of the first movies I reviewed, in 1967. I did not think I understood it. A third of a century later, I know most of what I am ever likely to know about films, and I think I understand that the best approach to *Persona* is a literal one.

It is exactly about what it seems to be about. "How this pretentious movie manages to not be pretentious at all is one of the great accomplishments of *Persona*," says a moviegoer named John Hardy, posting his comments on the Internet Movie Database. Bergman shows us everyday actions and the words of ordinary conversation. And Sven Nykvist's cinematography shows them in haunting images. One of them, of two faces, one frontal, one in profile, has become one of the most famous images of the cinema.

Elisabeth (Liv Ullmann) stops speaking in the middle of *Electra* and will not speak again. A psychiatrist thinks it might help if Elisabeth and nurse Alma (Bibi Andersson) spend the summer at her isolated house. Held in the same box of space and time, the two women somehow merge. Elisabeth says nothing, and Alma talks and talks, confessing her plans and her fears, and eventually, in a great and daring monologue, confessing an erotic episode during which she was, for a time, completely happy.

The two actresses look somewhat similar. Bergman emphasizes this similarity in a disturbing shot where he combines half of one face with half of the other. Later, he superimposes the two faces, like a morph. Andersson told me she and Ullmann had no idea Bergman was going to do this, and when she first saw the film, she found it disturbing and frightening. Bergman told me, "The human face is the great subject of the cinema. Everything is there."

Their visual merging suggests a deeper psychic attraction. Elisabeth, the patient, mute and apparently ill, is stronger than Alma, and eventually the nurse feels her soul being overcome by the other woman's strength. There is a moment when her resentment flares and she lashes back. In the sunny courtyard of the cottage, she picks up the pieces of a broken glass and then deliberately leaves a shard where Elisabeth might walk. Elisabeth cuts her foot, but this is essentially a victory for the actress, who has forced the nurse to abandon the discipline of her profession and reveal weakness.

Elisabeth looks at Alma, seeming to know the glass shard was not an accident, and at that moment Bergman allows his film to seem to tear and burn. The screen goes blank. Then the film reconstitutes itself. This sequence mirrors the way the film has opened. In both cases, a projector lamp flares to life, and there is a montage from the earliest days of the cinema: jerky silent skeletons, images of coffins, a hand with a nail being driven into it. The middle "break" ends with the camera moving in toward an eye, and even into the veins in the eyeball, as if to penetrate the mind.

The opening sequence suggests that *Persona* is starting at the beginning, with the birth of cinema. The break in the middle shows it turn-

ing back and beginning again. At the end, the film runs out of the camera and the light dies from the lamp and the film is over. Bergman is showing us that he has returned to first principles. "In the beginning, there was light." Toward the end, there is a shot of the camera crew itself, with the camera mounted on a crane and Nykvist and Bergman tending it; this shot implicates the makers in the work. They are there, it is theirs, they cannot separate themselves from it.

Early in the film, Elisabeth watches images from Vietnam on the TV news, including a Buddhist monk burning himself. Later, there are photographs from the Warsaw Ghetto, of Jews being rounded up; the film lingers on the face of a small boy. Have the horrors of the world caused Elisabeth to stop speaking? The film does not say, but obviously they are implicated. For Alma, horrors are closer to home: She doubts the validity of her relationship with the man she plans to marry; she doubts her abilities as a nurse; she doubts she has the strength to stand up to Elisabeth.

But Elisabeth has private torments too, and Bergman expresses them in a sequence so simple and yet so bold we are astonished by its audacity. First there is a dream sequence (if it is a dream; opinions differ) in which Elisabeth enters the room of Alma in the middle of the night. In a Swedish summer, night is a finger drawn by twilight between one day and the next, and soft pale light floods the room. The two women look at one another like images in a mirror. They turn and face us, one brushing back the other's hair. A man's voice calls, "Elisabeth." It is her husband, Mr. Vogler (Gunnar Björnstrand). They are outside. He caresses Alma's face and calls her "Elisabeth." No, she says, she is not Elisabeth. Elisabeth takes Alma's hand and uses it to caress her husband's face.

Inside, later, Alma delivers a long monologue about Elisabeth's child. The child is born deformed, and Elisabeth leaves it with relatives so she can return to the theater. The story is unbearably painful. It is told with the camera on Elisabeth. Then it is told again, word for word, with the camera on Alma. I believe this is not simply Bergman trying it both ways, as has been suggested, but literally both women telling the same story—through Alma when it is Elisabeth's turn, since Elisabeth does not speak. It shows their beings are in union.

The other monologue in the movie is more famous: Alma's story of sex on the beach involving herself, her girlfriend, and two boys. The imagery of this monologue is so powerful that I have heard people describe the scene as if they actually saw it in the film. In all three monologues, Bergman is showing how ideas create images and reality.

The most real objective experiences in the film are the cut foot and the threat of boiling water, which by "breaking" the film show how everything else is made of thought (or art). The most real experience Alma has ever had is her orgasm on the beach. Elisabeth's pain and Alma's ecstasy were able to break through the reveries of their lives. Most of what we think of as "ourselves" is not direct experience of the world, but a mental broadcast made of ideas, memories, media input, other people, jobs, roles, duties, lusts, hopes, fears. Elisabeth chooses to be who she is; Alma is not strong enough to choose not to be Elisabeth. The title is the key. *Persona*. Singular.

{ PICKPOCKET }

One of the early images in Robert Bresson's *Pickpocket* (1959) shows the unfocused eyes of a man obsessed by excitement and fear. The man's name is Michel. He lives in Paris in a small room under the eaves, a garret almost filled by his cot and his books. He is about to commit a crime. He wants to steal another man's wallet, and he wants his face to appear blank, casual. Perhaps it would, to a casual observer. But we know him and what he is about to do, and in his eyes we see the trancelike ecstasy of a man who is surrendering to his compulsion.

Or do we? Bresson, one of the most thoughtful and philosophical of directors, was fearful of "performances" by his actors. He forced the star of *A Man Escaped* (1956) to repeat the same scene some fifty times, until it was stripped of all emotion and inflection. All Bresson wanted was physical movement. No emotion, no style, no striving for effect. What we see in the pickpocket's face is what we bring to it. Instead of asking his actors to "show fear," Bresson asks them to show nothing, and depends on his story and images to supply the fear.

Martin LaSalle, the star of *Pickpocket*, plays Michel as an unexceptional man with a commonplace face. He is not handsome or ugly or memorable. He usually wears a suit and tie, disappears in a crowd, and has few friends. To one of them, in a café, he wonders aloud if it is all right for an "extraordinary man" to commit a crime—just to get himself started.

Michel is thinking of himself. He could probably get a job in a day if he wanted one. But he does not. He gathers his narcissism around himself like a blanket. He sits in his garret and reads his books, and treasures an image of himself as a man so special that he is privileged to steal from others. Also, of course, he gets an erotic charge out of stealing. On the Métro or at the racetrack, he stands as close as possible to his victims, sensing their breathing, their awareness of him. He waits for a moment of distraction and then opens their purses or slips their wallets from their coats. That is his moment of release, of triumph over a lesser person—although, of course, his face never reflects joy.

In this story, you may sense echoes of Dostoyevsky's *Crime and Punishment,* another story about a lonely intellectual who lived in a garret and thought he had a license, denied to common men, to commit crimes. Bresson's Michel, like Dostoyevsky's hero, Raskolnikov, needs money in order to realize his dreams and sees no reason why some lackluster ordinary person should not be forced to supply it. The reasoning is immoral, but the characters claim special privileges above and beyond common morality.

Michel, like the hero of *Crime and Punishment,* has a good woman in his life, who trusts he will be able to redeem himself. The woman in *Pickpocket* is named Jeanne (Marika Green). She is a neighbor of Michel's mother, and the lover of Michel's friend Jacques (Pierre Leymarie). She comes to Michel with the news that his mother is dying. Michel does not want to see his mother but gives Jeanne money for her. Why does he avoid her? Bresson never supplies motives. We can only guess. Perhaps she shames him with her simplicity. Perhaps she makes it impossible for him to think of himself as an extraordinary man, alone in the world. Does he avoid her because of arrogance, or fear?

Another character in the movie is a police inspector (Jean Pélégri), who has his eye on Michel. They play a delicate cat-and-mouse scene together in which the inspector implies that he knows Michel is a thief, and Michel more or less admits it. Together they examine an ingenious tool designed by a master pickpocket to slit open coat pockets. The inspector is on Michel's case, and Michel, we sense, wants to be caught.

Shoplifters and pickpockets operate in different emotional weather than more brazen thieves. They do not use strength, but stealth. Their thefts are intimate violations of the property of others; to succeed, they must either remain invisible or inspire trust. There is something sexual about it. It's no coincidence that when another pickpocket spots Michel at work and confronts him, it is in a men's room; their liaison involves money as a substitute for sex. And later, when a police decoy at the racetrack shows Michel a pocket full of cash, Michel suspects the man is a cop ("He didn't even bet on the winning horse!"). But he tries to pick his pocket anyway, and when the cop slaps on handcuffs, it's as if that's what Michel hoped for.

Robert Bresson (1907–99) had a talent that flowed freely in old age, like Buñuel and Rohmer. He made his last film, *L'Argent,* in 1983, and it won a special prize at Cannes. He has been called the most Christian of filmmakers. Most of his films deal, in one way or another, with redemption. In *Diary of a Country Priest* (1950), a dying young priest confronts his death by focusing on the lives of others. In *A Man Escaped* (1956), based on a true story of the French Resistance, an imprisoned patriot acts as if his soul is free. In the great *Mouchette* (1967), a young girl—an outcast in her village and a victim of rape—finds a way to shame her enemies. In addition to *Pickpocket*'s parallels of *Crime and Punishment,* Bresson made two films directly based on Dostoyevsky: *Une Femme Douce* (1969) and *Four Nights of a Dreamer* (1971).

Pickpocket is about a man who deliberately and self-consciously tries to operate outside morality ("Will we be judged? By what law"). Like many criminals, he does it for two conflicting reasons: because he thinks he is better than others and because—fearing he is worse—he seeks punishment. He avoids Jeanne because she is wholly good and therefore a threat to him. "These bars, these walls, I don't even see them," he tells her. But he does and is healed by the touch of her hand (the last line: "Oh, Jeanne, what a strange way I had to take to meet you!").

There is incredible buried passion in a Bresson film, but he doesn't find it necessary to express it overtly. Also great tension and excitement, tightly reined in. Consider a sequence in which a gang of pickpockets, including Michel, work on a crowded train. The camera uses close-ups of hands, wallets, pockets, and faces in a perfectly timed ballet of images that explains, like a documentary, how pickpockets work. How one distracts, the second takes the wallet and quickly passes it to the third, who moves away.

The primary rule: The man who takes the money never holds it. The three men work the train back and forth, at one point even smoothly returning a victim's empty wallet to his pocket. Their work has the timing, grace, and precision of a ballet. They work as one person, with one mind. And there is a kind of exhibitionism in the way they show their moves to the camera but hide them from their victims.

Bresson films with a certain gravity, a directness. He wants his actors to emote as little as possible. He likes to film them straight-on, so that we are looking at them as they look at his camera. Oblique shots and over-the-shoulder shots would place characters in the middle of the action; head-on shots say, "here is a man and here is his situation; what are we to think of him?"

{ PINOCCHIO }

When the Russian director Sergei Eisenstein saw Disney's *Snow White and the Seven Dwarfs*, he called it the greatest film ever made. High praise from a man whose *Battleship Potemkin* then topped lists of great films. In *Snow White* (1937), Eisenstein saw a new cinematic freedom: Cartoons could represent any visual an artist could imagine. They were no longer shorts for kids, but worthy to stand beside realistic feature films.

In 1940, Disney made his second and third cartoon features, *Fantasia* and *Pinocchio*, and they are generally considered to this day to be the best of all the studio's animated films. Perhaps they're so good because they came at just the right time in the development of animation.

The early pioneers (Walt Disney and Max Fleischer in particular) found ways to make their characters something more than just drawings on a screen—to make them seem to exist in a world of gravity and dimension. They experimented endlessly with how an animated character should move, finding a new kind of stylized realism that carried conviction without mirroring the real world. The animation expert Ernest Rister writes, "I wonder if they knew that finding a technique for investing a drawing with a sense of weight and volume would someday be used to create killer bugs or a giant snake in the Amazon."

After the breakthrough of *Snow White*, the Disney animators went back to their storyboards with a couple of innovations up their sleeves. One was the freedom to imply that there was space outside the screen. In "regular" movies, characters were half-seen at the edges, they entered and exited, and the camera panned and zoomed through additional space. Early animation tended to stay within the frame. In *Fantasia* and especially *Pinocchio*, Disney broke out of the frame, for example in the exciting sequence where Pinocchio and his father are expelled by the whale's sneeze, then drawn back again, then expelled again. There is the palpable sense of Monstro the Whale, offscreen to the right.

Another innovation was the "multiplane camera," a Disney invention that allowed drawings in three dimensions; the camera seemed to pass through foreground drawings on its way deeper into the frame. There is an aerial shot of Pinocchio's village in which the camera zooms past levels of drawings until it arrives at a close-up. This was much better than using only simple perspective to show depth.

These innovations were not much noticed by *Pinocchio*'s audiences: They were drawn in by the power of the narrative. The story of the little puppet and his quest to become a real boy is a triumph of storytelling with a moral. Has popular culture ever produced a more unforgettable parable about the dangers of telling a lie? The story is just plain wonderful. It contains elements that would be refined into the Disney formula (Figaro the cat and Cleo the goldfish would be recycled into countless comic-relief sidekicks), but its main story line is designed with almost diabolical cunning to reach children.

The key is Pinocchio's desire to become a "real little boy," not just a wooden puppet that can walk and talk without strings. At a very deep level, all children want to become real and doubt that they can. One of the film's inspirations is to leave Pinocchio more or less on his own in the process of becoming. He's supplied with a father figure in Geppetto, the kindly puppet-maker, but the old man is forgetful and easily distracted. And he has Jiminy Cricket, who applies for the job of being Pinocchio's conscience, and gets it, without being terribly well qualified. What Geppetto, the Blue Fairy, and Jiminy do is provide a vision for Pinocchio—an idea of what he should strive toward. But the Blue Fairy warns him she will only help so much, and the other two aren't much help at all.

Kids know they should be good and know they are weak when

tempted. Pinocchio stands for all of them as he sets off for school and allows himself to be diverted by Foulfellow and Gideon. This twist comes as a surprise: The movie has opened on a gentle, mellow tone, with "When You Wish upon a Star" and Geppetto's bedtime play with the puppet and friendship with Figaro and Cleo. The Blue Fairy's magical visit is enchanting. Jiminy is a cheerful new friend. And then suddenly Pinocchio is blindsided by the two con men who supply him to Stromboli, the vile puppeteer. He finds himself starring as a puppet song-and-dance man ("I've Got No Strings"). Jiminy, who is not a gifted analyst, shrugs and figures that since Pinocchio is a star he doesn't need him anymore ("What does an actor want with a conscience anyway?"). Why doesn't Jiminy know how worried Geppetto will be? Maybe crickets don't understand human love.

Pinocchio tries to escape, is locked in a cage by Stromboli, is visited by the Blue Fairy, and then (in one of the best movie scenes ever filmed) tells her lies and finds that his nose grows and grows and grows. Finally it sprouts leaves and gains a nest with two chirping birds in it. Glance sideways at children during this scene, and you'll see kids utterly fascinated by the confirmation of their guiltiest fears.

The Blue Fairy grants a reprieve, but Pinocchio lands back in the soup, scooped up by Foulfellow and shanghaied to Paradise Island, where little boys smoke, play pool, and are recycled into mules for the salt mines ("Give a bad boy enough room and he'll soon make a jackass of himself"). Through the poisons of tobacco and their sins, they grow ears, hooves, and a snout; how many kids decided right then and there never to smoke?

Pinocchio and Jiminy escape and return at last to Geppetto's, only to find (in a powerful and gloomy scene) that the old man is gone. Pinocchio feels abandoned, and in the audience the eyes of kids grow large and moist. The Blue Fairy, deus ex machina to the last, sends a dove with the information that Geppetto is captive in the belly of Monstro the Whale. That leads into the last great action sequence, where Pinocchio proves himself at last. The climax is a cascade of visual imagination. Everyone remembers Monstro's thrashings after Pinocchio sets a fire to make him sneeze. But the action is preceded by a long and magical sequence in which the puppet and the cricket wander the ocean floor, encountering fish, sea flowers, coral denizens, and other delicately drawn creatures.

Pinocchio is a parable for children, and generations have grown up remembering the words "Let your conscience be your guide" and "A lie keeps growing and growing until it's as plain as the nose on your face." The power of the film is generated, I think, by the fact that it is really about something. It isn't just a concocted fable or a silly fairy tale, but a narrative with deep archetypal reverberations. (*Cinderella* [1950], *Beauty and the Beast* [1991], and *The Lion King* [1994] share that quality, and so do the scenes involving Dumbo and his mother.)

Once we've grown up and learned, or ignored, the lessons of the film, why does it continue to have such appeal? It may be because of the grace of the drawing. Later Disney films would have comparable skill, but not the excitement of discovery. Is it possible to sense, through thousands of individual drawings by dozens of different artists, a collective creative epiphany? I think so. Disney's loyal animators had been there in the early days when Mickey Mouse cartoons were patronized by Hollywood as kid stuff from a dinky side-street shop. They must have known they were making something great. Their joy saturates the screen.

What the Disney shop did with its first animated features has resonated through film history. Ernest Rister says in a letter, "I cannot tell you how many of today's computer graphics artists have the book *Disney Animation: The Illusion of Life* at their work stations." All modern animated content in movies, from Jabba the Hut to *Toy Story*, springs from those years of invention at Disney, he says: "The same principles apply everywhere, and those principles were all discovered under one roof, decades ago, by a bunch of young punks jazzed up about creating something."

And that's no lie.

{ PSYCHO }

It wasn't a message that stirred the audiences,
nor was it a great performance . . . they
were aroused by pure film.

So Alfred Hitchcock told François Truffaut about *Psycho,* adding that it
"belongs to filmmakers, to you and me." Hitchcock deliberately wanted *Psy-cho* to look like a cheap exploitation film. He shot it not with his usual ex-pensive feature crew (which had just finished *North by Northwest*), but with
the crew he used for his television show. He filmed in black and white. Long
passages contained no dialogue. His budget, $800,000, was cheap even by
1960 standards; the Bates Motel and mansion were built on the back lot at
Universal. In its visceral feel, *Psycho* has more in common with noir quick-ies like *Detour* (1945) than with elegant Hitchcock thrillers like *Rear Win-dow* (1954) and *Vertigo* (1958).

Yet no other Hitchcock film had a greater impact. "I was directing
the viewers," the director told Truffaut in their book-length interview. "You
might say I was playing them, like an organ." It was the most shocking film
its original audience members had ever seen. "Do not reveal the surprises!"
the ads shouted, and no moviegoer could have anticipated the surprises
Hitchcock had in store: the murder of Marion (Janet Leigh), the apparent

heroine, only a third of the way into the film, and the secret of Norman's mother. *Psycho* was promoted like a William Castle exploitation thriller. "It is required that you see *Psycho* from the very beginning!" Hitchcock decreed, explaining, "The late-comers would have been waiting to see Janet Leigh after she had disappeared from the screen action."

These surprises are now widely known, and yet *Psycho* continues to work as a frightening, insinuating thriller. That's largely because of Hitchcock's artistry in two areas that are not as obvious: the setup of the Marion Crane story, and the relationship between Marion and Norman (Anthony Perkins). Both of these elements work because Hitchcock devotes his full attention and skill to treating them as if they will be developed for the entire picture.

The setup involves a theme that Hitchcock used again and again: the guilt of the ordinary person trapped in a criminal situation. Marion Crane does steal $40,000, but still she fits the Hitchcock mold of an innocent to crime. We see her first during an afternoon in a shabby hotel room with her divorced lover, Sam Loomis (John Gavin). He cannot marry her because of his alimony payments; they must meet in secret. When the money appears, it's attached to a slimy real estate customer (Frank Albertson) who insinuates that for money like that, Marion might be for sale. So Marion's motive is love, and her victim is a creep.

This is a completely adequate setup for a two-hour Hitchcock plot. It never for a moment feels like material manufactured to mislead us. And as Marion flees Phoenix on her way to Sam's hometown of Fairvale, California, we get another favorite Hitchcock trademark: paranoia about the police. A highway patrolman (Mort Mills) wakes her from a roadside nap, questions her, and can almost see the envelope with the stolen money. She trades in her car for one with different plates, but at the dealership she's startled to see the same patrolman parked across the street, leaning against his squad car, arms folded, staring at her. Every first-time viewer believes this setup establishes a story line the movie will follow to the end.

Frightened, tired, perhaps already regretting her theft, Marion drives closer to Fairvale but is slowed by a violent rainstorm. She pulls into the Bates Motel and begins her short, fateful association with Norman Bates. And here again Hitchcock's care with the scenes and dialogue persuades us that Norman and Marion will be players for the rest of the film.

He does this during their long conversation in Norman's "parlor," where savage stuffed birds seem poised to swoop down and capture them as prey. Marion has overheard the voice of Norman's mother speaking sharply with him, and she gently suggests that Norman need not stay here in this dead end, a failing motel on a road that has been bypassed by the new interstate. She cares about Norman. She is also moved to rethink her own actions. And he is touched. So touched, he feels threatened by his feelings. And that is why he must kill her.

When Norman spies on Marion, Hitchcock said, most audience members read it as Peeping Tom behavior. Truffaut observed that the film's opening, with Marion in a bra and panties, underlines the later voyeurism. We have no idea murder is in store.

Seeing the shower scene today, several things stand out. Unlike modern horror films, *Psycho* never shows the knife striking flesh. There are no wounds. There is blood, but not gallons of it. Hitchcock shot in black and white because he felt the audience could not stand so much blood in color (the 1998 Gus Van Sant remake specifically repudiates that theory). The slashing chords of Bernard Herrmann's sound track substitute for more grisly sound effects. The closing shots are not graphic but symbolic, as blood and water spin down the drain, and the camera cuts to a close-up, the same size, of Marion's unmoving eyeball. This remains the most effective slashing in movie history, suggesting that situation and artistry are more important than graphic details.

Perkins does an uncanny job of establishing the complex character of Norman, in a performance that has become a landmark. He shows us there is something fundamentally wrong with Norman, and yet he has a young man's likability, jamming his hands into his jeans pockets, skipping onto the porch, grinning. Only when the conversation grows personal does he stammer and evade. At first he evokes our sympathy as well as Marion's.

The death of the heroine is followed by Norman's meticulous mopping-up of the death scene. Hitchcock is insidiously substituting protagonists. Marion is dead, but now (not consciously but in a deeper place) we identify with Norman—not because we could stab someone, but because, if we had to clean up afterward, we would be consumed by fear and guilt, as he is. The sequence ends with the masterful shot of Bates pushing Marion's car (containing her body and the cash) into a swamp. The car sinks, then pauses. Norman watches intently. The car finally disappears under the surface.

Analyzing our feelings, we realize we *wanted* that car to sink, as much as Norman did. Before Sam Loomis reappears, teamed up with Marion's sister, Lila (Vera Miles), to search for her, *Psycho* already has a new protagonist: Norman Bates. This is one of the most audacious substitutions in Hitchcock's long practice of leading and manipulating us. The rest of the film is effective melodrama, and there are two jarring shocks. The private eye Arbogast (Martin Balsam) is murdered, in a shot that uses back projection to seem to follow him down the stairs. And the secret of Norman's mother is revealed.

For thoughtful viewers, however, an equal surprise is still waiting. That is the mystery of why Hitchcock marred the ending of a masterpiece with a sequence that is grotesquely out of place. After the murders have been solved, there is an inexplicable scene during which a long-winded psychiatrist (Simon Oakland) lectures the assembled survivors on the causes of Norman's psychopathic behavior. This is an anticlimax taken almost to the point of parody. If I were bold enough to reedit Hitchcock's film, I would include only the doctor's first explanation of Norman's dual personality: "Norman Bates no longer exists. He only half existed to begin with. And now, the other half has taken over, probably for all time." Then I would cut out everything else the psychiatrist says, and cut to the shots of Norman wrapped in the blanket while his mother's voice speaks ("It's sad when a mother has to speak the words that condemn her own son"). Those edits, I submit, would have made *Psycho* very nearly perfect. I have never encountered a single convincing defense of the psychiatric blather; Truffaut tactfully avoids it in his famous interview.

What makes *Psycho* immortal, when so many films are already half-forgotten as we leave the theater, is that it connects directly with our fears: our fears that we might impulsively commit a crime, our fears of the police, our fears of becoming the victim of a madman, and, of course, our fears of disappointing our mothers.

{ PULP FICTION }

Dialogue drives Quentin Tarantino's *Pulp Fiction*—dialogue of such high quality it deserves comparison with other masters of spare, hard-boiled prose, from Raymond Chandler to Elmore Leonard. Like them, Q.T. finds a way to make the words humorous without ever seeming to ask for a laugh. Like them, he combines utilitarian prose with flights of rough poetry and wicked fancy.

Consider a little scene not often mentioned in discussions of the film. The prizefighter Butch (Bruce Willis) has just killed a man in the ring. He returns to the motel room occupied by his girlfriend, Fabienne (Maria de Medeiros). She says she's been looking in the mirror and she wants a pot-belly. "You have one," he says, snuggling closer. "If I had one," she says, "I would wear a T-shirt two sizes too small, to accentuate it." A little later, she observes, "It's unfortunate what we find pleasing to the touch and pleasing to the eye are seldom the same."

This is wonderful dialogue (I have only sampled it). It is about something. The dialogue comes at a moment of desperation for Butch. He agreed to throw the fight, then secretly bet heavily on himself and won. He will make a lot of money—but only if he escapes the vengeance of Marsel-lus Wallace (Ving Rhames) and his hit men Jules and Vincent (Samuel L. Jackson and John Travolta). In a lesser movie, the dialogue in this scene would have been entirely plot-driven; Butch would have explained to Fabi-

enne what he, she, and we already knew. Instead, Tarantino uses an apparently irrelevant conversation to quickly establish her personality and their relationship. His dialogue is always load-bearing.

It is Tarantino's strategy in all of his films to have the characters speak at right angles to the action, or depart on flights of fancy. Remember the opening conversation between Jules and Vincent, who are on their way to a violent reprisal against some college kids who have offended Wallace and appropriated his briefcase. They talk about the drug laws in Amsterdam, what Quarter Pounders are called in Paris, and the degree of sexual intimacy implied by a foot massage. Finally Jules says, "Let's get in character," and they enter an apartment.

Tarantino's dialogue is not simply whimsical. There is a method behind it. The discussion of why Quarter Pounders are called Royales in Paris is reprised, a few minutes later, in a tense exchange between Jules and one of the kids (Frank Whaley). And the story of how Marsellus had a man thrown out of a fourth-floor window for giving his wife a foot massage turns out to be a setup: Tarantino is preparing the dramatic ground for a scene in which Vincent takes Mia Wallace (Uma Thurman) out on a date, on his boss's orders. When Mia accidentally overdoses, Vincent races her to his drug dealer, Lance (Eric Stoltz), who brings her back to life with a shot of adrenaline into the heart.

And *that* scene also begins with dialogue that seems like fun while it's also laying more groundwork. We meet Lance's girlfriend, Jody (Rosanna Arquette), who is pierced in every possible place and talks about her piercing fetish. Tarantino is setting up his payoff. When the needle goes into the heart, you'd expect that to be one of the most gruesome moments in the movie, but audiences, curiously, always laugh. In a shot-by-shot analysis at the University of Virginia, we found out why. Q.T. never actually shows the needle entering the chest. He cuts away to reaction shots in which everyone hovering over the victim springs back simultaneously as Mia leaps back to life. And then Jody says it was "trippy"—and we understand that, as a piercer, she has seen the ultimate piercing. The body language and the punch line take a grotesque scene and turn it into dark but genuine comedy. It's all in the dialogue and the editing. Also, of course, in the underlying desperation, set up by thoughts of what Marsellus might do to Vincent, since killing Mrs. Wallace is much worse than massaging her foot.

The movie's circular, self-referential structure is famous. The restaurant holdup with Pumpkin and Honey Bunny (Tim Roth and Amanda Plummer) begins and ends the film, and other story lines weave in and out of strict chronology. But there *is* a chronology in the dialogue, in the sense that what is said before invariably sets up or enriches what comes after. The dialogue is proof that Tarantino had the time-juggling in mind from the very beginning, because there's never a glitch; the scenes do not follow in chronological order, but the dialogue always knows exactly where it falls in the movie.

I mentioned the way the needle-to-the-heart scene is redeemed by laughter. That's also the case with the scene where the hit men inadvertently kill a passenger in their car. The car's interior is covered with blood, and the Wolf (Harvey Keitel) is called to handle the situation; we remember much more blood than we actually see, which is why the scene doesn't stop the movie dead in its tracks. Scenes of gore are deflected into scenes of the Wolf's professionalism, which is funny because it is so matter-of-fact. The movie does contain scenes of sudden, brutal violence, as when Jules and Vincent open fire in the apartment, or when Butch goes "medieval" (Marsellus's unforgettable word choice) on the leather guys. But Tarantino uses long shots, surprise, cutaways, and the context of the dialogue to make the movie seem less violent than it has any right to.

Howard Hawks once gave his definition of a good movie: "Three great scenes. No bad scenes." Few movies in recent years have had more good scenes than *Pulp Fiction*. Some are almost musical comedy, as when Vincent and Mia dance at Jackrabbit Slim's. Some are stunning in their suddenness, as when Butch returns to his apartment and surprises Vincent. Some are all verbal style, as in Marsellus Wallace's dialogue with Butch, or when Captain Koons (Christopher Walken) delivers a monologue to the "little man" about his father's watch.

And some seem deliberately planned to provoke discussion: What is in the briefcase? Why are there glowing flashes of light during the early shooting in the apartment? Is Jackson quoting the Bible correctly? Some scenes depend entirely on behavior (the Wolf's no-nonsense cleanup detail).

Many of the scenes have an additional level of interest because the characters fear reprisals (Bruce fears Wallace, Vincent fears Wallace, Jimmie the drug dealer wants the dead body removed before his wife comes home).

I saw *Pulp Fiction* for the first time at the Cannes Film Festival in 1994; it went on to win the Palme d'Or and to dominate the national conversation about film for at least the next twelve months. It is the most influential film of the decade; its circular timeline can be sensed in films as different as *The Usual Suspects, The Zero Effect,* and *Memento*—not that they copied it, but that they were aware of the pleasures of toying with chronology. But it isn't the structure that makes *Pulp Fiction* a great film. Its greatness comes from its marriage of original characters (essentially comic) with a series of vivid and half-fanciful events—and from the dialogue. The dialogue is the foundation of everything else.

Watching many movies, I realize that all of the dialogue is entirely devoted to explaining or furthering the plot, and no joy is taken in the style of language and idiom for its own sake. There is not a single line in *Pearl Harbor* you would want to quote with anything but derision. Most conversations in most movies are deadly boring—which is why directors with no gift for dialogue depend so heavily on action and special effects. The characters in *Pulp Fiction* are always talking, and always interesting, funny, scary, or audacious. This movie would work as an audio book. Imagine having to listen to *The Mummy Returns*.

{ RAGING BULL }

Raging Bull is not a film about boxing, but about a man with paralyzing jealousy and sexual insecurity, for whom being punished in the ring serves as confession, penance, and absolution. It is no accident that the screenplay never concerns itself with fight strategy. For Jake LaMotta, what happens during a fight is controlled not by tactics, but by his fears and drives.

Consumed by rage after his wife, Vickie, unwisely describes one of his opponents as "good-looking," he pounds the man's face into a pulp, and in the audience a Mafia boss leans over to his lieutenant and observes, "He ain't pretty no more." After the punishment has been delivered, Jake (Robert De Niro) looks not at his opponent, but into the eyes of his wife (Cathy Moriarty), who gets the message.

Martin Scorsese's 1980 film was voted in three polls as the greatest film of the decade, but when he was making it, he seriously wondered if it would ever be released: "We felt like we were making it for ourselves." Scorsese and Robert De Niro had been reading the autobiography of Jake LaMotta, the middleweight champion whose duels with Sugar Ray Robinson were a legend in the 1940s. They asked Paul Schrader, who wrote *Taxi Driver* (1976), to do a screenplay. The project languished while Scorsese and De Niro made the ambitious but unfocused musical *New York, New York* (1977) and then languished some more as Scorsese's drug use led to a crisis. De Niro visited his friend in the hospital, threw the book on his bed, and said, "I think we should make this." And the making of *Raging Bull,* with a screenplay further sculpted by Mardik Martin (*Mean Streets* [1973]), became therapy and rebirth for the filmmaker.

The movie won Oscars for De Niro and editor Thelma Schoonmaker, and nominations for best picture, director, cinematography, sound, and supporting actor (Joe Pesci) and actress (Moriarty). It lost for best picture to *Ordinary People,* but time has rendered a different verdict. At the University of Virginia, I was able to do a stop-action analysis of the film with Schoonmaker as my tour guide; the editor, who always knows all of a film's secrets, helped me see what meticulous detail and construction went into this brawling, painful story.

For Scorsese, the life of LaMotta was like an illustration of a theme always present in his work, the inability of his characters to trust and relate with women. The engine that drives the LaMotta character in the film is not boxing, but a jealous obsession with his wife, Vickie, and a fear of sexuality. From the time he first sees her, as a girl of fifteen, LaMotta is mesmerized by the cool, distant, blond goddess, who seems so much older than her age, and in many shots seems taller and even stronger than the boxer.

Although there is no direct evidence in the film that she has ever cheated on him, she is a woman who at fifteen was already on friendly terms with Mafiosi, who knew the score, whose level gaze, directed at LaMotta during their first date, shows a woman completely confident as she waits for Jake to awkwardly make his moves. It is remarkable that Moriarty, herself nineteen, had the presence to so convincingly portray the later stages of a woman in a bad marriage.

Jake has an ambivalence toward women that Freud named the "Madonna-whore complex." For LaMotta, women are unapproachable, virginal ideals—until they are sullied by physical contact (with him), after which they become suspect. During the film, he tortures himself with fantasies that Vickie is cheating on him. Every word, every glance, is twisted by his scrutiny. He never catches her, but he beats her as if he had; his suspicion is proof of her guilt.

The closest relationship in the film is between Jake and his brother, Joey (Joe Pesci). Pesci's casting was a stroke of luck; he had decided to give up acting when he was asked to audition after De Niro saw him in a B

movie. Pesci's performance is the counterpoint to De Niro's, and its equal; their verbal sparring has a kind of crazy music to it, as in the scene where Jake loses the drift of Joey's argument as he explains, "You lose, you win. You win, you win. Either way, you win." And the scene where Jake adjusts the TV and accuses Joey of cheating with Vickie: "Maybe you don't know what you mean." The dialogue reflects the Little Italy of Scorsese's childhood, as when Jake tells his first wife that overcooking the steak "defeats its own purpose."

The fight scenes took Scorsese ten weeks to shoot instead of the planned two. They use, in their way, as many special effects as a science fiction film. The sound track subtly combines crowd noise with animal cries, bird shrieks, and the grating explosions of flashbulbs (actually panes of glass being smashed). We aren't consciously aware of all we're listening to, but we feel it. The fights are broken down into dozens of shots, edited by Schoonmaker into duels consisting not of strategy, but simply of punishing blows. The camera is sometimes only inches from the fists; Scorsese broke the rules of boxing pictures by staying inside the ring and by freely changing its shape and size to suit his needs—sometimes it's claustrophobic, sometimes unnaturally elongated.

The brutality of the fights is also new; LaMotta makes Rocky look tame. Blows are underlined by thudding impacts on the sound track, and Scorsese uses sponges concealed in the gloves and tiny tubes in the boxers' hair to deliver spurts and sprays of sweat and blood; this is the wettest of boxing pictures, drenched in the fluids of battle. One reason for filming in black and white was Scorsese's reluctance to show all that blood in a color picture.

The most effective visual strategy in the film is the use of slow motion to suggest a heightened awareness. Just as *Taxi Driver*'s Travis Bickle saw the sidewalks of New York in slow motion, so LaMotta sees Vickie so intently that time seems to expand around her. Normal movement is shot at twenty-four frames a second; slow motion uses more frames per second, so that it takes longer for them to be projected. Scorsese uses such subtle speeds as thirty or thirty-six fps, and we internalize the device so that we feel the tension of narrowed eyes and mounting anger when Jake is triggered by paranoia over Vickie's behavior.

The film is bookmarked by scenes in which the older Jake La-Motta, balding and overweight, makes a living giving "readings," running a nightclub, even emceeing at a Manhattan strip club. It was De Niro's idea to interrupt the filming while he put on weight for these scenes, in which his belly hangs over his belt. The closing passages of the film include Jake's crisis of pure despair, in which he punches the walls of his Miami jail cell, crying out, "Why! Why! Why!"

Not long after, he pursues his brother down a New York street, to embrace him tenderly in a parking garage, in what passes for the character's redemption—that, and the extraordinary moment where he looks at himself in a dressing room mirror and recites from *On the Waterfront* ("I coulda been a contender"). It's not De Niro doing Brando, as is often mistakenly said, but De Niro doing LaMotta doing Brando doing Terry Malloy. De Niro could do a "better" Brando imitation, but what would be the point?

Raging Bull is the most painful and heart-rending portrait of jealousy in the cinema—an *Othello* for our times. It's the best film I've seen about the low self-esteem, sexual inadequacy, and fear that lead some men to abuse women. Boxing is the arena, not the subject. LaMotta was famous for never being knocked down in the ring. There are scenes where he stands passively, his hands at his side, allowing himself to be hammered. We sense why he didn't go down. He hurt too much to allow the pain to stop.

$\Big\{$ RED RIVER $\Big\}$

When Peter Bogdanovich needed a movie to play as the final feature in the doomed small-town theater in *The Last Picture Show,* he chose Howard Hawks's *Red River* (1948). He selected the scene where John Wayne tells Montgomery Clift, "Take 'em to Missouri, Matt!" And then there is Hawks's famous montage of weathered cowboy faces in close-up and exaltation, as they cry "Hee-yaw!" and wave their hats in the air.

The moment is as quintessentially western as any ever filmed, capturing the exhilaration of being on a horse under the big sky with a job to do and a paycheck at the other end. And *Red River* is one of the greatest of all westerns when it stays with its central story about an older man and a younger one, and the first cattle drive down the Chisholm Trail. It is only in its few scenes involving women that it goes wrong.

The film's hero and villain is Tom Dunson (Wayne), who heads West with a wagon train in 1851 and then peels off for Texas to start a cattle ranch. He takes along only his wagon driver, Nadine Groot (Walter Brennan). Dunson's sweetheart, Fen (Coleen Gray), wants to join them, but he rejects her almost absentmindedly, promising to send for her later. Later, from miles away, Tom and Nadine see smoke rising: Indians have destroyed the wagon train. Nadine, a grizzled codger, fulminates about how Indians "always want to be burning up good wagons," and Tom observes that it

would take them too long to go back and try to help. Their manner is surprisingly distant, considering that Dunson has just lost the woman he loved.

Soon after, the men encounter a young boy who survived the Indian attack. This is Matt Garth, who is adopted by Dunson and raised as
the eventual heir to his ranch. Played as an adult by Montgomery Clift (his
first screen role), Matt goes away to school, but returns in 1866 just as Dunson is preparing an epic drive to take nine thousand head of cattle north to
Missouri.

I mentioned that Dunson is both hero and villain. It's a sign of the
movie's complexity that John Wayne, often typecast, is given a tortured,
conflicted character to play. He starts with "a boy with a cow and a man with
a bull" and builds up a great herd. But then he faces ruin; he must drive the
cattle north or go bankrupt. He's a stubborn man; all through the movie
people tell him he's wrong, and usually they're right. They're especially right
in wanting to take the cattle to Abilene, which is closer and reportedly has
a railroad line, instead of on the longer trek to Missouri. As the cattle drive
grows grueling, Dunson grows irascible, and finally whiskey and lack of
sleep drive him a little mad; there are attempted mutinies before Matt finally rebels and takes the cattle to Abilene.

The critic Tim Dirks has pointed out the parallels between their
conflict and the standoff between Captain Bligh and Fletcher Christian in
Mutiny on the Bounty. And indeed the Borden Chase screenplay makes
much of the older man's pride and the younger one's need to prove himself.
Also established, but never really developed, is a rivalry between young
Matt and a tough cowboy named Cherry Valance (John Ireland), who signs
up for the cattle drive and becomes Matt's rival. "There's gonna be trouble
between those two," old Groot predicts, but the film never delivers, leaving
them stranded in the middle of a peculiar ambivalence that drew the attention of *The Celluloid Closet* (1995), a documentary about hidden homosexuality in the movies. ("You know," Cherry says, handling Matt's gun, "there
are only two things more beautiful than a good gun. A Swiss watch, or a
woman from anywhere. You ever had a Swiss watch?")

The shifting emotional attachments in the movie are tracked by a
silver bracelet, which Dunson gives to Fen before leaving her. It later turns
up on the wrist of an Indian he kills, and Dunson then gives it to Matt, who

later gives it to Tess Millay (Joanne Dru), a woman he rescues and falls in love with. The three scenes with Tess are the movie's low points, in part because of her prattle (listen to how she chats distractingly with Matt during an Indian attack), in part because she is all too obviously the deus ex machina the plot needs to avoid an unhappy ending. The final scene is the weakest in the film, and screenwriter Borden Chase reportedly hated it, with good reason: Two men act out a fierce psychological rivalry for two hours, only to cave in instantly to a female's glib tongue-lashing.

What we remember with *Red River* is not, however, the silly ending, but the setup and the majestic central portions. The tragic rivalry is so well established that somehow it keeps its weight and dignity in our memories, even though the ending undercuts it.

Just as memorable are the scenes of the cattle drive itself, as a handful of men control a herd so large it takes all night to ford a river. Russell Harlan's cinematography finds classical compositions in the drive, arrangements of men, sky, and trees, and then in the stampede scene he shows a river of cattle flowing down a hill. It is an outdoor movie (we never go inside the ranch house Dunson must have built), and when young Matt steps inside the cattle buyer's office in Abilene, he ducks, observing how long it's been since he was under a roof.

Hawks is wonderful at setting moods. Notice the ominous atmosphere he brews on the night of the stampede—the silence, the restlessness of the cattle, the lowered voices. Notice Matt's nervousness during a night of thick fog, when every shadow may be Tom, come to kill him. And the tension earlier, when Dunson holds a kangaroo court. And watch the subtle way Hawks modulates Tom Dunson's gradual collapse. John Wayne is tall and steady at the beginning of the picture, but by the end his hair is gray and lank, and his eyes are haunted; the transition is so gradual we might not even notice he wears a white hat at the outset but a black one at the end. Wayne is sometimes considered more of a natural force than an actor, but here his understated acting is right on the money; the critic Joseph McBride says that John Ford, who had directed Wayne many times, saw *Red River* and told Hawks, "I never knew the big son of a bitch could act."

Between Wayne and Clift there is a clear tension, not only between an older man and a younger one but between an actor who started in 1929 and another who represented the leading edge of the Method. It's almost as if Wayne, who could go over a flamboyant actor, was trying to go under a quiet one: He meets the challenge and matches it.

The theme of *Red River* is from classical tragedy: the need of the son to slay the father, literally or symbolically, in order to clear the way for his own ascendancy. And the father's desire to gain immortality through a child (the one moment with a woman that does work is when Dunson asks Tess to bear a son for him). The majesty of the cattle drive, and all of its expert details about "taking the point" and keeping the cowhands fed and happy, is atmosphere surrounding these themes.

Underlying everything else is an attitude that must have been invisible to the filmmakers at the time: the unstated assumption that it is the white man's right to take what he wants. Dunson shoots a Mexican who comes to tell him "Don Diego" owns the land. Told the land had been granted to Diego by the king of Spain, Dunson says, "You mean he took it away from whoever was here before—Indians, maybe. Well, I'm takin' it away from him." In throwaway dialogue, we learn of seven more men Dunson has killed for his ranch, and there's a grimly humorous motif as he shoots people and then "reads over 'em" from the Bible. Dunson is a law of his own, until Matt stops a hanging and ends his reign. If most westerns are about the inevitable encroachment of civilization, this is one where it seems like a pretty good idea.

{ SCHINDLER'S LIST }

Schindler's List is described as a film about the Holocaust, but the Holocaust supplies the field for the story, rather than the subject. The film is really two parallel character studies—one of a con man, the other of a psychopath. Oskar Schindler, who swindles the Third Reich, and Amon Goeth, who represents its pure evil, are men created by the opportunities of war.

Schindler had no success in business before or after the war, but used its cover to run factories that saved the lives of more than one thousand Jews. (Technically the factories were failures too, but that was his plan: "If this factory ever produces a shell that can actually be fired, I'll be very unhappy.") Goeth was executed after the war, which he used as a cover for his homicidal pathology.

In telling their stories, Steven Spielberg found a way to approach the Holocaust, which is a subject too vast and tragic to be encompassed in any reasonable way by fiction. In the ruins of the saddest story of the century, he found not a happy ending, but at least one affirming that resistance to evil is possible and can succeed. In the face of the Nazi charnel houses, it is a statement that has to be made, or we sink into despair.

The film has been an easy target for those who find Spielberg's approach too upbeat or "commercial," or condemn him for converting Holocaust sources into a well-told story. But every artist must work in his medium, and the medium of film does not exist unless there is an audience between the projector and the screen. Claude Lanzmann made a more profound film about the Holocaust in *Shoah* (1985), but few were willing to sit through its nine hours. Spielberg's unique ability in his serious films has been to join artistry with popularity—to say what he wants to say in a way that millions of people want to hear.

In *Schindler's List* (1993), his brilliant achievement is the character of Oskar Schindler, played by Liam Neeson as a man who never, until almost the end, admits to anyone what he is really doing. Schindler leaves it to "his" Jews, and particularly to his accountant, Itzhak Stern (Ben Kingsley), to understand the unsayable: that Schindler is using his factory as a con game to cheat the Nazis of the lives of his workers. Schindler leaves it to Stern, and Spielberg leaves it to us; the movie is a rare case of a man doing the opposite of what he seems to be doing, and a director letting the audience figure it out itself.

The measure of Schindler's audacity is stupendous. His first factory makes pots and pans. His second makes shell casings. Both factories are so inefficient they make hardly any contribution to the Nazi war effort. A more cautious man might have insisted that the factories produced fine pots and usable casings, to make them invaluable to the Nazis. The full measure of Schindler's obsession is that he wanted to save Jewish lives *and* produce unusable goods—all the while wearing a Nazi Party badge on the lapel of his expensive black-market suit.

The key to his character is found in his first big scene, in a nightclub frequented by Nazi officers. We gather that his resources consist of the money in his pocket and the clothes he stands up in. He walks into the club, sends the best champagne to a table of high-ranking Nazis, and soon has the Nazis and their girlfriends sitting at *his* table, which swells with late arrivals. Who is this man? Why, Oskar Schindler, of course. And who is that? The Reich never figures out the answer to that question.

Schindler's strategy as a con man is to always seem in charge, to seem well connected, to lavish powerful Nazis with gifts and bribes, and to stride, tall and imperious, through situations that would break a lesser man. He also has the con man's knack of disguising the real object of the con. The Nazis accept his bribes and assume that his purpose is to enrich himself

through the war. They do not object, because he enriches them too. It never occurs to them that he is actually saving Jews. There is that ancient story about how the guards search the thief's wheelbarrow every day, unable to figure out what he is stealing. He is stealing wheelbarrows. The Jews are Schindler's wheelbarrows.

Some of the most dramatic scenes in the movie show Schindler literally snatching his workers from the maw of death. He rescues Stern from a death train. Then he redirects a trainload of his male workers from Auschwitz to his hometown in Czechoslovakia. When the women's train is routed to Auschwitz in error, Schindler boldly strides into the death camp and bribes the commandant to ship them back out again. His insight here is that no one would walk into Auschwitz on such a mission if he were not the real thing. His very boldness is his shield.

Stern, of course, quickly figures out that Schindler's real game is not to get rich, but to save lives. Yet this is not said aloud until Schindler has Stern make a list of some eleven hundred workers who will be transported to Czechoslovakia. "The list is an absolute good," Stern tells him. "The list is life. All around its margins lies the gulf."

Consider now Commandant Amon Goeth (Ralph Fiennes), the Nazi who has power over the Krakow Ghetto and later over the camp where the Jews are moved. He stands on the balcony of his ski chalet and shoots Jews as target practice, destroying any shred of hope they may have that the Nazi policies will follow some sane pattern. If they can die arbitrarily at his whim, then both protest and adherence are meaningless and useless.

Goeth is clearly mad. War masks his underlying nature as a serial killer. His cruelty twists back on his victims: He spares a life only long enough to give his victim hope and then shoots him. Seeing *Schindler's List* again recently, I wondered if it was a weakness to make Goeth insane. Would it have been better for Spielberg to focus instead on a Nazi functionary—an "ordinary" man who is simply following orders? The terror of the Holocaust comes not because a monster like Goeth could murder people, but because thousands of people snatched from their everyday lives became, in the chilling phrase, Hitler's willing executioners.

I don't know. The film as Spielberg made it is haunting and powerful; perhaps it was necessary to have a one-dimensional villain in a film whose hero has so many hidden dimensions. The ordinary man who was just "following orders" might have disturbed the focus of the film—although he would have been in contrast with Schindler, an ordinary man who did not follow orders.

Schindler's List gives us information about how parts of the Holocaust operated, but does not explain it, because it is inexplicable that men could practice genocide. Or so we want to believe. In fact, genocide is a commonplace in human history and has happened recently in Africa, the Middle East, Afghanistan, and elsewhere. The United States was colonized through a policy of genocide against native peoples. Religion and race are markers that we use to hate one another, and unless we can get beyond them, we must concede we are potential executioners. The power of Spielberg's film is not that it explains evil, but that it insists that men can be good in the face of it, and that good can prevail.

The film's ending brings me to tears. At the end of the war, Schindler's Jews are in a strange land—stranded but alive. A member of the liberating Russian forces asks them, "Isn't a town over there?" and they walk off toward the horizon. The next shot fades from black and white into color. At first we think it may be a continuation of the previous action, until we see that the men and women on the crest of the hill are dressed differently now. And then it strikes us, with the force of a blow: *Those are Schindler's Jews.* We are looking at the actual survivors and their children as they visit Oskar Schindler's grave. The movie began with a list of Jews being confined to the ghetto. It ends with a list of some who were saved. The list is an absolute good. The list is life. All around its margins lies the gulf.

{ THE SEVEN SAMURAI }

Akira Kurosawa's *The Seven Samurai* (1954) is not only a great film in its own right but the source of a genre that flowed through the rest of the century. The critic Michael Jeck suggests that this was the first film in which a team is assembled to carry out a mission—an idea that gave birth to its direct Hollywood remake, *The Magnificent Seven,* as well as *The Guns of Navarone, The Dirty Dozen,* and countless later war, heist, and caper movies. Since Kurosawa's samurai adventure *Yojimbo* (1961) was remade as *A Fistful of Dollars* and essentially created the spaghetti western, and since this movie and Kurosawa's *The Hidden Fortress* (1958) inspired George Lucas's Star Wars series, it could be argued that this greatest of filmmakers gave employment to action heroes for the next fifty years, just as a fallout from his primary purpose.

That purpose was to make a samurai movie that was anchored in ancient Japanese culture, and yet argued for a flexible humanism in place of rigid traditions. One of the central truths of *The Seven Samurai* is that the samurai and the villagers who hire them are of different castes and must never mix. Indeed, we learn that these villagers had earlier been hostile to samurai—and one of them, even now, hysterically fears that a samurai will make off with his daughter. Yet the bandits represent a greater threat, and so the samurai are hired, valued and resented in about equal measure.

Why do they take the job? Why, for a handful of rice every day, do

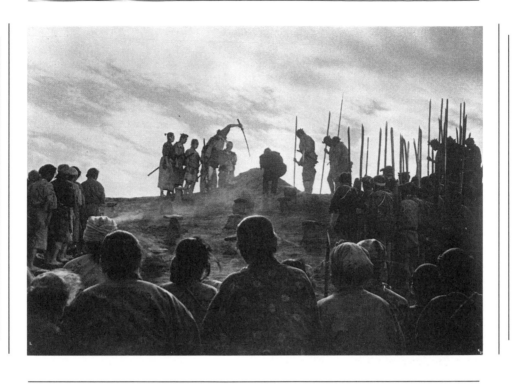

they risk their lives? Because that is the job and the nature of the samurai. Both sides are bound by the roles imposed on them by society, and in *To the Distant Observer*, his study of Japanese films, Noel Burch observes that "masochistic perseverance in the fulfillment of complex social obligations is a basic cultural trait of Japan." Not only do the samurai persevere but so do the bandits, who continue their series of raids even though it is clear that the village is well defended, that they are sustaining heavy losses, and that there must be unprotected villages somewhere close around. Like characters in a Greek tragedy, they perform the roles they have been assigned.

Two of the movie's significant subplots deal with rebellion against social tradition. Kikuchiyo, the high-spirited samurai played by Toshiro Mifune as a rambunctious show-off, was not born a samurai, but has jumped caste to become one. And there is a forbidden romance between the samurai Katsushiro (Isao Kimura) and a village girl (ironically the very daughter whose father was so worried). They love one another, but a farmer's daughter cannot dream of marrying a ronin; when they are found together on the eve of the final battle, however, there are arguments in the village to "understand the young people," and an appeal to romance—an appeal designed for modern audiences and unlikely to have carried much weight in the 1600s when the movie is set.

Kurosawa was considered the most Western of great Japanese directors (*too* Western, some of his Japanese critics sniffed). *The Seven Samurai* represents a great divide in his work. Most of his earlier films, Jeck observes, subscribe to the Japanese virtues of teamwork, fitting in, going along, conforming. All his later films are about misfits, noncomformists, and rebels. The turning point can be seen in his greatest film, *Ikiru* (1952), in which a bureaucrat spends his days in the rote performance of meaningless duties but decides when he is dying to break loose and achieve at least one meaningful thing.

That bureaucrat was played by Takashi Shimura—who, incredibly, also plays Kambei, the leader of the seven samurai. He looks old and withered in the 1952 picture, tough and weathered in this one. Kurosawa was loyal to his longtime collaborators and used either Shimura or Mifune, or often both of them, in every movie he made for eighteen years. In *The Seven Samurai*, both actors are essential. Shimura's Kambei is the veteran warrior, who in an early scene shaves his head to disguise himself as a priest, in order to enter a house where a hostage is being held. (Did *this* scene create the long action-movie tradition of opening sequences in which the hero wades into a dangerous situation unrelated to the later plot?) He spends the rest of the movie distractedly rubbing his bristling head during moments of puzzlement. He is a calm, wise leader and a good strategist, and we follow the battles partly because he (and Kurosawa) map them out for us, walk us through the village's defenses, and keep count as the forty bandits are whittled down one by one.

Mifune's character, Kikuchiyo, is an overcompensator. He arrives equipped with a sword longer than anyone else's and swaggers around holding it over his shoulder like a rifleman. He is impulsive, brave, a show-off who quickly assembles a fan club of local kids who follow him around. Mifune was himself a superb athlete and does some difficult jumps and stunts in the movie, but his character is shown to be a hopeless horseman (as a farmer's son, Kikuchiyo would not have had an opportunity as a youth to learn to ride). One running gag involves Kikuchiyo's inability to master an unruly local horse; there is a delightful moment where horse and rider disappear behind a barrier together and emerge separately.

The movie is long (207 minutes), with an intermission, and yet it moves quickly because the storytelling is so clear, there are so many sharply defined characters, and the action scenes have a thrilling sweep. Nobody could photograph men in action better than Kurosawa. One of his particular trademarks is the use of human tides, sweeping down from higher places to lower ones, and he loves to devise shots in which the camera follows the rush and flow of an action, instead of cutting it up into separate shots. His use of close-ups in some of the late battle scenes was perhaps noticed by Orson Welles, who in *Falstaff* conceals a shortage of extras by burying the camera in a Kurosawan tangle of horses, legs, and swords.

Repeated viewings of *The Seven Samurai* reveal visual patterns. Consider the irony, for example, in two sequences that bookend the first battle with the bandits. In the first, the villagers have heard the bandits are coming, and rush around in panic. Kambei orders his samurai to calm and contain them, and the ronin run from one group to the next (the villagers always run in groups, not individually) to herd them into cover. Later, after the bandits have been repulsed, a wounded bandit falls in the village square, and now the villagers rush forward with delayed bravery, to kill him. This time the samurai hurry about pushing them back. Mirrored scenes like that can be found throughout the movie.

There is also an instinctive feeling for composition. Kurosawa constantly uses deep focus to follow simultaneous actions in the foreground, middle, and background. Often he delineates the distance with barriers. Consider a shot where the samurai, in the foreground, peer out through the slats of a building and across an empty ground to the sight of the bandits, peering in through the slats of a barrier erected against them. Kurosawa's moving camera often avoids cuts in order to make comparisons, as when he will begin on dialogue in a close-up, sweep through a room or a clearing, and end on a close-up of another character who is the point of the dialogue.

Many characters die in *The Seven Samurai*, but violence and action are not the point of the movie. It is more about duty and social roles. The samurai at the end have lost four of their seven, yet there are no complaints because that is the samurai's lot. The villagers do not much want the samurai around once the bandits are gone because armed men are a threat to order. That is the nature of society. The samurai who fell in love with the local girl is used significantly in the composition of the final shots. First he is seen with his colleagues. Then with the girl. Then in an uncommitted place not with the samurai, but somehow of them. Here you can see two genres at war: the samurai movie and the western, with which Kurosawa was quite familiar. Should the hero get the girl? Japanese audiences in 1954 would have said no. Kurosawa spent the next forty years arguing against the theory that the individual should be the instrument of society.

{ THE SEVENTH SEAL }

A knight returning from the Crusades finds a rude church still open in the midst of the Black Death and goes to confession there. Speaking to a hooded figure half-seen through an iron grille, he pours out his heart: "My indifference has shut me out. I live in a world of ghosts, a prisoner of dreams. I want God to put out his hand, show his face, speak to me. I cry out to him in the dark but there is no one there." The hooded figure turns and is revealed as Death, who has been following the knight on his homeward journey.

Images like that have no place in the modern cinema, which is committed to facile psychology and realistic behavior. In many ways, Ingmar Bergman's *The Seventh Seal* (1957) has more in common with the silent film than with the modern films that followed it—including his own. Perhaps that is why it is out of fashion at the moment. Long considered one of the masterpieces of cinema, it is now a little embarrassing to some viewers, with its stark imagery and its uncompromising subject, which is no less than the absence of God.

Films are no longer concerned with the silence of God, but with the chattering of men. We are uneasy to find Bergman asking existential questions in an age of irony, and Bergman himself, starting with *Persona* (1966), found more subtle ways to ask the same questions. But the directness of *The*

Seventh Seal is its strength: This is an uncompromising film, regarding good and evil with the same simplicity and faith as its hero.

All of Bergman's mature films, except the comedies, are about his discontent with the ways that God has chosen to reveal himself. But when he made *The Seventh Seal,* he was bold enough to approach his subject in a literal manner—to actually show the knight playing chess with Death, an image so perfect it has survived countless parodies. And he had the confidence to end his film not with a statement or a climax, but with an image. "The strict lord Death bids them dance," says the young actor, directing the attention of his wife to the horizon, against which Death leads his latest victims in a macabre parade.

Seeing *The Seventh Seal* again after many years, I was reminded of the richness of detail about Europe in the early Middle Ages, when plague swept the land and the Crusaders returned. The knight (Max von Sydow) shares the story with many other characters, not least his squire (Gunnar Björnstrand), a realistic, down-to-earth man who has a lively dislike of women and a sardonic relationship with his master (he has a silent little snarl to show his discontent). As the two of them travel home to the knight's castle, the knight is challenged by Death ("I have been at your side for a long time"). He offers Death a bargain: They will play chess for the knight's soul. The game continues during the entire film.

Continuing on their way, the knight and squire encounter a troupe of performers, including a couple named Joseph and Mary who have a young child. They visit a seemingly deserted farmstead, where the squire catches a man named Raval trying to steal the bracelet of a plague victim. This Raval is the very theologian who, years earlier, convinced the knight to join the Crusades.

The plague has inspired extreme behavior. A group of flagellants files past, some carrying heavy crosses, others whipping themselves, doing penance. The knight and squire encounter a young girl (Gunnel Lindblom), held in a cage, who is going to be burned at the stake; her captors explain that she slept with the devil, drawing down the plague. The knight questions the girl about the devil, who should know if God exists. "Look in my eyes," the woman says. "The priest could see him there, and the soldiers— they would not touch me." She is almost proud. "I see nothing but terror,"

the knight says. Later, as the woman is being prepared for burning, the squire says, "Look into her eyes. She sees nothing but emptiness." "It can't be," says the knight. We are left, almost until the end, with the possibility that although Death exists as a supernatural figure, there is no larger structure in which God plays a part.

Some filmmakers are born. Ingmar Bergman was made. Born in Uppsala in 1918, he was the son of a Lutheran minister whose strict upbringing included the punishment (recalled in the films) of the small boy being locked in a cupboard "with things that will eat your toes." His first postwar films, not much seen today, are uneasy mixtures of Italian neorealism and Hollywood social drama, and even the titles (*It Rains on Our Love* [1946], *Night Is My Future* [1948]) suggest their banality. He was not at ease in the world of small realistic gestures and everyday behavior, and only when he drew back into more serious issues did he begin to find his genius, in films like *To Joy* (1950) and *Sawdust and Tinsel* (1953). *The Seventh Seal* and *Wild Strawberries*, both released in 1957, mark his coming of age as an artist. Both are about men near the ends of their lives, on a journey in search of meaning.

Bergman's spiritual quest is at the center of the films he made in the middle of his career. *The Seventh Seal* opens that period, in which he asked, again and again, why God seemed absent from the world. In *Through a Glass Darkly* (1961), the mentally ill heroine has a vision of God as a spider. In the austere *Winter Light* (1963), Björnstrand and von Sydow appear again, in the story of a country priest whose faith is threatened by the imminence of nuclear catastrophe. In *Persona* (1966), televised images of war cause an actress to simply stop speaking. In the masterpiece *Cries and Whispers* (1972), a woman dying of cancer finds a faith that her sisters cannot understand or share.

The last four films in Bergman's career look inside for the answers to his haunting questions. All autobiographical, they are *Fanny and Alexander* (1984), the last film he directed, and three more he wrote the screenplays for: *The Best Intentions* (1992), *Sunday's Children* (1992), and *Faithless* (2000). *Sunday's Children*, based on a memory of a summer vacation in the country with a young man and his father, a dying minister, was directed by Bergman's own son, Daniel—perhaps as a way of allowing Daniel to deal with the same kinds of questions Ingmar has had. And *Faithless* was directed by the actress Liv Ullmann, who had an affair and a daughter with Bergman, never married him, always remained close to him, and here was presented by him with a screenplay about an old man named Bergman, who lives in Bergman's house, works at Bergman's desk, and mercilessly questions his immoral behavior in a relationship from years ago. Here is a man who, in his eighties, continues to ask Life the same questions, still not content with the answers. If Bergman never makes another film, *Faithless* will be as close to closure as he was ever likely to come.

Bergman's work has an arc. The dissatisfied young man considers social and political issues. In middle age, he asks enormous questions about God and existence. In old age, he turns to his memories for what answers there are. And in many of these films, there is the same kind of scene of reconciliation. In *The Seventh Seal*, facing the end of his own life and the general destruction of the plague, the knight spends some time with Joseph and Mary and their child, and says, "I will remember this hour of peace. The dusk, the bowl of wild strawberries, the bowl of milk, Joseph with his lute." Saving this family from Death becomes his last gesture of affirmation. In *Cries and Whispers*, a journal left by the dead sister recalls a day when she was feeling a little better, and the sisters and a maid walked in the sunlight and sat in a swing on the lawn: "I feel a great gratitude to my life," she wrote, "which gives me so much."

And *Scenes from a Marriage* (1973) tells the story of a couple whose marriage disintegrates but whose love and hope do not quite disappear; after many years apart, they visit a country house where they were once happy. The woman awakens with a nightmare, the man holds and comforts her, and in the middle of the night in a dark house, surrounded by hurt and fear, this comforting between two people is held up as mankind's best weapon against despair.

THE SHAWSHANK
REDEMPTION

It is a strange comment to make about a film set inside a prison, but *The Shawshank Redemption* creates such a warm hold on our feelings because it makes us a member of a family. Many movies offer us vicarious experiences and quick superficial emotions. *Shawshank* slows down and looks. It uses the calm, observant voice of the narrator to include us in the story of men who have formed a community behind bars. It is deeper than most films; about continuity in a lifetime, based on friendship and hope.

Interesting that although the hero of the film is the convicted former banker Andy Dufresne (Tim Robbins), the action is never seen from his point of view. The film's opening scene shows him being given two life sentences for the murder of his wife and her lover, and then we move, permanently, to a point of view representing the prison population and particularly the lifer Ellis "Red" Redding (Morgan Freeman). It is his voice remembering the first time he saw Andy ("looked like a stiff breeze would blow him over") and predicting, wrongly, that he wouldn't make it in prison.

From Andy's arrival on the prison bus to the film's end, we see only how others see him—Red, who becomes his best friend, Brooks the old librarian, the corrupt Warden Norton, guards, and prisoners. Red is our surrogate. He's the one we identify with, and the redemption, when it comes, is Red's. We've been shown by Andy's example that you have to keep true to yourself, not lose hope, bide your time, set a quiet example, and look for

your chance. "I guess it comes down to a simple choice, really," he tells Red. "Get busy livin' or get busy dyin'."

The key to the film's structure, I think, is that it's not about its hero, but about our relationship with him—our curiosity, our pity, our admiration. If Andy had been the heroic center, bravely enduring, the film would have been conventional and less mysterious. But we wonder about this guy. Did he really kill those two people? Why does he keep so much to himself? Why can he amble through the prison yard like a free man on a stroll, when everyone else plods or sidles?

People like excitement at the movies, and titles that provide it do well. Films about "redemption" are approached with great wariness; a lot of people are not thrilled by the prospect of a great film—it sounds like work. But there's a hunger for messages of hope, and when a film offers one, it's likely to have staying power even if it doesn't grab an immediate audience.

The Shawshank Redemption premiered at the Toronto Film Festival in September 1994 and opened a few weeks later. It got good reviews but did poor business. Its $18-million original gross didn't cover costs; it took in only another $10 million after winning seven Oscar nominations, including best picture.

There wasn't much going for it. It had a terrible title, it was a "prison drama" and women don't like those, it contained almost no action, it starred actors who were respected but not big stars, and it was long at 142 minutes. Clearly this was a movie that needed word of mouth to find an audience, and indeed business was slowly but steadily growing when it was yanked from theaters. If it had been left to find its way, it might have continued to build and run for months, but that's not what happened.

Instead, in one of the most remarkable stories in the history of home video, it found its real mass audience on tapes and discs and through TV screenings. Within five years, *Shawshank* was a phenomenon, a video best-seller and renter that its admirers feel they've discovered for themselves. When *The Wall Street Journal* ran an article about the *Shawshank* groundswell in April 1999, it was occupying first place in the Internet Movie Database worldwide vote of the 250 best films; it's usually in the top five.

Polls and rentals reflect popularity but don't explain why people valuc *Shawshank* so fervently. Maybe it plays more like a spiritual experience than like a movie. Of course it has entertaining payoff moments (as when the guards from another prison, wearing their baseball uniforms, line up to have Andy do their taxes). But much of the movie involves quiet solitude and philosophical discussions about life. The moments of violence (as when Andy is sexually assaulted) are seen objectively, not exploited. The movie avoids lingering on Andy's suffering; after beatings, he's seen in medium and long shots, tactfully. The camera doesn't focus on his wounds or bruises, but, like his fellow prisoners, gives him his space.

The Morgan Freeman character is carrier of the film's spiritual arc. We see him at three parole hearings, after twenty, thirty, and forty years. The first hearing involves storytelling trickery; the film has opened with Andy's sentencing, and then we see a parole board and expect it's about to listen to Andy's appeal. But, no, that's when we first see Red. In his first appeal, he tries to convince the board he's been rehabilitated. In the second, he just goes through the motions. In the third, he rejects the whole notion of rehabilitation, and somehow in doing so he sets his spirit free, and the board releases him.

There's an underlying problem. Behind bars, Red is king. He's the prison fixer, able to get you a pack of cigarettes, a little rock pick, or a Rita Hayworth poster. On the outside, he has no status or identity. We've already seen what happened to the old librarian (James Whitmore), lonely and adrift in freedom. The last act of the movie, in which Andy helps Red accept his freedom, is deeply moving—all the more so because, once again, Andy operates at a distance, with letters and postcards, and is seen through Red's mind.

Frank Darabont wrote and directed the film, basing it on a story by Stephen King. His film grants itself a leisure that most films are afraid to risk. The movie is as deliberate, considered, and thoughtful as Freeman's narration. There's a feeling in Hollywood that audiences have short attention spans and must be assaulted with fresh novelties. I think those movies, which cut to the next shot before interest is established in the present one, are slower to sit through than a film like *Shawshank*, which absorbs us and takes away the awareness that we are watching a film.

Deliberate, too, is the dialogue. Tim Robbins makes Andy a man of few words, quietly spoken. He doesn't get real worked up. He is his own man, capable of keeping his head down for years and then indulging in a grand gesture, as when he plays an aria from Mozart's *The Marriage of Figaro* (the overhead shot of the prisoners in the yard, spellbound by the music, is one of the film's epiphanies). Because he does not volunteer himself, reach out to us, or overplay his feelings, he becomes more fascinating: It is often better to wonder what a character is thinking than to know.

Roger Deakins's cinematography is tactful, not showy. Two opening shots, one from a helicopter, one of prison walls looming overhead, establish the prison. Shots follow the dialogue instead of anticipating it. Thomas Newman's music enhances rather than informs, and there is a subtle touch in the way deep bass rumblings during the early murder are reprised when a young prisoner recalls another man's description of the crime.

Darabont constructs the film to observe the story, not to punch it up or upstage it. Upstaging, in fact, is unknown in this film; the actors are content to stay within their roles, the story moves in an orderly way, and the film itself reflects the slow passage of the decades. "When they put you in that cell," Red says, "when those bars slam home, that's when you know it's for real. Old life blown away in the blink of an eye. Nothing left but all the time in the world to think about it." Watching the film again, I admired it even more than the first time I saw it. Affection for good films often grows with familiarity, as it does with music. Some have said life is a prison, we are Red, Andy is our redeemer. All good art is about something deeper than it admits.

THE SILENCE
OF THE LAMBS

A fundamental difference between *The Silence of the Lambs* (1991) and its sequel, *Hannibal* (2001), is that the former is frightening, involving, and disturbing, while the latter is merely disturbing. It is easy enough to construct a geek show if you start with a cannibal. The secret of *Silence* is that it doesn't start with the cannibal—it arrives at him, through the eyes and mind of a young woman. *The Silence of the Lambs* is the story of Clarice Starling, the FBI trainee played by Jodie Foster, and the story follows her without substantial interruption. Dr. Hannibal Lecter lurks at the heart of the story, a malevolent but somehow likable presence—likable because he likes Clarice and helps her. But Lecter is the sideshow, and Clarice is in the center ring.

The popularity of Jonathan Demme's movie is likely to last as long as there is a market for being scared. Like *Nosferatu*, *Psycho*, and *Halloween*, it illustrates that the best thrillers don't age. Fear is a universal emotion and a timeless one. But *The Silence of the Lambs* is not merely a thrill show. It is also about two of the most memorable characters in movie history, Clarice Starling and Hannibal Lecter, and their strange, strained relationship ("People will say we're in love," Lecter cackles).

They share so much. Both are ostracized by the worlds they want to inhabit—Lecter, by the human race, because he is a serial killer and a cannibal, and Clarice, by the law enforcement profession, because she is a woman. Both feel powerless—Lecter because he is locked in a maximum security prison (and bound and gagged like King Kong when he is moved) and Clarice because she is surrounded by men who tower over her and fondle her with their eyes. Both use their powers of persuasion to escape from their traps. Lecter is able to rid himself of the pest in the next cell by talking him into choking on his own tongue, and Clarice is able to persuade Lecter to aid her in the search for the serial killer named Buffalo Bill. And both share similar childhood wounds. Lecter is touched when he learns that Clarice lost both her parents at an early age, was shipped off to relatives, was essentially an unloved orphan. And Lecter himself was a victim of child abuse (on the DVD commentary track, Demme says he regrets not underlining this more).

These parallel themes are mirrored by patterns in the visual strategy. Note that both Lecter in his prison cell and Buffalo Bill in his basement are arrived at by Starling after descending several flights of stairs and passing through several doors; they live in underworlds. Note the way the movie always seems to be *looking* at Clarice: The point-of-view camera takes the place of the scrutinizing men in her life, and when she enters dangerous spaces, it is there waiting for her instead of following her in. Note the consistent use of red, white, and blue: not only in the FBI scenes but in the flag draped over the car in the storage shed, other flags in Bill's lair, and even the graduation cake at the end (where the U.S. eagle in the frosting is a ghastly reminder of the way Lecter pinned a security guard spread-eagle to the walls of his cage).

The movie's sound track also carries themes all the way through. There are exhalations and sighs at many points, as when the cocoon of the gypsy moth is taken from the throat of Bill's first victim. Much heavy breathing. There are subterranean rumblings and faraway cries and laments, almost too low to be heard, at critical points. There is the sound of a heart monitor. Howard Shore's mournful music sets a funereal tone. When the sound track wants to create terror, as when Clarice is in Bill's basement, it mixes her frightened panting with the sound of Bill's heavy breathing and the screams of the captive girl—and then adds the dog's frenzied barking, which psychologically works at a deeper level than everything else. Then it adds those green goggles so he can see her in the dark.

Ken Regan

Jodie Foster and Anthony Hopkins won Oscars for best actress and actor. The movie also won for best picture, for Demme's direction and Ted Tally's screenplay, and was nominated for editing and sound. It is remarkable that the Academy would remember, let alone single out, a film released thirteen months before the Oscarcast; it usually votes for films that are still in theaters or new on video. But *Silence* was so clearly one of a kind that it could not be ignored.

Hopkins's performance has much less screen time than Foster's, but it made an indelible impression on audiences. His "entrance" is unforgettable. After Clarice descends those stairs and passes through those doors and gates (which all squeak), the camera shows her POV as she first sees Lecter in his cell. He is so . . . still. Standing erect, at relaxed attention, in his prison jumpsuit, he looks like a waxwork of himself. On her next visit, he is erect, and then very slightly recoils, and then opens his mouth, and I at least was made to think of a cobra. His approach to Lecter's personality, Hopkins says on his commentary track, was inspired by HAL 9000 in *2001:* He is a dispassionate, brilliant machine, superb at logic, deficient in emotions.

Foster's Clarice is not only an orphan but a disadvantaged backwoods girl who has worked hard to get where she is and has less self-confidence than she pretends. Noticing the nail polish on one of Bill's victims, she guesses that the girl is from "town," a word used only by someone who is not. Her bravest moment may come when she orders the gawking sheriff's deputies out of the room at the funeral home ("Listen here now!").

One key to the film's appeal is that audiences *like* Hannibal Lecter. That's partly because he likes Starling, and we sense he would not hurt her. It's also because he is helping her search for Buffalo Bill and save the imprisoned girl. But it may also be because Hopkins, in a still, sly way, brings such wit and style to the character. He may be a cannibal, but as a dinner party guest he would give value for money (if he didn't eat you). He does not bore, he likes to amuse, he has his standards, and he is the smartest person in the movie.

He bears comparison, indeed, with such other movie monsters as Nosferatu, Frankenstein's (especially in *Bride of Frankenstein*), King Kong, and Norman Bates. They have two things in common: They behave according to their natures, and they are misunderstood. Nothing that these monsters do is "evil" in any conventional moral sense, because they lack any moral sense. They are hardwired to do what they do. They have no choice. In the areas where they do have choice, they try to do the right thing (Nosferatu is the exception in that he never has a choice). Kong wants to rescue Fay Wray, Norman Bates wants to make pleasant chitchat and do his mother's bidding, and Dr. Lecter helps Clarice because she does not insult his intelligence, and she arouses his affection.

All of these qualities might not be enough to assure the longevity of *Silence* if it were not also truly frightening (*Hannibal* is not frightening, and for all of its box office success it will have a limited shelf life). *Silence* is frightening first in the buildup and introduction of Hannibal Lecter. Second in the discovery and extraction of the cocoon in the throat. Third in the scene where the cops await the arrival of the elevator from the upper floors. Fourth in the intercutting between the exteriors of the wrong house in Calumet City, Illinois, and the interiors of the right one in Belvedere, Ohio. Fifth in the extended sequence inside Buffalo Bill's house, where Ted Levine creates a genuinely loathsome psychopath (notice the timing as Starling sizes him up and reads the situation before she shouts, "Freeze!"). We are frightened both because of the film's clever manipulation of story and image and for better reasons—we like Clarice, identify with her, and fear for her. Just like Lecter.

{ SINGIN' IN THE RAIN }

There is no movie musical more fun than *Singin' in the Rain,* and few that remain as fresh over the years. Its originality is all the more startling if you reflect that only one of its songs was written new for the film, that the producers plundered MGM's storage vaults for sets and props, and that the movie was originally ranked below *An American in Paris,* which won a best picture Oscar. The verdict of the years knows better than the Academy: *Singin' in the Rain* is a transcendent experience, and no one who loves movies can afford to miss it.

The film is above all lighthearted and happy. The three stars—Gene Kelly, Donald O'Connor, and nineteen-year-old Debbie Reynolds—must have rehearsed endlessly for their dance numbers, which involve alarming acrobatics, but in performance they're giddy with joy. Kelly's soaking-wet "Singin' in the Rain" dance number is "the single most memorable dance number on film," Peter Wollen wrote in a British Film Institute monograph. I'd call it a tie with Donald O'Connor's Mixmaster "Make 'Em Laugh" number, in which he manhandles himself like a cartoon character. Kelly and O'Connor were established stars when the film was made in 1952. Debbie Reynolds was a newcomer with five previous smaller roles, and this was her big break. She has to keep up with two veteran hoofers, and does; note the determination on her pert little face as she takes giant strides when they all march toward a couch in the "Good Morning" number.

Singin' in the Rain pulses with life. In a movie about making movies, you can sense the joy they had in making this one. It was codirected by Stanley Donen, then only twenty-eight, and Kelly, who supervised the choreography. Donen got an honorary Oscar in 1998 and stole the show by singing "Cheek to Cheek" while dancing with his statuette. He started in movies at seventeen, in 1941, as an assistant to Kelly, and they collaborated on *On the Town* (1949) when he was only twenty-five. His other credits include *Funny Face* (1957) and *Seven Brides for Seven Brothers* (1954).

One of this movie's pleasures is that it's really about something. Of course it's about romance, as most musicals are, but it's also about the film industry in a period of dangerous transition. The movie simplifies the changeover from silents to talkies but doesn't falsify it. Yes, cameras were housed in soundproof booths, and microphones were hidden almost in plain view. And, yes, preview audiences did laugh when they first heard the voices of some famous stars; "Garbo Talks!" the ads promised, but her costar, John Gilbert, would have been better off keeping his mouth shut. The movie opens and closes at sneak previews, has sequences on soundstages and in dubbing studios, and kids the way the studios manufactured romances between their stars.

When producer Arthur Freed and writers Betty Comden and Adolph Green were assigned to the project at MGM, their instructions were to recycle a group of songs the studio already owned, most of them written by Lennie Hayton, with Nacio Herb Brown. Comden and Green noted that the songs came from the period when silent films were giving way to sound, and they decided to make a musical about the birth of the talkies. That led to the character of Lina Lamont (Jean Hagen), the blond bombshell with the voice like fingernails on a blackboard.

Hagen, in fact, had a perfectly acceptable voice, which everyone in Hollywood knew; maybe that helped her win an Academy nomination for best supporting actress. (In a cheeky irony, she dubbed Debbie Reynolds's singing voice in the scene where Debbie's character is shown behind the screen singing for Hagen!) Hagen plays a caricatured dumb blonde, who believes she's in love with her leading man, Don Lockwood (Kelly), because she read it in a fan magazine. She gets some of the funniest lines ("What do they think I am? Dumb or something? Why, I make more money than Calvin Coolidge put together!").

Kelly and O'Connor had dancing styles that were more robust and acrobatic than the grand master, Fred Astaire. O'Connor's "Make 'Em Laugh" number remains one of the most amazing dance sequences ever filmed—a lot of it in long, unbroken takes. He wrestles with a dummy, runs up walls and does backflips, tosses his body around like a rag doll, cartwheels on the floor, runs into a brick wall and a lumber plank, and crashes through a backdrop.

Kelly was the mastermind behind the final form of the "Singin' in the Rain" number, according to Wollen's study. The original screenplay placed it later in the film and assigned it to all three stars (who can be seen singing it together under the opening titles). Kelly snagged it for a solo and moved it up to the point right after he and young Kathy Selden (Reynolds) realize they're falling in love. That explains the dance: He doesn't mind getting wet, because he's besotted with romance. Kelly liked to design dances that grew out of the props and locations at hand. He dances with the umbrella, swings from a lamppost, has one foot on the curb and the other in the gutter, and in the scene's high point, simply jumps up and down in a rain puddle.

Other dance numbers also use real props. Kelly and O'Connor, taking elocution lessons from a voice teacher, do "Moses Supposes" while balancing on tabletops and chairs (it was the only song written specifically for the movie). "Good Morning" uses the kitchen and living areas of Lockwood's house (ironically a set built for a John Gilbert movie). Early in the film, Kelly climbs a trolley and leaps into Kathy's convertible. Outtakes of the leap show Kelly missing the car on one attempt and landing in the street.

The story line is suspended at the two-thirds mark for the movie's set piece, "Broadway Ballet," an elaborate fantasy dance number starring Kelly and Cyd Charisse. It's explained as a number Kelly is pitching to the studio, about a gawky kid who arrives on Broadway with a big dream ("Gotta Dance!") and clashes with a gangster's leggy girlfriend. MGM musicals liked to stop the show for big production numbers, but it's possible to enjoy "Broadway Ballet" and still wonder if it's really needed; it stops the headlong energy dead in its tracks for something more formal and considered.

The climax ingeniously uses strategies that the movie has already planted, to shoot down the dim Lina and celebrate fresh-faced Kathy. After a preview audience cheers Lina's new film (her voice substituted backstage by Kathy), she's trapped into singing onstage. Kathy reluctantly agrees to sing into a backstage mike while Lina mouths the words, and then her two friends join the studio boss in raising the curtain so the audience sees the trick. Kathy flees down the aisle—but then, in one of the great romantic moments in the movies, she's held in foreground close-up while Lockwood, onstage, cries out, "Ladies and gentlemen, stop that girl! That girl running up the aisle! That's the girl whose voice you heard and loved tonight! She's the real star of the picture—Kathy Selden!" It's corny, but it's perfect.

The magic of *Singin' in the Rain* lives on, but the Hollywood musical didn't learn from its example. Instead of original, made-for-the-movies musicals like this one (and *An American in Paris* [1951] and *The Band Wagon* [1953]), Hollywood started recycling presold Broadway hits. That didn't work, because Broadway was aiming for an older audience (many of its hits were showcases for ageless female legends). Most of the good modern musicals have drawn directly from new music, as *A Hard Day's Night, Saturday Night Fever, Pink Floyd the Wall,* and *Purple Rain* did. Meanwhile, *Singin' in the Rain* remains one of the few movies to live up to its advertising. "What a glorious feeling!" the posters said. It was the simple truth.

{ SOME LIKE IT HOT }

What a work of art and nature is Marilyn Monroe. She hasn't aged into an icon, some citizen of the past, but still seems to be inventing herself as we watch her. She has the gift of appearing to hit on her lines of dialogue by happy inspiration, and there are passages in Billy Wilder's *Some Like It Hot* where she and Tony Curtis exchange one-liners like hot potatoes. Poured into a dress that offers her breasts like jolly treats for needy boys, she seems totally oblivious to sex while at the same time melting men into helpless desire. "Look at that!" Jack Lemmon tells Curtis as he watches her adoringly. "Look how she moves. Like Jell-O on springs. She must have some sort of built-in motor. I tell you, it's a whole different sex."

Wilder's 1959 comedy is one of the enduring treasures of the movies, a film of inspiration and meticulous craft, a movie that's about nothing but sex and yet pretends it's about crime and greed. It is underwired with Wilder's cheerful cynicism, so that no time is lost to soppiness and everyone behaves according to basic Darwinian drives. When sincere emotion strikes these characters, it blindsides them: Curtis thinks he wants only sex, Monroe thinks she wants only money, and they are as astonished as delighted to find they want only each other.

The plot is classic screwball. Curtis and Lemmon play Chicago musicians who disguise themselves as women to avoid being rubbed out after they witness the St. Valentine's Day Massacre. They join an all-girl orchestra on its way to Florida. Monroe is the singer, who dreams of marrying a millionaire but despairs, "I always get the fuzzy end of the lollipop." Curtis lusts for Monroe and disguises himself as a millionaire to win her. Monroe lusts after money and gives him lessons in love. Their relationship is flipped and mirrored in low comedy as Lemmon gets engaged to a real millionaire, played by Joe E. Brown. "You're not a girl!" Curtis protests to Lemmon. "You're a guy! Why would a guy want to marry a guy?" Lemmon: "Security!"

The movie has been compared to Marx Brothers classics, especially in the slapstick chases as gangsters pursue the heroes through hotel corridors. The weak points in many Marx Brothers films are the musical interludes—not Harpo's solos, but the romantic duets involving insipid supporting characters. *Some Like It Hot* has no problems with its musical numbers because the singer is Monroe, who didn't have a great singing voice but was as good as Sinatra at selling the lyrics.

Consider her solo of "I Wanna Be Loved by You." The situation is as basic as it can be: a pretty girl standing in front of an orchestra and singing a song. Monroe and Wilder turn it into one of the most mesmerizing and blatantly sexual scenes in the movies. She wears that clinging, see-through dress, gauze covering the upper slopes of her breasts, the neckline scooping to a censor's eyebrow north of trouble. Wilder places her in the center of a round spotlight that does not simply illuminate her from the waist up, as an ordinary spotlight would, but toys with her like a surrogate neckline, dipping and clinging as Monroe moves her body higher and lower in the light with teasing precision. It is a striptease in which nudity would have been superfluous. All the time, she seems unaware of the effect, singing the song innocently, as if she thinks it's the literal truth. To experience that scene is to understand why no other actor or actress has more sexual chemistry with the camera than Monroe.

Capturing the chemistry was not all that simple. Legends surround *Some Like It Hot*. Kissing Marilyn, Curtis famously said, was like kissing Hitler. Monroe had so much trouble saying one line ("Where's the bourbon?") while looking in a dresser drawer that Wilder had the line pasted inside the drawer. Then she opened the wrong drawer. So he had it pasted inside every drawer.

Monroe's eccentricities and neuroses on sets became notorious, but studios put up with her long after any other actress would have been black-balled, because what they got back on the screen was magical. Watch the final take of "Where's the bourbon?" and Monroe seems utterly spontaneous. And watch the famous scene aboard the yacht, where Curtis complains that no woman can arouse him, and Marilyn does her best. She kisses him not erotically, but tenderly, sweetly, as if offering a gift and healing a wound. You remember what Curtis said, but when you watch that scene all you can think is, Hitler must have been a terrific kisser.

The movie is really the story of the Lemmon and Curtis characters, and it's got a top-shelf supporting cast (Joe E. Brown, George Raft, Pat O'Brien), but Monroe steals it, just as she walked away with every movie she was in. It is an act of the will to watch anyone else while she is on the screen. Tony Curtis's performance is all the more admirable because we know how many takes she needed—Curtis must have felt at times like he was in a pro-am tournament. Yet he stays fresh and alive in sparkling dialogue scenes like their first meeting on the beach, where he introduces himself as the Shell Oil heir and wickedly parodies Cary Grant. Watch his timing in the yacht seduction scene and the way his character plays with her naiveté. "Water polo? Isn't that terribly dangerous?" asks Monroe. Curtis: "I'll say! I had two ponies drown under me."

Watch, too, for Wilder's knack of hiding bold sexual symbolism in plain view. When Monroe first kisses Curtis while they're both horizontal on the couch, notice how his patent-leather shoe rises phallically in the middistance behind her. Does Wilder intend this effect? Undoubtedly, because a little later, after the frigid millionaire confesses he has been cured, he says, "I've got a funny sensation in my toes—like someone was barbecuing them over a slow flame." Monroe: "Let's throw another log on the fire."

Jack Lemmon gets the fuzzy end of the lollipop, in the parallel relationship. The screenplay by Wilder and I.A.L. Diamond is Shakespearean in the way it cuts between high and low comedy, between the heroes and the clowns. The Curtis character is able to complete his round-trip through gender, but Lemmon gets stuck halfway, so that Curtis connects with Monroe in the upstairs love story while Lemmon is downstairs in the screwball department with Joe E. Brown. Their romance is frankly cynical: Brown's character gets married and divorced the way other men date, and Lemmon plans to marry him for the alimony.

But they both have so much fun in their courtship! While Curtis and Monroe are on Brown's yacht, Lemmon and Brown are dancing with such perfect timing that a rose in Lemmon's teeth ends up in Brown's. Lemmon has a hilarious scene the morning after his big date, lying on his bed, still in drag, playing with castanets as he announces his engagement. (Curtis: "What are you going to do on your honeymoon?" Lemmon: "He wants to go to the Riviera, but I kinda lean towards Niagara Falls.") Both Curtis and Lemmon are practicing cruel deceptions—Curtis has Monroe thinking she's met a millionaire, and Brown thinks Lemmon is a woman—but the film dances free before anyone gets hurt. Both Monroe and Brown learn the truth and don't care, and after Lemmon reveals he's a man, Brown delivers the best curtain line in the movies. If you've seen the movie, you know what it is, and if you haven't, you deserve to hear it for the first time from him.

{STAR WARS}

To see *Star Wars* again after twenty years is to revisit a place in the mind. George Lucas's space epic has colonized our imaginations, and it is hard to stand back and see it simply as a motion picture, because it has so completely become part of our memories. It's as goofy as a children's tale, as shallow as an old Saturday afternoon serial, as corny as Kansas in August—and a masterpiece. Those who analyze its philosophy do so, I imagine, with a smile in their minds. May the Force be with them.

Like *The Birth of a Nation* and *Citizen Kane*, *Star Wars* was a technical watershed that influenced many of the movies that came after. These films have little in common, except for the way they came along at a crucial moment in cinema history, when new methods were ripe for synthesis. *The Birth of a Nation* brought together the developing language of shots and editing. *Citizen Kane* married special effects, advanced sound, a new photographic style, and a freedom from linear storytelling. *Star Wars* combined a new generation of special effects with the high-energy action picture; it linked space opera and soap opera, fairy tales and legend, and packaged them as a wild visual ride.

Star Wars effectively brought to an end the golden era of early-1970s personal filmmaking and focused the industry on big-budget special effects blockbusters, blasting off a trend we are still living through. But you

can't blame it for what it did; you can only observe how well it did it. In one way or another, all the big studios have been trying to make another *Star Wars* ever since (pictures like *Raiders of the Lost Ark, Jurassic Park, Independence Day,* and *The Matrix* are its heirs). It located Hollywood's center of gravity at the intellectual and emotional level of a bright teenager.

It's possible, however, that as we grow older we retain, buried within, the tastes of our earlier selves. How else to explain how much fun *Star Wars* is, even for those who think they don't care for science fiction? It's a good-hearted film in every single frame, and shining through is the gift of a man who knew how to link state-of-the-art technology with a deceptively simple but really very powerful story. It was not by accident that George Lucas worked with Joseph Campbell, an expert on the world's basic myths, in fashioning a screenplay that owes much to mankind's oldest stories.

By now the ritual of classic film revival is well established: An older classic is brought out from the studio vaults, restored frame by frame, rereleased in the best theaters, and then relaunched on home video. With the 1997 "special edition" of the Star Wars trilogy, Lucas went one step beyond.

His special effects were so advanced in 1977 that they spun off an industry, including his own Industrial Light & Magic Co., the computer wizards who do many of today's best special effects. In 1997, Lucas put IL&M to work touching up the effects, including some that his limited 1977 budget left him unsatisfied with. Most of the changes are subtle; you'd need a side-by-side comparison to see that a new shot is a little better. There's about five minutes of new material, including a meeting between Han Solo and Jabba the Hut that was shot for the first version but not used. (We learn that Jabba is not immobile, but sloshes along in a kind of spongy undulation.) There's also an improved look to the city of Mos Eisley ("a wretched hive of scum and villainy," says Obi-Wan Kenobi). And the climactic battle scene against the Death Star has been rehabbed.

The improvements are well done, but they point up how well the effects were done to begin with. If the changes are not obvious, that's because *Star Wars* got the look of the film so right in the first place. The obvious comparison is with Kubrick's *2001: A Space Odyssey,* made ten years earlier, in 1967, which also holds up perfectly well today. (One difference is that Kubrick went for realism, trying to imagine how his future world would really look, while Lucas cheerfully plundered the past. Han Solo's Millennium Falcon has a gun turret with a hand-operated weapon that would have been at home on a World War II bomber, but too slow to hit anything at space velocities.)

Two Lucas inspirations started the story with a tease: He set the action not in the future, but "long ago," and jumped into the middle of it with "Chapter 4: A New Hope." These seemingly innocent touches were actually rather powerful. They gave the saga the aura of an ancient tale and an ongoing one.

As if those two shocks were not enough for the movie's first moments, I learn from the critic Mark R. Leeper that this was one of the first films to pan the camera across a star field: "Space scenes had always been done with a fixed camera, and for a very good reason. It was more economical not to create a background of stars large enough to pan through." As the camera tilts up, a vast spaceship appears from the top of the screen and moves overhead, an effect reinforced by the surround sound. It is such a dramatic opening that it's no wonder Lucas paid a fine and resigned from the Directors Guild rather than obey its demand that he begin with conventional opening credits.

The film has simple, well-defined characters, beginning with the robots C-3PO (fastidious, a little effete) and R2-D2 (childlike, easily hurt). The evil Empire has all but triumphed in the galaxy, but rebel forces are preparing an assault on the Star Destroyer. Princess Leia (pert, sassy Carrie Fisher) has information pinpointing the Star's vulnerable point and feeds it into C-3PO'S computer. When her ship is captured, the robots escape from the Star Destroyer and find themselves on Luke Skywalker's planet, where soon Luke (Mark Hamill as an idealistic youngster) meets the wise, old, mysterious Ben Kenobi (Alec Guinness) and they hire the freelance space jockey Han Solo (Harrison Ford, already laconic) to carry them to Leia's rescue.

The story is advanced with spectacularly effective art design, set decoration, and effects. Although the scene in the intergalactic bar is famous for its menagerie of alien drunks, there is another scene, when the two robots are thrown into a hold with other used droids, that equally fills the screen with fascinating throwaway details. And a scene in the Death Star's garbage bin (inhabited by a snake with a head curiously shaped like E.T.'s) is also well done.

Many of the planetscapes are startlingly beautiful and owe something to Chesley Bonestell's imaginary drawings of other worlds. The final assault on the Death Star, when the fighter rockets speed between parallel walls, is a nod in the direction of *2001*, with its light trip into another dimension: Kubrick showed, and Lucas learned, how to make the audience feel it is hurtling headlong through space.

Lucas fills his screen with loving touches. There are little alien rats hopping around the desert, and a chess game played with living creatures. Luke's weather-worn "Speeder" vehicle, which hovers over the sand, reminds me uncannily of a 1965 Mustang. And consider the details creating the presence, look, and sound of Darth Vader, whose fanged face mask, black cape, and hollow breathing are the setting for James Earl Jones's cold voice of doom.

Seeing the film the first time, I was swept away, and have remained swept ever since. Seeing the restored version, I tried to be more objective, and noted that the gun battles on board the spaceships go on a bit too long; it is remarkable that the Empire marksmen never hit anyone important; and the fighter raid on the enemy ship now plays like the computer games it predicted. I wonder, too, if Lucas could have come up with a more challenging philosophy behind the Force. As Kenobi explains it, it's basically just going with the flow. What if Lucas had pushed a little further, to include elements of nonviolence or ideas about intergalactic conservation? (It's a great waste of resources to blow up star systems.)

The films that will live forever are the simplest-seeming ones. They have profound depths, but their surfaces are as clear to an audience as a beloved old story. The way I know this is because the stories that seem immortal—the *Odyssey, The Tale of Genji, Don Quixote, David Copperfield, Huckleberry Finn*—are all the same: a brave but flawed hero, a quest, colorful people and places, sidekicks, the discovery of life's underlying truths. If I were asked to say with certainty which movies will still be widely known a century or two from now, I would list *2001,* and *The Wizard of Oz,* and Keaton and Chaplin, and Astaire and Rogers, and probably *Casablanca . . .* and *Star Wars* for sure.

{ SUNSET BLVD. }

Billy Wilder's *Sunset Blvd.* is the portrait of a forgotten silent star, living in exile in her grotesque mansion, screening her old films, dreaming of a comeback. But it's also a love story, and the love keeps it from becoming simply a waxworks or a freak show. Gloria Swanson gives her greatest performance as the silent star Norma Desmond, with her grasping talons, her theatrical mannerisms, her grandiose delusions. William Holden tactfully inhabits the tricky role of the writer half her age who allows himself to be kept by her. But the performance that holds the film together, that gives it emotional resonance and makes it real in spite of its gothic flamboyance, is by Erich von Stroheim, as Norma's faithful butler, Max.

The movie cuts close to the bone, drawing so directly from life that many of the silent stars at the movie's premiere recognized personal details. In no character, not even Norma Desmond, does it cut closer than with Max Von Mayerling, a once-great silent director, now reduced to working as the butler of the woman he once directed—and was married to. There are unmistakable parallels with von Stroheim, who directed Swanson in *Queen Kelly* (1928) and whose credits included *Greed* and *The Merry Widow* (both 1925), but who directed only two sound films and was reduced to playing Nazi martinets and parodies of himself in other people's films.

In *Sunset Blvd.* (1950), Desmond screens one of her old silent classics for Joe Gillis, the young writer played by Holden. Max runs the projec-

tor. The scene is from *Queen Kelly*. For a moment, Swanson and von Stroheim are simply playing themselves. Later, when Gillis is moved into the big mansion, Max shows him to an ornate bedroom and explains, "It was the room of the husband." Max is talking about himself; he was the first of her three husbands and loved her so much he was willing to return as a servant, feeding her illusions, forging her fan mail, fiercely devoted to her greatness.

In one of the greatest of all film performances, Swanson's Norma Desmond skates close to the edge of parody. Swanson takes enormous chances with theatrical sneers and swoops and posturings, holding Norma at the edge of madness for most of the picture, before letting her slip over. We might not take her seriously. That's where Max comes in. Because he believes, because he has devoted his life to her shrine, we believe. His love convinces us there must be something worth loving in Norma Desmond, and that in turn helps explain how Joe Gillis can accept her.

Norma, of course, is not a wrinkled crone. She is only fifty at the time of the film, younger than stars like Susan Sarandon and Catherine Deneuve when they played nude scenes for grateful audiences. There is a scene during Norma's beauty makeover when a magnifying glass is held in front of her eyes, and we are startled by how smooth Swanson's skin is. Swanson in real life was a health nut who fled from the sun, which no doubt protected her skin (she was fifty-three when she made the film), but the point in *Sunset Blvd.* is that she has aged not in the flesh, but in the mind; she has become fixed at the moment of her greatness and lives in the past.

Billy Wilder and his cowriter, Charles Brackett, knew the originals of the characters. What was unusual was how realistic Wilder dared to be. He used real names (Darryl Zanuck, Tyrone Power, Alan Ladd). He showed real people (Norma's bridge partners, cruelly called "the waxworks" by Gillis, are the silent stars Buster Keaton, Anna Q. Nilsson, and H. B. Warner). He drew from life (when Norma visits Cecil B. DeMille at Paramount, the director is making a real film, *Samson and Delilah*, and calls Norma "little fellow," which is what he always called Swanson). When Max the butler tells Joe, "There were three young directors who showed promise in those days, D. W. Griffith, Cecil B. DeMille, and Max Von Mayerling," if you substitute von Stroheim for Von Mayerling, it would be a fair reflection of von Stroheim's stature in the 1920s—in his mind anyway.

Sunset Blvd. remains the best drama ever made about the movies because it sees through the illusions, even if Norma Desmond doesn't. When the silent star first greets the penniless writer inside her mansion, they have a classic exchange. "You used to be big," he says. Norma responds with the great line "I *am* big. It's the pictures that got small." Hardly anyone remembers Joe's next line: "I knew there was something wrong with them."

The plot has supplied Joe with a lot of reasons to accept Norma's offer of a private screenwriting job. He's broke and behind on his rent, his car is about to be repossessed, and he doesn't want to go back to his job as a newspaperman in Dayton. He is also not entirely unwilling to prostitute himself; Holden projects subtle weakness and self-loathing into the role. He goes through the forms of saying he doesn't want Norma's gifts, but he takes them—the gold cigarette cases, the platinum watch, the suits, the shirts, the shoes. He claims to be surprised on New Year's Eve when she throws a party just for the two of them, but surely he has known from the first that she wants not only a writer, but a young man to reassure her that she is still attractive.

The thing about Norma is that life with her isn't all bad. She isn't boring. Her histrionics and dramaturgy are entertaining, and she has a charming side, as when she stages a pantomime for Joe, playing a Mack Sennett bathing girl and then doing a passable version of Chaplin's Tramp. Joe is willing to be kept. The only thing the film lacks is more sympathy between Joe and Max, who have so much in common.

There is, of course, the young blond Paramount writer Betty (Nancy Olson), whom Joe meets early in the picture. She's engaged to be married (to a young Jack Webb), but as Joe begins sneaking out of the mansion to collaborate on a screenplay with Betty, she falls in love with him. He's attracted but pulls back, partly because he doesn't want her to discover the truth, but also because he likes the lifestyle with Norma. And . . . maybe because, like Max, he has fallen under her spell? His dialogue is sharp-edged and can be cruel (when she threatens suicide, he tells her, "Oh, wake up, Norma. You'd be killing yourself to an empty house. The audience left twenty years ago"). But there's a certain pity too. "Poor devil," he says, "still waving proudly to a parade which had long since passed her by."

I have seen *Sunset Blvd.* many times and even analyzed it a shot at a time at the University of Virginia. But on my latest viewing, I was struck by its similarity with the 1964 Japanese drama *Woman in the Dunes.* Both are about men who are trapped in the home, or lair, of a woman who simply will not let them out again. They struggle, they thrash a little, they look for the means of escape, but at some subterranean level they are content to be prisoners, and perhaps even enjoy it. Both women need a man to help them hold back the inexorable advance of the sands—in Norma's case, the sands of time.

Of all the great directors of Hollywood's golden age, has anybody made more films that are as fresh and entertaining to this day as Billy Wilder's? The credits are astonishing: *Double Indemnity* (1944), *Ace in the Hole* (1951), *Some Like It Hot* (1959), *The Apartment* (1960), *The Lost Weekend* (1945), *Stalag 17* (1953), *Witness for the Prosecution* (1957), *Sabrina* (1954). And who else can field three contenders among the greatest closing lines of all time? From *Some Like It Hot* there is "Nobody's perfect!" From *The Apartment*, "Shut up and deal." And from *Sunset Blvd.*, Norma Desmond's "There's nothing else. Just us, and the cameras, and those wonderful people out there in the dark. All right, Mr. DeMille, I'm ready for my close-up."

Sweet Smell of Success

The two men in *Sweet Smell of Success* relate to each other like junkyard dogs. One is dominant, and the other is a whipped cur, circling hungrily, his tail between his legs, hoping for a scrap after the big dog has dined. The dynamic between a powerful gossip columnist and a hungry press agent is seen starkly and without pity. The rest of the plot simply supplies events to illustrate the love-hate relationship.

When *Sweet Smell of Success* was released in 1957, it was seen as a thinly veiled attack on Walter Winchell, who for decades had been the most famous and reviled gossip columnist in America. Forty years later, Winchell is mostly forgotten (he died in 1972), but the film lives on—sharp-edged, merciless. The performances by Burt Lancaster and Tony Curtis have not dated or grown soft. Although both men were dismissed as studio stars at the time, can we think of a "serious actor" who could have played either role so well?

Lancaster plays J. J. Hunsecker, most powerful of the New York columnists, whose items can make a career or break one. Curtis is Sidney Falco, a press agent so marginal that his name isn't painted on his office door, but written on a sheet of paper and taped there. (The inner room is his bedroom.) Falco supports himself largely by getting items into Hunsecker's column, and recently Hunsecker has frozen him out. Why? Hunsecker asked Falco to break up a romance between Hunsecker's younger sister, Susan (Susan Harrison), and a jazz musician named Steve Dallas (Martin Milner), and Falco has so far failed.

Audiences at the time might have heard whispers that Walter Winchell did much the same thing, using his column to attack a man who wanted to marry his daughter, Walda (her name provides some measure of her father's ego). In *Sweet Smell of Success,* Falco hatches a scheme to convince another columnist—Hunsecker's bitter rival—to run the smear item, so that Susan won't suspect it comes from her brother's camp.

All of this is pitiless and cruel and reflects Hunsecker's personal style. He is a man apparently without sexuality of his own, although he seems delicately tuned to the weathers of Falco's moods. Falco is a very pretty boy, but J.J. is wary ("I'd hate to take a bite out of you," he tells the publicist at one point. "You're a cookie full of arsenic"). There are certainly suppressed incestuous feelings in J.J.'s odd household, where his sister lives firmly under his thumb and the columnist grows hysterical when another man seems about to take her away.

The movie, photographed by James Wong Howe in winter in black and white, takes place within a few blocks of Manhattan's midtown club district. Scenes are set in '21' and other nightspots, and those who notice will find a nice irony in the fact that Hunsecker lives in the Brill Building on Broadway, which for decades has housed showbiz offices and Tin Pan Alley composers—and has a long, empty entrance hall that was used for the loneliest shot in *Taxi Driver.*

Hunsecker knows his beat cold. "I love this dirty town," he says in an early scene. He calls all the maître d's and hatcheck girls by name, holds court for senators and call girls at his favorite booth, and doesn't miss a thing. Here is the kind of detail the movie notices: Falco leaves his office without his coat, to save on tips. Later, as he and Hunsecker leave '21' together, the columnist says, "Where's your coat, Sidney? Saving tips?" But we have just seen Hunsecker take his own coat without tipping. He never tips and never pays, and no one in this world would ever expect him to.

Although Falco is in exile as the story opens, Hunsecker cannot quite banish him from his sight, because he needs him. How does the top dog know he rules unless the bottom dog slinks around? Falco sits down at Hunsecker's table, and the columnist senses he's there without even need-

ing to look around. He holds up an unlit cigarette and in the movie's most famous line says, "Match me, Sidney."

The screenplay is cowritten by Clifford Odets, a playwright of left-wing social drama, whose hard take on American society led to *Golden Boy* (1939) and Robert Aldrich's *The Big Knife* (1955)—which did for a Hollywood screenwriter more or less what *Sweet Smell* did for the columnist. His cowriter, Ernest Lehman, based it on a story he'd written. The director was Alexander Mackendrick, from Britain, whose filmography consists mostly of comedies (*The Ladykillers* [1955], *The Man in the White Suit* [1951])—and then this one extraordinary American noir.

The movie is uncanny in its ability to capture that time and place just before the Beats introduced the modern anticonventional style. Jazz musicians wear suits and ties, hair is cropped short, and the trick is to always appear cool—a trick Hunsecker has developed into an act. The streets outside are filled with anonymous people, all in a hurry to get somewhere, and when Falco walks with them, he becomes part of the crowd. When Hunsecker walks, his limousine follows him. For pedestrians like Falco, he is the key to getting off the sidewalk and into the booth at "21."

Odets and Lehman pull off the neat trick of making the film seem hard-boiled and realistic while slipping in dialogue as quotable as it is unlikely. "You're dead, son," Hunsecker tells Falco. "Get yourself buried." And in a moment of introspection: "My right hand hasn't seen my left hand in thirty years." Falco is told by a club owner who is one of his clients, "It's a publicity man's nature to be a liar. I wouldn't hire you if you wasn't a liar." But Falco tells the truth when he confesses, "J. J. Hunsecker is the golden ladder to the place I want to get."

Falco wants to be Hunsecker. To live in the penthouse and wear the expensive clothes and be fawned upon by the next generation of Falcos. Neither man has any morals. That's dramatized in the heartless scam where Falco persuades Hunsecker's rival columnist to smear Susan's boyfriend. He lures the man to his office with promises of sex, and lures a cigarette girl (Barbara Nichols) there with the same promise, except that she expects to sleep with Sidney and not the slimy columnist. "Don't you have a kid in military school?" Sidney asks her pointedly, and after thinking it over, she agrees to prostitute herself.

The ingenues are, by contrast, pale and conventional. Susan Hunsecker and Steve Dallas occupy the margins of the picture, playing the hapless roles of innocent lovebirds. When Falco's planted item surfaces, it's a double play: Dallas is accused of being a dope fiend *and* a commie. Then Falco seals the deal by planting a reefer on the kid for Hunsecker's crooked cop friend, Harry Kello, to find. The ending of the film is coldly ironic, although marred a little by Falco's unnecessarily cruel speeches to Susan right at the close.

Sweet Smell of Success is one of those rare films where you remember the names of the characters because you remember *them*—as people, as types, as benchmarks. "Even today," the writer Ben Brantly wrote about this film, "I've heard theater publicity representatives speak wryly of going into their 'Sidney Falco mode.' " The film stands as the record of one of the most convincing and closely observed symbiotic relationships in the movies. Hunsecker and Falco. You can't have one without the other. "From now on," Falco says, "the best of everything is good enough for me." Well, at least he's the best flunky.

{ S W I N G   T I M E }

Of all the places the movies have created, one of the most magical and enduring is the universe of Fred Astaire and Ginger Rogers. To a series of movies made between 1933 and 1939, they brought such grace and humor that they became the touchstone of all things elegant. "Whenever any kind of question of style or taste comes up," the director Gregory Nava once told me, "I simply ask myself—what would Fred Astaire have done?"

Astaire and Rogers were, first of all, great dancers. So were a lot of other film performers, including Astaire's partners (Rita Hayworth, Eleanor Powell, Cyd Charisse) after Rogers turned to serious dramatic roles. But what Fred and Ginger had together, and what no other team has ever had in the same way, was a joy of performance. They were so good, and they knew they were so good, that they danced in celebration of their gifts.

Look at the final moment of their number "Isn't It a Lovely Day?" in *Top Hat* (1935). It begins with her mocking him, following him around a bandstand with her hands in her pockets. It escalates into a passionately physical dance in counterpoint to thunder and lightning, and then slows down into a sequence where they imitate each other's styles and moves. Finally, satisfied, they plop down on the edge of the bandstand and shake hands. I have always thought that handshake was between the dancers, not their characters.

More than any other dancers in the history of film, Astaire and

Rogers occupied real time. Godard told us that "the cinema is truth twenty-four times a second, and every cut is a lie." Astaire arrived at the same conclusion thirty-five years earlier. He believed every dance number should be filmed, as nearly as possible, in one unbroken take, always showing the full figures of the dancers from head to toes. There are no cutaways to an admiring audience—Astaire thought that was a distraction. No cuts, or very few, to different points of view (in *Swing Time,* the camera is on a crane to follow them up flights of stairs from a lower dance floor to a higher one). And no close-ups of the dancers' faces, for that would deny us the movement of their bodies. (After seeing the dance film *Staying Alive* in 1983, Miss Rogers told me, "The young people today—they think they can dance with their faces!")

When you see anyone—an athlete, a musician, a dancer, a craftsperson—doing something difficult and making it look easy and a joy, you feel enhanced. It is a victory for the human side, over the enemies of clumsiness, timidity, and exhaustion. The cynical line on Astaire and Rogers was, "She gave him sex; he gave her class." Actually they both had class, and sex was never the point. The chemistry between Fred and Ginger was not erotic, but intellectual and physical: They were two thoroughbreds who could dance better than anyone else, and they knew it. Astaire's later dance partners danced in his spotlight, but Ginger Rogers, the dance critic Arlene Croce wrote, "shed her own light."

Astaire was a painstaking craftsman who, usually working with the choreographer Hermes Pan, preplanned even the slightest gesture in his dances. Rogers was a performer, not a creator, but she was willing to rehearse until her feet bled ("I did everything Fred did—backwards and in heels"). There is the fiction in their films that the dance numbers between them just happen, as a spontaneous expression of their feelings. They look carefree, but they're tightly disciplined in timing and movement and required unimaginable hours of rehearsal.

Many of the Astaire-Rogers musicals involve Fred falling in love with Ginger at first sight, after which she backs cautiously away, only to be wooed in a series of dance numbers. When she has finally fallen in love, incredible plot contrivances make her think he's an adulterer, a philanderer, or engaged to somebody else. In film after film, she shies away from the undeniable love between them, only to be finally saved at the last moment during a dance scene of urgency and passion. "Only a very good girl could be quite so shrewd about life and so dumb about any man who threatens to race her blood," Murray Kempton wrote when she died in 1995.

The best of the Astaire-Rogers film is their fifth, *Swing Time* (1936), directed by George Stevens at a time when he was a king at RKO Radio Pictures (his other credits in that period included *Alice Adams* [1935] and *Gunga Din* [1939]). The plot, with its sly drolleries, is based like *Top Hat* on mistaken identities, but it's wittier and more cleverly written; it could have been devised by P. G. Wodehouse. It serves to link the great dance sequences, built around Jerome Kern songs and including the climactic "Never Gonna Dance" number that may be the high point of the Astaire-Rogers partnership.

This song, which comes at the end and emotionally resolves all of their problems, has always struck me as mirroring the act of lovemaking. It opens with Astaire, dejected by rejection, walking slowly across the floor of a deserted nightclub. Rogers follows him, just as depressed. Almost imperceptibly their walk gathers a quiet rhythm, until they are dancing without ever quite seeming to have started. They dance apart, together, apart. Astaire uses his trademark of changing tempo: Unrestrained passion changes suddenly to prolonged, drawn-out steps suggesting slow motion. Then the tempo revives again.

Another brilliant sequence is Astaire's solo, the "Bojangles of Harlem" number. Modern sensibilities are jarred by the sight of Astaire in blackface, but audiences at the time might have read the scene as a tribute to the great African American dancer Bill Robinson. Apart from the fact of the blackface itself, which is now intrinsically offensive, there is nothing in the sequence that can be seen as racist—quite the contrary.

The number includes a sequence in which Astaire dances in front of three back-projected shadows of himself. The four figures are all in perfect sync for most of the way, until the joke is revealed when one of the shadows breaks out of sync, and eventually all three exit—unable to keep up with him. How did he do this? The three background silhouettes have identical movements, and Astaire mirrors them so well they seem to be his shadows, but apparently he simply timed his live performance so well it mirrored the back projection. Such technical discipline is awesome.

There's also the great number "Waltz in Swing Time," in an astounding art deco nightclub, as a duet about new love. Their movements don't suggest physical passion, but that early stage of idealism in which lovers discover they're soulmates. And the movie's first dance number, "Pick Yourself Up," is funny for the way Astaire pretends to be unable to dance, gets lessons from a dance instructor (Rogers), gets her fired, and then dances a furiously energetic tap number with her to prove to the boss that she did teach him something.

Fred Astaire (1899–1987) had such a particular physical presence that he was easy for cartoonists to caricature—he'd already done their work for them, with his hair slicked back flat from a high forehead above his long, triangular face. He wore clothes as if he had been born in them. His legs flopped over the arms of chairs, as if sitting up straight was unnatural for him. His romantic rivals, on the other hand, wore evening dress as if they had hairshirts underneath.

Ginger Rogers (1911–95), almost as tall as Astaire, slender, athletic, with a face more cheerful than classically beautiful, was Astaire's ideal partner even when they weren't dancing. That's because they both knew, long before many of their contemporaries, that less is more. Big broad facial reactions and strong emotions would have destroyed these fragile films. Rogers survived her ludicrous plots by never quite seeming to believe them. She was sad, but not too sad; angry, but as an act, not an emotion.

When the genuine poignancy of their endangered romances had to be expressed, it was always through dance, not dialogue. That's why the "Never Gonna Dance" number is so wonderful: In their voices and movements, they make it clear that if they can't dance, they can't live. Well, maybe they can, but what fun would that be?

{ TAXI DRIVER }

Are you talkin' to me? Well I'm the only one here.
TRAVIS BICKLE

It is the last line, "Well I'm the only one here," that never gets quoted. It is the truest line in the film. Travis Bickle exists in *Taxi Driver* as a character with a desperate need to make some kind of contact somehow—to share or mimic the effortless social interaction he sees all around him, but does not participate in. The film can be seen as a series of his failed attempts to connect, every one of them hopelessly wrong. He asks a girl out on a date and takes her to a porno movie. He sucks up to a political candidate and ends by alarming him. He tries to make small talk with a Secret Service agent. He wants to befriend a child prostitute but scares her away. He is so lonely that when he asks, "Who you talkin' to?" he is addressing himself in a mirror.

Martin Scorsese's 1976 film doesn't grow dated or overfamiliar. I have seen it dozens of times. Every time I see it, it works. I am drawn into Travis's underworld of alienation, loneliness, haplessness, and anger. His utter aloneness is at the center of *Taxi Driver,* one of the best and most powerful of all films, and perhaps it is why so many people connect with it even though Travis Bickle would seem to be the most alienating of movie heroes. We have all felt as alone as Travis. Most of us are better at dealing with it.

It is a widely known item of cinematic lore that Paul Schrader's screenplay for *Taxi Driver* was inspired by *The Searchers,* John Ford's 1956 film. In both films, the heroes grow obsessed with "rescuing" women who may not, in fact, want to be rescued. They are like the proverbial Boy Scout who helps the little old lady across the street whether or not she wants to go.

The Searchers has Civil War veteran John Wayne devoting years of his life to the search for his young niece, Debbie (Natalie Wood), who has been kidnapped by Comanches. The thought of Debbie in the arms of an Indian grinds away at him. By the time he finally finds her, the Indians are her people, and she runs away. Wayne plans to kill the girl, for the crime of having become a "squaw." But at the end, he lifts her up (in a famous shot) and says, "Let's go home, Debbie."

The dynamic here is that Wayne thinks he has *forgiven* his niece, after having participated in the killing of the people who, for fifteen years or so, had been her family. As the movie ends, the niece is reunited with her surviving biological family, and the last shot shows Wayne silhouetted in a doorway, drawn once again to the wide-open spaces. There is, significantly, no scene showing us how the niece feels about what has happened to her.

In *Taxi Driver,* Travis Bickle (Robert De Niro) is also a war veteran, horribly scarred in Vietnam. He encounters a twelve-year-old prostitute named Iris (Jodie Foster), controlled by a pimp named Sport (Harvey Keitel). Sport wears an Indian headband. Travis determines to "rescue" Iris and does so, in a bloodbath that is unsurpassed even in the films of Scorsese. A letter and clippings from the Steensmas, Iris's parents, thank him for saving their girl. But a crucial earlier scene between Iris and Sport suggests that she was content to be with him, and the reasons why she ran away from home are not explored.

The buried message of both films is that an alienated man, unable to establish normal relationships, becomes a loner and wanderer and assigns himself to rescue an innocent young girl from a life that offends his prejudices. In *Taxi Driver,* this central story is surrounded by many smaller ones, all building to the same theme. The story takes place during a political campaign, and Travis finds himself with the candidate, Palantine, in his cab. He goes through the motions of ingratiating flattery, but we, and Palantine, sense something wrong.

Shortly after that meeting, Travis tries to "free" one of Palantine's campaign workers, a blonde he has idealized (Cybill Shepherd), from the Palantine campaign. That goes wrong with the goofy idea of a date at a porno movie. And then, after the fearsome rehearsal in the mirror, he becomes a walking arsenal and goes to assassinate Palantine. The Palantine scenes are like dress rehearsals for the ending of the film. With both Betsy and Iris, he has a friendly conversation in a coffee shop, followed by an aborted "date," followed by attacks on the men he perceived as controlling them; he tries unsuccessfully to assassinate Palantine and then goes gunning for Sport.

There are undercurrents in the film that you can sense without quite putting your finger on them. Travis's implied feelings about blacks, for example, which emerge in two long shots in a taxi drivers' hangout, when he exchanges looks with a man who may be a drug dealer. His ambivalent feelings about sex (he lives in a world of pornography, but the sexual activity he observes in the city fills him with loathing). His hatred for the city, inhabited by "scum." His preference for working at night, and the way Scorsese's cinematographer, Michael Chapman, makes the yellow cab into a vessel by which Travis journeys the underworld, as steam escapes from vents in the streets and the cab splashes through water from hydrants—a Stygian passage.

The film has a certain stylistic resonance with *Mean Streets* (1973), the first Scorsese film in which Keitel and De Niro worked together. In the earlier film, Scorsese uses varying speeds of slow motion to suggest a level of heightened observation on the part of his characters, and here that technique is developed even more dramatically. As the taxi drives through Manhattan's streets, we see it in ordinary time, but Travis's point-of-view shots are slowed down. He sees hookers and pimps on the sidewalks, and his heightened awareness is made acute through slow motion.

The technique of slow motion is familiar to audiences, who usually see it in romantic scenes, or scenes in which regret and melancholy are expressed—or sometimes in scenes where a catastrophe looms and cannot be avoided. But Scorsese was finding a personal use for it, a way to suggest a subjective state in a POV shot. And in scenes in a cabdrivers' diner, he uses close-ups of observed details to show how Travis's attention is apart from the conversation, is zeroing in on a black who might be a pimp. One of the hardest things for a director to do is to suggest a character's interior state without using dialogue; one of Scorsese's greatest achievements in *Taxi Driver* is to take us inside Travis Bickle's point of view.

There are other links between *Mean Streets* and *Taxi Driver* that may go unnoticed. One is the "priest's-eye view" often used in overhead shots, which Scorsese has said are intended to reflect the priest looking down at the implements of the Mass on the altar. We see, through Travis's eyes, the top of a taxi dispatcher's desk, candy on a movie counter, guns on a bed, and finally, with the camera apparently seeing through the ceiling, an overhead shot of the massacre in the red-light building. This is, if you will, the final sacrifice of the Mass. And it was in *Mean Streets* that Keitel repeatedly put his finger in the flame of a candle or a match, testing the fires of hell. Here De Niro's taxi driver holds his fist above a gas flame.

There has been much discussion about the ending, in which we see newspaper clippings about Travis's "heroism," and then Betsy gets into his cab and seems to give him admiration instead of her earlier disgust. Is this a fantasy scene? Did Travis survive the shoot-out? Are we experiencing his dying thoughts? Can the sequence be accepted as literally true?

I am not sure there can be an answer to these questions. The end sequence plays like music, not drama: It completes the story on an emotional, not a literal, level. We end not on carnage, but on redemption, which is the goal of so many of Scorsese's characters. They despise themselves, they live in sin, they occupy mean streets, but they want to be forgiven and admired. Whether Travis gains that status in reality or only in his mind is not the point. Throughout the film, his mental state has shaped his reality, and at last, in some way, it has brought him a kind of peace.

{ THE THIRD MAN }

Has there ever been a film where the music more perfectly suited the action than in Carol Reed's *The Third Man*? The score was performed on a zither by Anton Karas, whom Reed heard one night in a Vienna beerhouse. The sound is jaunty but without joy, like whistling in the dark. It sets the tone; the action begins like an undergraduate lark and then reveals vicious undertones.

The story begins with a spoken prologue ("I never knew the old Vienna, before the war"). The shattered postwar city has been divided into French, American, British, and Russian zones, each with its own cadre of suspicious officials. Into this sinkhole of intrigue falls an American innocent: Holly Martins (Joseph Cotten), alcoholic author of pulp westerns. He has come at the invitation of his college chum Harry Lime. But Lime is being buried when Martins arrives in Vienna.

How did Lime die? That question is the engine that drives the plot, as Martins plunges into the murk that Lime left behind. Calloway (Trevor Howard), the British officer in charge, bluntly says Lime was an evil man and advises Holly to take the next plane home. But Harry had a girl named Anna (Alida Valli), whom Holly sees at Lime's grave, and perhaps she has some answers. Certainly Holly has fallen in love with her, although his trusting Yankee heart is no match for her defenses.

The Third Man (1949) was made by men who knew the devastation

457

of Europe at first hand. Carol Reed worked for the British Army's wartime documentary unit, and the screenplay was by Graham Greene, who not only wrote about spies but occasionally acted as one. Reed fought with David O. Selznick, his American producer, over every detail of the movie; Selznick wanted to shoot on sets, use an upbeat score, and cast Noel Coward as Harry Lime. His film would have been forgotten in a week. Reed defied convention by shooting entirely on location in Vienna, where mountains of rubble stood next to gaping bomb craters, and the ruins of empire supported a desperate black-market economy. And he insisted on Karas's zither music ("The Third Man Theme" was one of 1950's biggest hits).

Reed and his Academy Award–winning cinematographer, Robert Krasker, also devised a reckless, unforgettable visual style. More shots, I suspect, are tilted than are held straight; they suggest a world out of joint. There are fantastic oblique angles. Wide-angle lenses distort faces and locations. And the bizarre lighting makes the city into an expressionist nightmare. (During a stakeout for Lime, a little balloon man wanders onto the scene, and his shadow is a monster three stories high). Vienna in *The Third Man* is a more particular and unmistakable *place* than almost any other location in the history of the movies; the action fits the city like a hand slipping on a glove.

Then there are the faces. Joseph Cotten's open, naive face contrasts with the "friends" of Harry Lime: the corrupt "Baron" Kurtz (Ernst Deutsch), the shifty Dr. Winkel (Erich Ponto), the ratlike Popescu (Siegfried Breuer). Even a little boy with a rubber ball looks like a wizened imp. The only trusting faces are those of innocents like the hall porter (Paul Hörbiger) who tells Holly "there was another man . . . a third man" and the beefy Sergeant Paine (Bernard Lee), Calloway's aide, who levels the drunken Holly with a shot to the chin and then apologizes. Even the resident exiles are corrupt. Crabbin (Wilfrid Hyde-White), the head of the discussion group, chatters about culture while smoothly maneuvering his mistress out of sight through doors and up stairs.

As for Harry Lime, he allows Orson Welles to make the most famous entrance in the history of the movies, and one of the most famous speeches. By the time Lime finally appears, we have almost forgotten Welles is even *in* the movie. The sequence is unforgettable: the meow of the cat in the doorway, the big shoes, the defiant challenge by Holly, the light in the window, and then the shot, pushing in, on Lime's face, enigmatic and teasing, as if two college chums had been caught playing a naughty prank.

The famous speech comes after an uneasy ride on a giant Ferris wheel. At one point, Lime slides open the door of the car they are riding in, and Holly uneasily wraps an arm around a post. On the ground again, Harry tries to justify himself: "You know what the fellow said: In Italy for thirty years under the Borgias they had warfare, terror, murder, and bloodshed, but they produced Michelangelo, Leonardo da Vinci, and the Renaissance. In Switzerland they had brotherly love—they had five hundred years of democracy and peace, and what did that produce? The cuckoo clock." (Greene says this speech was written by Welles.)

The emotional heart of the movie is Holly's infatuation with Anna, who will love Harry and be grateful to him no matter what she learns. The scenes between Holly and Anna are enriched by tiny details, as when they visit Harry's apartment and she opens a drawer without looking—because she already knows what will be inside. Or the way she sometimes slips and calls Holly "Harry." Everyone in the movie has trouble with names. Holly calls Calloway "Callahan," and Dr. Winkel insists on "*Vink*-ell!" And of course the name on Harry Lime's tombstone is wrong too.

The chase sequence in *The Third Man* is another joining of the right action with the right location. Harry escapes into the sewer system like a cornered rat, and Reed edits the pursuit into long, echoing, empty sewer vistas and close-ups of Lime's sweaty face, his eyes darting for a way out. Presumably there would be no lights in the Vienna sewers, but there are strong light sources just out of sight behind every corner, throwing elongated shadows, backlighting Harry and his pursuers.

The final scene in *The Third Man* is a long elegiac sigh. It almost did not exist. Selznick and Greene at first wanted a happy ending (Greene originally wrote, "her hand was through his arm"). Reed convinced Greene he was wrong. The movie ends as it begins, in a cemetery, and then Calloway gives Holly a ride back to town. They pass Anna walking on the roadside. Holly asks to be let out of the jeep. He stands under a tree, waiting for her. She walks toward him, past him, and then out of frame, never looking. After a long pause, Holly lights a cigarette and wearily throws away the match. Joseph Cotten recalled later that he thought the scene would end sooner. But Reed kept the camera running, making it an unusually long shot, and absolutely perfect.

The Third Man reflects the optimism of Americans and the bone-weariness of Europe after the war. It's a story about grown-ups and children: Adults like Calloway, who has seen at first hand the results of Lime's crimes, and children like the trusting Holly, who believes in the simplified good and evil of his western novels.

The Third Man is like the exhausted aftermath of *Casablanca.* Both have heroes who are American exiles, awash in a world of treachery and black-market intrigue. Both heroes love a woman battered by the war. But *Casablanca* is bathed in the hope of victory, while *The Third Man* already reflects the cold war years of paranoia, betrayal, and the bomb. The hero doesn't get the girl in either movie—but in *Casablanca,* Ilsa stays with the resistance leader to help in his fight, while in *The Third Man,* Anna remains loyal to a rat. Yet Harry Lime saved Anna, a displaced person who faced certain death. Holly will never understand what Anna did to survive the war, and Anna has absolutely no desire to tell him.

Of all the movies I have seen, this one most completely embodies the romance of going to the movies. I saw it first on a rainy day in a tiny, smoke-filled cinema on the Left Bank in Paris. It told a story of existential loss and betrayal. It was weary and knowing, and its glorious style was an act of defiance against the corrupt world it pictured. Seeing it, I realized how many Hollywood movies were like the pulp westerns that Holly Martins wrote: naive formulas supplying happy endings for passive consumption. I read the other day that they plan to remake *The Third Man.* Do you think Anna will cave in to Holly—or will she remain true to her bitter cynicism and unspeakable knowledge?

{ TROUBLE IN PARADISE }

When I was small, I liked to go to the movies because you could find out what adults did when there weren't any children in the room. As I grew up, that pleasure gradually faded; the more I knew, the less the characters seemed like adults. Ernst Lubitsch's *Trouble in Paradise* reawakened my old feeling. It is about people who are almost impossibly adult, in that fanciful movie way—so suave, cynical, sophisticated, smooth, and sure that a lifetime is hardly long enough to achieve such polish. They glide.

It is a comedy for three characters, plus comic relief in supporting roles. Herbert Marshall plays a gentleman jewel thief, Miriam Hopkins plays the con woman who adores him, and Kay Francis is the rich widow who thinks she can buy him but is content to rent him for a while. They live in a movie world of exquisite costumes, flawless grooming, butlers, grand hotels in Venice, penthouses in Paris, cocktails, evening dress, wall safes, sweeping staircases, nightclubs, the opera, and jewelry, a lot of jewelry. What is curious is how real they manage to seem in the midst of the foppery.

The romantic triangle was the favorite plot device of Lubitsch. The critic Greg S. Faller notes that the German-born director liked stories in which "an essentially solid relationship is temporarily threatened by a sexual rival." Here it's clear from the beginning that the gentleman thief Gaston Monescu (Marshall) and the lady pickpocket Lily Vautier (Hopkins) are destined for one another—not only because they like each other but because their professions make it impossible to trust civilians. When Gaston meets Mariette Colet (Francis), it is to return the purse he has stolen from her and claim the reward. She is attracted to him, and he gracefully bows to her lust, but there is an underlying sobriety: He knows it cannot last, and in a way so does she.

The sexual undertones are surprisingly frank in this pre-Code 1932 film, and we understand that none of the three characters is in any danger of mistaking sex for love. Both Lily and Mariette know what they want, and Gaston knows that he has it. His own feelings for them are masked beneath an impenetrable veneer of sophisticated banter.

Herbert Marshall takes ordinary scenes and fills them with tension because of the way he seems to withhold himself from the obvious emotional scripting. He was forty-two when he made the film, handsome in a subdued rather than an absurd way, every dark hair slicked close to his scalp, with a slight stoop to his shoulders that makes him seem to be leaning slightly toward his women, or bowing. His walk is deliberate and noticeably smooth; he lost a leg in World War I, had a wooden one fitted, and practiced so well at concealing his limp that he seems to float through a room.

He gives a droll, mocking richness to the dialogue by Samson Raphaelson, Lubitsch's favorite collaborator. He seems to know he's in a drawing room comedy, and the actresses speak in tune with him. There are exchanges so teasing that they're like verbal foreplay. Consider the early scene where Gaston, having stolen some jewels, returns to his hotel suite to host a private dinner for Lily. He poses as a baron. She poses as a countess.

"You know," says Lily, "when I first saw you, I thought you were an American."

"Thank you," Gaston gravely replies.

"Someone from another world, so entirely different. Oh! One gets so tired of one's own class—princes and counts and dukes and kings! Everybody talking shop. Always trying to sell jewelry. Then I heard your name and found out you were just one of us."

"Disappointed?"

"No, proud. Very proud."

And they kiss. But soon it is revealed that they have both been

busily stealing each other's possessions. She has his wallet, he has her pin, and it's like a game of strip poker in which, as each theft is revealed, their excitement grows, until finally Lily realizes she has been unmasked by another criminal and cries out, "Darling! Tell me, tell me all about yourself. Who are you?"

He is one of the boldest thieves in the world. He meets Mariette (Francis) by stealing her diamond-encrusted purse and then returning it. He insinuates himself into her trust, advising her on lipstick and on her choice of lovers (of course he has read the love letter in the handbag). The dialogue is daring in its insinuations:

"If I were your father, which fortunately I am not," he says, "and you made any attempt to handle your own business affairs, I would give you a good spanking—in a business way, of course."

"What would you do if you were my secretary?"

"The same thing."

"You're hired."

Turn up the heat under this dialogue, and you'd have screwball comedy. It's tantalizing the way Lubitsch and his actors keep it down to a sensuous simmer. In the low, caressing tones of Marshall and Francis, they're toying with the words—they're in on the joke. And Mariette is neither a spoiled rich woman nor a naive victim. She is a woman of appetites and the imagination to take advantage of an opportunity. She probably doesn't believe, even then, that this man is who he says. He has a way of smiling while he lies, to let his victims have a peek at the joke. But Mariette is an enormously attractive woman, not least because of her calm self-assurance, and he likes her even as he deceives her.

Their first meeting is a splendid example of "the Lubitsch Touch," a press agent's phrase that stuck, maybe because audiences sensed that the director *did* have a special touch, a way of transforming material through style. What happens, and you are surprised to sense it happening, is that in a drawing room comedy of froth and inconsequence, you find that you believe in the characters and care about them.

Ernst Lubitsch (1892–1947), short, plain, cigar-chewing, beloved, was born in Berlin, was on the stage by the time he was nineteen, worked as a silent film comedian, and in 1915 began to direct. His silent films often starred Pola Negri, who played Madame DuBarry in *Passion* (1919), which made their reputations in America. Mary Pickford brought him to Hollywood in 1923, where he quickly became successful. His best silent films include a version of Oscar Wilde's *Lady Windermere's Fan* (1925) that the critic Andrew Sarris argues actually improves on the original ("it seems incredible") by dropping Wilde's epigrams, "which were largely irrelevant to the plot."

Lubitsch ruled at Paramount in the late 1920s and 1930s (he was head of the studio for a year), embracing the advent of sound with a series of musicals that often starred Jeannette MacDonald. *Trouble in Paradise* is generally considered his best film, but there are advocates for his version of Noel Coward's *Design for Living* (1933), with Gary Cooper, Fredric March, and Miriam Hopkins; *Ninotchka* (1939), with Garbo, a definitive adult; *The Shop Around the Corner* (1940), with James Stewart and Margaret Sullavan as bickering coworkers who don't realize they're romantic pen pals; and *To Be or Not to Be* (1942), with Jack Benny and Carole Lombard in a comedy aimed squarely at Hitler.

Because "the Lubitsch Touch" was coined by a publicist, no one, least of all Lubitsch, ever really defined it. It is often said to refer to his fluid camera. Watching *Trouble in Paradise,* what I sensed even more was the way the comic material is given dignity by the actors; the characters have a weight of experience behind them that suggests they know life cannot be played indefinitely for laughs. Sarris, trying to define the Touch, said it was "a counterpoint of poignant sadness during a film's gayest moments." Consider the way Gaston and Mariette say good-bye for the last time, after it is clear to both of them that he loved her and stole from her. How gallantly they try to make a joke of it.

{UN CHIEN ANDALOU}

Luis Buñuel said that if he were told he had twenty years to live and was asked how he wanted to live them, his reply would be: "Give me two hours a day of activity, and I'll take the other twenty-two in dreams—provided I can remember them." Dreams were the nourishment of his films, and from his earliest days as a surrealist in Paris to his triumphs in his late seventies, dream logic was always likely to interrupt the realism of his films. That freedom gave them a quality so distinctive that, like those of Hitchcock and Fellini, they could be identified almost immediately.

His first film, written in collaboration with the notorious surrealist artist Salvador Dalí, was *Un Chien Andalou* (1928). Neither the title ("An Andalusian Dog") nor anything else in the film is intended to make sense. It remains the most famous short film ever made, and anyone halfway interested in the cinema sees it sooner or later, usually several times.

It was made in the hope of administering a revolutionary shock to society. "For the first time in the history of the cinema," wrote the critic Ado Kyrou, "a director tries not to please but rather to alienate nearly all potential spectators." That was then, this is now. Today its techniques have been so thoroughly absorbed even in the mainstream that its shock value is diluted—except for that shot of the slicing of the eyeball, or perhaps the shot of the man dragging the grand piano that has the priests and the dead donkeys on top of it . . .

It is useful to remember that *Un Chien Andalou* was made not by the Buñuel and Dalí that we see as crumbling old men in photographs, but by headstrong young men in their twenties, intoxicated by the freedom of Paris during the decade of the Lost Generation. There is a buried connection between the surrealists and the Sex Pistols, Buñuel and David Lynch, Dalí and Damien Hirst (the artist who exhibited half a lamb in a cube of plastic). "Although the surrealists didn't consider themselves terrorists," Buñuel wrote in his autobiography, "they were constantly fighting a society they despised. Their principal weapon wasn't guns, of course; it was scandal."

The scandal of *Un Chien Andalou* has become one of the legends of the surrealists. At the first screening, Buñuel wrote in his autobiography, he stood behind the screen with his pockets filled with stones, "to throw at the audience in case of disaster." Others do not remember the stones, but Buñuel's memories were sometimes a vivid rewrite of life. When he and his friends first saw Eisenstein's revolutionary Soviet film *Battleship Potemkin*, he claimed, they left the theater and immediately began tearing up the street stones to build barricades. True?

Un Chien Andalou was one of the first handmade films—movies made by their creators on a shoestring budget, without studio financing. It is an ancestor of the works of Cassavetes and today's independent digital movies. Buñuel (1900–83), a Spaniard lured to Paris by vague dreams of becoming an artist, found employment in the film industry, learned on the job, was fired for insulting the great director Abel Gance, and drifted into the orbit of the surrealists.

He went to spend a few days at the house of Dalí, a fellow Spaniard, and told him of a dream he'd had, in which a cloud sliced the moon in half, "like a razor blade slicing through an eye." Dalí countered with his own dream about a hand crawling with ants. "And what if we started right there and made a film?" he asked Buñuel, and they did. They wrote the screenplay together, and Buñuel directed, taking only a few days and borrowing the budget from his mother.

In collaborating on the scenario, their method was to toss shocking images or events at one another. Both had to agree before a shot was included in the film. "No idea or image that might lend itself to a rational explanation of any kind would be accepted," Buñuel remembered. "We had to open all doors to the irrational and keep only those images that surprised us, without trying to explain why."

The image of the moon was followed by the image of a man with a razor (Buñuel) slicing a woman's eye (actually a calf's eye—although legend has transformed it into a pig). The hand crawling with ants was followed by a transvestite on a bicycle, a hairy armpit, a severed hand on the sidewalk, a stick poking the hand, a silent-movie-style sexual assault, a woman protecting herself with a tennis racket, the would-be rapist pulling the piano with its bizarre load, two apparently living statues in sand from the torso up, and so on. To describe the movie is simply to list its shots, since there is no story line to link them.

And yet we try to link them nevertheless. Countless analysts have applied Freudian, Marxist, and Jungian formulas to the film. Buñuel laughed at them all. Still, to look at the film is to learn how thoroughly we have been taught by other films to find meaning even when it isn't there.

Buñuel told an actress to look out the window at "anything—a military parade, perhaps." In fact, the next shot shows the transvestite falling dead off the bicycle. We naturally assume the actress is looking at the body on the sidewalk. It is alien to everything we know about the movies to conclude that the window shot and the sidewalk shot simply happen to follow one another without any connection. In the same way, we assume that the man pulls the piano (with the priests, dead donkeys, etc.) across the room *because* his sexual advance has been rebuffed by the woman with the tennis racket. But Buñuel might argue the events have no connection—the man's advance is rejected, and then, in an absolutely unrelated action, he picks up the ropes and starts to pull the piano.

While looking at *Un Chien Andalou*, it is useful to look with equal attention at ourselves as we watch the movie. We assume it is the "story" of the people in the film—these men, these women, these events. But what if the people are not protagonists but merely models—simply actors hired to represent people performing certain actions? We know that the car at the auto show does not belong to (and was not designed or built by) the model in the bathing suit who points to it. Buñuel might argue that his actors have a similar relationship to the events surrounding them.

Buñuel made another surrealist film, *L'Age d'Or* (1930), which was accused of sacrilege and suppressed for many years. He was a journeyman for MGM at one point, supervising the Spanish-language versions of Hollywood movies. He made many movies in Mexico, some of them, like *The Young and the Damned* (1950) and *The Criminal Life of Archibaldo de la Cruz* (1955) highly valued. At sixty-one, he had a worldwide hit with *Viridiana* (1961), with its shocking scene modeled on the Last Supper, and for the next seventeen years, a period of inspired productivity, produced one astonishing film after another, such as *The Exterminating Angel* (1962), *Diary of a Chambermaid* (1964), *Belle de Jour* (1967), *Tristana* (1970), *The Discreet Charm of the Bourgeoisie* (1972), *The Phantom of Liberty* (1974), and *That Obscure Object of Desire* (1977).

Un Chien Andalou is a curtain-raiser: In a way, he was never unfaithful to it. A movie like this is a tonic. It assaults old and unconscious habits of moviegoing. It is disturbing, frustrating, maddening. It seems without purpose (and yet how much purpose, really, is there in seeing most of the movies we attend?). There is wry humor in it, and a cheerful willingness to offend. Most members of today's audiences are not offended, and maybe that means the surrealists won their revolution: They demonstrated that art (and life) need not follow obediently within narrow restrictions that have been decreed since time immemorial. And that in a film that is alive and not mummified by convention, you never know what you might see when you look out the window.

THE "UP"
DOCUMENTARIES

The "Up" documentaries, they're called. Every seven years, since 1964, the British director Michael Apted revisits a group of people whose lives he has been chronicling since they were children. As he chats with them about how things are going, his films penetrate to the central mystery of life, asking the same questions that Wim Wenders poses in *Wings of Desire:* Why am I me and why not you? Why am I here and why not there?

They always strike me as an inspired, even noble, use of the film medium. No other art form can capture so well the look in an eye, the feeling in an expression, the thoughts that go unspoken between the words. To look at these films, as I have every seven years, is to meditate on the astonishing fact that man is the only animal that knows it lives in time.

"The child is father of the man," Wordsworth wrote. That seems literally true as we look at these films. The seven-year-olds already reveal most of the elements, good and bad, that flower in later life. Sometimes there are surprises: A girl who is uptight and morose at twenty-one, vowing never to marry, blossoms in the later films into a cheerful wife and mother.

And consider Neil, who for most followers of the series has emerged as the most compelling character. He was a brilliant but pensive boy, who at seven said he wanted to be a bus driver so he could tell the passengers what to look for out the windows; he saw himself in the driver's seat, a tour guide for the lives of others. What career would you guess for him? An educator? A politician?

In later films, he seemed to drift, unhappy and without direction. He fell into confusion. At twenty-eight, he was homeless in the Highlands of Scotland, and I remember him sitting outside his shabby house trailer on the rocky shore of a loch, looking forlornly across the water. He won't be around for the next film, I thought: Neil has lost his way. He survived, and at thirty-five was living in poverty on the rough Shetland Islands, where he had just been deposed as the (unpaid) director of the village pageant; he felt the pageant would be going better if he were still in charge.

In a way, I didn't expect him to be back for the next film. But the latest chapter in Neil's story is the most encouraging of all the episodes in *42 Up*, and part of the change is because of his fellow film subject, Bruce, who was a boarding school boy, studied math at Oxford, and then gave up a career in the insurance industry to become a teacher in London inner-city schools. Bruce has always seemed one of the happiest of the subjects. At forty, he got married. Neil moved to London at about that time, was invited to the wedding, found a job through Bruce, and today—well, I would not want to spoil your surprise when you find the unlikely turn his life has taken.

Some lives seem to proceed with a certain inevitability. Tony at seven wants to be a jockey, at fourteen is a stableboy, and at twenty-one has actually ridden in the same race with the great Lester Piggott. Speculating that he might not be able to make a career as a jockey, he talks about taxi driving, and at twenty-eight he is content as a London cabbie, happy with a wife and two children, talking about his annual holidays in Spain, thinking about opening a pub. Because he is doing what he wants to be doing, he likes his life.

That seems to be the key: doing what you like. There are two subjects who go into teaching. Bruce, Neil's friend, sees his decision to teach in poor schools in positive terms, speaks of his socialist ideals, seems happy. Another subject teaches in a similar position but sees the job as a dead end. You can sense fundamental differences in their personalities and see that the most overworked clichés may indeed be valid—that it helps to look on the

sunny side. It is not the job that makes you unhappy. It is whether you want to be doing it.

Looking again at the *28, 35*, and *42 Up* films (1985, 1991, and 1998), I noticed more than before the roles of the spouses. Although modern feminism came of age during the making of the series, the men in these couples essentially define the conditions under which a couple lives, and the women still essentially raise the children. There is much talk about task-sharing, but in the smiles and shrugs of the women, and their glances into the distance, we read the rest of the message.

One subject, an Oxford graduate, took a job at the University of Wisconsin, to pursue his research on fusion. His wife, also an academic, came along into exile, but talks winsomely of visiting England only once every two years; she realizes she can expect to see her family members perhaps only ten more times in her lifetime. Talking about raising a family, she says optimistically (in 1984) that a computer in the home may help her juggle work and domestic duties. Another wife, the mate of the unhappy teacher, doesn't want children because they will limit her choices; on the basis of the lives of the others in the film, she's right. Still, we see subjects dubious about children at twenty-one but treasuring them in later years.

Because all of the subjects are British, there are qualities that leap out for an American viewer. One is how articulate the subjects are; from the three working-class girls in a pub to the well-born graduate of the best schools, from the taxi driver to the Cockney who moved with his wife to Australia, they're all good at self-expression. They speak with precision, and often with grace and humor. One ponders the inarticulate murkiness, self-help clichés, sports metaphors, and management truisms that clutter American speech.

It is also evident that class counts for more in Britain than in America. One woman says she believed when she was younger that there were "opportunities," but now sees that she was deceived. We sense those in the middle are the least content. The working classes seem sure of themselves, confident in their idiom, realistic and humorous. The fortunate also seem to have found interesting options (an upper-class twit at twenty-one refused to be interviewed at twenty-eight—but by thirty-five, amazingly, had flowered into a worker for a relief project in eastern Europe). Those caught in the middle seem more trapped, unless education has released them; the nuclear physicist relaxes on the shores of a Wisconsin lake and talks about how American universities open up new opportunities for every generation.

Watching the films again, I became more aware of the role the countryside plays in British lives. Many of the subjects live or visit the country, and are at home with gardening and the outdoors; during one interview the camera casually changes focus to show the subject's dog, in the background, capturing a rabbit.

The subjects are good sports. At seven, they didn't volunteer for this project, but now they're stuck with it. The series plays on British television, so their notoriety is renewed on a regular basis; it doesn't help to grow gray, because the cameras keep up with them. Some refer to the project ruefully, but there have been fewer dropouts than one would imagine, and one subject came back in from the cold. Even Neil, the loner who is the most worrisome of the subjects, comes forward. They accept that they're part of an enterprise larger than themselves: Their films exploit, more fully than any others, the use of cinema as a time machine. I feel as if I know these subjects, and indeed I do know them better than many of the people I work with every day, because I know what they dreamed of at seven, their hopes at fourteen, the problems they faced in their early twenties, and their marriages, their jobs, their children, even their adulteries.

Apted says in his introduction to the book *42 Up* that if he had the project to do again, he would have chosen more middle-class subjects (his sample was weighted toward the upper and working classes) and more women. He had a reason, though, for choosing high and low: The original question asked by the series was whether Britain's class system was eroding. The answer seems to be yes—but slowly. Andrew Sarris, writing in the *New York Observer*, delivers this verdict: "At one point, I noted that the upper-class kids, who sounded like twits at seven compared to the more spontaneous and more lovable lower-class kids, became more interesting and self-confident as they raced past their social inferiors. It was like shooting fish in a barrel. Class, wealth and social position did matter, alas, and there was no getting around it."

None of the fourteen have died yet, although three have dropped out of the project (some drop out for a film and are back for the next one). By now many have buried their parents. Forced to look back at themselves at seven, fourteen, twenty-one, twenty-eight, and thirty-five, they seem mostly content with the way things have turned out. Will they all live to forty-nine? Will the series continue until none are alive? Revisiting these now-familiar faces, I think of my own life. Curious how, at seven or eight, I wanted to be a newspaperman, and how today I am one. Anyone watching these films goes through a similar process of self-examination. Why am I me and why not you? Why am I here and why not there?

{ VERTIGO }

Did he train you? Did he rehearse you?
Did he tell you what to do and what to say?

This cry from a wounded heart comes at the end of Alfred Hitchcock's *Vertigo,* and by the time it comes we are completely in sympathy with it. A man has fallen in love with a woman who does not exist, and now he cries out harshly against the real woman who impersonated her. But there is so much more to it than that. The real woman has fallen in love with him. In tricking him, she tricked herself. And the man, by preferring his dream to the woman standing before him, has lost both.

Then there is another level, beneath all of the others. Alfred Hitchcock was known as the most controlling of directors, particularly when it came to women. The female characters in his films reflected the same qualities over and over again: They were blondes. They were icy and remote. They were imprisoned in costumes that subtly combined fashion with fetishism. They mesmerized the men, who often had physical or psychological handicaps. Sooner or later most Hitchcock women were humiliated.

Vertigo (1958), which is one of the two or three best films Hitchcock ever made, is the most confessional, dealing directly with the themes that controlled his art. It is *about* how Hitchcock used, feared, and tried to control women. He is represented by Scottie (James Stewart), a man with physical and mental weaknesses (back problems, fear of heights), who falls obsessively in love with the image of a woman—and not any woman, but the quintessential Hitchcock woman. When he cannot have her, he finds another woman and tries to mold her, dress her, train her, change her makeup and her hair, until she looks like the woman he desires. He cares nothing about the clay he is shaping; he will gladly sacrifice her on the altar of his dreams.

But of course the woman he is shaping and the woman he desires are the same person. Her name is Judy (Kim Novak), and she was hired to play the dream woman, "Madeleine," as part of a murder plot that Scottie does not even begin to suspect. When he finds out he was tricked, his rage is uncontrollable. He screams out the words I began with. Each syllable is a knife in his heart, as he spells out that another man shaped the woman that Scottie thought to shape for himself. The other man has taken not merely Scottie's woman but Scottie's dream.

That creates a moral paradox at the center of *Vertigo*. The other man (Gavin, played by Tom Helmore) has, after all, only done to this woman what Scottie also wanted to do. And while the process was happening, the real woman, Judy, transferred her allegiance from Gavin to Scottie, and by the end was not playing her role for money, but as a sacrifice for love.

All of these emotional threads come together in the greatest single scene in all of Hitchcock's works. Scottie, a former San Francisco policeman hired by Gavin to follow "Madeleine," has become obsessed with her. Then it appears Madeleine has died. By chance, Scottie encounters Judy, who looks uncannily like Madeleine but appears to be a more carnal, less polished version. Of course he does not realize she is exactly the same woman. He asks her out, Judy unwisely accepts, and during their strange, stilted courtship she begins to pity and care for him, so that when he asks her to remake herself into Madeleine, she agrees, playing the same role the second time.

The great scene takes place in a hotel room. Judy has arrived, not looking enough like Madeleine to satisfy Scottie, who wants her in the *same* dress, with the *same* hair. His eyes burn with zealous fixation. Judy realizes that Scottie is indifferent to her as a person and sees her as an object. Because she loves him, she accepts this. She locks herself into the bathroom,

does the makeover, opens the door, and walks toward Scottie out of a haunting green fog that is apparently explained by the hotel's neon sign, but is in fact a dreamlike effect.

As Hitchcock cuts back and forth between Novak's face (showing such pain, such sorrow, such a will to please) and Stewart's (in a rapture of lust and gratified control), we feel hearts being torn apart: They are both slaves of an image fabricated by a man who is not even in the room—Gavin, who created "Madeleine" as a device to allow himself to get away with the murder of his wife.

As Scottie embraces "Madeleine," even the background changes to reflect his subjective memories instead of the real room he's in. Bernard Herrmann's score creates a haunting, unsettled yearning. And the camera circles them hopelessly, like the pinwheel images in Scottie's nightmares, until the shot is about the dizzying futility of our human desires, the impossibility of forcing life to make us happy. This shot, in its psychological, artistic, and technical complexity, may be the one time in his entire career that Alfred Hitchcock completely revealed himself, in all of his passion and sadness. (Is it a coincidence that the woman is named Madeleine—the word for the French biscuit which, in Proust, brings childhood memories of loss and longing flooding back?)

Alfred Hitchcock took universal emotions, like fear, guilt, and lust, placed them in ordinary characters, and developed them in images more than in words. His most frequent character, an innocent man wrongly accused, inspired much deeper identification than the superficial superman in today's action movies.

He was a great visual stylist in two ways: He used obvious images, and he surrounded them with a subtle context. Consider the obvious ways he suggests James Stewart's vertigo. An opening shot shows him teetering on a ladder, looking down at a street below. Flashbacks show why he left the police force. A bell tower at a mission terrifies him, and Hitchcock creates a famous shot to show his point of view: Using a model of the inside of the tower, and zooming in while at the same time physically pulling the camera back, Hitchcock shows the walls approaching and receding at the same time; the space has the logic of a nightmare. But then notice less obvious ways that the movie sneaks in the concept of falling, as when Scottie drives down San Francisco's hills, but never up. And note how truly he "falls" in love.

There is another element, rarely commented on, that makes *Vertigo* a great film. From the moment we are let in on the secret, the movie is equally about Judy: her pain, her loss, the trap she's in. Hitchcock so cleverly manipulates the story that when the two characters climb up that mission tower, we identify with both of them, and fear for both of them, and in a way Judy is less guilty than Scottie.

"Hitchcock was very exact in telling me exactly what to do," Kim Novak remembered when I talked with her after the 1996 restoration. "How to move, where to stand. I think you can see a little of me resisting that in some of the shots, kind of insisting on my own identity. I think there was a little edge in my performance that was trying to suggest that I would not allow myself to be pushed beyond a certain point—that I was there, I was me."

The danger is to see Judy, played by Novak, as an object in the same way that Scottie sees her. She is, in fact, one of the most sympathetic female characters in all of Hitchcock. Over and over in his films, Hitchcock took delight in literally and figuratively dragging his women through the mud— humiliating them, spoiling their hair and clothes as if lashing out at his own fetishes. Judy, in *Vertigo*, is the closest he came to sympathizing with the female victims of his plots. And Novak, criticized at the time for playing the character too stiffly, has made the correct acting choices: Ask yourself how you would move and speak if you were in unbearable pain, and then look again at Judy.

{ THE WILD BUNCH }

We all dream of being a child again, even the
worst of us, perhaps the worst most of all.

In an early scene of *The Wild Bunch,* the bunch rides into town past a crowd of children who are gathered with excitement around their game. They have trapped some scorpions and are watching them being tortured by ants. The eyes of Pike (William Holden), leader of the bunch, briefly meet the eyes of one of the children. Later in the film, a member of the bunch named Angel is captured by Mexican rebels and dragged around the town square behind one of the first automobiles anyone there has seen. Children run after the car, laughing. Near the end of the film, Pike is shot by a little boy who gets his hands on a gun.

The message here is not subtle, but then Sam Peckinpah was not a subtle director, preferring bold images to small points. It is that the mantle of violence is passing from the old professionals like Pike and his bunch, who operate according to a code, into the hands of a new generation that learns to kill more impersonally, as a game, or with machines.

The movie takes place in 1913, on the eve of World War I. "We gotta start thinking beyond our guns," one of the bunch observes. "Those days are closing fast." And another, looking at the newfangled auto, says, "They're gonna use them in the war, they say." It is not a war that would

have meaning within his intensely individual frame of reference; he knows loyalty to his bunch and senses it is the end of his era.

The video versions of *The Wild Bunch,* restored to its original running time of 144 minutes, include several scenes not widely seen since the movie had its world premiere in 1969. Most of them fill in details from the earlier life of Pike, including his guilt over betraying Thornton (Robert Ryan), who was once a member of the bunch but is now leading the posse of bounty hunters on their trail. Without these scenes, the movie seems more empty and existential, as if Pike and his men seek death after reaching the end of the trail. With them, Pike's actions are more motivated: He feels unsure of himself and the role he plays.

I saw the original version at the world premiere in 1969, during the golden age of the junket, when Warner Bros. screened five of its new films in the Bahamas for 450 critics and reporters. It was party time, and not the right venue for what became one of the most controversial films of its time—praised and condemned with equal vehemence, like *Pulp Fiction.* At a press conference the morning after the premiere, Holden and Peckinpah hid behind dark glasses and deep scowls; it was rumored that Holden had been appalled when he saw the film. After a reporter from the *Reader's Digest* got up to ask, "Why was this film ever made?" I stood up and called it a masterpiece; I felt, then and now, that *The Wild Bunch* is one of the great defining moments of modern movies.

But no one saw the 144-minute version for many years. It was cut, not because of violence (only quiet scenes were removed), but because it was too long to be shown three times in an evening. It was successful, but it was read as a celebration of compulsive, mindless violence; see the uncut version, and you get a better idea of what Peckinpah was driving at.

The movie is, first of all, about old and worn men. Holden and his fellow actors (Ernest Borgnine, Warren Oates, Edmond O'Brien, Ben Johnson, and the wonderful Robert Ryan) look lined and bone-tired. They have been making a living by crime for many years, and although Ryan is now hired by the law, it is only under threat that he will return to jail if he doesn't capture the bunch. The men provided to him by a railroad mogul are shifty and unreliable; they don't understand the code of the bunch.

And what is that code? It's not very pleasant. It says that you stand by your friends and against the world, that you wrest a criminal living from the banks, the railroads, and the other places where the money is, and that while you don't shoot at civilians unnecessarily, it is best if they don't get in the way.

The two great violent set pieces in the movie involve a lot of civilians. One comes through a botched bank robbery at the beginning of the film, and the other comes at the end, where Pike looks at Angel's body being dragged through the square and says, "God, I hate to see that," and then later walks into a bordello and says, "Let's go," and everybody knows what he means, and they walk out and begin the suicidal showdown with the heavily armed rebels. Lots of bystanders are killed in both sequences (one of the bunch picks a scrap from a woman's dress off of his boot), but there is also cheap sentimentality, as when Pike gives gold to a prostitute with a child, before walking out to die.

In between the action sequences (which also include the famous scene where a bridge is bombed out from beneath mounted soldiers), there is time for the male bonding that Peckinpah celebrated in most of his films. His men shoot, screw, drink, and ride horses. The quiet moments, with the firelight and the sad songs on the guitar and the sweet tender prostitutes, are like daydreams, with no standing in the bunch's real world. This is not the kind of film that would likely be made today, but it represents its set of sad, empty values with real poetry.

The undercurrent of the action in *The Wild Bunch* is the sheer meaninglessness of it all. The first bank robbery nets only a bag of iron washers—"a dollar's worth of steel holes." The train robbery is well planned, but the bunch cannot hold on to their takings. And at the end, after the bloodshed, when the Robert Ryan character sits for hours outside the gate of the compound, just thinking, there is the payoff: A new gang is getting together, to see what jobs might be left to do. With a wry smile he gets up to join them. There is nothing else to do, not for a man with his background.

Seeing this restored version is like understanding the film at last. The missing pieces flesh out the characters. It is all there: why Pike limps, what passed between Pike and Thornton in the old days, why Pike seems tortured by his thoughts and memories. Now, when we watch Ryan, as

Thornton, sitting outside the gate and thinking, we know what he is remembering. It makes all the difference in the world.

The movie was photographed by Lucien Ballard, in dusty reds and golds and browns and shadows. The editing, by Lou Lombardo, uses slow motion to draw the violent scenes out into meditations on themselves. Every actor was perfectly cast to play exactly what he could play; even the small roles need no explanation. Peckinpah possibly identified with the wild bunch. Like them, he was an obsolete, violent, hard-drinking misfit with his own code, and did not fit easily into the new world of automobiles and Hollywood studios.

Sam Peckinpah (1925–84) was a marine in World War II, apprenticed in Hollywood under the action director Don Siegel, and did more than anyone else to bring the traditional western into the gloom of a modern, ironic age. He was an iconoclast, warred with the studios, was often drunk, fought even with his actors, but achieved in *The Wild Bunch* and *Bring Me the Head of Alfredo Garcia* (1974) a fusion of the western myth and the existential hero. I met him twice, once on the set of *Pat Garrett and Billy the Kid* (1973), once in a hotel room when he was touring to publicize *Alfredo Garcia,* which then and now was not seen as the great film it is. Both times he seemed tremulous, and I had the impression of almost uncontrollable discomfort. He was clearly drunk (on the set in Mexico, he sat on a chair in the sun, shielded by an umbrella, hat, dark glasses, relaying instructions to his assistant director). I cannot pretend to know what he was thinking, but I look at the films and I surmise that they represent a continuing parable about a professional doing what he does well in the face of personal and professional agony. Certainly that is a theme of *The Wild Bunch.*

{ WINGS OF DESIRE }

The angels in *Wings of Desire* are not merely guardian angels, placed on earth to look after human beings. They are witnesses and have been watching for a long time—since the beginning. Standing on a concrete riverbank in Berlin, they recall that it took a long time before the primeval river found its bed. They remember the melting of the glaciers. They are a reflection of the solitude of God, who created everything and then had no one to witness what he had done; the role of the angels is to see.

In Wim Wenders's film, they move invisibly through the divided city of Berlin, watching, listening, comparing notes. Often they stand on high places—the shoulder of a heroic statue, the tops of buildings—but sometimes they descend to comfort an accident victim or to put a hand on the shoulder of a young man considering suicide. They cannot directly change events (the young man does kill himself), but perhaps they can suggest the possibility of hope, the intuition that we are not completely alone.

The film evokes a mood of reverie, elegy, and meditation. It doesn't rush headlong into plot, but has the patience of its angels. It suggests what it would be like to see everything but not participate in it. We follow two angels: Damiel (Bruno Ganz) and Cassiel (Otto Sander). They listen to the thoughts of an old Holocaust victim, and of parents worried about their son, and of the passengers on trams and the people in the streets; it's like turning the dial and hearing snatches of many radio programs. They make notes about the hooker who hopes to earn enough money to go south, and the circus aerialist who fears that she will fall because it is the night of the full moon.

You're seduced into the spell of this movie, made in 1987 by Wenders, who collaborated on the screenplay with the German playwright Peter Handke. It moves slowly, but you don't grow impatient because there is no plot to speak of and so you don't fret that it should move to its next predictable stage. It is about being, not doing. And then it falls into the world of doing, when the angel Damiel decides that he must become human.

He falls in love with the trapeze artist. He goes night after night to the shabby little circus where she performs above the center ring. He is touched by her doubts and vulnerability. He talks with Cassiel, the other angel, about how it would feel to feel: to be able to feed a cat or get ink from a newspaper on your fingers. He senses a certain sympathy from one of the humans he watches, an American movie actor (Peter Falk, playing himself). "I can't see you, but I know you're here," Falk tells him. How can Falk sense him? Sometimes children can see angels, but adults are supposed to have lost the facility.

The answers to these questions are all made explicitly clear in the 1998 Hollywood movie *City of Angels,* which is a remake of *Wings of Desire* and spells out what the original film only implies. After seeing the new film, which stars Nicolas Cage as the angel and Meg Ryan as the woman (now a heart surgeon rather than an aerialist), I went back to *Wings of Desire* again. It reminded me of the different notes that movies can strike. *City of Angels* is a skillful romantic comedy and I enjoyed it, but it all stayed there on the screen, content to be what it was. *Wings of Desire* is so much more. It doesn't release its tension in a smooth plot payoff. It creates a mood of sadness and isolation, of yearning, of the transience of earthly things. If man is the only animal that knows it lives in time, the movie is about that knowledge.

It is a beautiful film, photographed by the legendary cinematographer Henri Alekan, who made the characters float weightlessly in Cocteau's *Beauty and the Beast* (the circus in the movie is named after him). When he shows the point of view of the angels, he shoots in a kind of blue-tinted monochrome. When he sees through human eyes, he shoots in color. His camera seems liberated from gravity; it floats over the city or glides down

the aisle of an airplane. It does not intrude; it observes. When the angel follows the trapeze artist into a rock club, it doesn't fall into faster cutting rhythms; it remains detached. The critic Bryant Frazer observes that Cassiel, the other angel, "leans against the wall and closes his eyes, and the stage lights cast three different shadows off his body, alternating and shifting position and color as though we're watching Cassiel's very essence fragmenting before our eyes."

Bruno Ganz has a good face for an angel. It is an ordinary, pleasant, open face, not improbably handsome. Like a creature who has been observing since the dawn of time, he doesn't react a lot. He has seen it all. Now he wants to feel. "I'm taking the plunge," his angel tells the other one. He will descend into time, disease, pain, and death, because at the same time he can touch, smell, and be a part of things. All that he desires is summed up in the early dawn at an outdoor coffee stand when Peter Falk tells him, "To smoke, and have coffee—and if you do it together, it's fantastic. To draw, and when your hands are cold you rub them together." The children in the streets call Falk "Columbo," and indeed the character Columbo, in his dirty raincoat, enters people's lives and stands around and observes and eventually asks questions. And the angels, who wear long black topcoats, do the same things, although their questions are not easily heard.

Wenders is an ambitious director who experiments with the ways in which a movie can be made. I didn't think his 1991 film *Until the End of the World* was a success, but I admired his audacity in following two lovers in a story improvised over five months in twenty cities in seven countries on four continents. His *Kings of the Road* (1976) was a three-hour odyssey in which two men wander the border between East and West Germany in a VW bus, sharing confessions and insights, learning that they cannot live with women and cannot live without them. It's like an intellectual, metaphysical version of Promise Keepers. His *Paris, Texas* (1984) was a modern remake of *The Searchers,* in which a loner played by Harry Dean Stanton tries to track down a lost girl in a landscape that seemed to forbid human connections.

Like many directors who make films of greater length, Wenders is not a perfectionist. He will include what a perfectionist would leave out, because of intangible reasons that are more important to him than flawlessness. Consider, for example, the first time the trapeze artist (Solveig Dommartin) encounters Peter Falk at that coffee stand. Her performance is almost giddy; she seems like an actress pleased to meet a star she's seen on TV, and the scene's reality is broken by her vocal tone and body language. They both seem to be doing an ill-prepared improvisation. That may make it a "bad" scene in terms of the movie's narrow purposes, but does it have a life of its own? Yes, for the same reasons it's flawed. Movies are moments of time, and that is a moment I am happy to have.

Wings of Desire is one of those films movie critics are accused of liking because they're esoteric and difficult. "Nothing happens, but it takes two hours and there's a lot of complex symbolism," complains Peter van der Linden in a comment on the Internet Movie Database. In the fullness of time, perhaps he will return to it and see that astonishing things happen and that symbolism can only be evocative by being complex; simple symbolism is like a flag, which tells you one obvious thing very well. For myself, the film is like music or a landscape: It clears a space in my mind, and in that space I can consider questions. Some of them are asked in the film: Why am I me and why not you? Why am I here and why not there? When did time begin and where does space end?

{ THE WIZARD OF OZ }

As a child I simply did not notice whether a movie was in color or not. The movies themselves were such an overwhelming mystery that if they wanted to be in black and white, that was their business. It was not until I saw *The Wizard of Oz* for the first time that I consciously noticed b&w versus color, as Dorothy was blown out of Kansas and into Oz. What did I think? It made good sense to me.

The switch from black and white to color would have had a special resonance in 1939, when the movie was made. Almost all films were still being made in b&w, and the cumbersome new color cameras came with a "Technicolor consultant" from the factory, who stood next to the cinematographer and officiously suggested higher light levels. Shooting *The Wizard of Oz* in color might have been indicated because the film was MGM's response to the huge success of Disney's pioneering color animated feature *Snow White and the Seven Dwarfs* (1937).

If *Wizard* began in one way and continued in another, that was also the history of the production. Richard Thorpe, the original director, was fired after twelve days. George Cukor filled in for three days, long enough to tell Judy Garland to lose the wig and the makeup, and then Victor Fleming took over. When Fleming went to *Gone with the Wind,* again following Cukor, King Vidor did some of the Munchkin sequences and the Kansas scenes.

There were cast changes too. After Buddy Ebsen, as the Tin Man, had an allergic reaction to the silvery makeup, he was replaced by Jack Haley. Musical numbers were recorded and never used. Margaret Hamilton (the Wicked Witch of the West) was seriously burned when she went up in a puff of smoke. Even Toto was out of commission for two weeks after being stepped on by a crew member.

We study all of these details, I think, because *The Wizard of Oz* fills such a large space in our imagination. It somehow seems real and important in a way most movies don't. Is that because we see it first when we're young? Or simply because it is a wonderful movie? Or because it sounds some buried universal note, some archetype or deeply felt myth?

I lean toward the third possibility, that the elements in *The Wizard of Oz* powerfully fill a void that exists inside many children. For kids of a certain age, home is everything, the center of the world. But over the rainbow, dimly guessed at, is the wide earth, fascinating and terrifying. There is a deep fundamental fear that events might conspire to transport the child from the safety of home and strand him far away in a strange land. And what would he hope to find there? Why, new friends, to advise and protect him. And Toto, of course, because children have such a strong symbiotic relationship with their pets that they assume they would get lost together.

This deep universal appeal explains why so many different people from many backgrounds have a compartment of their memory reserved for *The Wizard of Oz*. Salman Rushdie, growing up in Bombay, remembers that seeing the film at ten "made a writer of me." Terry McMillan, an African American who spent her childhood in northern Michigan, "completely identified when no one had time to listen to Dorothy." Rushdie wrote that the film's "driving force is the inadequacy of adults, even of good adults, and how the weakness of grown-ups forces children to take control of their own destinies." McMillan learned about courage, about "being afraid but doing whatever it was you set out to do anyway."

They're touching on the key lesson of childhood, which is that someday the child will not be a child, that home will no longer exist, that adults will be no help because now the child is an adult and must face the challenges of life alone. But that you can ask friends to help you. And that even the Wizard of Oz is only human and has problems of his own.

The Wizard of Oz has a wonderful surface of comedy and music, special effects and excitement, but we still watch it six decades later because its underlying story penetrates straight to the deepest insecurities of childhood, stirs them, and then reassures them. As adults, we love it because it reminds us of a journey we have taken. That is why any adult in control of a child is sooner or later going to suggest a viewing of *The Wizard of Oz*.

Judy Garland had, it is said, an unhappy childhood (there are those stories about MGM quacks shooting her full of speed in the morning and tranquilizers at day's end), but she was a luminous performer, already almost seventeen when she played young Dorothy. She was important to the movie because she projected vulnerability and a certain sadness in every tone of her voice. A brassy young child star (a young Ethel Merman, say) would have been fatal to the material because she would have approached it with too much bravado. Garland's whole persona projected a tremulous uncertainty, a wistfulness. When she hoped that troubles would melt like lemon drops, you believed she had troubles.

Her friends on the Yellow Brick Road (the Tin Man, the Scarecrow, the Cowardly Lion) were projections of every child's secret fears. Are we real? Are we ugly and silly? Are we brave enough? In helping them, Dorothy was helping herself, just as an older child will overcome fears by acting brave before a younger one.

The actors (Jack Haley, Ray Bolger, Bert Lahr) had all come up through a tradition of vaudeville and revue comedy and played the characters with a sublime unselfconsciousness. Maybe it helped that none of them knew they were making a great movie. They seem relaxed and loose in many scenes, as if the roles were a lark. L. Frank Baum's book had been filmed before (Oliver Hardy played the Tin Man in 1925), and this version, while ambitious, was overshadowed by the studio's simultaneous preparation of *Gone with the Wind*. Garland was already a star when she made *Wizard*, but not a great star—that came in the 1940s, inspired by *Wizard*.

The special effects are glorious in that old Hollywood way, in which you don't even have to look closely to see where the set ends and the backdrop begins. Modern special effects show *exactly* how imaginary scenes might look; effects then showed how we *thought* about them. A bigger Yellow Brick Road would not have been a better one, as *The Wiz* (1978) proved.

The movie's storytelling device of a dream is just precisely obvious enough to appeal to younger viewers. Dorothy, faced with a crisis (the loss of Toto), meets the intriguing Professor Marvel (Frank Morgan) on the road. She is befriended by three farmhands (Bolger, Haley, and Lahr). Soon comes the fearsome tornado. (What frightened me was that you could see individual things floating by—for months I dreamed I was circling around and around while seated at the little desk in my bedroom, looking at classmates being swept mutely past me.) Then, after the magical transition to color, Dorothy meets the same characters again, so we know it's all a dream, but not really.

There are good and bad adult figures in Oz—the Wicked Witches of the East and West, Glinda, the Witch of the North. Dorothy would like help from her friends, but needs to help them, instead ("If I Only Had a Brain" or a heart, or nerve, they sing). Arriving at last at the Emerald City, they have another dreamlike experience; almost everyone they meet seems vaguely similar (because they're all played by Morgan). The Wizard sends them on a mission to get the Wicked Witch's broom, and it is not insignificant that the key to Dorothy's return to Kansas is the pair of ruby slippers. Grown-up shoes.

The ending has always seemed poignant to me. Dorothy is back in Kansas, but the color has drained from the film, and her magical friends are mundane once again. "The land of Oz wasn't such a bad place to be stuck in," decided young Terry McMillan, discontented with her life in Michigan. "It beat the farm in Kansas."

{Woman in the Dunes}

"I love staying at local homes," the man says, accepting an offer of hospitality after he misses the last bus back to the city. He has been collecting insects in a remote desert region of Japan. The villagers lead him to a house at the bottom of a sand pit, and he climbs down a rope ladder to spend the night with the woman who lives there. She prepares his dinner and fans him as he eats. During the night, he wakens to observe that she is outside, shoveling sand. In the morning, he sees her sleeping, her body naked and sparkling with sand. He goes outside to leave. "That's funny," he says to himself. "The ladder is gone."

There is a harsh musical chord at this moment, announcing the painful surprise of *Woman in the Dunes* (1964), one of the rare films able to combine realism with a parable about life. The man (Eiji Okada) is expected to remain in the pit and join the woman in shoveling sand, which is hauled to the surface in bags by the villagers. "If we stop shoveling," the woman (Kyoko Kishida) explains, "the house will get buried. If we get buried, the house next door is in danger."

I am not able to understand the mechanics of that explanation. Nor do I understand the local economy. The villagers sell the sand for construction, the woman explains. It is too salty to meet the building codes, but they sell it cheap. Yes, but surely there are choices in life other than living in a pit and selling sand? Of course there is no logic beneath the story, and the director, Hiroshi Teshigahara, has even explained that sand cannot rise in steep walls like those on the sides of the pit: "I found it physically impossible to create an angle of more than thirty degrees."

Yet there is never a moment when the film doesn't look absolutely realistic, and it isn't about sand anyway, but about life. "Are you shoveling to survive, or surviving to shovel?" the man asks the woman, and who cannot ask the same question? *Woman in the Dunes* is a modern version of the myth of Sisyphus, the man condemned by the gods to spend eternity rolling a boulder to the top of a hill, only to see it roll back down again.

In a way the man has himself to blame. He makes his desert trips to escape the drumbeat of Tokyo. He seeks solitude and finds it. The film opens with a montage of fingerprints and signature stamps, and then there is a close-up of a grain of sand as big as a boulder, and then several the size of diamonds, and then countless grains, with the wind rippling their surface as if they were water. There has never been sand photography like this (no, not even in *Lawrence of Arabia*), and by anchoring the story so firmly in this tangible physical reality, the cinematographer, Hiroshi Segawa, helps the director pull off the difficult feat of telling a parable as if it is really happening. The score, by Toru Takemitsu, doesn't underline the action, but mocks it, with high, plaintive notes, harsh, like a metallic wind.

The first time I saw the film, it played like a psychosexual adventure. The underlying situation is almost pornographic: A wandering man is trapped by a woman, who offers her body at the price of lifelong servitude. There is a strong erotic undercurrent, beginning with the woman displaying her sleeping form, and continuing through hostility, struggle, and bondage to their eventual common ground.

More than almost any other film I can think of, *Woman in the Dunes* uses visuals to create a tangible texture—of sand, of skin, of water seeping into sand and changing its nature. It is not so much that the woman is seductive as that you sense, as you look at her, exactly how it would feel to touch her skin. The film's sexuality is part of its overall reality: In this pit, life is reduced to work, sleep, food, and sex, and when the woman wishes wistfully for a radio, "so we could keep up with the news," she only underlines how meaningless that would be.

The screenplay is by Kobo Abe, based on his own novel, and it re-

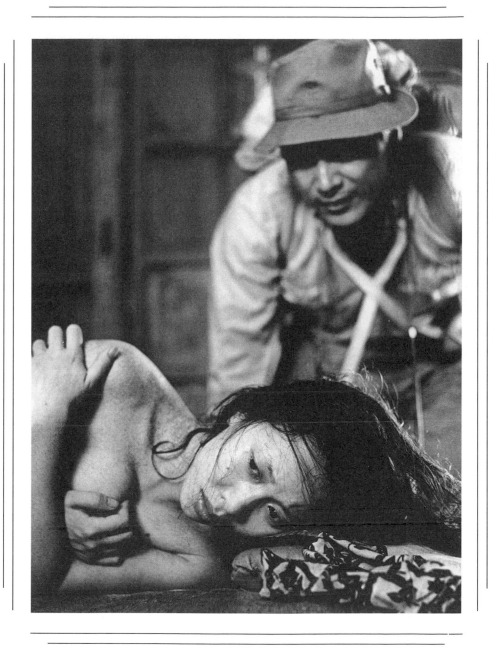

veals the enormity of the situation slowly and deliberately—not rushing to announce the man's dilemma, but revealing it in little hints and insights, while establishing the daily rhythm of life in the dunes. The pit-dwellers are serviced by villagers from above, who use pulleys to lower water and supplies and haul up the sand. It is never clear if the woman willingly descended into her pit or was placed there by the village; certainly she has accepted her fate and would not escape if she could. She participates in the capture of the man because she must: Alone, she cannot shovel enough sand to stay ahead of the drifts, and her survival—her food and water—depend on her work. Besides, her husband and daughter were buried in a sandstorm, she tells the man, and "the bones are buried here." So they are both captives—one accepting fate, the other trying to escape it.

The man tries everything he can to climb from the pit, and there is one shot, a wall of sand raining down, that is so smooth and sudden the heart leaps. As a naturalist, he grows interested in his situation, in the birds and insects that are visitors. He devises a trap to catch a crow, and catches no crows, but does discover by accident how to extract water from the sand, and this discovery may be the one tangible, useful, unchallenged accomplishment of his life. Everything else, as a narrative voice (his?) tells us, is contracts, licenses, deeds, ID cards—"paperwork to reassure one another."

Hiroshi Teshigahara (1927–2001) was thirty-seven when he directed *Woman in the Dunes,* which won the Jury Prize at Cannes and two Oscar nominations. His father had founded a famous school of flower arranging in Tokyo—a school where I once took a few classes, getting just a glimpse of the possibility that to arrange flowers harmoniously could be a triumph of art and philosophy, and a form of meditation. He was always expected to take over management of the school ("a situation ironically similar to that of the protagonist of *Woman in the Dunes,*" the film notes observe). He seemed intrigued by variety and made documentaries on the boxer José Torres and on a woodblock artist, worked in ceramics, directed opera, staged tea ceremonies, and directed seven other feature films. He also, according to plan, took over the flower arranging school.

Woman in the Dunes seemed to disappear for years. I tried to rent it for film classes and couldn't. At Teshigahara's school in Tokyo, I was told vaguely by a translator that the master had chosen to look in new directions, instead of back at his old work. But in 1998, a fresh print was released by Milestone, an American company dedicated to rescuing films, and seeing the film in 35mm, I found it as radical, hard-edged, and challenging as when I first saw it.

Unlike some parables that are powerful the first time but merely pious when revisited, *Woman in the Dunes* retains its power because it is a perfect union of subject, style, and idea. A man and a woman share a common task. They cannot escape it. On them depends the community—and, by extension, the world. But is struggle the only purpose of struggle? By discovering the principle of the water pump, the man is able to bring something new into existence. He has changed the terms of the deal. You cannot escape the pit. But you can make it a better pit. Small consolation is better than none.

A WOMAN
UNDER THE INFLUENCE

John Cassavetes is one of the few modern directors whose shots, scenes, dialogue, and characters all instantly identify their creator. Watch even a few seconds of a Cassavetes film, and you know whose it is, as certainly as with Hitchcock or Fellini. They are films with a great dread of silence; the characters talk, fight, joke, sing, confess, accuse. They need love desperately and are bad at giving it and worse at receiving it, but God knows they try.

Cassavetes (1929–89) is the most important of the American independent filmmakers. His *Shadows* (1960), shot in 16mm on a low budget and involving plausible people in unforced situations, arrived at the same time as the French New Wave and offered a similar freedom in America: not the formality of studio productions, but the spontaneity of life happening right now. Because his films felt so fresh, it was assumed that Cassavetes was an improvisational filmmaker. Not true. He was the writer of his films, but because he based their stories on his own emotional experience, and because his actors were family or friends, his world felt spontaneous. There was never the arc of a plot, but the terror of free fall. He knew that in life we do not often improvise, but play a character who has been carefully rehearsed for a lifetime.

A Woman Under the Influence (1974) is perhaps the greatest of Cassavetes's films (although a good case can be made for his last, *Love Streams*, in 1984). It stars his wife and most frequent collaborator, Gena Rowlands,

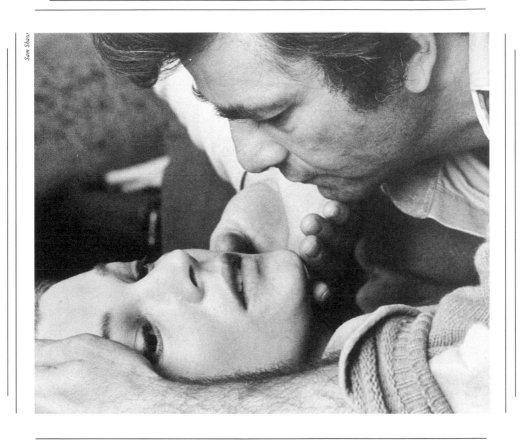

Sam Shaw

and his friend Peter Falk, in roles perhaps suggested by his own marriage (how closely may be guessed by the fact that the two characters' mothers are played by Lady Rowlands and Katherine Cassavetes).

Falk plays a construction foreman named Nick Longhetti, and Rowlands is his wife, Mabel. They have three children and live in a house with so little privacy that they sleep on a sofa bed in the dining room. (The bathroom door has a large sign: PRIVATE. People are always knocking on it.) Mabel drinks too much and behaves strangely, and during the film she will have a breakdown, spend time in a mental institution, and star at her own welcome-home party. Only by the end of the film is it quietly made clear that Nick is about as crazy as his wife is, and that in a desperate way their two madnesses make a nice fit.

Rowlands won an Oscar nomination for her performance, which suggests Erma Bombeck playing Lady Macbeth. Her madness burns amid the confusions of domestic life. Nothing goes easily. Her first words are "No yelling!" Sending the three kids to spend the night with her mother, she hops around the front yard on one foot, having lost her shoe. When her husband unexpectedly arrives home early in the morning with ten fellow construction workers, her response is direct: "Want some spaghetti?" But she tries too hard and is eventually embracing one embarrassed worker, asking him to dance, until Nick breaks the mood with "Mabel, you've had your fun. That's enough." The workers quickly clear their places and leave, while Mabel crumples into the ashes of another failed attempt to please.

Mabel has no room of her own. Her entire house belongs at all times to the other members of her family, to her relatives and in-laws, to the neighbors, to unexpected visitors like Dr. Zepp (Eddie Shaw), who turns up to eyeball her and decide if she's a suitable case for treatment. There is a quiet early moment in the film when Mabel is left alone for a while and stands in the middle of the front hallway, smoking, thinking, listening to opera, drinking, and making gestures toward the corners of the rooms, as if making sure they are still there. Later we see her guzzling a beaker of whiskey in a bar and spending the night with a guy she can't get rid of. (The guy leaves just before Nick arrives with his crew; Cassavetes avoids the obvious payoff of having them meet, while establishing the possibility that such meetings with stray men may have occurred in the past.) Nick and

Mabel, alone for a moment, are fond and loving, but soon the kids burst in and join them on the bed, along with Mabel's mother, and Nick leads everyone in the manic whistling of "Jingle Bells."

Waves of noise and chaos sweep in and out of this house. "In her view," writes the critic Ray Carney, "for things to stop moving even for a pulsebeat is for them to begin to die." True enough, and true of most of Cassavetes's characters. Living in constant dread of silence or insight, unsure of her abilities as wife or mother, rattled by booze and pills, Mabel tries to enforce a scenario of happiness. Just meeting the school bus is a daily crisis, and in the house the kids are always being prompted to perform, to play, to sing, to bounce, to *seem happy*. "Tell me what you want me to be," she tells Nick. "I can be anything."

"She's in love with him," Rowlands told me in 1975, when she and Cassavetes were distributing the film personally, "but in the whole movie, she never once expresses a statement that's really hers, anything she really thinks for herself. Nobody can do that forever and not crack up. She says she'll be whatever her husband wants, but who can do that?"

While Mabel is offstage, we see Nick's own madness, masked by macho self-assurance. Consider the scene where he arrives at his children's school in a city truck, yanks the kids out of class, and takes them to the beach, where they are instructed to run up and down and have a good time. On the way home, he even lets them have sips from his six-pack. Nothing Mabel has done is as crazy as this.

And consider the welcome that Nick stages for Mabel on her return from the institution. It is strained in countless ways, but underneath everything is the sense of an actress returning to reclaim the role she made her own, in a long-running play. She may be well, she may still be ill, but the people in her life are relieved that at least she is back, taking up the psychic space they are accustomed to her occupying. A dysfunctional family is not a nonfunctional family. It functions after its fashion, and in its screwy routine there may even be a kind of reassurance.

There is no safe resolution at the end of any of Cassavetes's films. You have the feeling that the tumult of life goes on uninterrupted, that each film is a curtain raised on a play already in progress. The characters seek to give love, receive it, express it, comprehend it. They are prevented by various addictions: booze, drugs, sex, self-doubt. Self-help gurus talk about "playing old tapes." Cassavetes writes characters whose old tapes are like prison cells; their dialogue is like a call for help from between the bars.

Ray Carney, who assembled *Cassavetes on Cassavetes,* the closest thing we will have to an autobiography, believes that *A Woman Under the Influence* is the middle film of a "marriage trilogy." The first in the emotional sequence is *Minnie and Moskowitz* (1971), with Rowlands and Seymour Cassel in the goofy intoxication of first love, and the third is *Faces* (1968), with Rowlands and John Marley in the last stages of a disintegrating marriage. *A Woman Under the Influence* comes in the full flood of marriage and parenthood, with an uncertain balance between hope and fear.

Cassavetes cut many other films from the bolt of his quest and exhilaration. I thought *Husbands* (1970) was unconvincing, with Cassavetes, Falk, and Ben Gazzara mourning a friend by holding an extended debauch. *The Killing of a Chinese Bookie* (1976), with Gazzara as the operator of a strip club, is the sleeper, never given adequate distribution, a portrait of an ingratiating, shifty, charming operator. *Opening Night* (1977) stars Rowlands in one of her best performances, as an alcoholic actress coming to pieces on the first night of a new play. *Gloria* (1980) is more conventional, with Rowlands as a mob-connected woman who hides a kid whose parents have been rubbed out. Then comes the greatness of *Love Streams* (1984), but by then Cassavetes's health was failing, and after a few more jobs he descended into a painful terminal illness.

One of the things we can ask of an artist is that he leave some record of how it was for him, how he saw things, how he coped. Movies are such a collaborative medium that we rarely get the sense of one person, but Cassavetes at least got it down to two: himself and Rowlands. The key to his work is to realize that it is always Rowlands, not the male lead, who is playing the Cassavetes role.

{ Written on the Wind }

Opinion on the melodramas of Douglas Sirk has flip-flopped since his key films were released in the 1950s. At the time, critics ridiculed them and the public lapped them up. Today most viewers dismiss them as pop trash, but in serious film circles Sirk is considered a great filmmaker—a German who fled Hitler to become the sly subverter of American postwar materialism.

One cold night in January 1998, I went up to the Everyman Cinema in Hampstead, north of London, to see a revival of a restored print of Sirk's *Written on the Wind* (1956). This is a perverse and wickedly funny melodrama in which you can find the seeds of *Dallas, Dynasty,* and all the other prime-time soaps. Sirk is the one who established their tone, in which shocking behavior is treated with passionate solemnity, while parody burbles beneath.

All the reviews of this movie seem to include lists: It's about wealth, alcoholism, nymphomania, impotence, suicide, and veiled elements of incest and homosexuality. Yet the theme song, by Sammy Cahn, is sung by the Four Aces. The pieces are in place for a film you can mock and patronize. But my fellow audience members sat in appreciative silence (all right, they snickered a little when Rock Hudson is told it's time to get married and he replies, "I have trouble enough just finding oil").

To appreciate a film like *Written on the Wind* probably takes more sophistication than to understand one of Bergman's masterpieces, because

Bergman's themes are visible and underlined, while with Sirk the style conceals the message. His interiors are wildly over the top, and his exteriors are phony—he wants you to notice the artifice, to see that he's not using realism, but an exaggerated Hollywood studio style. The Manhattan skyline in an early scene is obviously a painted backdrop. The rear-projected traffic uses cars that are ten years too old. The swimming hole at the river, where the characters make youthful promises they later regret, is obviously a tank on a soundstage with fake scenery behind it.

The actors are as artificial as the settings. They look like *Photoplay* covers and speak in the clichés of pulp romance. Sirk did not cast his films by accident, and one of the pleasures of *Written on the Wind* is the way he exaggerates the natural qualities of his actors and then uses them ironically.

The film stars Rock Hudson as Mitch Wayne (think about that name), who grew up poor on the Texas ranch owned by oil millionaire Jasper Hadley (Robert Keith). He's been raised with Jasper's son, Kyle (Robert Stack), and daughter, Marylee (Dorothy Malone). Now Mitch holds an important post in the Hadley Oil empire, which requires him to wear a baseball cap and park a yellow pencil over his ear, while studying geological maps. Kyle has turned into a drunken playboy, and Marylee into a drunken nympho.

As the film opens, Mitch and Kyle are in New York, where they both fall in love with the trim, intelligent Lucy Moore (Lauren Bacall). When she tells Kyle she wants to work in advertising, he picks up the phone to buy her an agency. She demurs. All three have lunch at '21,' and then Kyle sends Mitch to buy cigarettes while he whisks Lucy off in a cab to the airport, where Mitch (who knows his tricks) is there ahead of them on the Hadley plane. Kyle pilots it himself, flying them to Miami Beach while confessing to Lucy, "I drink too much" and "Nobody has ever listened to me the way you do." Of Mitch Wayne, he says, "He's eccentric. He's poor." The terms are synonymous.

In Miami Beach, they check into a Hadley hotel, where the manager announces "Miss Moore's suite" while the music swells in materialistic ecstasy, and Kyle shows Lucy closets full of designer gowns, drawers full of purses and trays of jewelry, and asks her to prepare for dinner. Half an hour later (after dressing with Mitch in the suite they . . . share), Kyle enters

Lucy's suite, calling out, "Are you decent?" Discovering she has left for the airport, he muses, "I guess she was."

Miami Beach was a painted backdrop. Texas, apart from a few shots of sports cars racing past oil derricks, is all built on the back lot. The plot heats up. Marylee has had a crush on Mitch since childhood and wants to marry him. So great is her need, indeed, that when she sashays around in low-cut dresses, her knees almost buckle under the weight of her lust (Malone won an Oscar for the performance).

Kyle goes on the wagon, until a doctor unwisely informs him he is impotent. Well, not completely impotent—there is a "problem," but a baby is "possible." Kyle doesn't wait for the footnotes before racing to the country club to resume his boozing, and when Lucy tells him she's pregnant, he assumes the father is Mitch—a suspicion encouraged by Marylee, who wants Lucy off the ranch so she can regain possession of her childhood friends.

If I smile as I synopsize the plot, surely Sirk was smiling when he directed it; he's subverting the very lifestyle he celebrates. His use of artificial and contrived effects, colors and plot devices, is "a screaming Brechtian essay on the shared impotence of American family and business life" (Dave Kehr). Well, yes, but it's possible to enjoy Sirk's subtleties as simple entertainment too. Films like this are both above and below middlebrow taste. If you only see the surface, it's trashy soap opera. If you can see the style, the absurdity, the exaggeration, and the satirical humor, it's subversive of all the 1950s dramas that handled such material solemnly. William Inge and Tennessee Williams were taken with great seriousness during the decade, but Sirk kids their Freudian hysteria (that Williams's work survives is a tribute to his poetry, not his common sense).

One test of satire is: At what point do we realize the author is kidding? There's a clue here in an early remark by Mitch to Lucy: "Are you looking for laughs? Or are you soul-searching?" And in the way the old swimming hole represents lost innocence and promise for Marylee. In one of the film's more lurid sequences, Sirk uses a close-up of her face in orgiastic nostalgia, as we hear little Mitch's childish voice piping out a promise to marry Marylee when they grow up. "How far we've come from the river!" Mitch later tells her.

There's a broad wink and nudge at the end. Old Jasper Hadley is often seen behind his desk, which holds a large bronze model of an oil derrick (a portrait on his wall shows him at the same desk with the same bronze—a barbershop mirror effect). At the end of the film, after Marylee's rivals have won, she is left alone in her father's office, where she caresses the erect derrick—first sadly, then tenderly.

To appreciate the trashiness of *Written on the Wind* is not to condescend to it. To a greater degree than we realize, our lives and decisions are formed by pop clichés and conventions. Films that exaggerate our fantasies help us to see them—to be amused by them and by ourselves. They clear the air.

Douglas Sirk (1900–87) had two careers. His first thirty-seven years were spent in Germany, where he worked as a stage director, specializing in classics. His first American film was *Hitler's Madmen* (1943), and his critical reputation is based on a series of enormously popular melodramas he made for Universal, including *All I Desire* (1953), *Magnificent Obsession* (1954), *All That Heaven Allows* (1955), and *Imitation of Life* (1959). He also made westerns, musicals, and war stories, working with Hudson more often than any other star—perhaps appreciating the way Hudson's concealed homosexuality worked subtly to subvert the stock characters he often played.

Rainer Werner Fassbinder, another German obsessed with American forms of melodrama, said Sirk was the greatest influence on his work. Certainly Sirk was the father of prime-time TV soaps. "I have seen *Written on the Wind* a thousand times," the Spanish director Pedro Almodóvar said, "and I cannot wait to see it again." Sirk's style spread so pervasively that nobody could do melodrama with a straight face after him. In countless ways visible and invisible, Sirk's sly subversion skewed American popular culture and helped launch a new age of irony.

ABOUT THE AUTHOR

Roger Ebert was born in Urbana, Illinois, and attended local schools and the University of Illinois, where he was editor of *The Daily Illini*. After graduate study in English at the universities of Illinois, Cape Town, and Chicago, he became film critic of the *Chicago Sun-Times* in 1967, winning the Pulitzer Prize for criticism in 1975. The same year, he began a long association with Gene Siskel on the TV program *Siskel & Ebert*. After Siskel's death in 1999, the program continued with Richard Roeper on *Ebert & Roeper*. Ebert has been a lecturer on film in the University of Chicago's Fine Arts Program since 1969, is an adjunct professor of cinema and media studies at the University of Illinois, and received an honorary doctorate from the University of Colorado, where for thirty years he has conducted an annual shot-by-shot analysis of a film at the Conference on World Affairs. In 1999 he started an Overlooked Film Festival at the University of Illinois, selecting films, genres, and formats he believes deserve more attention. His reviews are collected in an annual *Movie Yearbook*, and he has published a dozen other books. He lives in Chicago with his wife, Chaz Hammelsmith Ebert, an attorney.